Jack Bruce
COMPOSING HIMSELF

Jack Bruce
COMPOSING HIMSELF

THE AUTHORISED BIOGRAPHY
BY HARRY SHAPIRO

Foreword by
ERIC CLAPTON

"Two roads diverged in a wood, and I –
I took the road less travelled by,
And that has made all the difference."

The Road Not Taken, ROBERT FROST

"Music does not depend on being right, on having good taste and education and all that."

"Indeed, then what does it depend on?"

"On making music, Herr Haller, on making music as well and as much as possible and with all the intensity of which one is capable. That is the point, monsieur."

Steppenwolf, HERMAN HESSE

Jack Bruce COMPOSING HIMSELF
THE AUTHORISED BIOGRAPHY BY HARRY SHAPIRO

Unlike Robert Frost, I have not been a lone traveller; the right true path has always been clearly marked, and so this book is dedicated to Kay, my heart, my soul, and my walking partner.

A GENUINE JAWBONE BOOK
First Edition 2010
Published in the UK and the USA by Jawbone Press
2a Union Court,
20–22 Union Road,
London SW4 6JP,
England
www.jawbonepress.com

ISBN 978-1-906002-26-8

DESIGN Paul Cooper Design
EDITOR Thomas Jerome Seabrook
EDITORIAL DIRECTOR Tony Bacon

Printed by Everbest Printing Co Ltd, China.

1 2 3 4 5 14 13 12 11 10

Contents

CLOCKWISE FROM TOP LEFT: Jack in his Bellahouston Academy school uniform, aged around 11; with Dick Heckstall-Smith (left) and Cyril Davies in Alexis Korner's Blues Inc, 1962; Ginger Baker, photographed by Jack; playing 'As You Said' with Cream, 1968; during Cream's farewell concerts at the Royal Albert Hall, London, November 1968; with The Graham Bond Organisation, 1963.

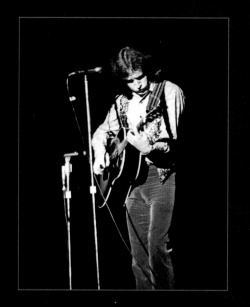

MAIN PICTURE: Jack with Carla Bley during the recording of *Escalator Over The Hill*.
OPPOSITE: with Tony Williams in Lifetime, 1970; with Leslie West in West Bruce & Laing.
RIGHT: with Mick Taylor, being interviewed by Bob Harris on *The Old Grey Whistle Test*, January 1975; backstage at the Palladium, New York, where Jack played his first show after the death of John Lennon in December 1980.

CLOCKWISE FROM TOP LEFT: Jack as Hoss in *The Tooth Of Crime*, 1987; with Margrit in Germany, early 80s; at The Belushi Bar with John Belushi, 1982; with Walter Quintus and Kurt Renker of CMP, 1987; with Robin Trower, 1981; enjoying an ice cream with Ginger and Ginger's then wife, Karen, in Israel, 1990.

CLOCKWISE FROM TOP LEFT: Jack with Charles Neville, Bill Graham, and Ginger Baker, Israel, 1990; with Don Pullen, Paris, 1985; with Gary Moore at one of the concerts arranged to celebrate Jack's 50th birthday, Cologne, 1993; with Dick Heckstall-Smith at the same event; the Bruce family, with Jack's mum, Betty (right), during the late 80s; with Simon Phillips and Blues Saraceno, Japan, 1993; with Kip Hanrahan.

CLOCKWISE FROM TOP LEFT: Jack with his favourite bass, the Warwick; reunited with Cream at the Royal Albert Hall, 2005; at Savage Sound Studios, San Francisco, with Bernie Worrell and Jo Bruce, 1989; backstage at Madison Square Garden with Eric Clapton, Ahmet Ertegun, and Ginger Baker, 2005; playing with a mic stand, Israel, 1990.

CLOCKWISE FROM TOP LEFT: Jack with Pete Brown at the BMI Awards, London, November 2005; performing with Ginger at the Zildjian Drummers Achievement Awards, London, December 2008; in Scotland with Natascha, Kyla, Margrit, and Corin during the mid 90s.

Foreword by ERIC CLAPTON

My beginning years in the English music world were punctuated by numerous moments of awakening. Perhaps the most significant and yet most obvious of these was the realisation that great music could be experienced live, in person, as well as on record. As naive as this sounds, all through my early teens I had been listening to imported blues records and was absolutely convinced that this was the only way to experience the music I had come to love. It was possible of course to see some of the famous rock'n'roll acts of the day on tour, but for the most part it was packaged and promoted hoo-hah, and consequently pretty disappointing.

The first real opportunity I had to hear and see the real thing in the flesh was when I saw Buddy Guy, and later on Little Walter, at the Marquee club. What hit me right away was that here was something happening spontaneously, right in front of me, that had never taken place before, anywhere, and that did not refer to or rely on any of the recorded work of the two artists in question. It was absolutely 'in the moment' music. I was stunned and moved to the core; I had no idea that anything like this existed.

Shortly after, I began to meet and play with musicians who were not only aware of this concept but could achieve it, too. In fact it seemed to be their desired way of playing – and also, for the most part, their way of living. Which of course brings me to Jack.

The first time I saw Jack play was with Ginger, in Alexis Korner's band, and it had a profound effect on me. This was also at the Marquee club, and it was clear, even to my young ears, that these guys were larger than life and that they were barely constrained by their responsibilities as a rhythm section. I was intrigued. Up until then my interest was centred more on recorded work; now I was being introduced to something totally new, the reality of improvised, live music, created out of thin air.

Years went by, and I found my way into John Mayall's band. Not long

17

after I joined, Jack replaced John McVie on bass and my life was never the same again. It was not volume, or technique, or virtuosity that defined Jack's presence on stage, it was his obvious desire to make the most of every musical opportunity, combined with the power that is always present when a musician is absolutely convinced of, and secure with, his capabilities. Most important of all, for me, was the joy I felt from being able to play over the solid foundation that he created. The music, and the experience of playing it, took me to another dimension.

The rest, as they say, is history. Ginger asked if I would join him in forming a band, and I said yes, but only on the condition that Jack was part of it. In all the years that we have known and played with each other, I have to say I have never really been sure what Jack's main calling is. He is definitely in tune with the concept of playing blues – how could he not be; he was already a formidable jazz musician when we met. He was also deeply drawn to and conversant in classical music, and would often refer to the modern composers like Schoenberg, Webern, and Cage. Not surprising, then, that Cream's early collective listening, as a group, was extremely eclectic, ranging from country-blues to avant-garde jazz. It does seem then, considering the many directions he is able to go in, that Jack is probably best considered a jazz musician, but in truth, I would have to say he transcends any categorisation, and I'm sure he is happiest being considered that way.

If I had to reluctantly commit to naming his most defining quality as an artist, it would be that he intuitively knows how to step into, and gather from, all of the genres that he has focused on. His ability to see beyond the normal limits of any musical framework is astounding. I have often stood at the doorway and watched him disappearing in the dust of his own endeavours.

We have had many laughs together, and even spoken in tongues on odd occasions. He is a deep and thoughtful man and I am glad to know him. Best of all I have been honoured and privileged to have been able to soar from time to time on his rock-steady and burning bottom line.

Introduction

Think about this. How many musicians can you name who would genuinely tick all the following boxes: a world-class pioneer in his main instrument; a composer of some of the most enduring and recognisable rock songs of our time; an accomplished classical, jazz, and Latin musician; one of popular music's most distinctive and evocative voices. One reviewer of the recent Jack Bruce boxed set cut to the chase. "If Clapton was God," wrote Marco Rossi in *Shindig!* magazine, "what the fuck was Jack Bruce?"

Yet when I told a bass-playing friend of mine I was writing a biography of Jack, his immediate response was: "That'll be a short book."

"Why?"

"Well, what are you going to write about after Cream?"

I proceeded to reel off album titles from Jack's 40-year solo career, but apart from a flicker of recognition at the mention of *Songs For A Tailor*, the rest were met with a blank stare. Other friends wondered if Jack was still alive – perhaps only the Cream reunion in 2005 reminded people that this was still very much the case, although it was a pretty close run thing. I can't say that I was that surprised at the response because this book was borne from my frustration at the lack of profile for Jack and an extraordinarily diverse career regularly punctuated by albums and touring bands of the highest quality.

So what happened? Why has Jack Bruce, so well known in the 60s, been hidden in plain sight? Jack has always aspired to be a leading-edge musician, his work informed by a musical landscape that includes Scottish folksong, Bach, Messiaen, Mingus, the bass runs of Motown legend James Jamerson – and attempting to create a new music which is all of these things and yet none of them. In doing so, he has reduced the warp and weft of their complexities to songs of sublime simplicity – always the hallmark of a great composer. This is what gives Jack's music its substance, freshness, and permanence.

But pioneers never have it easy. Cream were a pioneering band, but nobody thought they would be as successful as they were. As Jack notes, being the right band in the right place at the right time was critical to their commercial success. "If we had come along 18 months before or after ... who knows?"

Jack Bruce COMPOSING HIMSELF

Nobody was expecting Jack's first solo album, *Songs For A Tailor* (1969), to sound anything like it did, and he has continued to confound expectations ever since, switching effortlessly between rock trios, avant-garde jazz, and Latin ensembles. He is a restless spirit and one who gets bored easily. It has been hard even for his diehard fans to keep up and follow the train of thought. But as his long-term writing partner Pete Brown says: "Jack's music is just music, it goes where it needs to go. It's hard for people to understand somebody doing that. But they should understand that if you are an artist, and if you can do all these things, blues, jazz, rock, whatever, you want to do them."

And yet Jack has never set out to be deliberately anti-commercial. If your taste is in driving riffs, then songs such as 'Bird Alone', 'Smiles And Grins', and 'Life On Earth' stand proud next to 'White Room', 'Politician', or 'Sunshine Of Your Love'. And a compilation of heart-melting Bruce Ballads – 'Make Love', 'Out Into The Fields', and 'Folk Song' are but three of them – could form a whole new soundtrack to the desperate nights of bedsitter angst.

Jack has always carried around a reputation for being difficult to deal with, something he readily admits to and which in part is an inevitable product of his background. Underlying all stereotypical images and clichés are the germs of a truth, and in Jack's case it's the fiery Scot – not just any Scot but a native of Glasgow. In his travelogue, *Heart Of Scotland*, published in 1934, George Blake declared that the Glaswegian man has "the furious quality of the Scot in its most extreme form … [he] hates pretence, ceremonial form … He likes to be alone, is reticent, and does not mix so readily with his fellow man … he glories in being outspoken sometimes without realising that the … ill-advised remark is not rendered less the … ill-advised for being candid."

In 1946 the writer Charles Oakley characterised the man of Glasgow as somebody who would jaywalk, travel in a crowded bus when there was an empty one behind, and deliberately ask for toothpaste that was out of stock, simply to "preserve his individuality". Jack not only refuses to compromise but is also a perfectionist who will always speak his mind. The passion and intensity that he brings to his music is integral to his personality. He never gives less than 100 per cent and expects the same from the musicians around him. He is also fiercely competitive and again, by his own admission, "egotistical". And yet as a creative artist it would be surprising if he weren't egotistical: you have to live inside your head much of the time and be the centre of your own universe.

Of course, in a business ridden with ego (much of it utterly unjustified), this can cause friction and bad feeling. And it is in Jack's nature to take anything he sees as a betrayal very much to heart. There are a few musicians he hasn't spoken to for decades. So Jack does have a reputation, and in a business that can be vengeful this can easily be turned against the artist to stifle and hamper a career. But none of it can really excuse the neglect of Jack's work. It is a testament to his indomitable spirit that he has survived both the worst that the business can throw at a musician and the best efforts of his personal demons to finish him off completely.

Which takes us to the nub of the matter – the nature of the music business itself. Through a combination of bad luck, apathy, incompetence, and downright theft, Jack has been badly served by a succession of managers, agents, and record companies who have done little or nothing to promote his work. It doesn't matter how good the material is: if the record isn't in the shops by the time of the tour, or it doesn't get airplay, then it is a short step to the remainder racks. And in this business, failure becomes a self-fulfilling prophecy. If your last album didn't sell well there is even less support for the next one – which in turn means that it too is likely to fail. One of Jack's albums, *Jet Set Jewel*, was buried for 20 years.

○

This is the first biography I have written in collaboration with the subject, a project I approached with both anticipation and trepidation. I did interview Jack in 1978 for my biography of Graham Bond and spent an afternoon at his 'rock star' mansion, where both Jack and his first wife Janet were warm and friendly, with Jack eager to talk about a musician who was so important to him. But this would be a very different venture. Could I earn his trust? How much would he tell me? My fears were quickly allayed, and I like to think we made a good team – me filling in the gaps with names and events that Jack couldn't immediately recall, Jack correcting many of the mistaken assumptions I had carried with me from the general rock mythology that surrounds him and his career.

Jack was very open and candid about his life, enjoying the interviewing sessions and, as he says, using them as "free therapy". And while there have been dark times, as we talked, Jack's craggy, expressive face would often light up at the memory of some rock'n'roll madness, the tale often punctuated by self-deprecating dry humour, an impish grin, and a fit of the giggles. Jack gave many days of his time to this book and his close involvement opened the doors to important individuals who might otherwise have declined to be interviewed. Many thanks are also due to Jack's wife and manager Margrit for her willingness to share memories and for generally making me very welcome on my trips to their house deep in the English countryside.

But any attempt at a comprehensive biography demanded that the net be cast as widely as possible: family, fellow musicians, and others telling their stories and bringing perspective to Jack's life and work. Therefore I would like to extend my thanks to: Bob Adcock, Liz Baker, Nettie Baker, Norman Beaker, Jeff Berlin, Carla Bley, Sandra Brockington, Pete Brown, Charlie Bruce, Corin Bruce, Janet Bruce, Kyla Bruce, Malcolm Bruce, Eric Clapton, Clem Clempson, Billy Cobham, Larry Coryell, Natascha Eleonore, David English, Charles Evans, Stu Goldberg, Bob Hall, Kip Hanrahan, Arthur Heckstall-Smith, Horacio 'El Negro' Hernandez, Steve Hunter, Gary Husband, Tony Hymas, Paul Jones, Andy Johns, Corky Laing, Ronnie Leahy, Henry Lowther, Dennis Mackay, Mike Mandel, John Marshall, Gary Moore, John Mumford, Bill Oakes, Tony Palmer, Andy Park, Simon Phillips, Bud Prager, Kurt Renker, Phil Ryan, David Sancious, Blues Saraceno, Robert Somerville, Chris Spedding, Steve Swallow, Art Themen, Godfrey Townshend, Robin Trower, Keith Turner, Justin de Villeneuve, Dennis Weinreich, Martin Wesson, Bob Wishart, Bernie Worrell, and Chris Youle.

Very special thanks to Bob Elliott for compiling the discography and the gig list. Thanks also to Phil Beards, Peter Brkusic, Terry Horbury, Mitchell Kane,Mark Powell, David Spurlock, Robert Schatzle, and Stephanie Thorburn – and also Gareth Morgan and Otis Wolstenholme for technical insights into Jack's bass playing. John Powles and all the library staff at Glasgow Caledonian University were very helpful. A big thank you goes to Cecil Offley followed by a round of applause to Tony Bacon, Nigel Osborne, Tom Seabrook, Mark Brend, and all the folks at the Jawbone Press.

Thanks to William Pryor at Clear Books for permission to quote from Dick Heckstall-Smith's autobiography *The Safest Place In The World* (updated as *Blowing The Blues*) – and to Pete Brown for permission to quote his poem, 'Few'. Finally a sly nod to my friend Damon – he knows why.

○

Only Jack Bruce would do this. In front of hundreds of German rock fans, many on the edge of their seats waiting for 'White Room' or 'Sunshine Of Your Love', Jack walked out with a chair and a cello and for the first three minutes of the concert regaled the audience with a spirited dose of Bach's preludes. Apologising to the long dead composer, he then moved to the piano for a solo piece called 'FM' – For Margrit – written for his second wife and business manager who, back in the 80s when they first met, had wanted to take up the piano again and needed some pieces to play. It was Margrit who had arranged this event, on November 2–3 1993 at the E-Werk, one of the largest music venues in Cologne, to celebrate Jack's 50th year. "It was superbly organised," Jack says. "When she does something like that, she doesn't put a foot wrong … one of the best weeks of my life."

'FM' was the first of three songs in a very personal opening to what was to be a journey through Jack's musical history. It was entirely appropriate to start with cello, the instrument Jack first took up at secondary school when he was just 12 years old. He followed 'FM' with 'Can You Follow' from his second solo album, *Harmony Row*, a song devised by Jack and Pete Brown as a look back to their roots, with just Jack on piano and vocal. Drummer/keyboardist Gary Husband then joined Jack for 'Runnin' Thro' Our Hands' from *Out Of The Storm*, Jack's most autobiographical and paradoxically titled album, recorded at a time when he was very far from being sheltered against personal and career turmoil.

Jack ended this section of the performance with 'Childsong', written for his eldest son, Jo. Jo and his brother Malcolm, both accomplished musicians in their own right, supported Jack on stage across the two nights. If Jack's sons represented his real family, then the first ensemble pieces of the event featured those special musicians who could be called Jack's 'musical family'. His musical dad, as he puts it, was the late and much-missed saxophonist Dick Heckstall-Smith. It was back in 1962 that Jack, an acoustic bass-player of barely 19 years old, persuaded Dick and Ginger Baker to let him join them on the stand in a dingy Cambridge cellar. He blew through their attempts to catch him out and then disappeared into the night. Dick, who would later become known as 'the rowing captain' for his ability to bring talented musicians together, then tracked Jack down in London and brought him into Alexis Korner's Blues Incorporated. And there began a historic rhythm partnership unequalled in its influence on rock music or the intensity of its 'sibling rivalry'.

Here in 1993, Ginger was, well, Ginger. He had arrived in Germany from Colorado having made no arrangements about his drums and proceeded to have a row with Jack about drum solos, but was generally on his best behaviour until another incident occurred. "That was hilarious," says Pete Brown with a laugh. "Ginger always calls Jack 'Jekyll and Hyde', but it's the pot calling the kettle black. Ginger and I were standing together and it was probably the only time for years that we were actually having a reasonable conversation, standing there waiting to rehearse.

"There were lots of relatively young people running the gig and they couldn't do enough for you: 'What would you like to eat?' 'What would you like to drink?' 'Would you like to sit down? Stand up? Chair, prop, crutch, anything, you know?' And suddenly Ginger mutates into this Nazi Officer: 'Wolfgang! Helmut!' He just turned into a fuckin' Nazi. The vibe went arrgghhh and everybody froze. It was terrible."

Jack introduced Dick to the stage but the cheers for Ginger went on and on, prompting Jack to call out: "Come on, it'll go to his head. He'll get a swollen head." The trio launched into a straight-ahead jazz selection from Jack's *Things We Like* LP, but not before Jack gave a fleeting insight into the past mischief between him and Ginger. With the drummer still standing next to his kit, drink in hand, Jack said: "I'll start now before you sit down." Then, almost to himself: "That's the stuff we used to do. We're very nice now; we're friends now," he continued, pulling a face to the camera filming the event. Finally, and more loudly, he said: "He hasn't attacked me once with a knife today," before the three of them headed off into a jazz improvisation that morphed into 'Over The Cliff', Jack's tribute to bassist Cliff Barton.

Jack and lyricist/poet Pete Brown have often described their relationship as a marriage. From Cream's first single in 1966 onward they have fought, laughed, and nearly drowned together, and in the process produced a unique body of work as creative as that of any writing partnership in popular music.

When Jack invited Pete to his 50th it was the first time they had spoken in about four years.

The vibe in Cologne was good. "Everybody stayed in the same hotel and we had a party for a week," Jack recalls. "Nobody wanted it to end." Musicians gathered, rehearsed, drank, reminisced, and sang 'Happy Birthday' to Jack as a chocolate birthday cake did the rounds backstage. Among the other guests was trombonist John Mumford, who had shared a place in London with Jack when he first arrived in 1962 to stake his claim in the jazz scene. Trumpet player Henry Lowther had played with him in Manfred Mann and the Group Sounds modern-jazz line-ups. Like John and Henry, altoist Art Themen appeared on Jack's first solo album, *Songs For A Tailor*, and also toured with Jack in 1971 in a band that featured Chris Spedding, John Marshall, and Graham Bond. Jack had chosen Simon Phillips, then only 19, to play drums in his 1977 band with Tony Hymas and Hugh Burns, while guitarist Clem Clempson had begun a long association with Jack in 1980 after stints in Colosseum and Humble Pie.

In putting together his 1989 tour band, Jack had unexpectedly brought in two guys from the world of George Clinton and deep funk: keyboard player Bernie Worrell and singer Gary 'Mudbone' Cooper. Bernie and Jack have a very special relationship and during their songs on stage bounced little musical jokes off each other, laughing and grinning. But they still took things seriously, too. Bernie recalls that while the event was "fabulous, it was also very intense. There was a lot of work putting it together." On the second night, Gary Moore took over on lead guitar in preparation for what would be a high profile but shortlived trio with Jack and Ginger.

The audience was treated to a number of songs that had rarely been performed live, including 'Never Tell Your Mother She's Out Of Tune' with full horn section, and 'Rope Ladder To The Moon' and 'As You Said' with Jack on acoustic guitar accompanied by two young German cellists. Jack has taken some criticism for continuing to play Cream classics such as 'White Room', 'Politician', and 'Sunshine Of Your Love', the accusation being, why trade on old glories when there are so many other great self-penned songs he could play? Jack doesn't see it like that at all. "This is my music, which I am very proud of," he says. "[It just] happened to be played by Cream." It would be impossible to imagine then that for this of all concerts he wouldn't give these songs an airing – especially with audience expectation high and Ginger Baker in the line-up. In fact, Eric had been invited as well, and would have come had he not been touring in Japan, although it's possible that having Cream on stage would have overshadowed the whole event. So with Ginger's solo segueing to 'NSU', the concert thundered toward a rousing finale with everybody on stage for 'Sunshine' and a Willie Dixon composition, 'Blues You Can't Lose'.

Given the breadth of Jack's musical repertoire, he wasn't able to cover everything. One missing piece of the pie was his long-standing involvement with Latin musicians, which began in the early 80s and transmuted into his latest band, The Cuicoland Express. To give the musicians a break, a compere came on stage to conduct interviews with two individuals who could articulate their special relationship with Jack. One was Pete Brown; the other was Kip Hanrahan, a Brooklyn-born, half-Irish, half-Jewish producer-auteur-lyricist, fan of West Ham United, architect of Jack's introduction to and continued involvement with Latin music, and king of the unfinished sentence and the elliptical conversation. Asking Kip in all innocence about Jack's music, the compere stood in awkward bewilderment as Kip took off, hardly drawing breath as the words came tumbling out.

"I can't answer that in two minutes especially as you expect me to speak English slowly," he began. "Not a fuckin' chance. I can answer to something else. There's this thing going through my blood and it's thicker than Haitian rum or something. It burns stronger than … what? … Haitian sun. Fuck those motherfuckers because every one of those guys up there I have envy for because it burns, man … Husband and Clempson and Dick and the horns and Mudbone. I envy them with a passion that hurts. They can show Jack through their playing what they feel about him. Fuck you for being so lucky … so blessed. The rest of us … words can go through your fingers like sand; it doesn't mean the same thing. If you're fully [into] Jack's music, his music isn't ephemeral. He builds these fuckin' buildings, these cities, they're made of shadows and gold and diamonds – and if you have a dick or a pussy or soul or a heart, you end up living in Jack's buildings. The last thing about him, you can't talk about him in words, you can talk about him with emotions."

To his credit, the compere went in for a repeat performance the following night. He asked the question again, and Kip responded as if hearing it for the first time. "Fuck that," he roared and said he's been asked to give nice television-friendly, short, neat, concise answers about Jack Bruce. "Fuck that … with that intense emotion inside you that Jack's music brings on, there is no such fuckin' thing as a short, neat answer about it. If there was, then the motherfuckers on stage wouldn't be here for Jack, you motherfuckers wouldn't be here on stage, if there is a neat short answer for it." Then he railed at Jack for being "so fuckin' good and for making songs that make us feel emotions that we thought we would know how to do … I must go and get a drink."

It all made sense in a Kip kind of way – it *is* all about listening to the music and taking from it what your heart tells you. As Dick Heckstall-Smith said at the event, "words are words, music is music" – and it is damn near impossible for one to do justice to the other.

O

On one of those nights in Cologne, Jack told the audience that he was taking them on "a very long epic journey" and that he "hope[d] to see you all at the end". But first we need to go back to the beginning. A few weeks after the party left town, Cologne was battered by the worst storms in a century when the Rhine rose to its highest level in two hundred years. The old part of town was flooded out; 50,000 people were driven from their homes as torrents of icy rain lashed down. There was even a minor earthquake, registering 2.5 on the Richter scale.

Rewind 50 years and Cologne was being devastated by a very different kind of storm. From 1941 onward, tons of Allied bombs rained down on the city reducing it to rubble. But Charlie Bruce, a member of Glasgow's Auxiliary Fire Service, could afford to relax a little. Glasgow had been quiet for two months and no more German bombs would be falling. There would be no more incendiary fires to fight. He could turn his attention to his sick wife and the birth of his second child.

a man's a man for a' that

CHAPTER 1

The headlines in the Glasgow press for May 14 1943 brought encouraging news from the War. Victory was secured in North Africa following the fall of Tunisia, while Allied bombers continued to pulverise German cities amid rumours of imminent invasion and riots in Berlin.

As one of Britain's most important industrial cities and ports, Glasgow had taken its share of punishment from the German Luftwaffe. The first raids were in 1940, but the worst came between March 13–15 and April 7–8 1941. Since then the bombing had been sporadic, with nothing since March 1943.

Charlie Bruce was 30 at the outbreak of war. As a grocery delivery driver, he avoided conscription – 'food distribution' was a reserved occupation – but was instead recruited by the Auxiliary Fire Service. Firemen on the Home Front had an especially dangerous job, caught up in the full rage of the bombing raids, trying to rescue people from burning buildings on the verge of collapse. Charlie even found himself setting fires on the Campsie Fells, a range of hills that stretched from Stirling down to East Dunbartonshire on the northwest outskirts of Glasgow, as a ruse to draw German bombers away from the city centre.

On May 14, however, Charlie's attention was focused on home. Upstairs in their small, end-of-terrace house at 67 Beaufort Gardens in Bishopbriggs, to the north of the city, his wife Betty was about to give birth to a boy, John

Simon Asher Bruce. Simon Asher was Betty's father, his name suggesting a Jewish connection; John would quickly become 'Jack'.

The birth went well but there were complications. Betty had contracted double pneumonia, and as Jack's older brother Charlie, aged eight at the time, recalls: "It was touch and go. I remember her being taken to hospital in an ambulance and my father breaking down. Me and Jack were both looked after by our step-grandmother and others" – a shift system of their father's sisters.

Betty Bruce was an immensely strong character. Her son Charlie says that when he was taken to see her in hospital, he was "shocked how thin and drawn she was. But she made a quick recovery when she was released." "After that she was quite unstoppable," Jack adds. "She had so much energy, it was quite phenomenal."

Betty had already survived one bout of pneumonia as a child. Glasgow was notorious for the poor health of its working classes, many of whom lived in the most abject poverty and deprivation, particularly in and around the squalid tenements of the Gorbals in the south of the city. The city was badly hit by the 'flu pandemic that swept across the world in 1918–19 – in fact, medical historians think that Glasgow was quite literally the port of entry for the disease into Britain.

Influenza normally takes its course over a few days: the person feels terrible but then recovers. What happened in 1918 was more like a Hollywood horror movie. Perfectly fit people would go to work feeling a bit under the weather and be dead by the evening. There was a chronic shortage of doctors because many of them were still assigned to military units. In Glasgow one doctor died at a patient's bedside; another just collapsed in the street on his rounds. In less than a year, an estimated one million Scots were infected, and nearly 80,000 died. Tuberculosis and rickets – classic diseases of bad housing and poor diet – were also rampant in Glasgow. "Everybody knew or had a relative who died or suffered from TB," says Jack, "and I think my dad suffered from rickets as a child."

Betty's strength of character seemed genetic. Her family originally came from fiercely independent Highland stock, from Tain in Ross-shire, but by the time of her birth in 1909 they had moved to Springburn, about two miles up the road from Bishopbriggs. Like many other families they had come to the lowlands in search of work at a time when Glasgow's growing industrial might led to it being called 'the second city of the Empire'. Glasgow was the fastest growing city in Europe during the 19th century; in built up areas, the population increased tenfold.

Betty's mother had died in a bizarre accident when Betty herself was only 18 months old. In the cramped working-class houses of the day, the only way to dry clothes indoors was to hang them over a rack in the kitchen and hoist it up out of the way. One day, Betty's mother was reaching up when she hit her head on the rack and died of a brain haemorrhage. (Her father subsequently remarried, and her only sister, Isabella, would die before she turned 60.)

Betty's family lived close to the huge railways works at St Rollox, where her father was a coach painter. Because he was a skilled craftsman the family was quite well off by the standards of the time, although working in a closed environment inhaling paint fumes all day certainly contributed to his death.

Charlie Bruce's family were not so well found. They lived on Crown Street on the south side near the Gorbals, although their tenement was a bit better than most. As the younger Charlie recalls, they had "a flat with three or so rooms with a toilet inside which was quite something in those days." They would have needed the space: Charlie, also born in 1909, was the oldest of seven children. He had a brother, Jimmy, and five sisters, Mary, Kathy, Louisa, Peggy, and Millie. Peggy died around the age of 30, while Millie didn't see her 50th birthday.

Charlie's family had their roots in Ayrshire but they too had moved in search of employment. Jack and Charlie's grandfather (also called Charlie) was a pattern-maker at Braby's, where he carved the wooden moulds for the manufacture of metal machine tools, but having been gassed at Ypres and sustained an eye injury, he was in poor health. Working at Braby's didn't help: the working conditions there were among the worst in the city, which is saying something. Workers handled chemicals with no gloves, and many of the industrial processes gave off noxious fumes against which there was no protection. Jack recalls him as being (understandably) quite miserable. His wife, Jack's paternal grandmother, was very religious. "She got into this sect, the Church Of Christ, I think it was called. My grandfather hated religion; the family story goes that when he came back from the war, he kicked the priest down the stairs."

Jack's dad was a pretty smart kid and was offered a scholarship to Hutchesons' Grammar School, which the Bruces could see from their kitchen window. But in a story familiar to many intelligent yet poor working-class children, the window was as close as Charlie would ever get. The family wasn't destitute, but with Charlie Sr unable to work, both his sons were expected to make their contribution. So young Charlie focussed on his passions, one of which was dancing.

Glasgow's first dance hall, named the Albert Ballroom in honour of Queen Victoria's consort, opened in 1905. Located on Bath Street in the city centre, this beautiful, ornate hall was the first ballroom in Scotland to hold dances six nights a week. The Albert's popularity soared during the 20s as the introduction of new risqué dances like the Charleston brought more and more young Glaswegians flocking to the dance floor. Similarly, the Locarno Ballroom on Sauchiehall Street opened in 1926 and quickly became a Glasgow institution. It was named after the town in Switzerland where a year earlier the European powers signed a treaty agreeing the new frontiers of Europe following the First World War, raising false hopes of a lasting peace. Over on the other side of town, the original Dennistoun Palais opened in 1922, but was destroyed by fire in 1936. It reopened in 1938 as the biggest dance hall in Glasgow with a capacity of 1,800. It was said that ten times around the dance floor represented a mile.

These were just the most famous of the many dance halls dotted right across the city. It was in one of these that Betty and Charlie first met in the early 30s. There followed courtship, marriage, and the birth of Charlie, Jack's brother, in 1935.

As well as swirling around the ballroom to the dance crazes of the day, Betty and Charlie shared another more profound passion: left-wing politics. The combination of rapid industrialisation, appalling living conditions, and the passionate nature of the immigrant population from the Highlands and Ireland meant that Glasgow was already a hotbed of political activity before the Great War. Even so, the skilled working-class groups tended to back Lloyd George and the Liberal Party, and many of the poorer groups didn't even have the vote.

The War changed everything. The workers went flat out to support the war effort in the factories and docks. Scotland supplied more soldiers, proportionally, than any other part of Britain, and suffered very heavy casualties. To begin with there was a strong patriotic feeling about "a just war against The Boche". But the horrific waste of life, with countless families left without fathers and towns and villages losing their working men, caused many to turn against the Liberals, who in turn were beginning to regard any dissent as undermining the fight.

In 1915 there were rent strikes in Glasgow against greedy landlords. These were supported by the Labour Party, trade unions, and left-wing suffragettes, but much less so by the government. Four years later there was another strike to campaign for a 40-hour working week; 100,000 people marched and the riot that followed was crushed by 12,000 troops armed with machine guns and backed up by tanks. Many working-class soldiers coming back to 'the land fit for heroes' found it unfit for dogs.

In 1922 the Labour Party won ten out of 15 seats in the city and there were mass rallies to see the new MPs off to London. As the trains steamed off into the distance, both 'The Red Flag' and Psalm 24 – Scotland's Psalm of Deliverance – were sung. (Psalm 24 was written to celebrate the deliverance of the Jews from Babylonian captivity, and was taken up in the late 17th century as a Scottish nationalist battle hymn against English oppression under Charles II and James II.)

For some, inspired by the example of the Soviet Union, the Labour Party just wasn't left wing enough. There was a split between those who saw the ballot box as a road for change and those who in growing numbers were pushing for more radical action. When the Communist Party Of Great Britain was formed in 1920, Glasgow quickly became the most active city for British communism; both Charlie and Betty signed up as card-carrying members in the early 30s. Left-wing activists like Charlie concerned themselves with campaigns for rent control and improved housing and also the plight of the unemployed. Since the War, the region had become dangerously reliant on heavy industry. As the world slipped into Depression, unemployment rose at an alarming rate at a time when a family could literally starve to death if the man was out of work.

Even so, there was much division between more conservative skilled workers, many of them engineers, and the unskilled masses – and also between the various left-wing groups of the sort parodied in Monty Python's *The Life Of Brian*: the Socialist Democratic Federation, the Social Democratic Party, the Socialist League, the Socialist Labour Party, the Socialist Party Of Great Britain, and then all kinds of Marxist-Leninist-Trotskyist factions within the Communist Party. An attempt to start a separate Scottish Communist Party shortly after the formation of the British party collapsed in a welter of infighting.

Moreover, while Charlie and other Communist activists signed up to the utopian dream of a universal brotherhood of workers, there was no real evidence that most had the stomach for a bloody revolution. Like many of Scotland's politicised workers, Charlie Bruce's outlook can best be summed up by Robert Burns's five-verse song, 'A Man's A Man For A' That,' written in the Ayrshire dialect. In it Burns declared that money and social class should not be the measure of a man's true worth; that honesty and self-respect do not come from inherited wealth, fancy clothes, or airs and graces. The song ends with the hope that in the future we might all live together in trust and mutual respect. Looking forward to a time when rank and power would be dramatically diluted as the common man gained equality, it was essentially a creed of human rights, civil liberties, and natural justice.

But even if Charlie Bruce and his fellow travellers were not engaged in bringing down the government, being a member of The Party (as they called it) in the 30s could be very risky. The battle against unemployment was the main item on the Communist agenda, but many in the Communist-led National Unemployed Workers Movement were arrested, with libel charges brought against activists for attacking Labour MPs. Although there were vestiges of anti-war feeling in The Party, most communists were in favour of the war against Hitler even in the face of the Nazi-Soviet pact of 1939. Some members recalled the horrors of the war against the fascists in Spain; closer to home, some Party members had done battle in the streets with members of Oswald Mosley's New Party (a forerunner of the British Union Of Fascists), which had been launched in Glasgow in 1931.

Like Charlie, Betty came from a political background. Her father was a member of the Independent Labour Party, which was founded in 1893 by Keir Hardie and which laid the foundations for the modern Labour Party (while still retaining its own membership among those who felt that the Labour Party was too timid and modest in its aims on behalf of working people).

Despite their passion for the wellbeing of all working people, the Communists – like the other political groups of the time – saw politics as the work of men, especially since so much activity was centred around trade unionism and the workplace. The role of Party women was still largely confined to making tea and sandwiches for the meetings. Speaking of his father, Jack says: "Like all of us, he was a guy who was full of contradictions – far-sighted politically, but with the prejudices of his background and his time – and we are all prisoners of that, to some extent." But women had been the main organisers of the Rent Strikes, and were obviously very involved in the various suffrage organisations. With her innate self-confidence, Betty was just as likely as her husband to speak up at meetings, attend the rallies, go on the marches, and read the pamphlets and newspapers.

O

Politics were not put on hold during the Second World War. From the time that Hitler invaded Russia in 1941, membership of the Party grew from a few hundred in 1939 to thousands as the War progressed and Stalin became a national hero. Charlie and Betty would have been among the throng who attended a rally on Glasgow Green in support of the Allies opening up the Second Front to go to Uncle Joe's aid. By then, Charlie's brother Jimmy had been captured at Dunkirk and was a POW in one of the Stalags. He told Jack stories of eating rats to survive, but by all accounts he was something of a wheeler-dealer and delighted Jack's brother by bringing him back a genuine German helmet – much to the envy of his schoolmates.

For Jack and Charlie – and many other children in the city – the War became the backdrop to life and could even have its high spots. After their school was flattened by a bomb, every day was a holiday for Charlie and his mates. "I remember on the day War broke out, my mother got down on her knees and started crying," he recalls. "But the War was part of my growing up. There were shortages, but we were never really hungry. We grew up to love spam and dried eggs. There was no sense of deprivation."

With Betty ill and then convalescing, young Charlie had to do his share of looking after his baby brother. "It could be a nuisance," he says, "but there was no resentment. He was your wee brother and you loved him." Even so, Charlie's idea of 'looking after' Jack could sometimes be a bit cavalier. "We had this great big dog, a sable collie," he recalls. "I was taking the pram out and all my mates were out playing. So I hitched up the dog to the pram and whoosh, off it went. Everything was fine until it came to the kerb, then zoooom, Jack went flying out of the pram. We hadn't the wit to strap him in and he got a bump on the head that day." Jack's earliest memories are of being out with his dad on his delivery rounds at the age of about three. "He drove one of the little three-wheel vans. I remember delivering chocolate – big blocks of chocolate, so you could chip little bits off."

As Betty regained her strength she began to plan for the family; what she lacked in inches, she made up for with her forceful personality. "She was a powerful influence, and also a very controlling influence," says Jack. "In any situation she was in, she felt she needed to be in control. No doubt about it. My father made the important decisions, like who was going to win the Korean War, while my mother made all the other decisions – like what was going to happen, all the time! She was the reason we all emigrated to Canada. I don't think my father wanted to do that."

When it came to political arguments or any issue on which Charlie thought he was right, however, "He would *never* give way on a single point. One time when the family were all having tea round the table, my dad remarked that something had been delivered by 'fright' train. My brother said the word was 'freight', but my dad absolutely insisted the pronunciation was 'fright'. He never gave in on this, and I realise now he was just winding us up."

Betty Bruce had high ambitions for her family. She might have been fully committed to Communist ideals, but nevertheless was of the view that her family could aspire to a better life; that her family was 'a cut above' to the extent that some of the neighbours apparently dubbed her Queen Elizabeth III. Charlie's job as a grocery van driver had no prospects, and while it is likely that his move into selling insurance came at the behest of his wife, he really wasn't cut out for the job. His son Charlie remembers days when "he just wouldn't go out. You've got to be insincere and tell lies." Betty thought that they could all do better by going abroad. And in that, she was not alone; although Britain had been victorious in the War, the country was on its knees in the immediate post-war years, and Glasgow was just as poor and miserable as it had always been.

After the Second World War, many British families decided to start new lives in Australia. Old passenger liners and even a few converted 'Liberty Ships' were used to take large numbers of emigrants to Australia from Europe. The cost of this was subsidised by various agencies and by Australian State governments, and set at a low, affordable figure. Typically this was about £10 (about $40 at the time), and as the British were known as 'poms' in Australia, the nickname 'ten pound poms' was frequently applied to the new settlers.

There was no such plan for families moving to Canada, so the Bruces had to set about selling their house in Beaufort Gardens to raise the money. The house had two bedrooms upstairs with a quite large living room downstairs and a big kitchen at the back. "It was a nice house – very posh by a lot of standards," says Charlie. Selling it, however, was the start of their troubles. "There were these people who were injured in the War who wore a blue uniform with white shirts and red ties. That signified that they were ex-service who'd been wounded. There were loads of these people wandering about. This couple came to look at the house and they were both dressed in this regalia. And they got the house for less because they came out with all this spiel. I think my parents got £1,400 when they should have managed £1,600. It was only a couple of hundred pounds, but that was a lot of money in those days."

For Charlie and Jack, emigrating was a great adventure. "There was great excitement when I found out we were going to Canada," says Jack, who was about four years old at the time. "There were great crowds of people at Glasgow Central Station seeing us off. We went to London and then to Southampton and then onto the USS United States. It was beautiful inside, and really for the first time we began to realise what we had been deprived of. They had bread that was so white you couldn't believe it. All this food and fruit! How the other half lived!

"I do remember being on this ship and being very sea-sick – and seeing the first black person I had ever seen," Jack continues. "She was a stewardess, and when I felt better she brought me this big pile of sandwiches with all the crusts cut off, on a silver platter – so posh. I hadn't seen anything like it before. I remember seeing an iceberg. Every night I went to listen to the ship's orchestra. They would put me on a chair and I would conduct the orchestra."

The Bruces arrived in New York in the spring of 1947 and went through immigration. It was, Jack says, "not Ellis Island" but a "very similar situation – long lines of people coming off the ship. We went on a train to Toronto and arrived very early in the morning. We went for breakfast that was the best breakfast I had ever had – fried egg with yellow, yellow yolks and bacon. The place was run by a Chinese couple, and I had never seen Chinese people either."

After a short stay in a rather sleazy hotel, the family ended up in Weston, a small town in Northwest Toronto (since incorporated into the Toronto metropolitan area) and an important industrial centre for the whole region. Some would have it that the town was the home of the Wagon Wheel biscuit, but the story seems to have been garbled in the telling. Garry Weston was born in Toronto and took over his father's international food business chain, inventing the Wagon Wheel in 1949. But the town of Weston had nothing to do with the Weston family. It was named in 1815 by James Farr, a prominent local mill owner who came originally from Weston in Hertfordshire (about 40 miles north of London).

The Bruce family still had money from the house sale but the need to find work was urgent. Charlie bluffed his way into an engineering factory as a machine tool setter. The factory had huge machines called punch presses – capable, for example, of punching out car body panels – and Charlie's job was to set them up. Betty did some waitressing, and they took in a couple of construction workers as lodgers.

Jack had a great time. "I loved the whole experience," he says. "I loved the weather – it was either hot or very thick snow. I had a great time. I went to kindergarten. And I think I had just started proper school when we left. I was just this little Canadian boy with what they called a 'semi-crew' haircut. I would have been fine. I could have grown up to be Joni Mitchell!"

Charlie on the other hand felt very different. "School was a slight disaster for me," he recalls. "In Weston I went to the school at the end of the road and the headmaster said I should be in the High School. So they kicked me up to this other school and these kids were older and I was right out of my depth socially. And there was this 'limey' thing as well. So I was a bit of an outcast in some respects. And there was nobody else there in my situation."

The boys' father carried on his political activities both as a trade unionist and in the Canadian equivalent of the Communist Party, the Labour Progressive Party. Because some of the unions were cross-border – the AFL-CIO was connected to the motor industry, for example – Charlie attended conferences and events in the States at the height of the McCarthy era and came smack up against the ugly, corrupt face of American trade unionism, which was determined to exert maximum influence over any naive British trade unionists. In Milwaukee Charlie was confronted by henchmen of union boss Walter Reuther – a socialist in the 30s but a virulent anti-communist by the 40s – and told to keep his mouth shut and support the 'right' candidates. He was stopped and questioned at the border on his way home, and when news of his political activities got back to the factory bosses in Weston, Charlie lost his job and couldn't find another.

By then the Bruce family had already grown increasingly demoralised and homesick. This was not uncommon among families who emigrated – some spent the 50s moving backward and forward trying to work out where they really wanted to be. This wasn't an option for the Bruces, whose nest egg was running out. Early in 1949, scraping together what money they could, they came back to Glasgow.

CHAPTER 2 morning story

Charlie and Betty knew life was going to be hard when they got back. Charlie's experience as a machine tool setter in Canada counted for nothing in Scotland and he struggled to find work. "The poverty we faced was pretty grim," says Jack. The family was forced to live in what could only be described as a byre – a cow shelter – in a farming area near Bishopbriggs. They moved to a cottage with two rooms and a bit stuck out the back for a kitchen where they stayed for some while – "until the farmer who owned the cottage found out about my dad's politics and chased us out with a shotgun". The family then found lodgings in Lambhill, north of the river; then, after Betty laid siege to the local housing department, they finally landed the downstairs of a corporation house on a new housing estate in Pollok, on the south side of Glasgow. By then Charlie had found work with British Railways and family life began to settle down.

Those early years weren't easy for Jack. He had left the country when he was four, had a great time in Canada, but was now back in a place where he had no real friends. This was made worse by having to attend one school after another both because the family moved about so much and because of the rebuilding programme going on in Glasgow. Housing was the main social issue in post-war Glasgow, but while new housing estates were starting to spring up, there was no proper infrastructure of schools, shops, employment, or recreation – and in a vain attempt to control the legendary heavy drinking and alcoholism, there seemed to be a deliberate policy of not building any pubs. Charlie had to travel miles to work on a succession of buses, as did Jack depending on what school he was going to at the time. As such Jack was often quite isolated, geographically, from his classmates, but the divisions ran deeper than that.

"There were some local kids who I had some quite difficult relationships with," he recalls. "I think they thought I was a bit stuck-up, and just the way I talked as well – I had this Canadian accent which took a long time to wear off. I remember the first day I had a problem with kids physically attacking me. I was walking down near where I lived wearing a Parka with the fur hood, because that was normal in Canada, and they all said, 'you're a girl' because they'd all be wearing shorts and wellies. I very quickly adapted to the shorts-and-wellies look. Backing onto the houses where we lived was what remained of this beautiful wood and they would destroy the trees. And I'd say things like 'those things are alive, too' and that became another big thing – 'oh, he's talking to the trees'. I was just different to them."

Many of the kids in Pollok came from the Gorbals tenements. Betty was not keen on her Jack playing with ruffians, so tended to over-protect him. "If I was going to go out without a jacket or jumper, she'd say, 'you'd better put that on because you are not like those other boys, they're hardy annuals.' So I grew up with this idea that I was a bit more fragile than the other kids, but I wasn't in the least – I was a strong little kid. But I did get ill several times. I think I had an illness that went undetected, probably rheumatic fever. I was sent up to the shops and I collapsed in this shop and just went to bed for a while – but I think there was something seriously wrong."

Being rather an outsider from an early age, and with a brother who was eight years older than him, Jack tended to fall back on his own resources and lived life – as he saw it – as an only child. "I started reading very early. I taught myself to read by looking at my father's books. He had a collection of political books and I remember he had a thesaurus, which I still have – it was quite a famous family story. I'm sitting there probably three or four, so the first thing I worked out was *Hartrampf's Vocabulary*. 'Does that say *Hartrampf's Vocabulary*, dad?' I had a go at *The Ragged Trousered Philanthropists* as well. I loved comics – the *Dandy*, the *Beano*, the *Hotspur*, the *Wizard*, and all that. Tuesday for the *Dandy* and Thursday for the *Beano*, those were the big days. I had to hide those because DC Thompson, who printed these in Dundee, was a non-union organisation. So my father wouldn't allow them in the house and

I had to sneak them in. I joined the library and just read everything – *Treasure Island* and *Coral Island* and all those adventure books, which I really loved."

And then there was music. In the days before television, music was the hub around which much of family and community life revolved. Jack's paternal grandfather had a piano in his house, and from his visits there as a child, Jack's brother Charlie saw his grandfather playing a melodeon and dabbling on harmonica. He also had a go at a Jew's harp, following a family holiday in Troon, but that wasn't quite so successful. "I remember quite vividly my grandfather enthusiastically buying this Jew's harp that he saw in a shop window," Charlie recalls. "He had to take it back for a refund because, as he explained, he had 'nae teeth!'"

There was a strong emphasis in left-wing circles of not just raising political consciousness but also enriching the lives of working people through cultural activities. Both Betty and her sister Isabella had excellent singing voices and joined the Glasgow Socialist Choristers. Jack's brother was also in a choir, and both boys were excellent musicians. Jack remembers his dad as "a brilliant self-taught piano player in the style of Fats Waller. He was the life and soul of the party. As well as the piano, my father played the mandolin unbelievably. There was a lot of socialising in those days, pre-television. I remember all the parties we had at our house and other people's places. We would have social evenings and he would be playing all the tunes. He'd always have a fag hanging out of his mouth and the ash would get longer and longer.

"A lot of the gatherings would be to do with 'The Party'. But there was also a local community spirit. As kids we would organise little talent competitions in the back gardens. If you had a party or a social, everybody would sit around the walls in a circle and you'd go round and everybody would have to do their party piece – tell a joke or sing a song. We were quite a talented family: my brother played really great George Shearing jazz piano, my mother was a wonderful singer – it was she who encouraged me to sing. She sang Scottish folk songs and a lot of Robert Burns, which she taught me."

Jack absorbed music from wherever he could hear it. "My brother got a record player later on when he was a teenager. He and his friends were all into Frank Sinatra – *Songs For Swinging Lovers*. I used to look up to Charlie, so sophisticado! And I used to love listening to the radio. The Goons were a favourite. My father would say, 'Shut that bloody racket off.' He couldn't get it at all. But I also loved listening to The Third Programme, as it was then. If I could, I would come home at lunchtime, be on my own having a sandwich, and put my head right against this old radio listening to the orchestras,

Schubert, Bach. I can still smell the Bakelite and valves heating up. I don't really know why I got into that music – just twiddling the knobs on the radio and something would grab my attention. I really felt something – the power and depth of it."

Jack's earliest attempts at music were on the house piano, which had been bought by his parents for his brother. When Jack was ten, Charlie went into the RAF to do his national service; Jack just started improvising at the piano. Rock'n'roll came along a bit later; Little Richard and Elvis Presley could be heard just coming out of the houses as Jack walked around the streets. He never cared much for Presley, but still sent away "for an Elvis Presley guitar. It looked really good in the picture. When it came it was a little plastic ukulele with a terrible picture of Elvis on it which I scraped off, but I think bits of Elvis's foot were left."

It was as a singer that Jack's talent first became apparent. "I could always sing," he says. "When I was very young, my mother would make me do a turn, not just at a social, but even if she just had somebody round. I remember visiting her great aunt in the Highlands and singing for her. She went away and brought back half-a-crown – my first payment, I suppose."

On one memorable occasion, shortly after the family's return from Canada in 1949, Jack sang for Paul Robeson. The famous singer and left-wing activist was on one of his many trips to Britain – before the FBI took his passport away – and had come to Glasgow to sing and meet with Scottish socialists. It was after the formal events of the evening that young Jack was pushed forward.

"My mother was very much aware that I had this amazing voice – she started to encourage that and found me private teachers. The first one she found didn't charge her anything: there were people around who just wanted to nurture talent and weren't in it for the money. I went to this big old tumble-down house and the teacher there, Mrs McDonald, was very helpful."

Betty and Mrs McDonald also encouraged Jack to take part in singing competitions. "I was going in for a lot of competitions and I won the Glasgow Festival, the Lanarkshire Festival, and The Glasgow Mod, a competition singing in Gaelic. But I used to get very nervous and throw up. I didn't really enjoy the competitions – too nerve-wracking. Some of the adjudicators had great things to say. Herbert Howells – a very neglected composer – really saw what was in me and was very encouraging to me. But I remember one guy who was very critical because I was tapping my foot while I was singing. Also there were a couple of other boys who were in my league – and there was one in particular – he would either win and I would come second or the other way

41

round. There was tremendous competition between us – and the mums. I worked very hard at it, but if you had that kind of talent, that's what you did. I went along with all of this."

Like his mother and brother, Jack sang in a Sunday School Socialist Choir. "I was a member of a kiddie version of the Young Communist League Choir conducted by this amazing guy called Jimmy Callan. He told me that when I wrote music, it wouldn't be 'my' music as music belonged to the world and couldn't be owned." Jack didn't actually attend the Socialist Sunday School – "not Left enough for my parents!" – but he did manage to earn some money from his singing. Putting the family's atheism aside, he donned a surplice to join a church choir, then sang in Bizet's *Carmen* with the Carl Rosa opera company when it visited Glasgow, and on a BBC radio young musician's show.

Jack's last junior school in his tour of the Glasgow education system was Cardonald Primary. He went there aged 11 for a year of preparation for the 'quali' or 11-plus, the exam which determined the calibre of secondary school he would attend.

"There was a guy called Douglas Burney who was a wonderful bloke," he recalls. "And he was the teacher doing that year with us. The first day we got there, he came in with this record player and without a word put Louis Armstrong on and we were all shocked. It really was a shocking sound to hear in school in those days. Then he put on some Mozart straight after that. He obviously believed in the power of music to develop children. Because then he brought in these harmonicas, gave one to everybody and started teaching us. It was an Educator 2 – a special one that Hohner did. As soon as I got it, I just played all these melodies without even thinking about it. So he took a special interest in me."

Douglas Burney's interest in Jack was critical. He wanted Jack to go to the Bellahouston Academy, a rambling, Hogwarts-style Victorian building on Paisley Road West, where Jack's obvious talents as a musician could be developed. Jack was already composing music by then. "I think the first thing I wrote was the setting for a Dylan Thomas poem, 'This Bread I Break'," he says.

In true *Billy Elliot*-style, Burney went round to Jack's house and told his parents that the boy was really talented and should be sent to Bellahouston. Jack's dad wasn't keen: "He thought I should just go to the Junior Secondary School and get an apprenticeship. My father was quite against it – maybe a touch of jealousy because he'd had to go out to work to support the family and not take up the scholarship, or something about 'going above your station', that kind of thing."

Betty Bruce was naturally all in favour of the idea, and of course won the argument. But her work wasn't finished yet. Jack didn't do well enough on the 'quali', and looked to be headed instead for a newly built Comprehensive, Crookston Castle School in Pollock. "We had a look round and it was all new with a swimming pool," Jack recalls. "I would have loved to have gone there. But my mother quite rightly got me into Bellahouston because it was very famous for music."

Jack's first few days at Bellahouston were something of a trauma. "They said you've got to have gym shorts. So my mum said, 'Oh just use your brother's old RAF shorts, they're fine.' My brother was eight years older than me and I'm just a wee boy having to wear these heavy blue RAF shorts. Everybody took the piss out of me big time as you can imagine. It was so embarrassing, like Spike Milligan's drawing of Eccles with the long shorts and knobbly knees."

There was also the issue of what instrument Jack would play at the school. Most of the other kids were from middle class professional families who could afford to buy instruments for their children. Jack's mum and dad couldn't compete, but fortunately "in the corner at school was an old double bass. I just started playing it. I really enjoyed it – it's a very tactile instrument, a sensual feeling. And that was the only instrument that was going to be free. So they brought in this teacher – a really old man, at least in his sixties, maybe older. He'd offer you these sweeties out of his pocket and they'd all be covered in lint, fluff, and tobacco. He said, 'To be quite honest, you aren't big enough.' My hands weren't big enough to play properly. So he said, 'Come back in a year when you've grown a bit.'

"I was very downcast about that and so the music teacher said 'I think we can find you a cello'. So I started learning on that. I had a very good teacher - he was the lead cello for the Scottish National Orchestra."

Jack's prowess on cello earned him a place in the Glasgow Schools Orchestra conducted by Norman Del Mar, which he recalls "involved going for two weeks at Toward Castle near Dunoon and learning a concert repertoire". But while Jack's mother deserves much credit for fighting on his behalf to get him into a school from which this and other opportunities flowed, he still feels that she could have done more to make his first trip away from home a little easier.

"They said 'you've got to have a white shirt and grey shorts' or something like that – and I only had the one pair," he recalls. "And you know what it's like when you're a kid, I was in such a state. I just had the one pair and I thought, 'How am I going to get these pressed and looking half-decent?' Luckily I found this girl who did them for me and I had to hide while she did it. You'd think a mum would pack the suitcase and say, 'There's your shorts for every day and here's a spare in case you have an accident and here are the ones for the concert.' My mum thought she was protective of me, but she wasn't really."

Happily, the musical experience that followed was nothing but positive. "We did [Dvořák's] *New World Symphony*, a Beethoven symphony, and some stuff by [Swedish composer] Dag Wirén. You'd have individual lessons on cello, then the whole string section, then the full orchestra leading up to a concert. And the standard was very high. One evening, I was just improvising on piano and Norman Del Mar suddenly appeared in the room, listened for a while, and told me he was really impressed because a lot of classical musicians just can't improvise like that. If it's not written down, it doesn't exist." Jack also wrote "some compositions that were played by a string quartet – little concerts we did in the evenings". Jimmy Callan, conductor of the Glasgow Socialist Choir, asked him to play cello for the main Young Communist League choir at the Edinburgh Festival, "where we did Beethoven settings of Burns". Callan turned down offers of recording contracts in Britain because he refused to drop 'Communist' from the name of his award-winning choir.

○

As Jack moved into his teens the strands of his character began to come together. The constant moving around the city, the problem he had with friendships, and what he regarded as his mother's benign neglect led him to become quite self-sufficient. And because money was always tight, he knew if he wanted any luxuries, he'd have to go and find a job. To earn the money for his first record player, Jack got himself a milk round when he was only 11; he would get up at six and do a two hour round before going to school.

He also had to learn to look after himself on the streets. When he was 14, the family moved to a very modern apartment block called Moss Heights, the first high-rise to be built in Glasgow. In the upstairs of their first house in Pollok had lived an ex-tenement family who brought their habits with them. They spent most of the time arguing and getting drunk on fortified wine. One Saturday night, Jack's dad complained about the noise and they beat him up so badly he was hospitalised. Jack's brother took matters in hand and got his family moved away from Pollok. But it all meant more travelling about the city, and Glasgow could be a very dangerous place – especially if you were a little guy lugging a cello through the dark streets, which Jack often was as he went from school to home to orchestra practice, recitals, and so on. The city was notorious for the drink-fuelled violence between the gangs who carved up chunks of the city into their 'territory' as readily as they carved up each other with razors and broken bottles, inflicting the infamous 'Glesga grin'. But anybody could be a victim: as the writer William McIlvanney put it, Glasgow was "the city of the stare". Jack was once set upon at a bus stop in a completely unprovoked attack. So he unscrewed the spike from the end of his cello, sharpened it, and kept it handy in case of trouble. "I also had a flick-knife, which I kept in the lining of my jacket for years," he notes. But while he did get into a few situations where he needed to reach for a weapon, he never had to use it in anger.

At school Jack found little to hold his attention besides English and Music and instead began to hold court as leader of the class rebels. Now at a settled school, he had more chance to make friends. "There would be the swots and the rebels," he says. "We used to sit up the back and make stupid remarks. But the trick was to be cleverer than the swots, which I was in the subjects I liked. There was a big attic at the top of the school that ran right across. They had an old piano and a double bass up there and loads of books. When I got chucked out of the Science class, I'd go up there – it was my own pad – music, girls, and if I was skint I'd sell some of the books. I got about 3/9d a week for school dinners. But across the road from the school was a bit of a tuck shop and I'd spend the lot on fags and cream slices on Monday and starve the rest of the week."

Jack skipped Lower Music studies and went straight for his Higher Music exams. His Higher English essay earned him the highest mark in the whole of Scotland. He also studied Russian because he loved the sound of a different language and the look of the strange Cyrillic alphabet. He would clearly have been university material, had he carried on into the sixth form at Bellahouston. But he had other ideas.

Music was taking up increasing amounts of Jack's time. In 1958, aged 15, he won a part-time scholarship to the Royal Scottish Academy Of Music And Drama, where he went after school (and sometimes during school time) to improve his music theory, except all he learnt from his male composition teacher was how to avoid his groping hands. Jack felt eventually that both Bellahouston and the Academy were holding him back with their very traditional views on teaching classical music, which didn't allow for improvisation. "I was not the kind of musician they wanted," he says. "My music teacher saw a potential there, she said that I could be a Franz Lehar

[Austrian composer of operettas], which was quite an intelligent thing to say, but to me that would be like Andrew Lloyd Webber. I wanted to be more cutting-edge, more esoteric. I always felt that it was because of my background that they thought I couldn't possibly be anything great. It was very unusual for a working class kid to be in that situation – as far as I knew, I was the only one."

Just as he was finding formal music tuition increasingly uncomfortable, Jack discovered jazz. "My dad loved jazz, but my brother was my main guy," he says. "He was quite a jazz fan and I went to concerts to see The Modern Jazz Quartet, Sonny Stitt, Ella Fitzgerald, and Oscar Peterson. And of course, I loved the bass players. Percy Heath from the MJQ was the first person I really heard playing amazing bass. It was at St Andrew's Hall, which got destroyed by fire later on – I was sitting right in the back row and I could hear every note really clearly.

"Then there was Ray Brown with Oscar Peterson. I had my own record player by then and the first record I bought was an EP of 'The Golden Striker' by the MJQ. John Lewis was a fabulous pianist. They would do improvisations on classical-sounding pieces, which I could recognise. And because of my classical training, I was very attracted by the 'gimmick' of the MJQ, dressing up in evening dress with black ties and dinner jackets."

By the age of 16, Jack had grown enough to be able to handle the double bass. Bringing all his cello skills to bear, inspired by the jazz musicians he saw in concert and heard on record, and sure in the knowledge that he was going to leave education behind, Jack began to look for openings to earn money as a musician.

"I met some guy and he worked in this big dance band – a rehearsal band, no money involved – and he said 'Why don't you come along and play?' Through that I got offered some work, which then turned into full-time work while I was still at school. So I was working six nights and two afternoons as well and doing my A-Levels. By that time I had more or less given up singing – my voice had changed, and also you find that most people who are instrumentalists, they give up singing. I didn't really want to be a singer at that time. I wanted to be Charlie Haden. It took me many years – really until Cream – for me to find out what my voice was."

Like many port cities, Glasgow had a vibrant music scene that sucked up influences from across the world – everything from dance and show bands, jazz, rock'n'roll, through to country & western, skiffle, Scottish country dancing, and classical music sessions. Jack tried them all: so long as he walked out with some cash, he didn't care.

His first paid gig was with Freddie Riley. It should have paid £15, but Jack was told that he'd only get £10 because of his age. He soon appeared on many of the bandstands like the Locarno and the West End Ballroom where his parents had conducted their courtship. But violence was always simmering under the surface; the ballrooms were often venues where the gangs would congregate to call each other out for a 'rammy'. There was even cold-bloodied murder. "I was in a pub one night drinking at the bar and a guy came up and said to me 'Stand aside, I've got no argument with you,'" Jack recalls. "He shot the guy standing next to me." When Jack went back next day to collect something he'd left behind, he got hauled in by the police to take part in an identity parade – and got paid 2/6d (about £2 or $3 today) for his trouble.

Before too long, Jack was earning £16 a week while his father was getting £14 working in a factory doing overtime. Jack was able to indulge in one of his passions: cars. "I was driving to school in a car," he says, when even his teachers couldn't afford one. He drove his red Sunbeam Talbot illegally for some months before passing his test first time, just after his 17th birthday.

How then did Jack's parents react to their son's newfound sense of independence, his money, and the direction his life was taking? "My mother always had faith in me, thought I would do something – she had done her bit and I think assumed I would go on to do something successful in music. My father was slightly more complicated. He came round when it was hugely successful. In fact he probably realised this when I was getting £16 at the Dennistoun Palais. To his credit, he was quite positive about it – a 'you must be in the right game' sort of thing – when I was earning more than he was." By contrast, Jack's schoolmates doing apprenticeships on the docks or in factories would be lucky to be earning £4 a week.

Jack was happy to play anything he could get paid for, but he was keenest on modern jazz – the more way-out the better. There was no modern jazz circuit in Glasgow, but Jack became friends with those very few musicians in the city who were interested in the music. He got to know a pianist called Kenny Crawford – "a lovely player and far ahead of anything I was doing" – and Andy Park, an art teacher and self-taught pianist who introduced Jack to the music of Thelonious Monk. Park had a small rehearsal band with whom he played Monk and Horace Silver at a place called the Cell, an attic above a stage-set design studio next to the Mitchell Library on the Kent Road. To get to the tiny club, you went down a cobbled side street to a door that led up a long flight of stairs to the attic above the main building. As Andy recalls: "We played Fridays, Saturdays, and Sundays 9pm–6am. Many of those who sat in came from the dance bands, including Jack. It was like America, it had an attitude – we'd be in semi-darkness, someone would come in, pull out an alto sax and say 'Can I sit in?' We were so fuckin' desperate to be hip."

Like most Britons, the young people of Glasgow were besotted with American culture. For Jack's brother and his friends it was the ultra-cool Frank Sinatra, lounging against a lamppost, trilby at an angle, cigarette dangling from his lips, while for many kids of Jack's age it was Elvis Presley and rock'n'roll. But for Jack and his jazz friends it got no better than Thelonious Monk, Dizzy Gillespie, and Charlie Parker. "When I first met Jackie, as we called him, we were living in a world dominated by America – music, cinema and architecture," Andy recalls. "Jackie was then living in a part of the city called Moss Heights. These were the highest blocks in Glasgow, like skyscrapers, so for us, Moss Heights and anybody who lived in there was American – and so they had to be good at something."

Not yet 18, Jack certainly *was* really good at something – playing the bass. Park says that he was the only bass player who could get near what he, his saxophonist friend Bob Wishart, and the other Cell musicians were hearing on Blue Note or Riverside Records.

"Jackie was fantastically fast and *correct*," Andy says when discussing the improvisational sections of the arrangements they played. "He went in fast, but stayed correct and came out of it in the right place – it was just fantastic. Jackie was so highly regarded during the brief time he was playing with us, a light shining right through what we were trying to do. It mattered to us that Jackie was there. It was a good time and people played better because he was here."

On one occasion Jack sneaked Andy, Bob, and the others into the Academy for a rehearsal. He got away with it a few more times, but when the Academy learned that he had pulled in a bunch of outsiders to play jazz, they gave him a very hard time and wanted to chuck him out. But Jack could have cared less and just left of his own accord. He had already said goodbye to Bellahouston, returning only to collect a prize for his Higher English essay. Even then he clashed with authority. As his prize Jack had selected James Joyce's controversial and difficult novel *Ulysses* but the school at first refused to let him have what they thought was a "dirty book".

O

In the summer of 1961 Jack went on his first trip away from home as a professional musician. The occasion was the summer season at Dunoon, a popular holiday resort, about 30 miles from Glasgow and reachable by ferry on the Cowal Peninsula in Argyll – or a more scenic 70-mile drive via Loch Lomond. This was a period of high tension in the area because Dunoon was close to the submarine naval base at Holy Loch, where the first of the American Polaris nuclear missiles had arrived in March. Holy Loch became the scene of frequent demonstrations by the Campaign For Nuclear Disarmament.

The invitation to play in Dunoon came from a drummer who had been kicked out of the Scottish Variety Orchestra and was in the process of putting together a band starring a one-legged trombonist, a tenor sax player who had lung trouble and ran out of puff, and a female singer (lusted after by the drummer). As Jack recalls: "I remember him coming to the house and talking to my mother and saying, 'Oh it will be good for the boy to do it. I'll look after him.' It turned out to be mind-boggling in many ways. We played every night except Sunday and played outside in the afternoons for talent shows. I did some arrangements for the band and some pretty free-form things that had them scratching their heads while they were trying to play this during a dance – but I also did some straight ahead things like 'Lonesome Road' by Frank Sinatra."

If cars were one of Jack's passions, the other was girls. He had the kind of boyish good looks, charm, and sense of humour with an undercurrent of shyness and vulnerability that women seemed to find irresistible. "I had a few girlfriends," he says, "but not really a steady girlfriend. I wasn't that type. There was a Jewish girl called Rene and a lovely girl called Maureen Ferry. She wanted to be a ballet dancer and I think she did that professionally – until she married a vet! It wasn't a 'full' relationship – in those days that kind of thing hardly ever existed, although not for the want of me trying, I hasten to add. But she fought off all my advances. I dumped her for her best friend Joyce and one day there was a knock at the door and my mum answered:

"Oh, it's Maureen Ferry's dad come to see you."

"Oh no ..."

Jack was preparing for his escape, but Mr Ferry had not come baying for blood. "You've got to come and talk to her," he said.

"OK," Jack said, and went round to her house to find her languishing in bed. "I talked to her," he recalls, "but I was a bit naughty with Joyce, and I did feel bad about that. But I was only 16."

While he was in Dunoon, Jack met a girl from Paisley who he recalls was "down on holiday ... we had a sort of holiday romance. She was very sweet, only she took it very seriously and invited me to meet her parents. I showed up, but she was really embarrassed because I wasn't wearing a suit and tie. So I thought that maybe this wasn't the right situation for me."

49

Jack also got talking to Bob Wishart's wife Anne. She and her friend Olive were on a summer trip to Dunoon and came to watch the band at the Pier Ballroom. One of the musicians took a shine to Olive and they started getting serious. Jack and this guy were mates so Jack got talking to Anne. She remembers him as a "very smart guy, well read, funny, and obviously intelligent" and recalls that he took pride in telling her about the success of his Higher English essay.

Another of Jack's encounters in Dunoon proved to be fraught with danger. The presence of US sailors in the area drew women into the town like a magnet, and those who were already there took full advantage.

"I was staying with this titled lady, Sheila, who ran this big boarding house and she had a boyfriend in the US Navy," Jack recalls. "That was a bit tricky because there was a slight involvement and a slight running away. There was a lot of tension between the Americans and the locals – I remember the stage manager of the pier show got beaten up and I was attacked by some Americans. It all got very nasty. I had to run away from that boarding house because I'd got involved with Sheila – 'You'd better clear off or you're a dead man.' I went off to try and find some new digs – one of those prefab houses and this very attractive young woman opened the door – 'Aw no, here we go again!'"

After he got back from Dunoon, Jack would pop up in bands all over Glasgow, sometimes for a residency or maybe just a one-night spot. He even played *The White Heather Club* – an incredibly cheesy traditional Scottish variety show cited by British television presenter and author Jeremy Paxman in 2007 as proof that there was no golden age of British television. Bandleader Frank Pantrini had a new gig over at Victoria Park on the south side of the city in the basement of a hotel – a quintet with Pantrini on tenor, plus vibes, piano, drums, and Jack on bass. After that Jack appeared in East Kilbride, an overspill area for Glasgow. The first bowling alley in Scotland was built there on two storeys. Charlie Bruce (now working for Rolls Royce) and his fellow trade unionists held meetings in the bar downstairs. They didn't know what to do with the upper floor, so they turned it into a ballroom. Jack was hired to play there as the bass player in Tommy Maxwell's band; Andy and Bob were also invited to play. But as Andy recalls: "We came in to do the gig and Jack was ne' there. He'd upped and left."

12-bar
in
CHAPTER 3 beef

Despite the many opportunities to play in and around Glasgow, Jack knew he needed to broaden his horizons and find his way to London. In the autumn of 1961, an advert in *Melody Maker* for a vacancy in a Maynard Ferguson-style big band caught his eye. The leader was Murray Campbell, a star trumpeter who had played in a number of British dance-band orchestras of the 50s, including Oscar Rabin's Orchestra and The Basil Kirchen Band (which at various times boasted a stellar line-up of British jazz musicians such as Bobby Orr, Duncan Lamont, and Stan Tracey). Campbell also appeared on one of British television's most high profile variety shows, *Sunday Night At The London Palladium*. He would come out as a solo artist and play high register interpretations of classical pieces like Grieg's 'Piano Concerto'.

At one point Andy Park had auditioned for Murray up in Glasgow. "I was playing this ballroom gig," he recalls, "and somebody in the band came in one night and said he was leaving because there was a new band starting up at the Dennistoun Palais and they were holding auditions."

Andy went down to suss it out and then told his fellow musicians: "Jesus Christ, this band is unbelievable! You should hear the charts. He's not playing for dancing, he's tearing it up in there."

"Who is it?" they asked.

"Oh, he's come up from the south, name of Murray Campbell."

Andy did get in the band and had the chance to go on tour to Australia, but by then had already begun a teaching career.

For a while now Jack had wanted to invest in a decent bass. Walking through the city centre, he caught sight of a William Tarr double bass in the window of McCormick's music shop. Jack was determined to scrape together the deposit money, but when he went back to the shop clutching the cash, the bass had gone – sold to one of Jack's heroes, Ray Brown – so Jack persuaded his mother to buy him another bass instead. Much later, Brown said he would give Jack the much-coveted Tarr, but never did.

Now he was set. "I did play it a bit in Glasgow," he says, "but it was really bought for the audition." The advert that Jack saw would require him to move to Coventry, where Murray was now based. Jack presented his parents with what amounted to a *fait accompli* about leaving home to go south. "I'd brought my parents up pretty well," he says; his brother Charlie doesn't recall any argument about it.

Jack wouldn't be cutting his family ties altogether. It was arranged that he would stay with his aunt Mary, one of his dad's sisters, who had moved to 57 Summerhill Road in Ladywood, a district of Birmingham. Mary and her husband had nine children living in the house but they still found room for Jack, who shared the attic with the oldest boys, Charles and Terry. Charles, who now lives in Canada, remembers going out on the town with Jack, and Jack "being a bit of a flirt with the ladies. Once as we were getting off a bus he ripped off his coat and spread it on the ground for an attractive girl to walk on. Seems a bit corny now but at the time it was quite impressive. Jack borrowed my best and only winklepicker shoes for his audition and I never got them back!" Charles's sister Sandie was about 14 at the time and remembers Jack being "a very private kind of person", noting that he bought her a tube of Margo's hair spray out of his wages.

Jack has good memories of the time he spent with the family. "I was staying with my auntie, and my grandfather was staying there as well, which was really special because I had never spent much time with him. He was like a different person and we used to go out together for a pint. He had always been very morose up in Scotland. He would sit there and say nothing, just sit and spit. They were really warm people. I suddenly had all these cousins. This was all new to me and made me feel really good."

For his audition with Murray Campbell, Jack was to play Ray Brown's solo 'One Bass Hit'. "The bass solo was all written out," he recalls, "so, not being long out of college, I was able to sight read that note for note." Jack got the gig and soon found that Murray's men played at a much higher standard than the average Palais band. After playing for a while in Coventry, however, Campbell announced he was ending the big band and planning instead to take a smaller, five or six-piece band to play cine-variety and club dates in Italy.

"We went by train from Victoria to Milan," Jack recalls. "That's when I found out that we had to wear kilts – that was our gimmick. I was the only Scotsman in the bloody band and I didn't wear a kilt, that's Highlander dress. Murray's doing high-note trumpet solos in his kilt on his knees, cabaret stuff. Cine-variety was a very Italian form of entertainment. You went in and you saw a stage show then a movie. The entire audience was male – women never went out."

It wasn't long before Jack got his first taste of the double-dealings of the music business. "Our manager was a really beautiful woman, and she split with all the money, leaving us stranded with no way of getting home. We finished up making illegal vegetable stews on a primus stove in our room in a pension that was actually a brothel. Once I knew this, it worked very well to my advantage – the ladies were very kind to me and looked after me because I was still only a kid. But the owners wanted the bill paid. Eventually we had to be repatriated by the British Embassy in Milan. They gave us a one-way train ticket to London, but when we got there they impounded our passports until we paid back the money."

Once they all got home, Campbell must have felt a bit protective toward Jack after what had happened because he invited him to stay at his lovely house in Brighton. From there Murray and Jack would go to Archer Street in London's Soho, where musicians hung out in and around the Harmony Café looking for work.

This might have been Jack's big break into the London music scene but instead he got an offer to go back to Italy to join a band playing the US Airforce base in Aviano. The details seemed suspiciously casual: the deal was that Jack, who had sold himself as an experienced driver, had to get to Saumur in central France, pick up the band, and drive the car through France and over the Alps to Aviano. But first he had to get to Paris to connect with some guy who would give him the money and the ticket to get to Saumur.

Jack travelled light. "I had just a suitcase, my double bass in a soft case, and I always kept my dress suit in with the double bass." With no idea what he was walking into (and making sure he had his knife handy), Jack met his dubious contact in Paris, who had no money or ticket for him and who left him stranded yet again.

"I took my stuff to an American Express office and asked them if I could leave it there, then went again to the British Embassy. Fortunately it was this really young and very attractive woman interviewing me. I explained everything and she just gave me the money out of her purse – just enough to buy a ticket. So I got a late night slow train to Saumur and met the band. I then had this rather frightening drive with a trailer and a pre-war Mercedes. We got there in the end, after about two days."

The band was led by Bill Barron, a baritone sax player, with a pianist who doubled on vibes, a drummer, and a girl singer – "who of course I fell in love with, but she didn't want to know because she was with the pianist". They played in the Sergeants' Mess, doing pretty undemanding material. "We did standards and requests every night, plus some afternoons, and once a week we did a jazz night."

When Jack wasn't playing he had an unprecedented opportunity to study jazz. "They had a fantastic record library on the base and they had a room that was just full of every kind of musical instrument," he says. "I fell in with a load of jazz fans, mainly black guys. I became very friendly with them, and that's when I first heard Charles Mingus." Mingus's music came as a revelation to Jack and would prove to be very influential in his development, not just as a bass player but even more so as a composer with a strong affinity for folk and roots music.

As Jack saw it, being a serviceman on a military base during peacetime couldn't have been much easier. "Those guys were really pampered. A lot of them were really wealthy and there was still conscription, so if you had money you could opt for what was considered a cushy number. They worked on the weather side – skivers really, they all had their cars brought over from the States. This was all pre-Vietnam."

For Jack it was "like winning the pools". He was earning a staggering $200 a week (about $1,400 today) for a gig where his accommodation in the Batchelor Officers' quarters was only $1 a night, a packet of cigarettes was 25 cents, and a meal was 50 cents. The biggest battle the troops had to face was boredom, and for that there was cheap booze. American beer flowed like water, although Jack was more of a whisky and soda man.

Jack's family were not particularly heavy drinkers. His dad was definitely not a hard drinker, and while his mum enjoyed her drink nobody ever saw her drunk, however much had gone down. Of his brother Charlie and his friends, Jack recalls: "Could they drink! I don't think many of them are alive now. I think the thing that saved my brother was that he passed out fairly early in the evening." There was a bar across the road from Bellahouston Academy that played host to some of Jack's underage drinking, but now, in Italy, he was in with the big boys.

On his previous trip to Italy Jack was looked after by the hookers. Now he was in effect the Master Sergeants' mascot. These were the older guys who had spent their whole lives in service and who went in for some pretty heavy drinking sessions (topped up with Benzedrine amphetamines). They would go off on trips to Venice and take Jack with them. "One time we went to Harry's Bar in Venice and there were Spike Milligan, Peter Sellers, and some other actors," he recalls. "We got into a really drunken evening with those guys." (Jack would later appear on the soundtrack to Sellers's film *After The Fox*.)

Sometimes Jack would borrow Bill Barron's car and drive to Venice or Trieste. As a kid he often took his bike and cycled into the country alone or with friends to get out of the grime and greyness of the city and enjoy the cleaner air and rolling countryside. Later on, as a musician on the road, he would go off alone to soak up the local atmosphere or just for some solitude rather than hanging about in studios and hotels.

As he had found out in Dunoon, however, there was a dark side to the military, not noted for its tolerant attitudes or respect for the community they found themselves in. "Some bad things happened," he says. "One of my best friends was a black private. He was very interested in jazz and our relationship became very intense and close, not sexual, just the sort of attachments you can get at that age. I remember seeing him outside the sergeant's or the officer's mess where I was playing one night. I invited him to come and have a drink and he said, 'No, I can't go in there, I'm not allowed to go in there.' I kept asking him and he came with me and he instantly got into trouble – I think eventually he got drummed out. There was a lot of racism going on."

Out on the road, the Master Sergeants would take great pleasure in running local farmers into a ditch. Jack was also having problems with the bandleader – and, of course, there was a woman. This one was a local girl from a wealthy family who owned a knitwear factory. As ever the girl was more serious than Jack, but this was Italy, and she had brothers who were keen for Jack to do the honourable thing simply because the two of them had been out together – not, as rumoured, because the girl was pregnant (something Jack emphatically denies).

Having been abroad for about nine months, Jack had been thinking about leaving anyway and picking up his career in London. Then something happened that swiftly ended his time in Italy and sent him back to Glasgow. "I was having this drunken night with the older guys," he recalls. "One of them gave me a Zippo lighter and told me I would need to fill it up. But being drunk, I managed to pour petrol up my arm and when I lit it I got really badly burnt. They wouldn't do anything on the base because I wasn't a serviceman so I had to go off to get some medical attention. I went to this hospital where I was very well looked-after by these nuns. But I couldn't play so I went back home."

○

Jack was still only 18 when he got home in early 1962. He'd seen an awful lot of life for a boy of his age, out on the road with guys much older than him trying to survive as a professional musician. But now, having reclaimed his old room (which had been rented out in his absence to a policeman), he was back with his family in Moss Heights to recuperate from a serious injury and consider his next move.

There was little work to be had so Jack fell in with some other unemployed musicians who had started a window cleaning business. This is how he came to know the drummer and clarinet player with Jim McHarg's Scotsville Jazzmen, a band operating at the tail end of the trad-jazz boom. Jim McHarg had been in the Clyde Valley Stompers, but was famously sacked by his own band, leaving a vacancy for Jack. Very soon after, Jim left for Canada, where he would continue his music career until his death in 2003.

The Scotsville Jazzmen played all over the UK, including a date in Elgin on February 15 at the Red Shoes Ballroom. But it was in June '62, following a gig at the Cambridge May Ball, that a chance meeting set Jack on a whole new path into history. Taking a break from blasting trad jazz at the champagne-drenched Cambridge students in all their finery, he wandered outside and heard a very different kind of music coming from a nearby marquee. He went to investigate.

As a Cambridge old boy himself, tenor sax player Dick Heckstall-Smith had received a call from the university's social secretary asking if he wanted to put a band together to play at the ball. At the time Dick and drummer Ginger Baker, both freelancers on the hand-to-mouth London jazz scene, had been playing with trumpet player Bert Courtley. Bert was the leader but Dick rang him up to ask if he could borrow the band for the night, inviting Bert on trumpet. Bert didn't fancy being a sideman in his own band so Dick brought in John Hockeridge, with Maurice Salvat on bass, Kathy Stobart on sax, Colin Purbrook (another ex-Cambridge student who shared a flat with Dick) on piano, and Ginger on drums. They were just coming to the end of the first set when, as Dick wrote in his autobiography:

This little bloke came to the stage and in a powerful Scottish accent asked if he could play with us.

'What do you play?' I asked.

'Ah plee be-ass' he answered.

There are all sorts of possible responses when a total stranger asks for a sit-in. If you're a complete nutter, you can of course say yes, no matter what, and end up collapsing under a plague of loonies who don't know they can't play ... Or you can simply play it thick, and always say no – the risks are a great deal less, but it's a bit, well, unadventurous. Best is to use a combination of tactics and instinct. The standard approach – unless the gig's a jam session anyway – is to make it difficult but not impossible for the sitter-in, both logistically and musically, until you've got the smell of him.

So I said, 'No, not now. It's too late.'

'Are ye playin' anither sait?' he asked.

'Well, yes.'

'Can ah plee wi' ye thain?'

'Mmm,' I said. 'OK.'

Well, he was persistent anyway. I took pity – the second set wasn't in the marquee, and I couldn't see the poor bugger bringing his bloody bass all the way to the wrong place. 'It's in the cellars somewhere,' I said. 'I don't know exactly where, but bring your own bass eh? Our bass player won't want to lend you his, I don't think.'

'O-kee' said the little guy, nodding grimly, and off he went. He was about eighteen, if that.

And lo, he showed up in the cellars at half past one, visible at first only by the top end of a string bass moving slowly through a dense area of bobbing, shrieking hoorays. Eventually he surfaced by the stone flagging we were playing on.

Ginger and I exchanged a look. Tactic 17b was indicated. 'Hullo,' I said after we'd finished what we were playing.

'D'you want to play then?' Better get it over with.

'Aye,' he said.

Maurice stepped out for a fag and a smash at one of the hooray girls. He was good at girls.

'Twelve-bar in beef,' I called, and counted in 'Blue'n'Boogie', which is normally a fastish, vaguely boppy riff; a nice, neat, simple hook to hang long solos on, so that whether it's good or bad depends almost entirely on how well it's played. That night it went at an absolutely fiendish tempo. I counted it in *as fast as my fingers would move. It was so goddam fast that the choruses came and went before you could blink – it must have been eight or nine choruses a minute. And holy shit the little guy stormed into it like there was no tomorrow, heads down and no prisoners from the off. It was demonic. I remember exchanging a soul-awakening wow-here-we-go glance with the grinning Ginger a few bars in; after that it was straight through the roof and devil take the hindmost. It was glorious. It swung like the clappers.*

Nobody said anything afterward. He was much better than Maurice. 'OK,' I said, 'We'll do "Lover Man" in F.' You play the tune. Two, three, four ...' and by God he did! Beautifully. Faultlessly. Vibrato, in tune, the lot. All the changes.

Of course he did. He was Jack Bruce, only I didn't know that then. Neither did anybody else, anywhere, except I guess Jack.

Jack's abiding memory of the night was hearing Ginger for the first time. "He looked like a demon in that cellar, sitting down there with his red hair," he recalls. "He had this drum kit that he'd made himself. I never heard drums sound so good. I'd never seen a drummer like him and I knew then that I wanted to play with him."

○

Jack didn't have to wait long. He told Dick he was on his way to London to share a flat in Willesden with the clarinet player from The Scotsville Jazzmen, so the two men exchanged details. A few weeks later, Jack got a call from Dick inviting him to come down to the Marquee to consider joining Alexis Korner's Blues Incorporated.

Blues Inc was the brainchild of two diametrically opposed individuals who happened to share a deep love and knowledge of the blues. Alexis Korner was the black sheep of a Greek-Austrian business family. He was born in Paris and privately educated – sophisticated, erudite, cut-glass upper-class accent – but with an innate sense of what constituted good music. He played guitar and sang but was a much better bandleader, surrounding himself with the best musicians on the British jazz and burgeoning blues scene and always happy to give new blood a chance.

Cyril Davies was a rough diamond, a working-class panel-beater from West London. He was grumpy and opinionated, with a violent temper and an old fashioned sense of chivalry. He once smashed a guitar over the head of a guy in a queue for fish and chips for swearing in front of a lady. He also happened to be one of the best blues harmonica players Britain ever produced and was widely revered as among the country's most authentic bluesmen. Together the two men had started a skiffle club above the Roundhouse pub in Soho in the mid 50s, which then became Britain's first blues club. Many of the black American blues artists who visited Britain in the 50s came to play at the club – Bill Broonzy, Sonny Terry & Brownie McGhee, and Muddy Waters among them. Alexis and Cyril formed Blues Inc and performed interval spots with The Chris Barber band at the Marquee Club.

The central-London jazz-club scene was very elitist and dominated by a handful of owners, promoters, and musicians who came out of Britain's first modern jazz club, Club Eleven, in the late 40s, where Ronnie Scott was the leading light, so Alexis and Cyril decided to base themselves outside Soho. With the help of Art Wood – Ron Wood's older brother – they found a venue in Ealing, West London, beneath the ABC tearooms. It was a trad jazz place and an afternoon drinking club. Blues Inc took it over for Saturday nights. The bar takings went to the owner; the door-money went to the band.

The club opened on March 17 1962. On stage that night were Alexis and Cyril, Art Wood on vocals, a young commercial artist and drummer called Charlie Watts, and Charlie's mate from Hornsey Art College, Andy Hoogenboom, on bass. Word spread fast and the club was soon packed for its Saturday night gig. Over the coming weeks, budding blues musicians came from all over the country to sit in, each believing that American blues was a secret only they were privy to. Brian Jones came along from Cheltenham; Eric Burdon from Newcastle; Mick Jagger and Keith Richard from South London; Paul Jones from Oxford; and Eric Clapton, whom Dick Heckstall-Smith recalled as a "pale, sulky kid" who came on stage with no guitar, sang a couple of songs, and fled.

News of the club's success reached back to the owner of the Marquee Club, Harold Pendleton. He knew Blues Inc were popular because he had seen the audience reaction when they did the interval spot on Wednesdays at the Marquee. So he did a deal with Alexis to put on Thursday nights at the club. They opened on May 3 with a few changes. Blues Inc was organised more like a jazz band in that the line-up remained very fluid: Alexis and Cyril couldn't offer anything like a full date sheet, so musicians would come and go depending on their other commitments.

One very significant change was the arrival of Dick Heckstall-Smith, which brought to the fore the different visions Alexis and Cyril had for the band. Alexis was more eclectic in his tastes. He presented jazz programmes on the radio and wanted to include Mingus and Ellington compositions in the Blues

Inc repertoire. On that very first evening at the Ealing Club, they played Ellington's 'Dooji Wooji'. Cyril's idea was to simply re-create the Chicago Blues sound of Muddy Waters circa 1956, and he regarded the saxophone as an abomination. As far as he was concerned, jazz ended with The Fletcher Henderson Orchestra in the 30s. So when he turned up to a rehearsal and saw Dick there, he stormed across the room, swearing loudly as he went, and tipped his briefcase upside down on the piano, scattering a mountain of harmonicas in his wake. But Dick was one of Britain's very few blues saxophonists – and certainly the best of the bunch. Despite the awkward beginning, he soon realised that Cyril liked his playing. "He just didn't like what I was playing it on," he wrote.

Jack had his own reservations about Blues Inc. He remembers going to the Marquee and thinking, "It's rock'n'roll. I was so ignorant about real rhythm & blues and I was such a purist snob that I didn't really get it. It actually took me a long time to 'get' The Beatles. It was Dick who introduced me to them. Dick turned me onto everything. Once I started playing that music I got so sucked in, I really loved it. Playing a slow blues in E, that double bass tucked into your groin … such a great band."

In the ever-revolving Blues Inc line-up, Long John Baldry and then Ronnie Jones took on vocal duties, with Johnny Parker following Dave Stevens and Keith Scott on piano. Charlie Watts – who Jack recalls "had the grooves to end all grooves" – began to lose interest and was still undecided about his career, so Peter 'Ginger' Baker took over on drums.

Born in August 1939 just before the outbreak of war, Ginger grew up without his father, who was killed in action on the island of Leros in 1943. The British wanted the Germans to think that the Allies would be landing in Greece, not Sicily, so the Germans bombed the hell out of the island with 50 continuous air strikes. Frederick Baker, a signals operator, was buried there. Ginger's mother married a master bricklayer, George, whom she had given up to marry Frederick in the first place, and with whom she, Ginger, and Ginger's sister now lived in Eltham, South London. Ginger had aspirations to be a professional cyclist, but after his bike was flattened beyond redemption, he turned his attention to drumming, practicing for hours on end on a homemade kit in the derelict house next door.

Ginger eventually managed to bluff his way into Bob Wallis's Storeyville Jazzmen, where he first met Dick and, trawling his way through Bob's record collection, first heard Louis Armstrong's drummer Baby Dodds, one of his primary inspirations. He built up experience touring with Terry Lightfoot,

Acker Bilk, Diz Disley, and Sister Rosetta Tharpe, and then taught himself to sight-read in two weeks so he could join Ken Oldham's Showband. After coming home penniless from a European tour with Les Douglas, Ginger played in small jazz combos with Ronnie Scott, Joe Harriott, and Bert Courtly (again with Dick Heckstall-Smith) and did his time hanging round Archer Street – where, much to his disgust, he found himself having to play in a band backing female impersonator Danny La Rue. By the time he met up with Jack, he had been married to his girlfriend Liz for three years and had a young daughter, Nettie.

Finding work was always a struggle for Ginger. His loud, be-bop drumming style – which utilised heavy offbeats on the bass drum rather than a steady four-to-the-bar – met with stiff opposition, and he would often respond to criticisms with verbal or even physical ripostes drawn deep from the well of his Irish ancestry. Ginger was what would now be termed 'high maintenance'. He hardly seemed to 'like' anybody: suspicion and raised-brow scepticism were his default positions.

Charlie Watts knew that Dick wanted to get Ginger into Blues Inc. He was wary of chucking in his day job, but was convinced to hand over the reins after seeing Ginger play with Jack in The Johnny Burch Octet. "Ginger had this incredible sound," Watts recalls. "You could hear this thing that Jack and Ginger had between them – and I didn't want to get in the way of that."

Pianist John Burch founded his Octet as a rehearsal band, bringing in Dick, Jack, and Ginger with trombonist John Mumford, trumpeter Mike Falana, a rotating cast of saxophonists (Glenn Hughes, Miff Moule, and John Marshall), and keyboardist/alto saxophonist Graham Bond, who would shortly loom large in Jack's life. They rehearsed at the Marquee and the Partisan Club in Carlisle Street, and established a residency at the Plough Inn in Ilford, Essex. (As Jack notes: "The only time I ever met Ian Dury was toward the end of his life when I was playing in Belgium with Ringo and he came up to me, 'Oh, Jack, Jack, I've always wanted to meet you because I used to come down to the Plough. That was a great band.'") The Octet also managed a handful of other, more public gigs. They garnered a very good response at the Marquee, prompting Ginger to berate John Gee, the manager, over the paltry fee of £3 per musician and in the process earn himself the first of many bans from the club.

Playing in the Octet was a chance for Jack to debut some of his own jazz compositions, including 'Immortal Ninth' and 'HCKHH Blues'. "When I joined Alexis it was just two regular gigs a week," Jack says. "There was the

Marquee on a Thursday and the Ealing Club on a Saturday. Occasionally we'd do these one-off society gigs that Alexis could get because he'd been to St Paul's School and he was a definite 'hooray'."

In July 1962 Blues Inc played a society ball hosted by the Marquis and Marchioness of Londonderry. At one point, somebody approached Ronnie Jones and asked if he minded 'Mr Goodman' joining the band. Having put away a fair amount of whisky, Ronnie had no idea who Mr Goodman was until Alexis told him it was *Benny* Goodman, leaving Ronnie dumbstruck and unable to remember the words to the song they were going to play.

"We did another one for Baron Rothschild," Jack adds. "He had just bought an Argentinean polo team or something like that and wanted a party to show off. Prince Philip was there as the guest of honour with Jimmy Edwards as the MC. Hilarious. He'd say, 'Could you play a waltz?' 'Fuck Off!' 'Oh, thank you so much.'

"Cyril got very drunk, incredibly drunk. He threw up over this very valuable looking Persian rug. Eventually he collapsed, and it was our job to get him out into the van. We found out later he was dying – he knew about it and didn't tell anybody."

By the autumn a cold wind was blowing through Blues Inc – or at least from Cyril Davies's point of view. With Dick, Jack, and Ginger in the band the music was already drifting away from Chicago Blues toward a more Mingus-like approach. Now Graham Bond sat in occasionally on alto sax. He was a huge personality and a very impressive musician who looked like a white Cannonball Adderley. It all became too much for Cyril, who knew that there really wasn't room for two such strong personalities in the band. Matters came to a head just as the world stood on the brink of another global conflict. The Russians had moved missiles onto Cuba and were engaged in a frightening game of brinkmanship with the United States.

"During that couple of weeks, we all thought that the world would quite literally come to an end," Jack recalls. "We really thought that, because we had been brought up with that fear, the nuclear shadow hanging over our heads. I can remember going to play at the Ealing Club on a Saturday, being on the Central Line with my double bass, standing there like I did every Saturday and thinking, 'Why are we carrying on as normal?' Everybody on that quite crowded train had that same feeling – you could see them sleepwalking through what could have been the last weekend of the whole world."

Fortunately, the Russians backed down, and the Blues Inc Crisis resolved itself with the departure of Cyril, who set up the All Stars with Long John

Baldry, Nicky Hopkins, and Carlo Little. The bassist was another major young talent, Cliff Barton, one of the country's first fretless players. Sadly he died of a heroin overdose; Jack later wrote 'Over The Cliff' about him. Cyril himself died tragically early at the age of 32, his heart, weakened by pleurisy, giving out in January 1964.

○

By late 1962 Jack was getting his face known in London and the freelance work was steady. "Acker Bilk offered me a £100 a week to join – a vast fortune which I turned down because I didn't want to play that kind of music," he says. "Alexis was my main gig, two nights a week, not a lot of money, but it was okay and Alexis was always quite reasonable with paying. He wasn't a stingy guy. I was making a pretty good living."

Jack was part of a new wave of young jazz musicians who set themselves apart from the modern jazz establishment centred on Ronnie Scott's club. Dick, Ginger, pianist Mick Pyne, and trombonist John Mumford were still out there on the margins, part of a much more experimental and avant-garde wing. Dick's view of the London jazz scene was that it was much too safe and polite. "The kind of music I like is pushy, forward, full-bloodied, free of self-imposed restrictions," Dick recalled. "It takes risks … it battles its way through to expression. It is full of mistakes, but couldn't care a jot about them because it knows that mistakes are its life-blood … it doesn't care about good taste. But that is not to say it can't be beautiful. Its beauty is that of strength triumphing over ugliness."

Dick and Ginger got involved with the new generation of British poets, among them Mike Horowitz, Spike Hawkins, and Pete Brown. They joined together for jazz-poetry gigs where performance poetry – which Pete pretty much pioneered – would be read out to an accompaniment of modern jazz in small clubs for the young, middle class, black-clad bohemian cognoscenti. Pete hitched around the country performing his work and fell in love with Scotland, which would be an important touchstone in his later writing partnership with Jack.

In 1959, Pete wrote a poem called 'Few':

Alone tired half drunk hopeful
I staggered into the bogs
at Green Park station
and found 30 written on the wall

63

Appalled I lurched out
Into the windy, blaring neon Piccadilly night
Thinking surely,
Surely there must be more of us than that ...

Like Alexis Korner, Pete was the family rebel: the Jewish son who refused to become a tailor or sell shoes and instead entered a career offering plenty of opportunities to starve. Pete, Dick, and Ginger were the closest Britain had to the Beat poets and beboppers of America. They were hip and cool in the way that Andy Park and his friends back in Glasgow so urgently wanted to be. They knew about things that would never be discussed with anybody who wasn't hip – essentially everybody else.

With his gaunt, thin features, red hair, sharp clothes, and permanent fag, Ginger was a romantic figure to Jack, who looked up to Ginger and learnt much from him about rhythm and tone. Ginger had his own mentor, Phil Seaman, one of the best jazz drummers in the business and in effect Ginger's surrogate father. Phil taught him much about the drums and way too much about heroin. They would sit together in a club or a flat; Phil would show Ginger a new pattern he'd invented, rapping it out on a table or the back of a chair.

In those early London days, Jack was 'sofa-surfing' and shipped up for a while at Ginger and Liz's house in Braemar Avenue, Neasden, North London, kipping down on what Liz describes as a "a very uncomfortable Scandinavian sofa". But Jack didn't mind. He was where he wanted to be. He played occasional gigs with drummer John Stevens at the Little Theatre Club – what he describes as "free form improvisations with nobody in the audience. The fewer the better actually – that made us serious jazz musicians. We must be doing something right – nobody's come! The Little Theatre Club was perfect because you had to climb I don't know how many millions of stairs to get there. Once we had eight people. We probably thought we were getting too popular.

"The Ornette Coleman record *This Is Our Music* pretty much summed up our attitude," Jack adds. "We would be allowed to go into Ronnie Scott's and stand at the foot of the stairs, but not allowed to go in because we couldn't pay. I always tried to wear Ivy League jackets from Austin's of Shaftesbury Avenue and a shirt with a pin through the collar. It was very elitist: 'we're in the know and you're not'. There was Ginger and Dick – Dick was always a bit different because he was Dick and so unclassifiable, but still one of us. There was John Mumford and Mike Pyne – he was one of our group. We did piano and bass sessions together. I was always the youngest in that group and at that age a couple of years could make a vast difference."

But there was something else too – a refusal among these musicians to accept they had any reason to feel inferior to the Americans. "Some of those guys [in the jazz mainstream] felt that they weren't good enough because they were British, they had that chip on their shoulder that we didn't have," Jack says. "Maybe because there were great white bass players like Charlie Haden and Scott LaFaro, I felt that I had the potential to be good as anybody in the world. And then you had Phil Seaman, who was world class. So we didn't respect them because they didn't respect themselves. And they didn't like us because we wouldn't play the bebop changes."

By Christmas 1962 Blues Inc was at its peak, with Jack and Ginger becoming a powerful unit as they cemented their partnership with pianist Johnny Parker. Dick and Graham were wailing those searing blues sax riffs, perfect foils for Ronnie Jones's gutsy soul vocals. By the New Year, however, Graham was looking further afield. As well as being a top-flight saxophonist, he was a strong blues vocalist and an accomplished player of the thunderous Hammond organ. He could just imagine the kind of band he might form with Jack and Ginger roaring alongside him.

Graham persuaded Alexis to let them play intervals as The Graham Bond Trio, which went down a storm. Alexis drew the line at allowing Graham to use the Hammond during the main Blues Inc sets but John Burch let him play it in the Octet. There is one known tape of the band playing the Plough in March 1963. The sound is based on Johnny Griffin's Big Soul Band but with the influences of the individual members woven in: Horace Silver and Bud Powell from Johnny Burch; intricate bass soloing from Jack; and from Graham what would become his signature tune, 'Wade In The Water'.

Graham, Ginger, and Jack were absent from the next Octet gig at the Plough. They had secured a gig up in Manchester for which they earned £70 – a huge payday for a Blues Inc gig. Thanks to some eye-watering dope, they were in high spirits as they travelled back, but Jack and Ginger still had no plans to leave Alexis – at least until the day they arrived late for a rehearsal at the Flamingo Club in time to hear heated words between Alexis and Graham. "Graham came up to me and said, 'That's it, we've all quit,'" Jack recalls, adding that it took Alexis about 20 years to forgive him – even though he had nothing to do with it.

There was one thing though that Jack was happy to leave behind: Alexis's driving. "This guy was the world's scariest driver. We'd drive through the terrible smog of the time at 80 miles an hour. One time we're driving along, Ginger was the navigator, and Alexis fell asleep at the wheel. Ginger grabs the wheel and wakes Alexis, who calmly says, 'Thank you, Peter.' Another time we were driving down some other terrible road really fast because we were late. I thought I was going to die. Suddenly Alexis turns off the road and goes into this hospital, still going at 60 through the car park, round the back and then back on the road. So I started going by train. I couldn't take it anymore. That was the other thing. I was going to be the driver in the new band, so at least I could kill myself."

In April, the new trio became a quartet with the addition of John McLaughlin, a young guitarist from Yorkshire who had recently been in The George Fame band, and who Jack says played "slightly Wes Montgomery-style, a polite jazz style. He was very nervous at the time. We were playing the Leofric Hotel in Coventry. They had this little stage about 18 inches off the ground, and there was a guitar solo. I heard this very strange sound and saw John completely stiff but falling forward. He hit the ground and played this death chord and I actually thought he had died. He had smoked so much dope, he'd had a catatonic fit. That was the same day when we were doing a soundcheck, Ginger and me were eating daffodils – you get really high off daffodils but they really hurt your throat – and jumping from table to table."

All the while Graham had been trying in vain to get Dick to quit Alexis's band; Ginger meanwhile was getting fed up with John, who he accused not only of speeding up, but also of moaning too much about everything. By September John was gone and Dick was in.

yak
la
CHAPTER 4 bruze

Jack's move from trad jazz to rhythm & blues was symbolic of the way the music scene was changing in Britain through 1963 and into 1964. The work of Chris Barber and Alexis Korner in promoting live rhythm & blues and the increasing opportunities to hear the music on radio and on record had opened up the world of Bo Diddley, Chuck Berry, and Muddy Waters – right back into the pre-War country-blues era – to a whole new generation of music fans and aspiring musicians.

Three main strands developed: the organ-based, jazz-oriented rhythm & blues of The Graham Bond Organisation, Georgie Fame, and Brian Auger inspired by Ray Charles, Mose Allison, and Jimmy Smith; the commercial R&B/pop of The Rolling Stones and The Yardbirds; and what would eventually become a thread that Cyril Davies would have approved of – the re-creation of black urban blues by those involved in the 'British Blues Boom' (as spearheaded by John Mayall). A survey in *Melody Maker* told the story: between June and December 1963, 250 trad jazz clubs switched to rhythm & blues; by early '64 it was estimated that in London alone there were 100 R&B bands working the 28 clubs in the capital. And by popular consent the baddest live band on the block was the GBO.

"The original Alexis Korner band I first joined was a more laid back, 'in-the-groove' blues band," Jack recalls. "But this was a frighteningly intense band, hard-driving – in a bop way. Ginger was the most intense drummer I'd ever played with. He would bash the hell out of the cymbals and Graham had this screaming thing with the vocals."

Jack and Graham had huge respect and admiration for each other. "I have worked with musicians, just a few, who had a certain power," Jack says. "It was not a technical thing. Cyril Davies had it; he could play one note and bend it, and not only the band but the whole audience would be uplifted. He created an emotional experience. Graham certainly had this. You are like a tube, the music is not coming *from* you, but *through* you."

Graham in turn wrote a funny, affectionate poem about Jack in 'cod' Scottish, styled after The Goons' Spike Milligan:

Yak la bruze
Waz alwaz tide
Alwaz spruz

Until won dai
His father sed
Gi oop Jock mon
Goat etta bed
So up Jack got
So tired and pained
And wore pajamas till it rained
Cats ...

Played bass with CATZ
Until got cool
To show the world he was nae fool
Remained this way
So cool and scruffy
Until he met Will Bong and Duffy

○

During 1963–64 the GBO played 340 gigs in 480 days, taking their sound all over the UK and into pubs and clubs in provincial towns where this music was unknown. Where most touring bands were part of the ballroom pop-package tours, the GBO were out on their own, virtually creating the college circuit for rhythm & blues. They provided the complete antithesis of pop bands who could hardly play and created the cult of musical virtuosity. And as Jack says, they were phenomenally loud and exciting to watch with their own primitive light show, Ginger's solos, Jack's wild bass-playing, and Graham drilling audiences into the wall with the combined force of his voice, alto sax, and Hammond organ. The date sheets were full, the crowds ecstatic; this was a pioneering band in every sense, adored by fans, venerated by other musicians who held them in awe. Everything was great, except money caused endless rows in the band.

As bandleader Graham thought he was entitled to the lion's share of the money, and in a very Graham sort of way would use his considerable physical presence to charm, cheat, or threaten additional payments out of club owners and promoters. The band were originally managed by former Blues Inc manager Ronan O'Rahilly, who would become famous as the driving force behind pirate radio when he launched Radio Caroline in March 1964. He had set up an agency deal with Robert Masters at the Dick Charlesworth Agency, but Graham was an excellent hustler; he'd been a very successful salesman in his semi-pro days and still sold ovens and fridges to the owners of venues where they played. He made it a point of honour to get return bookings. None of this cut much ice with Ginger, and it got worse as Graham began to need more cash to feed a growing heroin habit. Eventually it was agreed that Ginger would look after the finances.

The GBO were clearly successful, but to take it to the next level they needed a hit record. O'Rahilly had signed them to a deal with EMI but the band hardly looked like pop stars. Graham weighed the wrong side of 200 pounds; Dick was balding with glasses; Ginger looked like he would eat your loved ones. Only Jack could have been a pin-up. So uninterested was the label in the band that their first single, 'Long Tall Shorty' / 'Long Legged Baby', and an EP called *The Graham Bond Organisation* were actually released on Decca. By 1965 The Graham Bond Organisation were in the hands of a 30-year-old Australian pop manager named Robert Stigwood, whose other charges included pretty boy pop singers John Leyton and Mike Sarne. The band recorded two albums, *Sound Of '65* and *There's A Bond Between Us*. Stigwood was listed as producer but did no real production work on either album, while the band were in and out of the studio in a few hours for both records. Nevertheless, each was chock full of excellent rhythm & blues standards from their live set.

Sound Of '65 includes Jack's first recorded compositions, 'Baby Be Good To Me' and 'Baby Make Love To Me'. Both have strong vocals; *There's A*

Bond Between Us also features his darkly sensual vocals on 'Hear Me Calling Your Name'. As folk legend Davy Graham remarked to the author some years ago: "One of the most marvellous things about Graham's band was the emergence of Jack Bruce as a singer."

The GBO records also feature embryonic versions of 'Traintime' and two Ginger Baker solos, which formed the basis of 'Toad'. Perhaps unsurprisingly, however, Stigwood's choice of single was a version of a dreary Debbie Reynolds hit, 'Tammy', from 1957. It didn't trouble the charts. The band also appeared on a Stigwood-promoted package tour headlined by Chuck Berry – a disaster that almost drove Stigwood into bankruptcy. The poorly attended show was littered with problems. The Organisation's set was plagued by horrendous feedback; Ginger broke two bass pedals, slinging the bits across the stage in anger; and during a rehearsal Graham managed to fall 15 feet off the stage into the orchestra pit.

Crippling too was the rapidly deteriorating relationship between Jack and Ginger. It is worth saying from the get-go that the problems in this band were not just between Jack and Ginger – during one fight between Ginger and Graham, about money, one sent his cymbals spinning in the air toward the other, who in turn actually attempted to pick up a Hammond organ and hurl it back. The difference of course is that the feud between Jack and Ginger went into rock mythology, and would periodically burst through like an active volcano for the next four decades. Asked if this has been hyped up over the years, Jack's answer is emphatic: "No."

So how did it all start? Everything was fine in the early days of Blues Inc. Jack had only just turned 19 when he joined; Ginger was not only four years older but was married with a young child. Ginger was a role model for Jack in many ways and they were good friends. But once the Organisation got underway, things became much more complicated.

The base line was inherent in their personalities. They were both incendiary characters: Ginger's short fuse was well established, while Jack – mistakenly dubbed 'the quiet one' – was always up for pranks but could explode under provocation. Life could be tough for any band on the road as much as the GBO were during the early 60s. They were cooped up together almost 24/7, travelling huge distances in vans held together with hope and string. When the agency was involved in booking there was no planning whatsoever – they might have a gig in London, then Middlesbrough, and on to Aberystwyth on consecutive nights, and that could go on for weeks and months on end. If they weren't travelling in the van or sleeping in it, they were eating horrible food together, squeezed into a toilet posing as a dressing room, or they were out on stage in the frontline, battling for audience appreciation and – as their competitive natures dictated – battling between themselves, one trying to outplay the other. They were thrown together like soldiers in a war zone who might have little in common other than the intensity of the lives they were living and the need to cling onto each other for survival.

Circumstances often soured the atmosphere. Not knowing if you would even arrive because the transport was so unreliable, dodgy equipment, hopeless PA systems (eventually they took their own) – all of these things conspired against the performance of musicians who were always striving for perfection. All the while Ginger was engaged in his own private war with heroin, and often felt like shit.

One specific bone of contention was Ginger's belief that Jack's basslines were too busy. "Maybe I was too busy because I was looking for a style and to introduce melody to the bass part in the same way as jazz bass players were playing countermelodies – that's what I wanted to do," Jack says. "Paul McCartney to an extent and certainly the great Motown bass players, like James Jamerson – that's what they were doing. On a lot of those Motown songs the bass guitar was playing the melody. I found that was encouraging because Ginger was getting me really down about this."

This difference of opinion sparked a massive blow up at the Golders Green Refectory. "I was playing a solo," Jack continues, "but Ginger was playing all over it. So I just looked at him, and he threw a drumstick at me, so I threw my bass and demolished the whole drum kit – in the middle of the gig. A lot more people came in actually. We were rolling around the stage and that's when I realised that I'm not really a fighter. I felt very silly about the whole thing" – not least because the crowd was singing "He Loves You, Yeh! Yeh! Yeh!"

In early 1964 the GBO were booked for a session with Jamaican guitarist Ernest Ranglin, who stipulated electric bass. Jack had previously been very much against the idea of electric bass but went out and hired one, discovering straight away that this was the instrument for playing rhythm & blues – quite apart from the luxury of no longer having to haul a double bass around on buses or the underground. With the six-string Fender bass he was using he was not just 'busy' but busy at a much higher volume, and more able to play melody lines. Ginger's blood pressure went up accordingly.

Jack was clearly inexperienced with electricity, however, and his story could have ended on April 1 at the 100 Club. "I electrocuted myself," he says. "I had an amp and a couple of speakers. I didn't know anything – I just tied the wires together." There was a mighty flash and Jack was hurled ten feet across the stage. The top of his guitar melted. It can't be said that the rest of the band leapt into action: "I had to kick the plug away myself, then they picked me up and carried me off. I was so stiff they laid me on top of an upright piano."

In retrospect, Jack wonders whether Ginger was really complaining about his playing or resentful that "this little kid" who looked up to him was now more assertive and self-assured. Where Graham or Dick might ignore a Ginger outburst, Jack would have to respond, causing a row. As his comments at the 50th birthday concert suggest, Jack could also be a bit mischievous in trying to catch Ginger out or making jokes at Ginger's expense that Ginger took the wrong way.

Some of this was Jack hitting back at what he saw as Ginger's attempt to undermine his confidence as a bass player. Although Jack knew he was an accomplished musician, to have Ginger of all people rubbish what he was doing had a devastating effect. "I remember going to Bobby Wellins when Ginger upset me once and he said, 'Just wait until you are better than him and you'll be all right,'" Jack recalls. In 1965, the band backed Marvin Gaye on some television appearances. "Marvin Gaye came round to my flat in West End Lane and we stayed up talking all night. He wanted me to join his band in the States; it was certainly very encouraging to hear somebody like that saying I was going in the right direction. That was wonderful."

It's possible too, Jack thinks, that as Ginger took control of the band it all somehow went to his head and he became a different person. There was certainly a complex set of factors underpinning Jack and Ginger's archetypal love/hate relationship. No doubt the sparks that flew between them ignited the music of the GBO, Cream, and other later pairings, but they also had a destructive and corrosive effect as well. It all could have ended in tragedy on two occasions when, with Jack driving and violent rows raging, the Organisation van nearly crashed.

Eventually Ginger took it upon himself to fire Jack, although he maintains that he was just doing the dirty work agreed by others. As Jack recalls: "I said, 'You can't fire me because I was one of the people who originated the band. You're not the boss.' So I just kept turning up to the gigs for a while. Then he did pull a knife on me. But I still don't think he had the right to fire me. Graham was very out of it and Dick was going through one of his 'I'm not involved' periods."

But Jack was out, and from there jumped straight into his next band. He had to. He needed the money – he was married.

◯

Janet Godfrey's background was remarkably similar to Jack's. She was born in Ashby de la Zouch in Leicestershire, during wartime, to respectable working-class parents who were both in the Communist Party. After the war the family returned to London, and after sharing a room with another family they settled in council accommodation in Boundary Road, Swiss Cottage, Northwest London.

In a household with no television, the radio and music were very important. Janet learnt piano from the age of six and loved The Goons. As a teenager in the late 50s she adopted the beatnik uniform, buying her duffle coat from Millet's and getting into the jazz of Dave Brubeck and Count Basie – as, like Jack, "the early Beatles didn't grab me". As rhythm & blues took off, Janet went with her friends to the clubs and dives around London where she met Alexis Korner's pianist, Johnny Parker, who must have been about 30 years old at the time. He regarded her as his 'girlfriend', but while Janet was excited by the attention and hanging around the band, she didn't "put out" for him (even though, she says, there were plenty of groupies around who would have).

During the hard British winter of 1962 – one of the harshest on record – Jack was renting a room at Johnnie Parker's place. There was no bed; Jack slept on an old couch using a curtain as a blanket, but the room did have a two-legged white grand piano (the third leg being a stack of books). It was here that Janet and Jack first met; for Janet, there was "instant chemistry", while for Jack, who'd spent the last few years fending off eager women, it was love at first sight.

"I wanted to spend as much time with Janet as possible," he recalls. "She was only 16 when we met and she was part of a group of girls who used to go to the Marquee. There was Janet; Carmen, who became tied up with Rohan O'Rahilly; Cleo, who became an actress; and Faith, who went to Camden School For Girls (where Janet went). I was with my friend Nick West at the time, a Scottish drummer I'd known for a while who was going to be the Stones drummer and then suddenly died of a brain haemorrhage. I was staying at Johnny Parker's and I think Nick may have staying there as well. We saw this really beautiful girl in school uniform. And we both thought it was really disgusting that this old man should have a 16-year-old girlfriend, so we decided we would split them up, because I fancied Janet. And that's what we did. And Johnny Parker was not my friend any more."

Janet became an important part of Jack's life. She was the secretary of the Graham Bond Fan Club and is credited as a co-author of both of Jack's songs on *Sound Of '65*. They found they had much in common and spent many hours getting to know each other. Janet says she found Jack "shy but very personable". She didn't tell her parents about Jack to begin with and then told them she was going out with a bus conductor because that sounded more respectable and secure than 'musician', and explained the strange hours he worked. Eventually they met and Jack was welcomed into the family, as were his parents – the political ties helping to bond them all together.

Janet went up to Glasgow as well. But while Betty Bruce enjoyed showing off 'Jack's girlfriend from London', she also showed Janet "quite clearly that no woman was going to be OK for her son". Janet confirms Jack's view that Betty had a "huge influence on Jack's life. Her whole focus was on Jack. He was everything." She also says she saw more of Betty than she did her own parents, who lived up the road.

Eventually Jack found a place with trombonist John Mumford – not the usual jazz hovel that most musicians inhabited, but a very nice flat on West End Lane in West Hampstead, Northwest London. "The solidly built Edwardian block was in good shape," John recalls, "and as the flat occupied the top floor, we had no-one clumping across the ceiling above us." They had a room each with a bathroom and a kitchen, but it was pretty spartan. "I think we owned a doormat," John adds. "And an empty fridge." To enhance the ambience, he made "stained glass windows" out of coloured paper.

Jack and John often went out to eat together. "I remember late one night in the Golden Egg in Leicester Square being much amused by Jack's radical treatment of a sub-standard strawberry gateau," John says. The two men respected each other's privacy: "We had a sort of unspoken agreement that we would take only one pace into each other's room, when communication was necessary."

John remembers Janet arriving on the scene and hearing "much laughter and bonhomie coming from their part of the flat". As Jack recalls: "We used to go and eat in this little place in Greek Street. It was very romantic." It wasn't the done thing in those days for couples to live together without getting married – both sets of parents would have been appalled, and Janet had already upset hers by dropping out of school. So on September 26 1964 – which also happened to be Dick Heckstall-Smith's 30th birthday – they were married at Hampstead Register Office. The ceremony was followed by a small reception at Janet's parents house paid for using money saved from Janet's job in the rag trade. Now a respectable couple, Jack and Janet moved into a self-contained flat in Bracknell Gardens, very close to the flat in West End Lane, and Janet Godfrey began her life as Mrs Jack Bruce. She gave up work to concentrate on homemaking and filling the flat with nice furniture and fittings, so when Jack got kicked out of the Organisation, he says he needed another job fast – "to pay off John Lewis".

$$\bigcirc$$

Toward the end of August 1965, Eric Clapton took a sabbatical from John Mayall's Bluesbreakers and set off with some mates for what was supposed to be a 'round the world' jaunt but which ended prematurely in Greece, where Eric had to extricate himself from a tricky situation with a local band and its management. With his star player off the scene, Mayall went through an assortment of guitarists, none of whom lasted more than a few gigs: John Weider, John Slaughter (from The Chris Farlowe Band), and finally Geoff Krivit from Jimmy Powell & The Five Dimensions, who kicked off his stint in the band at the Golders Green Refectory on September 10 1965.

It may have been that night that Jack turned up at the Manor House for his last attempt at gigging with the GBO, after which Ginger revealed his intentions with a sharp instrument. Jack was filling in with odd gigs when he got the call from John Mayall, who had heard that Jack was now a free agent. John had sacked his current bassist, John McVie, leaving him by the roadside after another argument about drinking. Jack and John got together over a plate of stew and potatoes and the deal was done.

The other members of the band were guitarist Geoff Krivit – who with The Five Dimensions had backed Chuck Berry on the Robert Stigwood package tour – and drummer Hughie Flint. The new line-up made its debut on September 11 and played about eight gigs before Peter Green stepped in, only to be told to step out again after a few days because Eric had called and wanted his old job back.

Jack's first gig with Eric was for London Airport staff on November 6 – a strange venue and audience for a blues gig. Jack says that although Eric had come down to see the Organisation, he had never heard Eric play before and was blown away by his style and technique. There was an instant rapport, he says, "which led us to having long chats together about what our aims and hopes were – I thought that although the blues was great ... there was more than that. It was the beginning rather than the end." Mayall recorded the following night's gig at the Flamingo. The surviving tapes are not of the highest quality, but there's some first rate playing (considering it was only their second gig together) and a fine representation of Eric's soaring blues runs, driven along by Jack's forceful basslines. Parts of the gig can be heard on the John Mayall albums *Looking Back* and *Primal Solos*.

Jack played about two dozen gigs with Mayall, and about ten of them were with Eric. The last show was at the Red Cross Hall in South London on November 21, where Jack played double bass for most of the show. In the audience was bassist Keith Tillman, who would later play with Mayall and Aynsley Dunbar, and who says that "with Bruce in the band, it tended to get very busy musically at times, and Mayall was sometimes upstaged by Clapton and Bruce. It was a strange period, as the live shows started to become looser, with Bruce and Clapton playing off each other and Mayall losing control over much of the proceedings … it almost became a mutual admiration thing between Bruce and Clapton, both of whom were on their best form, but already showing hints of things to come."

Jack also continued to demonstrate what a fine singer he was. On the GBO albums he sang in a low register because he didn't think he could capture the high notes of his boyhood. It took until Cream, he says, for him to "find his voice" again, although the strength of his vocals in the GBO and the Bluesbreakers suggest he wasn't giving himself enough credit as a vocalist. At that last gig, Keith Tillman says, "Jack sang a *fantastic* version of Clifton Chenier's 'Why Did You Go Last Night?' … Perfection. It was an all-time classic live performance."

Jack's time in the Bluesbreakers offered a wonderful opportunity to play with Eric and get to know him a bit, but when the chance came for more money, he took it. While there were plenty of gigs with the Bluesbreakers, the money was awful – probably no more than £5 a gig – "and you would drive to some bloody place that would take two days to get to, stay in some flea pit, or not even stay. Mayall was so stingy, we'd just drive straight back. We had this van which had a bunk bed built into it, which took up most of the room. He'd be in there with some bird that he'd picked up at the gig while the rest of us would be crammed on the engine cover."

○

On November 21 Jack played in a 'purist' blues band to a small but earnest audience of blokes in denim; within a week he was the bass player for a pop band at the Gaumont Cinema in Bradford in front of a horde of screaming teenage girls. Jack Bruce had joined Manfred Mann.

In 1965, Manfred Mann were a band in transition. Unlike most of the rhythm & blues-influenced pop bands of the era, they had their roots solidly in jazz. Keyboardist Manfred and drummer Mike Hugg had formed The Mann-Hugg Blues Brothers in 1962 and hit the road with a mixture of rhythm & blues, pop, and jazz, going through several line-ups and name changes. In 1964 they were asked to write the theme tune to a new television pop show, *Ready Steady Go!* '5-4-3-2-1' got to Number Five in the UK charts; 'Do Wah Diddy Diddy' did even better, not just in the UK but also in Canada and the USA. The band struggled to repeat that success, however. The search for another hit continued, but Manfred was looking for a change of direction. In early October 1965 he placed an advertisement in *Melody Maker* calling for "Jazzers who wish to sell out!" One of those who answered the call was a classically trained violinist and trumpet player, Henry Lowther. He was dubious about playing in a pop band, but says that "the attraction of joining Manfred Mann was that they had a reputation for playing jazz".

Henry went along to an audition at the Notre Dame Hall in Leicester Square. Sax player Dave Tomalin had told Henry about the auditions even before the ad appeared, but Dave never showed up, so Henry recommended Lyn Dobson.

Guitarist Mike Vickers had also left in the shake-up: Tom McGuinness gratefully switched back to guitar, leaving a vacancy for a bass player filled temporarily by Peter Burford. With Paul Jones remaining on vocals, Tom McGuinness, Mike Hugg on drums, and the new horn section, the band played a few dates in November before embarking on a package tour of the UK. The Marquee Show also featured The Yardbirds, The Mark Leeman Five, Gary Farr & The T-Bones (with Keith Emerson), and Goldie & The Gingerbreads.

The tour started on Thursday December 18, but after only one show Peter Burford was gone. The band's publicist told *Disc* that he left "because he found travelling too much for him", but Henry Lowther recalls: "It was obvious right from the beginning that this guy couldn't play. Somehow he'd got through the audition." David Hyde from The Mark Leeman Five stepped in for one show, but Manfred needed a permanent bassist – and fast.

At one time Henry Lowther had been invited by Graham Bond to join the GBO, but says he'd "heard about the band from Dick" and "didn't think it would suit my temperament". He knew Jack from the time they had spent together in The New Jazz Orchestra (led by Neil Ardley) and also Group Sounds Five, a pioneering free-form jazz outfit with Jon Hiseman and saxophonist Lyn Dobson, for whom Jack wrote a piece called 'Snow'. It was "a slow piece," Henry recalls, "but we freely improvised on it; we didn't play in any time or any harmony."

Group Sounds Five had a regular gig at the Regency Club in Stoke Newington, North London. (They sometimes played as GS4 or even GS3 because, Henry says, "Everyone fell out with Lyn.") The club was in the basement of a building containing a judo club, a Chinese restaurant, and a gambling den. "It was run by the Krays," Henry says. "The guy was a jazz fan. We had to stop playing when the gangsters came in at the end of the night about 11 because they wanted to play the jukebox."

Henry knew about the deal Jack was getting from John Mayall, so when Manfred Mann were in crisis he told them they "could probably get Jack Bruce. So I phoned Jack and asked if he wanted to join. I told him the money would be the same, but that, unlike the Mayall band, he would get a retainer so he would get paid whether the band worked or not."

Manfred Mann knew two things: first that Jack Bruce would need little or no rehearsal time to get to grips with a half-hour set that would be repeated night after night; and second that, in Jack, he had a schooled musician of the first rank who could do wonders for his new-look band. On that basis, Jack says, "I got promised all sorts of things by [manager/producer] Gerry Bron. I was going to be rich!"

Henry wasn't the only one lobbying for Jack. When Manfred had first announced he was looking for new blood, regulars Tom McGuinness and Paul Jones had both campaigned to get Jack Bruce in. Manfred resisted at first. Jack had only just joined John Mayall at that time, and John was Manfred's neighbour. It wasn't ethical to pinch musicians in that way, but Manfred was in the audience at the Flamingo on November 7 and according to Jack made the offer that night.

Manfred must also have known about the problems between Jack and Ginger, because Ginger has since said that Manfred called him up to ask him what Jack was like to work with. Whatever Ginger said, Jack was in, but his departure from Mayall's band clearly rankled. Shortly after Jack left, and during his spell with Immediate Records, Mayall wrote and recorded 'Double Crossing Time', which went unreleased until it appeared with overdubs on the famous *Bluesbreakers With Eric Clapton* LP.

With the Manfreds already on tour, Jack was thrown in at the deep end but took it all in his stride. "The first gig with Manfred was quite challenging," he says. "I played the whole set without a rehearsal, but after that it became incredibly boring to play."

There were odd moments of excitement, however, especially when the audience turned nasty. "I remember escaping from drunken people wanting to kill us," Jack says. "We were playing some place in the Welsh valleys. We were on stage behind the curtain; it was all fairly quiet in the audience and then they drew back the curtain, we started playing, and the whole place started fighting: 'There she was just a-walkin' down the street' – Biff! Boff! Everybody was fighting. The boys were kicking the shit out of each other with the girls standing round watching. Then for some reason they suddenly decided to get the band. 'Why should we be fighting each other when we could be killing the band?'"

Paul Jones recalls another lucky escape much closer to home for Jack. The band were up in Scotland, where a dodgy promoter swore blind that they could do two gigs in the same evening because the venues were very close together. "He lied," says Paul. "We turned up to the second gig really late and the audience were already disgruntled. Jack and I used to sing this Leadbelly song, 'Black Betty'. We put a Bo Diddley beat to it and shared lead vocals and harmonica – it was very exciting and I really looked forward to doing it. So we started the song and all the power failed. 'We're really sorry everybody, the power's gone. We'll be back in a minute just as soon as it's fixed.'

"Of course there was all this grumbling and mumbling from the audience, who were already pissed off at being kept waiting. So we came back on, started the song and the power went again. This time, they started throwing coins, those big old pennies. Manfred and Henry were the first to run because they were wearing glasses. Then we all ran and found ourselves holed up in the dressing room. The roadie ran to get the car and backed it up underneath the dressing room window on the first floor. We had to jump down several feet out of the window because the crowd were closing in and they were going to get us good. The last one to jump down was Jack, because up to then he'd been hiding in a cupboard. And we drove off with him hanging on the door and got about 200 yards down the road before we stopped to let him in. We set off again just as the first of the crowd caught up and started throwing coins again. Jack said, 'Right, let's have no more rubbish about Scottish people being mean – they must have thrown about six quid [pounds] back there.'"

The gruelling tour finished at the beginning of December. The band saw out the rest of the year with a handful of shows and two television appearances, leaving time for their first recording sessions with their new bass player. On December 7 they recorded seven tracks for BBC Radio's *Saturday Club* and then had three days booked before Christmas at Abbey Road with the aim of cutting a new single and some tracks for a new album.

Jack's first single was also released on Polydor. Recorded in October, before he joined Manfred Mann, 'I'm Getting Tired' / 'Rootin' Tootin" featured Don Rendell on sax and John Stevens on drums. *Record Mirror* gave it three out of four stars, but a lack of publicity or promotion meant no sales. It did however demonstrate Jack's keenness to develop as many strings to his bow as possible in the development of his career.

Although history – and Jack himself – has tended to gloss over this period as just a rent-paying prelude to Cream, the studio work in December 1965 and the early months of '66, dotted across Manfred Mann's subsequent releases, underlined Jack's growing stature as an all-round musician. Until then most of the band knew only that Jack was highly capable of playing through their set night after night; now they got a taste of the real Jack Bruce as the recordings took on a flavour much more to his taste. The band's versions of Cannonball Adderley's 'Tengo Tango' and Milt Jackson's 'Spirit Feel', with hot horn lines from Henry Lowther and Lyn Dobson and a scintillating bass solo, reveal a sophisticated and compelling side of Manfred Mann relatively unknown to many of their pop fans.

To herald the arrival of Jack, Henry, and Lyn, the band went back into the studio on January 12 1966 to record an EP of Jack's instrumental arrangements of hit records: The Who's 'My Generation', 'Still I'm Sad' by The Yardbirds, the Stones' 'Satisfaction', and Sonny and Cher's 'I Got You Babe'. With Jack highlighting throughout the potential of the Fender bass as lead instrument, *Instrumental Asylum* got to Number Three in the EP chart, prompting *Melody Maker* to call it "possibly the finest recording made by the Manfreds so far, or any other group for that matter", and Georgie Fame to declare that "Jack Bruce is the guv'nor bass player".

Encouraged by the success of *Instrumental Asylum*, the band recorded *Machines*, which did even better, topping the EP chart in the *New Musical Express*. Summing up the experience of playing with Jack in the studio, Tom McGuinness admits that Jack was "was quite impossible to play with at times ... we often literally couldn't follow him." But Jack could be inventive even when playing straightforward rhythm & blues, as Paul Jones explains: "Some people who play extra notes in the bar can drift a bit, but the thing about Jack is that his time is so utterly perfect that he can play seven or nine notes in the bar, but the most important four would be in exactly the right place."

The day after *Instrumental Asylum* was recorded, four members of the band and their driver were in a car accident on the way home from a gig at Hull University. Jack wasn't involved because there weren't enough places in the car; three of the band-members went in the van. Paul and Manfred were hospitalised; Paul broke his collarbone, but otherwise their injuries weren't serious. When Jack and the rest went to visit, Manfred was sitting up in bed eating an egg custard and was roundly mocked.

Interviewed by *Melody Maker* just before Christmas, Manfred Mann described Jack as "someone we have yet to exploit". Six months later he told the same publication that "Jack is the most forceful personality of the new guys. He's got a great wariness about being 'had'. But he's most cooperative when he's willing."

By then Jack felt that he had been well and truly exploited – and undoubtedly had been 'had' – and made his views known. The band finally achieved that elusive hit with 'Pretty Flamingo', released in April, for which Jack would have been paid a standard session fee. But they also had hit EPs where Jack had made a major contribution, yet he still only got the basic fee. The riches promised by Gerry Bron simply didn't materialise.

Jack stuck it out for the steady wage but found the tours very dull and wearing – and wearing itchy plaid trousers didn't help either. The last straw came at a gig in Walthamstow, Northeast London, when a beer bottle was thrown from the audience and bounced off his bass. Fortunately by then an exciting opportunity had presented itself to form "a nice little trio" that would change the face of rock music forever.

band of
CHAPTER 5 brothers

While Jack was gritting his teeth with Manfred Mann, Eric Clapton and Ginger Baker had reasons of their own to be restless. Eric was simply bored in Mayall's band and sometimes didn't even bother to turn up for gigs. At one of his no-shows, at the Woodhall Community Centre in Welwyn Garden City, a 17-year-old local, Mick Taylor, nervously played the second half on Eric's guitar. Eric wasn't even moonlighting – he was off watching The Lovin' Spoonful at the Marquee. He just missed playing with Jack. "Most of what we were doing with Mayall was imitating the records we got," he says, "but Jack had something else – he had no reverence for what they were doing and so he was composing new parts as he went along."

Eric was at a turning point in early 1966. Robert Johnson may truly have believed in a Devil waiting at the crossroads to trick the unwary, ambitious musician into trading his soul for the power of music, but it's more likely that the crossroads was simply a metaphor for freedom. If you could play, you could leave, but the world of choice could be scary and uncertain.

For Eric, the future really was uncertain. The people he knew as a child to be his parents turned out to be his grandparents, and when his real mother showed up he had to pretend she was his sister to save face with the neighbours – and then she was gone again. From this trauma grew a rather distant and aloof young man who felt himself to be an outsider surrounded by those with 'normal' families. His discovery of country-blues revealed to him a tough world of alienation and survival of the fittest, a world away from his life in the 'South London Delta'. Nonetheless, Eric related to the poetry of the blues, and as his guitar playing rapidly improved it became not just a source of escape but also a shield against the outside world. In 1962 he'd been the "pale skinny kid" that Dick Heckstall-Smith saw running off the stage at the Ealing Club; now, four years later, he was God. But part of him knew there were many better players – he would name-check several over the years – and he was disturbed by the fact that fans and the music press were treating him as if he had invented the blues. He had very publicly left The Yardbirds for their being too commercial, but resented their subsequent success with Jeff Beck on guitar. And yet he was flattered by the adulation: in 1966 he was still only 21, photogenic, fashionable, and always ready to talk to the new journalists of the music press like Chris Welch and Nick Logan, who wanted to promote new heroes for the younger generation.

Even so, he didn't know what to do next. He talked openly in January '66 of forming his own band; he spoke to Pete Quaife, bassist with The Kinks, and was also good friends with Stevie Winwood. And he carried on his discussions with Jack too about how the blues could be reinterpreted. "I remember having conversations with Eric," Jack says. "He wanted to play the blues. And I said, 'Well, I love the blues, but I see it as more of a language than a music.' I said, 'I don't think you can play the blues because you have to be black to do that, but you can use the language of the blues and write a new kind of music.' I distinctly remember talking to Eric about what we should be doing, how we do certain things." (Eric even contemplated leaving the UK altogether to pursue a blues career in Chicago close to the source of his inspiration.)

The two men grew close. Jack recalls one moment when his delight at seeing Eric overcame him. "I got banned from the Blue Boar Service Station on the motorway. Eric walked in and I was so excited I slung a whole greasy plate of beans, pie, bacon, and eggs at him. He ducked and it hit this woman in the face. I think I'm the only person to have been banned from the Blue Boar – with no dinner to boot!"

Eric didn't want to be a leader, but Ginger Baker on the other hand had no qualms on that front. Life for Ginger was much simpler; he had a chart on his wall showing the pattern of his earnings over time. At one point in the Organisation they peaked at £50 a week, but there was no progress. Jack had not been replaced; instead Mike Falana had come in on trumpet, with Graham doing the bass parts on the Hammond pedals. It just wasn't the same without Jack. There was still plenty of work, but with no hit records to boost earnings, the Organisation were losing ground to the new wave of guitar-led blues bands on the circuit. Ginger's chart was going nowhere but down and, with a wife and child to support, he knew it was time to go.

On Friday May 13 1966 Ginger travelled to Oxford Town Hall with his wife to sit in with the Bluesbreakers. They were travelling in Ginger's brand new yellow Rover, which he'd bought with the proceeds from 'Waltz For A Pig', a B-side he wrote for The Who under the name Harry Butcher that was performed by The Who Orchestra (aka The Organisation) as a product of The Who's messy legal dispute with producer Shel Talmy. In Oxford, Mayall's drummer Hughie Flint was more than happy to step aside to let Ginger take over and the result left both Eric and Ginger grinning. They had a conversation over a drink after the gig; Ginger asked Eric if he fancied forming a band. Eric inquired as to who the bass player might be. Ginger bounced the question back to Eric, who said "Jack Bruce". He knew there had been problems between Jack and Ginger but wasn't sure what it was all about. Ginger was very doubtful, but Eric says now: "I was insistent. It was Jack or no go." Ginger said he would have to think about it. He discussed it all the way back to London with Liz, who recalls: "I thought Jack was nice; he was a good musician, although I didn't realise how good. So I was all in favour."

Ginger eventually made the call. It was arranged that he would go not to Jack's place but to "neutral ground" – Janet's parents' flat – "in case he tried to knife me again". Jack was immediately impressed by Ginger's new car, but still the conversation went on for some time; Janet remembers putting out ashtrays because her parents were non-smokers, and says that they were full by the end of the evening.

"I never had any doubt about playing with Ginger again," Jack says. "Ginger is Ginger, but he is the greatest drummer to have come out of this country without any doubt, and in fact probably the greatest drummer there ever was in rock music – although he would never consider himself a rock musician (I would). Even now, no one comes close. And I didn't even think there would be problems because this would be a new band."

The next step was to gather at Ginger's house in Neasden, Northwest London, for a blow. The house backed onto an alley and beyond that fields going down to a local reservoir known as the Welsh Harp, so there was no problem about noise. They just set up and jammed 'something in D'. In subsequent interviews, Ginger and Eric have used the word 'magic' about that workout, and so it was for Jack. "We knew we had to play together," he says. Ominously, however, Eric recalls hearing an argument breaking out in another part of the house, with one telling the other "you're doing it again", suggesting that whatever had gone on in the past was unresolved.

But the drive to play together was over-powering. Jack remembers sitting in a little park in Notting Hill, near where Eric lived, the three of them chewing over all the details that needed sorting out. Would there be a fourth member? Was three enough? Jack and Ginger thought it was; and although some accounts have Eric wanting to bring in Stevie Winwood (and a passing collective thought about Graham Bond), it was never seriously discussed. Eric himself was attracted by the trio format. He had seen The Buddy Guy Trio a while back and marvelled at the space Buddy had to play in with just the rhythm section, although this was tempered by the realisation that he would have to handle both lead and rhythm, while Jack and Ginger were used to being in large bands with horn sections. In the end their prowess as musicians, Ginger's polyrhythmic onslaughts on his large kit, and the sheer volume would more than compensate for lack of numbers.

In the absence of any set plans, and before Ginger's approach, Eric may well have harboured thoughts of forming his own Chicago blues trio, especially as he was thinking of moving there. But he would have let that idea go straight away once he had teamed up with Jack and Ginger. In truth, there really was no 'vision' for the band at all. Eric saw the chance for more freedom to express himself; Jack was looking for a vehicle for his compositions; and Ginger just wanted to be successful, his view being that if England won the World Cup that year, Cream would be. The prime directive was to "have a blast playing together and see what happens" – and to show how nonsensical it was to think there was a real plan for the band. Jack later joked that Cream was meant to be The Ornette Coleman Trio with Eric as Ornette Coleman, "only we never told him".

The next issue was management. Eric had his ear bent by both Rik Gunnell, who booked the Bluesbreakers, and Giorgio Gomelsky, the ex-manager of the Stones and The Yardbirds; Ginger pushed for Robert Stigwood. Although the Chuck Berry tour had been a mess, Ginger saw in Stigwood a savvy entrepreneur who had a track record of managing successful pop stars, knew the business, and had the right contacts.

Jack was against the idea; Stigwood had done nothing for The Organisation and, moreover, Jack had "never trusted him from the start". Instead Jack wanted the band to manage itself – with an accountant and an agency for booking – and felt that he and Ginger had enough experience and strength of will to deal with most situations that would arise. But Ginger's view prevailed; he was also responsible for leaking the news to *Melody Maker*, which broke the story on Saturday June 11. Up until then, they had all been very wary of their plans leaking out; Ginger had declined an invitation to play on an Elektra white blues compilation called *What's Shakin'* because Eric and Jack were involved and he didn't want any exposure for the trio until they were ready.

In 1965 Jac Holzman, the head of Elektra Records, decided to appoint Joe Boyd, who had been working for the Newport Jazz Festival and tour-managing the American folk blues packages that had come to Britain, to run the label's new London office. At the time producer Paul Rothschild was trying to put together an album of Elektra artists to follow up the success of the label's *Blues Project* compilation, which featured white Greenwich Village musicians playing acoustic blues in the style of country artists who had recently been 'rediscovered' (Skip James, Sleepy John Estes, Son House, and so on).

Rothschild already had four tracks from an outfit called The Lovin' Spoonful, recorded before they signed to Kama Sutra, as well as demos from The Paul Butterfield Blues Band and tracks by Al Kooper and Tom Rush. Joe Boyd offered to get a British band together to finish it off but was having trouble finding any decent unsigned bands. He called Paul Jones. "Joe said he had phoned me because he had heard a rumour that I wanted to leave the Manfreds, which I denied, but he still asked me if I could put together an ad hoc blues band for this session. The first person I called was Jack who said he was up for it and he asked me who else was in it. I said, 'wouldn't it be great if we could get Eric Clapton and Ginger Baker?' and there was a slight pause and Jack said 'how much do you know?' Eric agreed, and so did drummer Pete York from Spencer Davis with Stevie Winwood, and Ben Palmer, a friend of both Paul and Eric and a first rate Chicago blues pianist. Joe arranged the necessary clearances, although Chris Blackwell insisted on a pseudonym for Winwood, who appeared as Steve Anglo. (Pete York became Pete Howard, and Paul Jones was billed as Jacob Matthews, the names of his two sons.)

Paul Jones chose to sing his own 'I Want To Know' with Steve, who wanted to do 'Steppin' Out'. Eric didn't want to sing but was keen on Albert King's 'Crosscut Saw'. Joe suggested 'Crossroad Blues' by Robert Johnson instead; Eric countered with 'Travelling Riverside Blues'. They ended up with a combination of the lyrics from one with a lick from the other. The renamed 'Crossroads' became a showpiece song that Eric would make his own.

In his autobiography, Joe Boyd has the band, now called Eric Clapton & The Powerhouse, going into the old Olympic Studios in George Street, central London, in mid January, while other accounts suggest early March. But Jack's comment to Paul about a secret band with Eric and Ginger suggests an even later date. The session went well and sounded very exciting on the playback, although Joe says that the resulting *What's Shakin'* didn't sound as good once Jac Holzman took the tapes back to the States to mix them.

When it came, the premature announcement of Cream left Jack and Eric mortified, since neither had yet said anything to their respective employers; Mayall went nuts and symbolically fired Eric, although he actually served out a notice period until mid-July. Jack carried on with Manfred Mann for a while, including a headlining appearance at the Uxbridge Blues Festival, where he was declared "a sheer delight on bass" by Nick Jones of *Melody Maker*; he was eventually replaced in the first week of July by Klaus Voorman. Ginger's place was taken by a young National Youth Jazz Orchestra drummer and trainee accountant, Jon Hiseman.

Eric came up with the name The Cream (later shortened to Cream), as announced by Stigwood at the end of June in a strangely worded press release: "The first is last and the last is first, but the first, the second, and the last are Cream. They will be called Cream and will be represented by me for agency and management. They will record for my Reaction label and will go into the studio next week to cut tracks for their first single. Their debut will be at the National Jazz And Blues Festival in July, when their first single would be released."

In reality Stigwood had even less idea about the band than the guys themselves. The first of three proper rehearsals took place in a church hall near Kensal Rise, not too far from Ginger's house, attended by Stigwood, *Melody Maker's* Chris Welch, and a group of dispossessed Brownies (junior Girl Guides) who had been kicked out to make way for a bunch of hairies about to make a loud noise, much to the chagrin of the caretaker. Using just part of a drum kit and a couple of amps, they ran through some blues numbers – not the usual British rhythm & blues fall-backs like 'Hoochie Coochie Man' or 'Smokestack Lighnin'' but songs culled from Eric's much broader knowledge of the blues, including Dr Ross's 'Cat's Squirrel' and Long 'Cleve' Reed's 'Lawdy Mama'. Then in an early demonstration of their eclecticism they ran through a Memphis Jug Band song, 'Take Your Finger Off It' – at which point Stigwood actually asked Chris if he thought they were any good.

Later on, over egg and chips, Chris asked the band what music they would play and got answers ranging from "blues ancient and modern" to "sweet and sour rock'n'roll". But it was precisely because there was no formula, no pre-set direction of travel, that the band, with its inclinations toward anarchy and mischief, could just please themselves. Eric in particular, concerned that people would be expecting to see a super-charged Bluesbreakers, suggested introducing visual elements such as dry ice, bubbles, and turkeys running around the stage. These thoughts quickly evaporated on the breeze when Eric admitted he didn't have the wit or imagination to pull it off, although a stuffed bear did make a brief appearance. Pete Brown calls this "Great British Rubbish – that old moth-eaten bear they carried around was part of that heritage plus pop imagery that had nothing to do with the blues, but everything to do with being bizarre. It was more James Robertson Justice than Buddy Guy."

So if Cream wouldn't be coming out of left-field visually, how else could it happen? The answer was in the music. Jack says those early days were fun. "We had a couple of nights where everybody came to our flat and we had these mad parties," he recalls. "We did 'The Ying Tong Song' (by The Goons) or I'd improvise some French thing on piano, like French film music, and Eric would join in on acoustic guitar – somewhere there are some tapes of this. It was really good fun. Pete came to one, and the idea was that Pete would write with Ginger – they started to write, but they didn't get anywhere. But Janet and Ginger did – they wrote 'Sweet Wine' one night – and I started to work with Pete. We hit it off almost instantly – we shared the sense of humour and a lot of common ground. I often say, jokingly, 'Ginger got my wife and I got Pete Brown.'"

Jack had already made his intentions clear by writing 'NSU' on his own for the early band rehearsals. "'NSU' was a very valid manifesto, my own personal manifesto, almost like a punk song ten years too early, very simple and tongue-in-cheek," he says. "I took a bit of Otis Redding when he's singing 'Respect' – in fours – da-a-da-a-da-a-da." Even on a simple song like this, the vocal comes in right across the beat where you don't expect it – a small point, maybe, yet indicative of Jack's thought processes as a composer.

Jack says he never had any discussions with Ginger about music in the way he did with Eric. Many years later, Eric told *Mojo* magazine: "I'd never known any kind of musical scale other than the strict blues scale – Jack brought with him an immense experience of classical, jazz and popular music." Even more tellingly, he added: "I'd seen myself as the front guy with Cream, but the reality was that Jack was easily the best equipped for that role. And that's how it immediately evolved."

On July 29 the band played two half-hour sets at the Twisted Wheel in Manchester as a warm-up for the National Jazz And Blues Festival at Windsor, where, true to the traditions of the Great British Summer, it poured with rain. Soaked but happy, the crowd of 15,000 cheering blues fans roared the band on as they played a brief and nervous showcase for each musician – 'Spoonful', 'Traintime', and 'Toad'.

Expectations were very high, but the structure of live music in the UK left the band little choice but to build their support on the very same circuit as the Organisation and the Bluesbreakers. Ginger took control of the business, booking gigs in association with the agent Robert Masters, but if he'd kept his chart going it wouldn't have looked that much healthier. Where the Organisation would play for £40, Cream simply added another £5 – and even then the Black Prince pub in Bexley wouldn't pay up. Ginger says he would sit in the agent's office goading him into asking for more money, and on the basis of this extra effort tried to get Jack and Eric to agree to a three-way royalty split on songwriting irrespective of the writer. They both said no. This would be a huge bone of contention for Ginger as it became clear that his arch nemesis Jack – and Pete – would ultimately earn the most from Cream in publishing royalties because they wrote the lion's share of the material, starting with the first single.

Stigwood's announcement of a summer single release was way off the mark but there is no doubt that Jack set out to write a commercial song. The examples of The Beatles, who influenced everybody, and the Stax and Motown labels showed Jack that you could create amazing songs of craft and substance lasting only two or three minutes. He makes the point that while it might seem incongruous for Cream to be playing 'Spoonful' on stage and 'I Feel Free' on television, "You could hear Howlin' Wolf doing 'Spoonful' on a jukebox. It was just a pop record for a different audience." Wolf, Muddy Waters, and the other blues greats might have been deified as purveyors of serious, 'authentic' music from the heart of the plantation by white academics, record producers, and fans, but in truth they just wanted hits on the chart and money in their pockets, same as any white pop musician.

Jack composed a slow, lilting blues ballad in need of lyrics. Ginger called up Pete and drove him at frightening speed to the Rayrik Studio in London, where he was played the master take of what became 'Wrapping Paper'. Explaining the song, Jack says: "We had been talked up as this particular sort of band, so I thought the answer to that was not to do what was expected – you should always do what was unexpected. It was a small hit, but it was a blues – the form of it was a blues, but it wouldn't sound like a strict 12-bar blues even though that's what it is. At the time I also wanted to play games with people. But we got attention, people talked about it because it wasn't what they expected."

Lyrically, Pete says he chose to fill 'Wrapping Paper' with movie images that just fell out onto the page, but feels in the end that the song didn't really work. "But it was something," he says. "It was a beginning. The music was peculiar as well. It's a strange old piece, it had an atmosphere which communicated itself." It made the UK Top 40 on its release in October, and if the idea was to shock people then mission accomplished: one reviewer suggested it might drive Cream fans to suicide. Good job, then, that they couldn't eavesdrop on band discussions about other possible singles, including a Tony Colton/Ray Smith composition, 'The Coffee Song', and a Bruce/Brown composition, 'Beauty Queen', which Pete says "had a nice tune, but the lyrics were shit".

Although Stigwood is listed as the producer on all the early Cream recordings, Jack was the unofficial musical director of the band. He came to the studio with all the parts for their next single, 'I Feel Free', written out and persuaded Ginger to pick up on the 'bom-bom' a cappella introduction with a tom-tom figure to kick the song into gear. "'I Feel Free' was inspired by the feeling of 'River Deep, Mountain High' and also an organ line by Steve Winwood from a Spencer Davis song," Jack explains. "That's the way it is – it's osmosis – people come up with inventions at the same time or painters influence each other in particular periods. It's the same with musicians.

"'I Feel Free' is actually a heavy song – the idea was that we could have very quiet singing over very heavy playing. The singing was very under-stated, so you have two emotions going at once. To me that's the magic of that song and the recording. There were extra harmonies that I overdubbed that got lost in the mix because it's only four-track. There's a canon on it that you can't hear clearly." Jack also says that Ginger was unhappy with the drum sound and wanted to re-record it. "I knew the feel of the recording couldn't be bettered," he says, "but Ginger wasn't pleased."

This time the press were mollified: 'I Feel Free' shot to Number 11 and stayed in the singles chart for 12 weeks. Over the years it has become the default track for film directors and advertising agencies wanting to express the spirit of the 60s, although Jack and Pete have refused to let the song be used either for a computer war game or to promote the GM seed manufacturer Monsanto, thereby losing out on six-figure payments.

Meanwhile, in between the usual slog around the UK, the band laid down the tracks for their first album. This time they used Ryemuse, a dinky little studio owned by the Spot Label and located above a chemists in central London. "You couldn't communicate through a window into the control booth," Jack recalls. "There was a TV monitor link – you had to talk into this camera. The first attempts at recording were done in an amateurish way. We just did them live, using the four tracks. It was not recorded as well as it might have been, but it was the way the band sounded."

The choice of tracks was not that difficult; they relied on the songs that comprised their current set plus original contributions: Jack's 'NSU' and 'Dreamin''; 'Sleepy Time Time' by Jack and Janet; and 'Sweet Wine' by Janet and Ginger. In keeping with his interest in country-blues and his determination to steer away from the more obvious covers, Eric chose 'Four Until Late' by Robert Johnson and 'I'm So Glad' by Skip James. To their eternal credit, Cream ensured that Skip James got his royalty payments, enabling him to die with some dignity in October 1969. (A few years later, Jack remembers a little old lady – Skip's widow – sitting backstage, flinching at the sound of a West Bruce & Laing soundcheck, but waiting patiently to thank him.)

The resulting album, *Fresh Cream*, was released in early December on the same day as 'I Feel Free'. Considering the inauspicious studio setting, the album was a triumph, with superb sonic dynamics, cleverly paced passages of light and shade, intelligent use of harmony and overdubbing, and, of course, individual musicianship of the highest calibre. Jack's nimble lead bass weaves in and out around Eric's clean, sharp lines, supported by the authority, power, and precision of Ginger's drumming. And while songs such as 'Sweet Wine' and 'Spoonful' were nothing like as long as they would become on stage, you can hear how the dynamics of the songs – the way Jack and Ginger would step back just before Eric launched into the guitar solo – set the framework for the extended improvisations that would define the band in the public imagination.

Fans wanting to see Jack and Ginger in the Organisation or Eric with John Mayall would pack the clubs. Now they were lining the streets; there were often as many locked out as were inside. Interviewed in late '66, London club managers Rik Gunnell and John Gee agreed that Cream were the top-drawing band of the year. And to their live success, they could add a Top Ten album: *Fresh Cream* reached Number Six in the UK and even sneaked into the US chart – a very creditable showing considering the band had made no appearances there (something Stigwood was looking to address as soon as possible).

Stigwood had already secured the band a deal with Atlantic Records, which released 'I Feel Free' on its Atco subsidiary label in January '67. *Fresh Cream* followed in March, with 'I Feel Free' replacing 'Spoonful'. Run by Ahmet and

Nesuhi Ertegun and producer Jerry Wexler, who had signed Charles Mingus, John Coltrane, Ray Charles, Wilson Pickett, and Aretha Franklin, Atlantic was the coolest jazz and rhythm & blues label in America. The company had Sonny and Cher, but it was looking for more white pop and rock acts to better compete with the likes of CBS. Ahmet Ertegun desperately wanted to sign Stigwood's latest acquisition, The Bee Gees. Stigwood agreed on one condition: if you want the Bee Gees, you have to sign Cream.

Ahmet agreed, but he had no idea about the band or what to do with them, even if the name Eric Clapton may well have rung a bell. As he told it, he was at the trendy Scotch Of St James nightclub in central London on March 9 1966, hosting a party for one of his stars, Wilson Pickett. At one point Ertegun heard some amazing blues guitar playing and complimented Wilson on his guitarist, only for the singer to point out the guy standing at the bar. The label boss turned to see Eric. Not only was he enamoured of his playing, he felt he was looking at a star in the making.

First, however, Cream had an internal crisis to deal with. One of the stipulations for getting the band off the ground was that Ginger would stop using heroin. He had been doing OK and stuck to the agreement, but by early December gigs were starting to get cancelled. Ginger failed to show up for the band's second set at the Agincourt Ballroom in Camberley, Surrey, on December 18, forcing Jack and Eric to play as a duo. It was rumoured that Ginger had disappeared because he refused to do another set for no extra money – even though Jack and Eric had apparently agreed to it. But for whatever reason, Ginger was nowhere to be seen. Jack says that he and Eric assumed that Ginger had gone off to score because he was upset. "We were quite worried about him," Jack says. But when Ginger re-appeared there was a showdown, during which Eric and Jack went through the motions of 'sacking' Ginger to shock him into quitting again.

Then on January 11 1967 Cream were booked to mime along to 'I Feel Free' on *Top Of The Pops*. "Eric and I were just mucking about because that's what you did," Jack says. "You deliberately sing and play out of time, hit huge chords, and nothing would happen (or the other way round). There were odd things going on with the union at that time – you had to sing live and mime to the record. But Ginger hated miming. He was dressed as a convict and got very upset about the rubber cymbals.

"We were leaving and went to the car. Eric had gone off separately and I asked the roadie, 'Where's Ginger? I'll go back and get him.' So I went back into the studio. He was in the dressing room and they had these wooden form benches with slats, very narrow. And he was stretched out along one. He was green and he was rattling. I knew immediately that he'd overdosed. So I went back to get the roadie and somehow we got him into the back of the car because he was as stiff as a board – he was sticking out the car window, I think. We drove him to the hospital in Willesden. I went back to see him next morning and he was lying in bed looking pretty miserable.

"'Oh, hi Ginger. How are you?'

"'You fuckin' cunt.'"

Whether Ginger was genuinely trying to end it all or was simply resentful that it was Jack who saved his life is open to question. But there was no doubt that if Jack hadn't gone looking for Ginger – and acted quickly – that could have been it. Game over.

○

Cream carried on touring Britain through February and March with trips to Northern Ireland and Europe, where at one point they shot a 'zany' short film of themselves prancing through fields dressed as monks and generally mucking about. They looked to be having a good time, and the film was destined to promote the single in the States, but was ultimately pulled, allegedly for fear of offending the Bible Belt.

In February the band played two shows at Brian Epstein's Saville Theatre – one of the rare occasions on which they performed at any of the larger UK venues. For Cream to play the Saville was symbolic of a new business relationship developing between Brian Epstein and Robert Stigwood. Much to the horror of his staff and associates, a tired and increasingly disillusioned Epstein was aiming to merge his business empire, NEMS, with Stigwood on terms that were hugely advantageous to the Australian.

Briefly energised by the idea of the new set-up and still driven by his deeply instilled work ethic, Epstein flew to New York to secure British tours for The Monkees and The Four Tops. He also arranged a trip for Cream and The Who (who had Stigwood as their agent) to play during Easter week at the RKO 58th Street Theater in Manhattan as part of a show promoted by the New York DJ Murray The K. Epstein also held court for the media and spoke enthusiastically about his company's exciting new interests: Cream, The Who, and The Bee Gees.

"It was a big deal going to New York in those days," says Jack. "It was like going home. The whole American culture was ingrained – comics, films. We stayed in the Gorham Hotel, which we thought was luxury – it was a fleapit actually. We were met by the limo, which was all done in lights with Union Jacks. The buzz of being there was amazing.

"The show started at 10am and went on until midnight. You got the little kids in the morning, and as the day wore on the audience got older, until by ten it was the drunks. The ambition was to do five shows in a day, but on the first day the show overran by six hours or something. I seem to recall us doing two or three songs – we were way down the bill. Wilson Pickett was top, then The Who. When it came to shortening the show, they said, 'You can only do one song.' I think we did 'I'm So Glad'. Then they said, 'You'll have to cut that.' So we ended doing a bit of 'I'm So Glad'. I think there were a few people who came to see us. It must have been a bit weird to come and see us do 16 bars of 'I'm So Glad' and that was it – abysmal, so boring. You had to be in there all day; Pete Townshend was going particularly mad.

"We had some time off, and I remember going to the home of the flute player from The Blues Project [Andy Kulberg]," Jack continues. "His wife made this amazing meal. I was pretty much a loner in those days, but I did hitch up with Al Kooper [also in The Blues Project]. It was the first time I took LSD without knowing it. That's quite frightening. We went to this 'Be-In' in Central Park and this little hippie girl came up with this bag of popcorn. So I started eating it and the guys were all looking at me and going 'wow'. So then we had to go round a few outpatient departments, but I had to do a load of shows with the effects of this happening.

"We had lots of plans for the last night, mainly hatched by Pete Townshend. Murray The K threatened that nobody would get paid if anything happened, but nobody did anyway."

At the end of this nonsense, Cream had a couple of days to spare before flying home. Perhaps to compensate for their dire experience at the hands of Murray The K (and to give Atlantic a chance for a brief introduction to the band), they went into the hallowed Atlantic Studios on April 3 to see what they could do in the time available. There they met two people who would prove critically important in their subsequent history: an engineer named Tom Dowd and a young, multi-talented musician looking for a foothold in record production, Felix Pappalardi.

Tom Dowd came from a highly musical family but seemed destined for a career as a physicist. He worked on the atom bomb in the 40s before making an abrupt career change after the war when he answered an advertisement for a recording engineer. He had a great ear for music and built a peerless career as the producer of the torrent of classic Atlantic jazz, rhythm & blues, and blues hits that poured out of the label in the following years, even if he was often only listed as the engineer. Moreover, he is credited with the development of the commercial use of stereo sound – together with the invention of the faders on recording consoles – and was the second person after Les Paul to have an eight-track Ampex recorder.

After studying classical music at the University of Michigan, Felix Pappalardi established himself on the mid-60s Greenwich Village folk scene as an accomplished bass guitarist, arranger, and producer for acts such as Tom Rush, Tom Paxton, Joan Baez, and The Youngbloods, and worked with John Sebastian in Fred Neil's club band. But by 1967 his career was in a rut and he was looking for a new opportunity. David Rubenson, an A&R guy at Columbia Records, had introduced Felix to a pop and country music manager, Bud Prager.

"Felix and I had an instant chemistry," Bud recalled, "and we decided to form a production company called Windfall. I knew Ahmet Ertegun going way back and I told Felix to hang out at Atlantic Records. Why there? Because there was a change going on. All the other record companies closed at five o'clock. But Atlantic had Ahmet – who didn't get up until two in the afternoon – and Jerry Wexler, who worked late, and they were an emerging rock label. For the musicians who don't get up until the afternoon, Atlantic was the only label where anything was happening in the evening – they had an eight-track studio in the same building as the label." (A few weeks after conducting this interview, Bud Prager passed away. He was 79 and had been suffering from cancer.)

Being a bright, charming guy, Felix hung out in the corridor between the studio and the offices, generally making himself useful, sorting out any problems that Arif Mardin, the other great Atlantic producer, might have. Then on that April day he met Robert Stigwood and Ahmet Ertegun, who asked: "Would you go into the studio and see if you could do anything with these guys?"

Like Stigwood, and in keeping with the thinking of the day, Ertegun was focused on the single after 'I Feel Free' – one that Atlantic could promote more easily now that Cream had shown their faces in the States (and with a full blown tour in the offing). But time was short. They ran through different interpretations of 'Lawdy Mama' – one in the style of Junior Wells (in the manner the song would usually be played live) and another more akin to the hard-edged sound of Albert King, whose records Eric played in the studio to get the sound right. Felix listened and then asked if he could take the tapes home overnight.

The next day 'Lawdy Mama' had morphed from 'Brain Stew' (its original title) into 'Strange Brew', with lyrics by Felix's wife, the troubled and volatile Gail Collins. Jack was very complimentary about Eric's guitar work but annoyed that it had been grafted onto the 'Lawdy Mama' backing track because it appeared – to a musician at any rate – that Jack had played a wrong note. In the blues you can play a 'long four' by going to the fourth chord on the fifth bar, or a 'short four', where you go to the fourth chord on the second bar. Jack played the long four on 'Lawdy Mama', but Eric played the 'short four' on 'Strange Brew', so with the guitar high in the mix, it sounded like Jack had gone wrong. This would prove to be just the start of Jack's problems at Atlantic.

Because of the shortage of original material, as a reasonable statement of the band at the time, and because of the expectations of the fans, it seemed acceptable for the first album to be littered with blues covers. But Cream had to progress, not least because Jimi Hendrix was storming the UK singles charts and had just released a debut album, *Are You Experienced*, full of original compositions. The album reached the Top Five in both the UK and the USA, boosted by Hendrix's landmark appearance at the Monterey Pop Festival.

It has since transpired that, while Stigwood can be blamed for many things in his management of Cream, the band's non-appearance at Monterey wasn't one of them. One of the organisers, Andrew Oldham, has since said that the band's name never came up in the planning, although one might argue that, as the agent of The Who (who did appear), Stigwood could have insisted that if the organisers wanted The Who, they had to have Cream as well. After all, it worked with Atlantic Records.

When Jimi Hendrix came to London in September 1966, the news spread fast among the community of musicians. "We'd all heard about Jimi from Linda Keith, one of Eric's girlfriends," Jack says. "She claimed to have discovered Jimi playing in New York and told Chas Chandler. Then she was back in London telling us about Jimi. There was definitely a buzz about him. We knew he was coming over and we were all very excited about seeing him."

Jimi had insisted to Chas that he wanted to meet Eric. It was Jack who made it happen. "We were playing at the Polytechnic Of Central London," he says. "I was having a drink in a pub and this guy came up to me and said, 'I'm Jimi Hendrix and I want to sit in with your band.' I took him over there, went into the dressing room. Eric was fine about it; Ginger wasn't keen and insisted Eric stayed on stage. So Jimi plugged into my amp, played 'Killin' Floor', and blew us all away. I don't think Eric was ever the same again."

As a guitarist and a fashion hound, Eric felt the (albeit friendly) rivalry with Jimi more acutely than did Jack or Ginger. It was Eric who adopted the Hendrix Afro – "fine by me," says Jack, "as long as I didn't have to have one. I think my hair had things living in it" – and was an early champion of the psychedelic finery in which neither Jack nor Ginger ever looked too comfortable. Jack says Jimi was just too nice a guy to be rivals with, and in any case, although Mitch was a great drummer, Noel wasn't really a bass player. And they were far more of a back-up rhythm section to Jimi, who sang and wrote all the songs as well.

Even so, Cream needed new and original material. Pete Brown says that, as an early devotee of 'world music', Ginger came up with a Polynesian song that went from 7/8 to 6/8, plus a melody line for a song that became 'Blue Condition'. Eric had composed a song, 'Tales Of Brave Ulysses', with lyrics written by his artist friend Martin Sharp, but he didn't want to sing it and didn't have any other material. So it was left to Jack and Pete, who often worked through the night because of the band's tour schedule, to write the songs. This is how it would be right to the end. It wasn't like The Beatles, who'd spend months in the studio making an album – touring just ruled that out, and Stigwood would never have spent the money anyway. Cream never had more than five straight days in a studio – they had to go with what they had. But in Jack and Pete they had a composer and a lyricist who turned in one timeless song after another – songs made all the more remarkable for the circumstances under which they were written.

After one particularly difficult night when nothing was happening, Jack just started playing a riff of syncopated eighth notes all on the offbeats, almost in a fit of desperation. Pete was looking out the window at the time, and muttered: "It's getting near dawn/When lights close their tired eyes." Jack had composed 'Sunshine Of Your Love', one of the most recognisable rock riffs of all time. (An early book on bass playing with a plastic disc at the back declared: "Learn this riff and you can send off for your union card.") The song didn't have an ending so Jack played it to Eric, who added the turnaround. A later dispute blew up over who devised the distinctive Native American-style drum pattern; Ginger claimed it was his idea and used it as an example of how he and Eric made contributions to songs that went uncredited. But in various interviews, Tom Dowd claimed that *he* came up with the pattern in the studio, and in fact a bootleg recording exists of a Ricky Tick Club gig in April before Cream went back to the States to record the song, where 'Sunshine' is played with a more conventional rock'n'roll beat.

Before leaving for the States to do the Murray The K show, Cream had gone into Ryemuse to demo more new material. They recorded an instrumental version of 'Blue Condition', for which Pete says he wrote the original lyrics only for Ginger to lose them and write his own, and five new Bruce/Brown songs: 'Take It Back', 'SWLABR (She Walks Like A Bearded Rainbow)', 'Hey Now Princess', 'Weird of Hermiston', 'The Clearout', and 'Theme For An Imaginary Western'. The first two would appear on the next album, but the rest were rejected by Eric and Ginger; Jack's view is that this was fuelled by a resentment that he and Pete were coming up with all these new songs. They were all first rate compositions – in 'Theme For An Imaginary Western' they had a song to die for, a beautifully constructed homage to life on the road – but in fact not only were the tapes rejected, they ended up 'lost' for decades. This version of 'Western' has never been found.

Things got worse when the band returned to Atlantic in mid-May for the five-day recording session for their next album, *Disraeli Gears*. Felix Pappalardi couldn't wait for them to come back; having heard *Fresh Cream* earlier in the year, he was thrilled to meet them in person and keen to get started. For his part, Ahmet Ertegun was thankful he had found a producer who could relate to whatever it was Cream were trying to do. But Ahmet wasn't convinced about 'Strange Brew' as a single. It reached the UK Top 20 in May, but when it dribbled out in the States in July there was no label support and it bombed.

While Cream were back in the UK, Felix had moved on from being a guy who merely helped out. He may have enjoyed hanging out with Greenwich Village types, but he was also ambitious. Windfall, his company with Bud Prager, had now signed a formal production deal with Atlantic to produce Cream using a new subsidiary company called One Toad, Two Frogs. So as Ahmet was now paying Felix, he had no compunction about putting the squeeze on him to come up with a single – and threatened to force a song on Cream if Felix couldn't deliver.

For his part Felix told Bud he would never just thrust a song on Cream like that. Felix became the go-between, doing his best to get the album tracks done while phoning Bud to ask advice on how to get Ahmet off his back. According to Bud, Felix took both 'Tales Of Brave Ulysses' and 'Sunshine Of Your Love' to Jerry Wexler; it was he, not Ahmet, who first demanded that Felix take off "that psychedelic hogwash". It is possible that Ahmet later repeated what Jerry had said, but knowing Jerry all those years, Bud was adamant that it would have been out of character – but not for Jerry, who would speak his mind without a second thought. Bud called Wexler "a rough, tough fucker – a very powerful record executive and the real fire behind that label".

Felix was so incensed by Wexler's response that when it came to finding a label for his band Mountain (co-founded by Leslie West) he refused to go with Atlantic. If Atlantic was just looking for a single release, Wexler might have had a point about 'Ulysses', but dismissing 'Sunshine' out of hand was incredibly misguided. When the song was eventually released in the States in 1968, it was the biggest-selling single Atlantic ever had, and the massive airplay helped guarantee full houses for Cream's final US tours that year.

Aside from the reaction to specific songs and the pressure to find a single, Ahmet Ertegun made it quite clear that he regarded Eric as the leader of the band. He wanted Eric to sing and Jack just to stand in the corner and play bass. So not only was the band becoming hostile to Jack's compositions, but their US label boss was equally dismissive. Only after the intervention of Otis Redding and Booker T. Jones – a respected Atlantic musician who heard 'Sunshine' and declared it a hit – was Jack able to salvage some self-esteem. It was indicative of just how much he was sidelined at that point that he is absent from the set of photos by Don Paulsen of Cream in the Atlantic offices and studio with Ahmet.

Jack was still upset over what had happened with 'Strange Brew' and was a bit wary of Felix, but says that they "got very close. We were real buddies; at one point I'd say he was my best friend in the world. I was the best man at his wedding." (Felix and Gail were married in London in 1969.)

For the new album, Felix and Gail wrote 'World Of Pain' alongside 'Tales Of Brave Ulysses', for which Jack improvised his vocal part in one take. Eric did an arrangement of 'Outside Woman Blues' by the obscure blues singer Arthur Reynolds, and there was also Ginger's 'Blue Condition', as well as 'Strange Brew' and 'Sunshine'. 'Dance The Night Away' was inspired by the jangly guitar sound of The Byrds; it employs a counter-melody against the vocals, with Jack's driving, semiquaver basslines building real tension before exploding in the chorus in a manner reminiscent of James Jamerson's playing on the Gladys Knight version of 'I Heard It Through The Grapevine'. For the ending, Jack just slides to the notes of an upbeat D-major chord to sign off Pete's romantic fantasy.

Jack says that he wrote the solo composition 'We're Going Wrong' while out walking on Hampstead Heath after a row with Janet, with a nod to the Gil Evans song 'Gone, Gone, Gone' from *Porgy & Bess*. The original intent behind 'Take It Back' was to write an anti-Vietnam song. It was, he says, "very explicit – I had some lyrics I had written about a guy getting a draft card in the States and tearing it up. But my version was more explicit – 'I don't want to go to war' was one of the lines. Then Pete took over and it got quite a bit more obscure – 'Don't go where the streams are red'. Maybe a bit inspired by Dylan – the oompah sound like 'Rainy Day Women' and a bunch of groupies whoopin' in the background."

'Mother's Lament' was an echo of the singsongs in the early Cream days, the working-class music hall and variety heritage they all grew up with, and some particularly drunken episodes in the bar beneath the studio. But did Jack mind a trivial ditty like this being on the album, considering the other songs Eric and Ginger had rejected? "No, I didn't mind," he says. "Anyway, I thought the band would go on and we might do those other songs in the future. I hadn't given up on those songs. Can you imagine 'Theme' with an Eric solo?"

those were the days

CHAPTER 6

Despite the creative problems he had faced, Jack could look back on his first year with Cream with some satisfaction. The band had taken off to universal acclaim and Jack had had his first taste of commercial success. His writing partnership with Pete Brown had blossomed and he was recording in Atlantic Studios with state of the art equipment and people like Tom Dowd and Felix Pappalardi, both of whom were sympathetic to his music and could make it sound great on record. And it was all still fun.

Back home, Martin Sharp had begun designing what would become the iconic pink Day-Glo cover of *Disraeli Gears* and asked photographer Bob Whitaker to take some shots of the band. Cream had a series of gigs planned in Scotland in July that would give Jack an opportunity to show off his country. "He was very proud of his heritage," said Whitaker. "He even carried a thistle in his hand. We travelled there in a couple of cars, including a green Mini Cooper that belonged to Jack." They drank in little pubs, bought candyfloss at a seaside resort, and would randomly leave the cars to take in the air and the sweep of the majestic scenery of which Jack was so proud.

It was Jack's idea for the band to scale Ben Nevis, the highest mountain in Britain; just to add a certain frisson to the climb, they were out of their heads on LSD. The plan was to shoot the cover shot from the top. "Eric was wearing pink boots and a purple cloak," Jack recalls. "It was hilarious when we had to sign autographs above the snow line for 'real' mountaineers wearing anoraks."

The weather was warm at the base but much colder as they climbed. They abandoned the attempt but found that coming down a steep mountainside on acid was no picnic either. Jack then took them all off to Glencoe, stopping on the way to hear the sounds of a piper who came striding over a hill. It was a magical day; Eric later described these shared experiences as "the peak of our mountain". Some of Bob Whitaker's photos were merged into the collage used on the cover but many remained unseen until they appeared in a beautiful book published in 2006 called *Cream: The Lost Scottish Tour*.

Back on the merry-go-round of clubs, ballrooms, universities, and television and radio appearances, the band previewed songs from the new album, although it became clear early on that only a few would feature regularly on stage: 'Sunshine' because it was such a compelling rock song; 'Tales Of Brave Ulysses' because it gave Eric a chance to use his new wah-wah pedal; and 'We're Going Wrong', which was aired occasionally as a vehicle for Jack's soaring vocals. On August 20 they played the Redcar Jazz Club in the north of England; the following day they were off to the USA. They were seen off with champagne at London Airport for the start of the tour not by Robert Stigwood but by Brian Epstein, who was giving some thought to becoming their 'hands-on' manager. That was never Stigwood's style. He was all about deals and contracts, although he would put in an occasional appearance at the more prestigious gigs. Stigwood's relationship with Cream was not straightforward. They would take the piss out of him mercilessly; once, when he came into the office proudly showing off a new suit, they proceeded to cut it to shreds with a scissors. When he arrived at the studio to 'produce' *Fresh Cream* they rolled him down the stairs in a bass drum case.

This wasn't quite the same as being dangled out of a window by the ferocious Don Arden – which really did happen when Arden thought Stigwood was trying to poach The Small Faces – but was still not the sort of treatment he expected from his charges. Apart from not understanding the music, Stigwood was much more comfortable with young boys – malleable teenage pop stars who did what they were told. He got on OK with Eric, but Jack and Ginger were out of his reach. He had lost interest in the band as a result, which meant that in the States they were on their own with just one man to sort things out: their road manager, Bob Adcock.

Up until early 1967 Cream's road manager was Eric's friend Ben Palmer. He started out on his own, driving the band's plush Austin Westminster (complete with a record player); later on he got help from a roadie, Mick

Turner, whose mangling of the racing-bike term 'Derailleur' helped name the band's new album. But really it was all too much for Ben, who hadn't bargained on humping gear and setting it up as well.

Bob Adcock had been the road manager of The Merseys, the band formed after the break-up of The Merseybeats. They moved to London to be looked after by The Who's management, and through them Bob came to know Brian Epstein and Robert Stigwood. Working with The Merseys was "good money but mind-numbingly boring", he says, but when Stigwood called to offer him the Cream job he turned it down. As something of a Mod, he "didn't want to be associated with a bunch of hippies". But Stigwood persisted, and eventually Bob agreed. He was pleasantly surprised. "If you did a gig with The Merseys," he says, "the audience would be teenyboppers, little girls trying to jump on the stage and little boys trying to beat you up because you were with the band. You could do exactly the same venue with Cream and it would be a totally different audience. All the people you met were there to listen to the music."

Driving up to the Floral Hall in Norfolk or the Kinema Ballroom in Dunfermline was one thing; touring the States in 1967 on an absolute shoestring was something entirely different. Bob remembers sitting in a diner not far from Kennedy Airport in a dodgy part of town. The airport was closed for lunch and he couldn't get the gear off the plane until 2pm, so he went for some lunch of his own. "I opened up this list of dates – and none of them meant a single thing to me," he says. "I'd heard of some of the cities in films, but other than that – nothing. We had no office in America, no backup or support of any kind. That was the scariest moment of my life. I sat there for an hour thinking, 'How the fuck do you do this?'"

Pete Brown wrote the lyrics to 'Theme For An Imaginary Western' with The Graham Bond Organisation in mind, but in fact it was more applicable to Cream. British groups like the Stones and The Beatles had toured the States, but those were pop tours with a business structure to support them. Cream literally struck out into the Wild West in a station wagon with another van for the gear.

Cream's US tour started on August 22 with the first of an incredible 12 nights at the very best place they could be in the summer of '67: Bill Graham's Fillmore Auditorium in San Francisco. Graham was one of rock's most influential and charismatic concert promoters. He knew how to treat his acts: there would be buckets of iced beer, tables groaning with food, wonderful sound, and no hassle getting paid. At first it might have seemed a hell of a gamble for an astute operator like Bill Graham to book a relatively unknown act for such a long residency at the start of a tour. But on the West Coast, Cream were better known than they might have thought. While the band were still back in Britain, Bud Prager and Felix Pappalardi had taken a trip to California with the unreleased album in Felix's luggage. When he got to San Francisco, Felix had a local station air some of the tracks. Atlantic sales managers started to get requests from all over the West Coast for large orders of an album that didn't yet exist. Jerry Wexler was furious, but in fact what Felix had done was to tee the situation up nicely for Cream's arrival in San Francisco. And when *Disraeli Gears* was eventually released simultaneously in the USA and UK in November, it went Top Five in both countries – all this without a single receiving airplay in the States.

On that first night at the Fillmore, Cream took the stage as they would be remembered down the years, with Jack playing his trademark growling Gibson EB3 and Eric using a Gibson SG painted by the Dutch design group The Fool. (Jack had also had his Fender VI bass painted by The Fool in time for the Murray The K shows earlier in the year. He didn't much like it because the neck felt 'tacky', but he did use it for a few television tapings.) Flanking the drums were two 100-watt Marshall stacks with four cabinets each; in the middle was Ginger with two bass drums, four toms, and a forest of cymbals. There were no stuffed bears, only Cream, red in tooth and claw.

The spirit of the times awaited them; a sea of around 2,000 people just wanting to hear them play, most sitting, some dancing, many stoned on time-warping marijuana that allowed them to get in, around, and behind the sounds. For the nascent San Francisco rock audience, Cream were a revelation. To hear such virtuosity from all the musicians was not unusual in jazz, but from a rock band it was unprecedented. Not one American band came close.

As the oft-told tale has it, the band played their usual set of around 45 minutes, with each song about four or five minutes long, and then announced that they had run out of songs. The crowd urged them to keep playing; flashing back to Ginger's house, where it all started, the band carried on, laying down the blueprint for the rest of their time on stage together as songs stretched to become platforms for improvisations.

Cream were certainly spoilt by starting at the Fillmore and then moving on to the Whisky A Go Go in Los Angeles – where, Jack says, "we were met at the airport by The Monkees". After that they had to travel to Boston for ten nights at the Psychedelic Supermarket, possibly one of the strangest rock venues ever. Situated down an alley off Kenmore Square, it was a damp parking garage by day – just a concrete space with pillars, no windows, and low ceilings like … a parking garage. In the evenings, even the pungent aroma of dope couldn't entirely overcome the smell of diesel fumes and oil.

Cream were one of the first bands to play at the Supermarket, and according to Jack the gig was "pretty disastrous for us. The sound was awful and the first night we played there about four people turned up. We were stuck there; it was a nightmare. It was the World Series and we couldn't go out; we were stuck in this really dismal hotel." With their long hair and weird clothes, the band dared not go out in a town full of 'All American' baseball fans. (It was here that Jack wrote 'Boston Ball Game 1967', as featured on his first solo album, *Songs For A Tailor*.)

The band next moved on to the Action House on Long Island, which was owned by Phil Basile, a reputed member of the Luchese crime family. The audience was again small but Cream were at least now in striking distance of New York City and their two-week residency at the Café Au Go Go, a Greenwich Village nightclub in the basement of 152 Bleeker Street. People were queuing round the block; these gigs were as important for the band in New York as the Fillmore had been for them on the West Coast. Many of the movers and shakers of the industry and the music press would be there.

"I remember getting into trouble with the promoter," Jack recalls. "He insisted we turned the audience around to make more money. It was the reverse of the problem Charlie Parker had. He used to promote his own gigs sometimes. In order to get two paying crowds he would have a country & western band on, just to get rid of the crowd, so that another lot of the same people would pay again to get back in. We had the opposite – people were coming in but they could only stay for one short set – and the promoter was making us play two shorts sets. So I made this speech: 'You are being exploited here!'"

With *Disraeli Gears* in the can, the band went back to Atlantic to finish tracks they had started back home and which were eventually destined for *Wheels Of Fire*: Howlin Wolf's 'Sittin' On Top Of The World' slowed down to almost funereal speed; 'Born Under A Bad Sign', brought to them by Felix even before it was released by Albert King; and a new Bruce/Brown song, 'White Room'.

The original lyrics for 'White Room' were based on an eight-page poem Pete wrote about his time recuperating from his smorgasbord of nasty habits. Jack still has his original score written out on manuscript paper, which he took into the studio so he could show Eric how to play the song. The unusual opening (in 5/4 time) takes us into another classic rock anthem that shows, in microcosm, Jack's subtle inventions as a bass player. He plays a simple fill at the end of the first verse, but instead of just repeating it at the end of each subsequent verse – as most bass players would do – he uses it as a foundation for myriad variations on a theme that acts like a classic blues 'call and response' device with his vocals. The responses change as the dialogue progresses, with Eric's wah-wah drifting over the top.

○

Cream came home at the end of October for more concerts and television/radio appearances in the UK and Europe, but by now their attention was increasingly focused on the States. Brian Epstein had died on August 27 with the group only a week into the American tour, and the London underground scene centred around clubs like UFO had pretty much passed them by. There was little to keep them here when American promoters who could book them into large venues were clamouring for their return – and when they could carry on recording at Atlantic with Felix and Tom. On February 10 1968 they played Manchester University – their last UK gig before the farewell concert at the Royal Albert Hall in November.

While the extended improvisations might have come about by accident, they were a dream for Jack and Ginger – the perfect setting to let rip, to be inventive and expressive, to conduct the Big Investigation of lengthy improvisation, and to paint a musical landscape with colours every bit as vivid as the palette of psychedelia swirling around them. It was tougher on Eric, who had not come from this tradition of jazz improvisation. He had never had to work so hard on stage, but some of his extended soloing left audiences breathless and Jack amazed. "I remember Eric doing long unaccompanied guitar passages without any real effects," he says. "Stuff like digital delay just wasn't around in those days – just ballsy guitar playing the like of which I'd never heard before or since."

Cream were at the Olympics every night, passing the baton from one member to the next. Ginger might pick up a pattern from Eric and riff around that, leaving Jack to be the bedrock, playing a traditional bass role; Jack might lead off, with Eric following, and skip away just as Eric got into the groove, leaving Ginger as anchor.

Eric was very happy to be in the spotlight off stage, giving media interviews, being seen at celebrity clubs, and hanging out; Jack was the "loner" who tended to go off on his own and generally felt uncomfortable with his celebrity status. But on stage the situation was reversed. An eyewitness to one of the band's two shows in May at The Scene in Milwaukee (another venue owned by Frank Baliesteri, one of the city's main crime bosses) said later that Eric was quite shy and retiring on stage but that Jack projected his personality right to the back of the hall, moving around the stage, belting out the songs, generally "in command of everything".

That may be true but they all paid a high price, physically and emotionally. They had to do this every night – sometimes twice a night – for months on end, and while the core of the set remained essentially the same, Cream's DNA demanded difference every night as well. There were inevitably plenty of below-par gigs, but no way they could they just turn up and coast. The expectations were too high, both within the band and from the audience.

The odds were stacked against them. Jack was particularly unhappy with the sound: the band had no monitors and were often reliant on the venue's totally inadequate PA system. You might get away with that in a small British club, but in front of 10,000 people it was horrendous. The band used volume to generate excitement and to fill out their sound but couldn't hear each other play, while Jack had to scream above the noise and says he lost his voice every night. He also maintains that, while he did have a double stack, this was more of an insurance against cabinets packing up – something that happened with tedious regularity – than some malicious desire to make Ginger's life miserable. Stories about how one would stop playing and others wouldn't notice have grown with the telling. Road manager Bob Adcock says he can only recall one time when Eric came to the side of the stage to complain, but it is a wonder that it didn't happen more often. In any case, they were feeling the music instinctively and didn't have to always be in visual contact. "If you are standing directly in front of your speakers, that's what you hear," Jack says. "But it says a lot for the musicianship that we played in tune and in time as much as we did. And that's the other thing about Cream – the improvisations were conversational. You don't have to look at people – sometimes you can hear it. It was all about musical conversation and proper improvisation."

Jack was very keen for the band to have their own PA system, like the Grateful Dead did, but says that Ginger vetoed the idea on cost grounds. Unlike the Dead, who would play for a week in one place, Cream were booked all over the place, and rarely for more than one night. They were constantly travelling, and to fit in all the one-night gigs being booked over enormous distances they had to be as mobile as possible and able to get all of their gear on planes just as excess baggage. A PA – especially one as sophisticated as the Dead's – would have meant more road travelling, a bigger entourage, more expenses, and less concert income. But Bob still had a lot of sympathy for Jack's concerns, even if "nobody [else] took Jack's complaint seriously".

Then there was the 'dartboard trail', as Bob calls it – the notion that a booking agent's idea of tour planning was to throw darts at a map and see where they landed. Doing this in the UK was bad enough; to subject Cream to such cavalier arrangements in the USA and Canada seemed insane. In early 1968 they went on from the West Coast to Wisconsin, Indiana, New Jersey, Connecticut, New York, and Texas; back to Indiana, Massachusetts, New York, and Canada; and then back to Connecticut, Florida, and Pennsylvania. They were then due to go back to Canada and then on to Detroit, but those shows were postponed until June because the band were about to implode with exhaustion. "We were sunburnt and frostbitten at the same time," Jack says.

"Having sent through the itinerary for America," says Bob, "nobody followed up to make sure it was possible" – either because they didn't care or because they had no idea how far apart all these places were. And as Cream piled on the gigs, word continued to spread, so more and more dates were added by promoters anxious to cash in. They would lose track entirely of where they were, especially out in the Midwest, where few British rock bands had been before. "We would go for a short 40 or 50 minute flight, come in, there'd be nothing except this long unending plain," he says. "Then you would see this little smudge in the distance and that would be the town. It would be the same town as we did yesterday. Bob Adcock would get the rental car, which he would trash that day, a big station wagon that he would drive to death. Bob did these amazing driving feats. There'd be a traffic jam or some sort of accident. Many times we'd get to the airport by driving very fast down the hard shoulder."

They were also criss-crossing a country in political turmoil. The summer of love had passed; now it felt more like the summer of hate, with race riots, assassinations, and demonstrations against an escalating war in Vietnam. For many Americans, those with long hair gravitated from being 'weirdos' to traitors and commie subversives with plans to burn the stars and stripes and eat mom's apple pie right off the window ledge. And Cream had a knack for being in the wrong place at the wrong time. On April 5, the night after Martin Luther King was shot, they were playing the Back Bay Theater in Boston. James Brown was due to perform across town on the same night and the police were freaking out at the thought of thousands of black and white kids all hitting the streets at the same time. They wanted to cancel the Cream gig, but in the end the concert times were staggered to keep the two audiences apart. After they'd finished playing, Cream got out of there as quickly as possible.

In June they were booked to play at Detroit's Grande Ballroom at the height of the race riots raging across America in the wake of Reverend King's murder. Bob Adcock and roadie Mick Turner were on their way to the venue to check it out. "We stopped the car opposite the stage door, got out, and this car screeched to a halt next to us," Bob recalls. "Three guys got out with knives. Mick was an ex-wrestler and started toward them – until we saw the knives, jumped back in the car, and left." Cream could also have been present at the assassination of Robert Kennedy, who was killed at the Ambassador Hotel in Los Angeles while celebrating his success in the California Democratic Presidential Primary, but they had turned down the gig because it was too political.

In riot-torn Chicago, whose mayor at the time was the notorious Richard J. Daley, the band had a run-in with the police. "We were driving back to the hotel and Bob accidentally went up a one-way street the wrong way," Jack recalls. "The police really came for us, arrested us all and took us all into the police station. And they were really horrible. They were threatening us – 'we can have you sent to this place we know about in the desert'. There were rumours at the time that they were picking up demonstrators and sending them off to camps."

Jack had some sticky moments of his own, too. After the soundcheck for the first Fillmore concert he thought he'd have a wander about and soak up the atmosphere, maybe find a bar and have a drink. The Fillmore was deep in the black part of town. Jack walked into a working-class bar dressed in a long black cloak and silver boots. Heads turn, voices drop, eyes stare – until Jack walks calmly over to the jukebox and cues up Howlin' Wolf's 'Natchez Burnin''. Yeah, all right, the kid's OK. On another occasion, he recalls: "A bunch of black guys came up to me and said, 'What do you think of the Vietnam War?' 'Err … I don't like it.'" Correct answer. "The accent gets you out of a lot of trouble in the States," he adds. "It certainly did then."

And of course bubbling away under the crust was the simmering hostility between Jack and Ginger, which was ready to burst through with volcanic force at a moment's notice. It had now metastasised into whole new areas. Ginger complained about songwriting credits and about the volume Jack played, and was convinced that Jack would do anything to get revenge from being fired from the Organisation. For his part, Jack was angry and frustrated that Ginger wouldn't agree to his idea of the band getting their own PA and outraged at Ginger's political views. Because he had lost his own father in the War, Ginger roundly abused a student journalist who was interviewing the band about Vietnam and had no sympathy for another student roughed up by the police during an anti-war demonstration.

Whatever the problems, it was just impossible for them to sit down and thrash it out. With Jack and Ginger it was either smouldering hostility or shouting, with nothing in between. After a film shoot in Copenhagen earlier in the year, Eric was reduced to tears by the intensity of the arguments. "I fell into a victim role in that band very quickly," he later said, but he also recognised the unique bond they had as musicians: "When things would go well musically between them, it was if they were one person, and no matter how close you thought you were to them, you were outside it." On the road, Eric was making increasingly desperate calls to Stigwood to get him out and steeling himself to announce, once they'd had their break in England, that he'd had enough, although as he says now, "It's hard for me to imagine that I would have had the nerve to broach that way back then."

Jack's recollection is that the fateful conversation took place in Chicago on April 27 after the band's concert at the Coliseum and during the recording of a radio jingle for Falstaff Beer. "Eric and I didn't want to do it but Ginger did because the band were breaking up and he was worried about money," Jack says, adding that Eric voiced what they were all feeling. It was maybe the first and only time they all agreed on something without an argument. Even the crew were relieved. And despite denying media speculation about the split until mid July, Stigwood didn't care either because it meant concert fees would now skyrocket – and, he believed, he would be left with three Creams instead of one.

If Eric had any lingering doubts about the decision, a shock awaited him the following week when he picked up the latest issue of *Rolling Stone*, which had him alone on the cover. The one paper you might expect to back Cream to the hilt took Eric apart, calling him "the master of the blues cliché". It was none too complimentary about Jack or Ginger either, but did say that there were few US bands even close to Cream. Felix was very dismissive of *Rolling Stone*, telling the British music paper *Sounds* in 1971: "They felt I meddled with Cream. They wanted an advanced Mayall's Bluesbreakers, but I didn't give a flying fuck what they wanted. I had a band in the studio and Jack Bruce was extremely important to that band, if not *the* driving force musically, and as producer I had to cope with what was happening there and not what I thought *Rolling Stone* wanted." This goes right back to the start of the band when Jack had impressed upon Eric that what they needed to do was create new music, using the blues simply as a starting point.

Despite the initial sense of relief, relations within the Cream camp didn't improve, and there was still a long way to go yet. For a start they had to spend time at Atlantic finishing off what was originally intended to be just a studio album. When they arrived in June Tom Dowd was shocked at how the demeanour of the band had changed. He knew there were problems, but later remarked that there were times during playbacks "when I thought they were going to kill each other". (To be fair, this was just another day at the office for Cream, and in their terms probably not that serious.)

Felix Pappalardi rightly believed that to ignore Cream's live performances would mean giving only a partial view of the band, so he pushed for them to release a double album – and to include some of the material recorded by Tom Dowd and Bill Levenson using the Wally Heider mobile studio at the Fillmore and Winterland in San Francisco. At the time live albums were regarded as the kiss of death. Ahmet Ertegun and Jerry Wexler refused even to consider releasing one, but Felix wouldn't budge. The decision was left to Nesuhi Ertegun, Atlantic's Head Of Albums (and Jazz), who eventually agreed.

Wheels Of Fire was released in the USA in July, albeit with Atlantic hedging its bets somewhat by issuing the material as two single albums as well. It was a chart smash on both sides of the Atlantic, earning Cream the very first platinum disc for sales of more than two million copies. While *Rolling Stone's* review was predictably cool, *Melody Maker* was effusive, singling out Jack as the star of the show: "Jack's contribution to the trio has been enormous through his writing, singing, and of course his superb bass playing."

The album provided the perfect opportunity to contrast the two sides of Cream. While Jack felt that the live performances captured on tape – here and on subsequent releases – failed to present Cream at their best, they remain a remarkable testament to the band in full flight. Jack sounds like two bass players at once: one driving the others impatiently along, the other zooming off with serpentine runs of his own. Some of his playing on 'I'm So Glad' is simply outrageous, as if Jack was trying to break free of the restrictions imposed by the song structure.

There are certainly no weak links on the studio album. It contains strong contributions from Ginger, who wrote the wonderfully quirky and humorous 'Pressed Rat And Warthog' with the much-respected British jazz pianist and composer Mike Taylor. The song is based on an old English folk tune, 'The Cutty Wren', and contains a reference to Eric as "the Bad Captain Madman". As Felix later recalled: "Jack and I worked on that and worked on it and worked on it into this amazing thing ... this huge orchestral sound." He used the song as an example of the 'meddling' he felt was so much resented by critics looking for power Delta blues.

Wheels Of Fire also includes four Bruce/Brown compositions: 'White Room', 'Politician', the underrated 'Deserted Cities Of The Heart', and 'As

111

You Said'. Jack says the latter song, perhaps the most interesting of the bunch, owed much to Richie Havens, whom he met backstage at the Village Theater (later the Fillmore East) in September 1967. "He showed me some open tunings in the dressing room, which were very important to me because I then wrote some songs using those tunings (including 'As You Said' and 'Deserted Cities Of The Heart'). A lot of people are quite protective about things like that because it is their thing. They are very straight open D tunings, but he showed me one that became 'Rope Ladder To The Moon', which is in a very unusual E minor seventh tuning."

'As You Said' also owes something to Debussy, who was himself inspired by the French Impressionist painters in the way, as Jack puts it, that "the whole composition is development, not like in classical music where you have resolution, a subject that resolves itself – a form that just expands itself. In theory, that song could go forever. So it was an attempt to do that without being too precious about it."

In the run-up to the release of the album, Felix gave *Crawdaddy* magazine his personal perspective on Jack as the creative driving force behind Cream. "The only one who is into composition is Jack, someone who would score things as he hears them," he said. "Jack's deeply into that ... he wrote this thing called 'As You Said'. To me it's totally original. It's scored for two acoustic guitars, two cellos, and vocal. His background is very much like mine. He's not a rock'n'roll musician – he's just a musician generically."

Felix went on to discuss the concept of orchestration in Cream and the layering of sounds and textures. He described 'Passing The Time' as "really breathtaking ... Cream are going like a house on fire and all of a sudden, there's this cello and viola duet that comes over them. The meter changes to 3/4 – or 3/4 over 4/4 implied – and it's a complete change of texture, beautiful. That came right out of Jack's head, it was so right, so obviously right, it just made it big and beautiful."

Asked where he thought the band would go next, Felix was remarkably prescient. "I see Jack growing into a bona-fide dynamite composer of such scope that I can only eagerly wait to hear what he's gonna do. Eric's my favourite guitarist; I still think he's got that drive to play the blues. Probably what he'll do is just play blues eventually, you know, go back. And Ginger ... he's such a phenomenal drummer that half the time I don't believe it. And I don't know what he's going to grow into ... a big green monster. But where they go has a lot to do with what they run into, between tomorrow and the next day."

Where Jack wanted to go the next day was straight back home. It had got so bad that even though he knew the end was in sight, and despite having just had a short break, he almost didn't make the final sessions at Atlantic. On June 5 the band had a gig at Massey Hall in Toronto. This was sacred turf for Jack – the scene of one of greatest live jazz recordings ever made, by the apotheosis of jazz supergroups: the Dizzy Gillespie Quintet with Charlie Parker, Max Roach, Bud Powell, and Charles Mingus. Jack was horrified to see Ginger hammering his drums into the beautiful oak stage and afterward was so stressed out, having lost his voice yet again, that he just fled to the airport and had to be coaxed back by Bob. How glad he must have been not to miss the Grande Ballroom concert in Detroit, an old ballroom with no windows where it got so hot they actually threw water over the band – a band with electric guitars and amps – to keep them cool. (It wasn't quite so bizarre, however, as the gig they'd played back in November 1967 at the Streatham Ice Rink in South London: "It was the weirdest gig I ever played in my life because the audience were skating past. There was a little bandstand and the ice was still there, so every now and again, people would skate by. I'm not making this shit up. Nobody ever believes me. That actually happened.")

Once the *Wheels Of Fire* sessions had finished the band took a much longer break. It lasted until the beginning of October and the start of a farewell tour of America, during which Cream would play some of the largest venues in the country and in one instance earn over $60,000 in one night. The *New Musical Express* calculated that the tour grossed over $700,000.

Coming back after such a long break was hard. *Rolling Stone* reported that the first rehearsal had ground to a halt after an hour, with each band-member sitting in a different corner of the room staring at the floor. It was "the ultimate in alienation. Antonioni should have been there to get it on film." Stories about separate hotels, cars, and dressing rooms have been exaggerated, however. Where they were offered separate dressing rooms, the band took them in preference to being squeezed in together, but they still travelled in a station wagon – unlike Deep Purple, who turned up as the support act for one gig in nine limos, with one for each of the band-members and managers. Separate hotels would have cost more; Bob Adcock says that, as they travelled around, the band never complained about rooms or asked for changes or upgrades.

In the end it was a tour of contrasts. "The crowds were generally well-behaved," Jack recalls, "more like stoners on the ground than into rushing the stage, but the excitement did build through the last tour. There was one big gig we played where we didn't get out before the crowd. We went out in our normal way and the entire audience was out there. I thought they were going to turn over the limo and kill us." On October 18 and 19 Cream played two sell-out nights at the LA Forum, with The Beatles in attendance; a day later at the San Diego Sports Arena the tumbleweed rolled through the empty spaces. To celebrate, Jack got himself arrested. He, Janet, and two roadies decided to head down to Mexico, with Bob at the wheel. After they'd done the usual touristy sightseeing, Jack said he wanted to go further, beyond Tijuana.

"We bought loads of mescalin," he recalls. "I told Bob to stop the car so we could go up this little hill. I bought these sandals made of car tyres – me and the roadies went up and came across a group of shepherds, one of whom was wearing a British navy hat. They invited us to this bar, which was not much more than a shed with a tin roof. We just spent hours in there drinking, getting completely trashed. Then somebody mentioned that we should be getting back."

"We got back through the Mexican side of the border all right. We got to the American side and I thought it would be a great idea to nick the car keys while they were checking our passports. So Bob couldn't start the car because he hadn't got the keys and we were causing a great disturbance because we couldn't get out of the way."

It was then that things turned nasty. The border guards tried to arrest Jack, who by then was railing against the USA; the roadies did their 'you'll never take him alive' act and battle ensued. Eventually they were arrested and slung into jail. Bob told a local radio station about what had happened and a load of kids showed up to shower the jail with flowers. Jack and his cohorts were let out in the end, but it was still "quite a nasty experience".

Jack was sprung just in time for the initial sessions for what would be Cream's final album, *Goodbye*. Recording began with two days at Wally Heider's Studio in Los Angeles and ended in November with a further four days back in London at IBC. The concept was simple: each band-member would compose one song, with the rest of the tracks to be selected from the bank of live recordings. Jack once again played a significant role in all of the studio tracks. About his own 'Badge', Eric admitted, "I owe that one to Jack. It was his influence."

Jack plays piano and organ and sings on Ginger's 'What A Bringdown', which has Felix on bass, offering an opportunity to compare his more straight-ahead approach with Jack's own playing. There was so little time for recording that Jack played his 'Doing That Scrapyard Thing' down the phone to Pete from his hotel, telling him simply that the song was "autobiographical"; Pete shot back some lyrics about being on the road in Britain.

On November 26 Cream played their last two concerts in the UK at the Royal Albert Hall. Fans queued for tickets for seven hours outside the venue. Having spent so much time in the States, Cream had attained mythical status back home. Once the band kicked off, the time passed in a haze that had nothing to do with dope. Just as the audience had begun to absorb the truth that Cream were on stage in front of them playing all those classic songs, it was all over and they were gone forever ... or so everybody thought.

Jack says there were no second thoughts about the split until the second show at the Albert Hall, which was "probably because we were being feted in our own country, although we had been very nervous about playing there". Tony Palmer filmed the concert for the BBC and says that the band hardly spoke to each other. There was no after-show party: Tony went off with Eric for a drink; Jack says he doesn't even recall saying goodbye. The whole thing was as much of a blur for Jack as it was for the audience. "I had to be reminded recently that we actually played a second show," he says.

Cream said their last goodbye over three nights at Madison Square Gardens. Even there, at the most prestigious venue in the most important music city, it was amateur hour as the band had to play on a revolving stage using the MSG PA. If the sound had been primitive before, imagine the effect as the band rotated and the music swirled out of range. As at the Albert Hall, nothing happened after the show. This seemed indicative of the band-members' desire to leave it all behind and also symbolic of the fact that, for all their time on the road in the States, they had hardly built any other friendships; no bolt holes for letting off steam. There were the usual female diversions – "I went to the odd orgy," Jack says – but for the most part they just worked and worked until they burnt themselves out.

In the run-up to the reunion in 2005, Eric revealed that he thought Cream "was going to be my band". He admits to having had "a childish fixation with what I wanted Cream to be versus what it turned out to be ... But this time around I had much more acceptance of what Cream was and actually – forgive me for saying this Ginger – it was Jack's band really."

As Bottom says in *A Midsummer Night's Dream*:

We will meet; and there we may rehearse most
obscenely and courageously. Take pains; be perfect: adieu.

beyond the white room

CHAPTER 7

I n the three years from 1965–68, Jack Bruce went from bassist-for-hire to international rock star with all the accoutrements of success. He and Janet had bought and tastefully decorated a fashionable five-storey townhouse in Chalk Farm, North London; parked outside was a $5,000 Stingray that Jack paid for in cash to the delight and astonishment of the Californian salesman. When that blew up – "It was a terrible car, really," he says – he bought his first Ferrari, then a green Bentley. Money seemed to be no object: whatever Cream asked for, the management obliged.

But the most famous rock band in the world had now broken up, and Jack would not have been human if, despite all the problems they'd had, he hadn't felt a pang of regret that it was all over. He still thinks it could have carried on in a different form: no more punishing tours, but occasional 'review' shows where each of the band-members could showcase their own influences and interests. For Eric it would be the blues; Ginger could front a band based around African music; and maybe Jack would lead a jazz-rock ensemble, with the three men coming together at the end for a performance as Cream. But it wasn't to be, and so the question remained: now what?

"After Cream finished, Ahmet Ertegun told me to get a couple of young musicians and go out on the road and do the Cream thing again," Jack says. "And yes, it might have been commercially successful for a while, but I wouldn't have stood up to the emotional strain of it and I wouldn't have been able to live with myself." Even so, it's interesting to note that at the time Jack seemed as though he could be a better commercial prospect than Eric, who was undoubtedly a world-class guitar hero but couldn't sing or compose anywhere near as well as Jack.

There were offers to join other bands, too, including one from Led Zeppelin bassist John Paul Jones. Exactly how Zeppelin would have worked with two bassists is uncertain; it seems most likely that Jones was looking to switch to keyboards. Jones followed up his visit with a letter, but Jack said no. At the other end of the spectrum came a call from Hank Marvin. You can just imagine the headline – 'Jack Bruce To Join Shadows Shock' – but once again Jack politely refused.

One offer he might have considered was the one from Stephen Stills to join Crosby Stills & Nash. The vocal harmony options would have been intriguing, but as Jack recalls: "He said, 'Oh no, we just want you to play bass.'" So that was that. (Stills's offer came in March 1969 at the filming of a 'super-show' at an abandoned linoleum factory in London. Also part of the show were Jack and Eric, who played together, plus Buddy Guy, Roland Kirk, Dick Heckstall-Smith, Buddy Miles, and The Modern Jazz Quartet.)

While some of the approaches themselves were surprising, the fact that major bands wanted Jack was not. But he needed some time out. He and Janet had recently moved into a new house, and Janet was due to give birth to their first child in February 1969. Jack wanted space to work on his own material without the pressure of touring – and for a while, he spent time reconnecting with his jazz inspirations in the company of accomplished, like-minded musicians.

As we have seen, Jack was always attracted to the cutting edges of jazz – free-form, avant-garde, whatever label you might want to put on it – and inspired by the music of Ornette Coleman and Charles Mingus. That kind of fringe jazz scene was so small that once Jack had moved to London he found it easy to hook up with the few musicians who shared his enthusiasm and commitment – John Stevens; the members of Group Sounds Five; Dick Heckstall-Smith; and jazz pianist Mike Taylor, who had co-written songs for Cream with Ginger.

Regarded by those who knew him as a visionary, Mike Taylor wrote over 300 compositions. Both Jack and bassist Ron Rubin appeared on his 1967 album *Trio*, alternating on some tracks and playing together on others. Jon Hiseman, Ginger Baker, Dave Tomalin, and Tony Reeves were among the other collaborators. But Mike was a strange, remote figure who refused to give interviews and became increasingly isolated. His style of jazz had no market in the UK – even in the more eclectic musical climate of the 60s. At one point Jon Hiseman had to rescue Mike's work from the fire after the pianist had flung it there in a fit of acute depression. He self-medicated on quantities of hash and LSD that drove him to the outer edges of communication – he went barefoot and 'spoke' only in hand signals. The end came in January 1969 when he walked into the sea off the Essex coast. Four months earlier, Jack had recorded Mike's 'Ballad' and his arrangement of Andrés Segovia's 'Study' for the New Jazz Orchestra album *Le Dejeuner Sur L'Herbe*. In May Jack took part in a BBC tribute to Mike as a member of the Dave Gelly Quintet alongside Jon Hiseman and his wife, the multi-instrumentalist and composer Barbara Thompson.

In the summer of '68, during his three-month break from Cream, Jack had organised a gig at the 100 Club in London's Oxford Street with Jon Hiseman and Dick Heckstall-Smith that evolved into a recording session at IBC studios for a jazz album called *Things We Like*. The title came from a reading primer given to Jack as a very young boy at school in Canada and pointed to a return to his musical past.

"The compositions I chose to record were partly those I had written when I was about 11 years old," he says. "I was keen to go back to my earliest compositions because I think it's when you are very young that you develop the ideas you continually re-work to form the basis for the rest of your life." 'HCKHH Blues' "was a nod to Mingus" while 'Ballad For Arthur' referred to Dick Heckstall-Smith's baby son. 'Statues' by contrast was influenced by someone he had discovered more recently, and whom he would refer to often later on: the French composer and organist Olivier Messiaen.

Jack has always been interested in the intervals between notes; Miles Davis once said those spaces were the most important part of his solos. Messiaen was fascinated by certain intervals – what he called 'limited' transpositions within the musical scales such as one Debussy used called the whole-tone scale. The technicalities of this are less important than the effect. It imparts a dreamlike quality to the composition – the music appears to float, rising and falling with no obvious resolution. Jack brought this to bear in 'As You Said' and later in 'Rope Ladder To The Moon', and here in Dick Heckstall-Smith's introduction to 'Statues', which was inspired by the 'Statue Theme' from Messiaen's *Turangalila Symphony*, a sweeping interpretation of the romance of Tristan and Isolde, the start of which invokes the terrible dread associated with the statues of Ancient Mexico.

Jack had intended for the album to be a trio recording until he saw an old friend on the way home from the first day in the studio. "I was driving along and saw John McLaughlin walking down the road with his guitar looking very disconsolate," he recalls. "John had had this offer to play with Tony Williams and Miles Davis, but he said he couldn't go because he didn't have the fare money." Jack offered him a spot in the sessions, resulting in some of the finest playing of this early part of his career. John got paid but he didn't go off with Williams immediately. He recorded his first solo album, *Extrapolation*, in London in January 1969 before arriving in New York in time for the recording of Miles Davis's *In A Silent Way* in February and then finally joining Tony Williams's new band, Lifetime, in May.

Things We Like was finished in three days but its release was delayed until the autumn of 1970 because Jack "didn't want it to come out as my first solo album and define me as a jazz bass player". Richard Williams of *Melody Maker* declared it "the purest jazz, a relaxed session with four names blowing on some stimulating skeletal arrangements, producing music which relies on the power of its content rather than decibels and facial grimaces ... The music is fast and difficult but full of lyricism." Heaping praise on John, Dick, and Jon, Williams adds that Jack "plays magnificently too, with completely unassuming drive and precision; listen to the beautiful fill he plays to introduce the penultimate chorus of 'Rill's Thrills' and his dark toned sonorous contribution to 'Arthur'." All in all, it was "a glorious album of listening music".

Asked by *Guitar* magazine in May 1990 if he thought the album was 'traditional' jazz, Jack replied "absolutely", but followed that with a significant qualification: "I would regard that album as kind of a Scottish bass player's version of the traditions of jazz ... because jazz is about the expression of individuals more than a music."

Jack went on to say, as he said to Eric about the blues, that in his view you couldn't actually make a 'traditional' jazz record unless you were Miles Davis or John Coltrane; it was much more to do with bringing your own interpretation and experiences to the music. "It has nothing to do with the notes," he continued, "or anything to do with music. It's something that's behind the music." This has been a recurring motif in Jack's work: you don't slavishly imitate but instead assimilate all the music in the ether to develop something that's new, unique – and yours.

With that in mind, Jack turned his attentions to developing the themes and ideas for his first solo album. Pete and Jack had established a style of working at Jack's house. This is where Jack has always worked best: quietly at home with a piano and a cup of tea. "I would play the music and he would write furiously," he says, "and eventually he would come up with something I didn't veto, because we did come up with bizarre beginnings, like [a version of] 'White Room' about cycling through France or selling fridges to Eskimos." When Jack changed the lyrics it was often to make a line easier to sing – putting open vowel sounds at the end of a line, for example, allows you to extend the notes.

Pete and Jack shared a very similar outlook on life. Their values and traditions were so in tune that it was hard to believe that the songs were not written and composed by the same person. How Pete came to know and understand Jack as a person is probably unique in songwriting partnerships. Jack could never sing anything he didn't really feel and believe in, and what Pete delivered were songs often full of poetic, surreal, sometimes obscure imagery. So Jack had to really understand Pete, and Pete needed to really understand Jack, or else the partnership was doomed. They had shown the world they could write commercial hit records and they could write classic heavy rock – now, as they say in the movies … this time it's personal.

O

Interviewed by *Melody Maker* in January 1969, Jack announced that his first solo album would be recorded at Atlantic and expressed a desire to work with Aretha Franklin's guitarist, Bobby Womack. Instead in April he went into Morgan Studios in Northwest London. A writing protocol with Pete was already in place; now he would establish a *modus operandi* for studio work that would stand him in good stead throughout this career.

Jack brought his trusted friend, Felix Pappalardi, to produce the album. "Felix played a bigger role on this record than the Cream records because he was around a lot of the time while I was planning it," he says. "He came up with some ideas that I actually listened to for once and he had quite a lot to do with the programming of the record."

The sessions were engineered by a 19-year-old guy just starting out in the business: Andy Johns, the younger brother of Glyn, who was already an established producer and engineer. "I thought Cream were as important as The Beatles and the Stones and here I am in a room with Jack Bruce doing his solo album," he recalls. "It was very intense for me, but Felix was very clever and very kind and Jack was a darling and kept complimenting me."

Many great live bands who have grown up together can get away with mistakes on stage – by and large it doesn't matter, it's all part of the anarchy of rock'n'roll. The guys tend to know what they are doing, but the volume, the adrenalin, and the fact that the crowd are there for a good time – and are probably drunk, stoned, or both – will hide a multitude of sins. But in a studio all the imperfections and blemishes are revealed. Keeping perfect time is critical – you can't have anybody, least of all the drummer, speeding up or slowing down. Much of the boredom and frustration of musicians in the studio comes from the time it takes to get these things right.

Jack never had a regular live band that he took into the studio; only once in a solo career spanning 40 years has he recorded two albums with the same line-up. But he turns up with a clear idea of what he wants – often with all the parts scored – and chooses schooled musicians who are able both to read the charts and to add their own interpretations to the music.

The idea behind Jack's debut solo album was to produce a collection of songs freed from the restrictions of writing for a three-piece rock band. Jack knew some of the musicians well – "it was a chance to play with mates" like Jon Hiseman, Dick Heckstall-Smith, Henry Lowther, and John Mumford. He augmented the horn section with two other stalwarts of the London jazz scene – trumpeter Harry Beckett and Art Themen, a remarkable tenor player who combined hot sax with a job as a hospital surgeon. Jack had recorded with the Mike Gibbs Orchestra for BBC Radio in February and was impressed with the drummer, John Marshall, who offered a contrast in style from Jon Hiseman. "John was playing more rock style," Jack says. "The sound of the drums reminded me of Ringo Starr."

Jack had a decision to make about the guitarist. Any of the heavyweights on the scene would have jumped at the chance to be on Jack Bruce's First Solo Album, but that's exactly what he didn't want. Instead he went to Pete Brown, now a bandleader in his own right. The guitarist in Pete's Battered Ornaments was Chris Spedding. "Pete thought Chris would be good for this because it was songs rather than long improvisations," Jack recalls. "I wanted to go a very spare route and not have a guitarist who was a Guitar God – the opposite from Cream. It should be about the songs, not the playing or the production. Very simple, very short, very little soloing."

Jack had a core of compositions to start with – songs rejected by Cream. Apparently Eric thought 'Theme For An Imaginary Western' sounded too much like The Band – whose first album *Music From Big Pink* was the catalyst in sparking his desire for a change of musical direction – but Jack says he'd been "playing around with it for years". It remains a towering achievement, and one seen by many as the best song Jack and Pete ever wrote. It captures beautifully the flawed romanticism of a band on the road and the madness and misery they can leave in their wake.

'Weird Of Hermiston' was inspired by Robert Louis Stevenson's unfinished novel *The Weir Of Hermiston* and tells the story of an upper class Edinburgh boy, estranged from his cruel father, who goes to live in Hermiston (on the outskirts of the city) and falls in love with a girl named Kirstie. In 'As You Said' Jack expresses the melancholic air that often hangs over Scottish history. As Pete observes in the foreword to Bob Whitaker's *Cream: The Lost Scottish Tour*: "There's a lament which captures that feeling, the ghosts of poverty and tragedy in the moaning of the wind." He adds that 'Hermiston' too "has a tremendous feeling of doom, the idea of parental repression and this guy going into the stews of Edinburgh to do stuff". Jack felt it could have been a hit for Cream, and recalls that "Sting told me he thought it was an incredibly commercial song and wanted to record it – but not the way I recorded it. That was deliberately pared down, almost like a diary, with very little production."

It was unusual for Pete to come up with lyrics ahead of the music, but that's how 'Rope Ladder To The Moon' happened. The result for Pete was astonishing. "I originally wrote the song for Arthur Brown," he says, "but he couldn't understand it, couldn't deal with it. As I recall, Jack came back with the music in about two days – just amazing, he just got the feeling of what I was trying to do. Absolute magic, perfect." (Jack actually wrote the music for a projected cartoon version of *Gulliver's Travels* by the company that made *Yellow Submarine*.)

'The Clearout' was an angry song about rejection, and another one previously dismissed by Eric and Ginger. It now had an extra edge for Jack because Eric and Ginger had formed Blind Faith with Stevie Winwood – and in May, right in the middle of the recording sessions, recruited bassist Ric Grech from Family. Martin Wesson, Robert Stigwood's Finance Director at the time, recalls Jack telling him how hurt he was about Blind Faith.

"I was a little pissed off with Eric and Ginger," Jack says now, "although Eric said that Ginger had forced his way into that band." He remains unsure if he would have accepted an offer to join because he was on his own path; he can't say for certain he would have ruled it out, but he had been aware of the dangers awaiting any attempt to recreate Cream.

For his part, Eric just wanted to get together with Stevie to try out some ideas. But then Ginger got involved, the eyes of the suits (even if they were wearing kaftans) lit up, the media started drooling over another 'supergroup', and Eric was caught on a rolling juggernaut he couldn't stop. The trauma of

Blind Faith began a process that would eventually drive him into seclusion for three years.

While Jack and his friends were working in the studio a tragic accident occurred that gave the album its title, *Songs For A Tailor*. During the early hours of Monday May 12 1969 the van carrying Fairport Convention back from a gig in Birmingham was involved in a crash that killed drummer Martin Lamble and Richard Thompson's girlfriend, Jeannie Franklin, an American designer who had made clothes for Cream. Jack remembers her mainly as "a close friend", although they were also lovers. She had written to Jack, encouraging him to "sing a few high notes for me"; he received the letter on his 26th birthday, May 14, two days after she died.

On its release there was much talk of the album being 'busy' and 'complex', but several songs bear out Jack's assertion that much of it was actually very simple. 'Tickets To Waterfalls', 'He The Richmond' – "a meaningless title that I dreamt," says Pete – and the Tolkien-esque 'To Isengard' all have a rural, pared-back folk feel. The melody from 'Isengard' was taken from a 1958 Kirk Douglas film called *The Vikings* – the sound of the three-note warning blown on a Viking horn. ("When I was growing up in Glasgow, the cinema was very popular and we used to go once or twice a week," Jack recalls. "You would always have to queue up, but we would go and see whatever was on. Once they were showing the Laurence Olivier *Hamlet*. We went anyway and my dad was watching this and said, 'What the bloody hell is this rubbish?'")

'Ministry Of Bag' was essentially 'Politician (Part 2)' and continued the theme of corruption in society that Jack and Pete would return to again later on. "In the 60s it was very likely that everybody would be turned into fucking neutrons," says Pete. "I did acquire a lot of political consciousness through Jack, who had [picked up] his point of view from his father in terms of seeing how things were and reading between the lines. I nearly got arrested in Trafalgar Square at a CND rally for insulting the Queen in the long version of 'Politician'."

The song that took most work in the studio was probably 'Never Tell Your Mother She's Out Of Tune'. As Pete recalls the title was not meaningless, but certainly had nothing to do with the song: "Chris [Spedding] came from a musical family and his mother used to sing in a choir. When we were in the Battered Ornaments, he went to a concert and made the mistake of telling her that some of the people in the choir were out of tune, and she went mad. The actual lyrics have nothing to do with it. It's more about cityscapes, Glasgow and the factories there. There were hundreds of drafts of that."

The main complexities were the syncopated horn parts that Art Themen recalls needed "many, many takes". There was also a surprise guest: George Harrison, who Jack decided to invite along as a result of his work on Cream's 'Badge'. "I had never thought of him as a great guitar player," Jack says. "I was wrong. I really did like his playing on 'Badge'. He did these high chord inversions and his sound was impressive."

Andy Johns remembers George being very nervous. "He turned up really early and came into the small control booth and said, 'So Andy, I hear Jack Bruce is really tough to work with.' So I thought I'd wind him up a bit, 'Yeah, yeah, he's really difficult, man. It's gonna be a tough night.' George was a bit petrified, but he got through it." There were no 'I am a Beatle' antics; George took it all very seriously, although afterward somebody from Apple rang up and demanded that George have a percentage of the whole album for just being on one track. The response was discouraging, which is why he is credited as Angelo Misterioso.

George wasn't the only nervous musician on the lot. Morgan Studios had been booked from midnight onward; on the first night drummer John Marshall turned up, he recalls, "I was trembling. When I arrived they were dubbing on the horns for 'Never Tell Your Mother She's Out Of Tune'. They were sitting in a square and there was this amazing rhythm track going and I thought, 'Oh, God. I'm out of my depth here."

John says that Felix was "very pleasant. We got on really well. He gave me some pointers for the feel he wanted on 'Rope Ladder'. Jack was very patient – he just books people he likes and lets them go. He didn't say much really. It was the jazz approach, you give people the shape and the changes you want, then you let them get on with it."

Chris Spedding meanwhile was unconcerned about being the first guitarist to work with Jack after Eric. "When I first heard Eric I thought, 'Wow, that guy has the blues thing sewn up,'" he recalls. "And I thought if I ever wanted to make an impression playing the guitar, I'd better forge a style that was the direct opposite. During this phase I thought extended soloing was self-indulgent and didn't help the songs. I just wanted to come up with parts that helped the music along – colours, sounds."

Chris concurs with John about how easy it was working with Jack in the studio. "Jack had a plan and a big part of that plan was to give us freedom. We'd cut tracks with Jack playing the piano part – no vocals or bass – and me playing along with the drummer [usually Jon Hiseman]. Jack wanted me to weave my parts in and out of his piano. I think we did achieve that nice floating effect. My being part of *Songs For A Tailor* marked the beginning of my session career. From then on the phone started ringing. I owe Jack a big debt of gratitude for starting me out."

"I was very proud of it," says Jack. "I knew it was a good record. At the time it was a shockingly fresh record in the sense that it was using elements that had not really been used in pop records or whatever you want to call it, like the Stravinsky-type horn parts and mirror-image writing – the same backward as forward – [mixed] in with folk songs."

Jack knew that as this was his first solo album a lot would be riding on it. Pointing out that Jack had (inevitably) delivered the unexpected, British reviewers recognised the album's unique qualities. One called it "a massive and impressive work" while another wrote that "these compositions are like nothing you've heard before". The album rose to Number Six on the UK album chart in September 1969 and made a particular impact among musicians. "I remember being phoned up by Paul McCartney who said how much he loved the record," Jack says. "I was asked round to the Apple offices to play it to them and Paul, Ringo, and George were all sitting there." Gary Moore was one of many other musicians to be bowled over by the album. "I remember me and Phil Lynott just sat and listened to this album over and over again," he recalls.

The response in America was less positive. The album only got as far as Number 55 on the chart while *Rolling Stone's* review was gratuitously vicious in its dismissal of "a patchwork affair lacking in any unifying thread, a baggy misfit made up of a shop-worn miscellany of jazz riffs, rock underpinnings, chamber music strings, [and] boringly baroque lyrics". In other words there were no guitar solos. The magazine would later revise that assessment, however. In a 1975 review of another album, Loyd Grossman called *Tailor* "a stunning recording with more than an ample amount of beautiful songs and excellent singing and playing".

O

After completing work on *Songs For A Tailor* Jack took his young family to Scotland, with Jo, then just six months old, stowed in a carrycot on the back seat of a 2+2 Ferrari. "We were staying at the hotel in Ullapool and I bought a paper and happened to see this place for sale near Oban," Jack recalls. The land included a private beach, a mountain, and its own stop on the railway. It was a chance, now that he could afford it, for Jack to have his own little piece of Scotland. "I jumped in the car and screeched down there but the woman wouldn't sell me the place. She wouldn't even let me in." Instead he bought Sanda, a four hundred acre island to the south of the Mull Of Kintyre. It was home to a few hundred sheep and The Ship lighthouse, with just one habitable house on the south side of the island. Jack had already added a boat to his fleet of vehicles and had also taken flying lessons, so the remote island would be more accessible.

Jack bought Sanda as a holiday home rather than somewhere to work; there were never any plans to build a studio. The setting was undoubtedly romantic and atmospheric. The Viking invasion of 1093 was led by the King of Norway, Magnus III, also known as Magnus Barefoot or Barelegs because he wore a Scottish kilt. In true Viking style, the invaders pillaged and burned whatever they came across and ended up controlling many of the Scottish Isles, the Isle Of Man, and bits of Ireland. Legend has it that in 1307, Edward, brother of Robert The Bruce, used it as a lookout to keep watch for the English while Robert fled to Rathlin Island off the coast of Northern Ireland. So Sanda was steeped in legend and history, but was also pretty bleak and primitive with no electricity in the house. With Jack away, Janet would spend the following summer there alone with Jo and pregnant with the couple's second child, Malcolm, who was born in September 1970.

After Tony Palmer made his film of Cream's Albert Hall Concert, the plan was to shoot individual documentaries on Jack, Ginger, and Eric. Jack wanted to show the beauty of Scotland but also the terrible conditions still suffered by many working-class people in Glasgow. His success and obvious material wealth engendered a sense of what he calls "working class guilt", especially as his father was still a dyed-in-the-wool Communist and militant trade union convenor whose faith had never wavered, not even after the Hungarian uprising of 1956 and Khrushchev's denunciation of Uncle Joe Stalin. Jack remembers his mother breaking down in tears in the kitchen. His parents still cherished the Communist dream offered up by *Soviet Monthly*: "glossy magazines with a beautiful blonde and a tractor on the front cover with a big field of wheat".

Jack took from his father an inherent dislike of the Establishment and all it stood for. He still recalls his sense of outrage at the age of ten at being made to stand in the boiling sun by his teacher to watch the newly crowned Queen and Prince Philip shoot down the Paisley Road. "They cut through these roundabouts so they wouldn't have to go round them," he says. "They put up huge billboards around the worst slums, worse than Harmony Row or Kinning Park, so the Queen and Prince Philip wouldn't see them. We stood there all day and they whizzed by at 50mph. That was it. Fuck that for a game of soldiers."

During the 60s Jack bought into the Age Of Aquarius zeitgeist up to a point but could never see the Establishment relinquishing power. He turned down an invitation to go to Paris to be a 'figurehead' of student revolt and had no time for the political pretensions of other rock luminaries. The authorities might have viewed the likes of John Lennon as a real political threat but Jack was unconvinced. Interviewed in September 1969 by Trevor Hyett, he said that The Beatles and the Stones "are not a political force. They have no basic political feelings. They might be upset by things rather than be motivated by politics.'"

Even so, Jack wanted his political sensibilities and traditions to be reflected in the film. Many of the old tenement slums in the Gorbals had been torn down, with former inhabitants moving on to the new estates like Pollok (where Jack had lived), Castlemilk, Drumchapel, and Easterhouse. But as we saw earlier, these estates had no facilities and were not enough to house all the needy families. So in the 60s the city council went for the fashionable high-rise option and built new slums for working people. The constructions were a disgrace – damp, badly built, no proper fire safety; it was a miracle they never fell down (as happened in London in 1968 when a block of similar construction partially collapsed following a gas explosion, killing four people). But the grim Gorbals tenements lived on, and would feature in Tony Palmer's film, *Rope Ladder To The Moon*.

In the initial discussions about the film, Jack pushed for more of a variety show than a straightforward documentary, but Tony convinced him it wouldn't work. "There was no formal script," Tony recalls. "Jack said, 'I want to be seen in Glasgow. I want it to be clear that I was at the Royal Academy Of Music And Drama.' And he wanted to include the island he'd just bought – he told me it represented 'a dream'. In fact when you see him and Pete Brown step off the boat, it's the first time he had set foot on the island."

Jack was anxious not to be seen leading an entourage around the city, so Tony used a small three-man crew. Jack was keen to be involved in the process: "As a classical musician, he understood that making a film was a formal process and yes, you can make it in a haze of pot, but in the end that's not going to help," Tony says. "There was nothing I asked him to do that he didn't do. In fact he was always suggesting things to me. We began with that clip of Attlee to show that in a socialist world, local boy could make good – and Jack quizzed me a lot about my background. I was nowhere near as working class as Jack, but nowhere near silver spoon in the mouth. Unless you have some sympathy with the person and they with you, it just doesn't work.

"Jack said, 'You haven't interviewed me.' I thought that would look wrong in this type of 'exploring' film, so I just gave him a tape recorder and said, 'You talk and I'll prompt you.' What you hear are those tapes and overall I think it is a real portrait of him at that time and what he believed."

Shooting took ten days between mid August and the beginning of September in Scotland. The musical sequences were filmed in London at the end of September. There was footage of Jack at the Albert Hall and extracts from *Songs For A Tailor* and *Things We Like* with musicians from the original recordings and Mike Pyne on piano.

The film was shown as part of the BBC's *Omnibus* art series on February 1 1970; the reviews were mixed. Music journalist Penny Valentine thought the film boring and felt that "Jack Bruce is a nice man and probably has a good story to tell … [but] a director should direct, not indulge. He should also come up with something that holds the attention: Palmer did neither, and that's a shame and a waste." By contrast television journalist Unity Hall implored viewers over the age of 30: "Don't Turn This Man Off … I think the most important result of *Rope Ladder To The Moon* is that it helps reveal the inner workings of a generation that baffles and angers its elders. … Even if older viewers do not understand, there is one moment for them – when Bruce plays the organ at the Albert Hall and plays it magnificently. I only hope they are not put off by the fact that he is wearing pale blue trousers and a pink velvet shirt at the time."

○

Songs For A Tailor might have fared better in America if Jack had been out there to promote it. But with RSO apparently too busy with Blind Faith, who toured the USA in July and August '69, no tour was arranged, and with no obvious single for airplay, sales suffered. Instead of touring on his own, Jack accepted an offer from up-and-coming guitarist Larry Coryell to fly to New York for a couple of gigs at Slugs on July 11 and 12. On that second night, while Jack was playing this dark, funky little jazz club on the Lower East Side, Blind Faith were performing at Madison Square Garden in front of 20,000 people. It was mayhem; a riot kicked off, Ginger got clubbed by a cop, and Winwood's piano was destroyed.

Jack came to know Larry from the Gary Burton Quartet, who supported Cream at Fillmore West. When the Quartet played at Ronnie Scott's in London, Cream came along and the two bands hung out together. Larry then invited Jack to play at Slugs alongside blind keyboardist Mike Mandel and drummer Steve Haas, both of whom had grown up with Larry in Seattle; Gary Burton's drummer Bob Moses and saxophonist Gato Barbieri also sat in.

Part of the problem with touring *Songs For A Tailor* was that Jack didn't have a band and couldn't use the key musicians who played on the album. Dick Heckstall-Smith and Jon Hiseman were engaged with Colosseum; Chris Spedding was in the Battered Ornaments, while John Marshall was committed to the jazz-rock band Nucleus. Jack mentioned Larry and Mike as potential band-members in an autumn interview, but nothing happened until late 1969 when Larry got a call to come to London to play with Jack Bruce & Friends. Larry then called Mike Mandel, who remembers being told that he "might get a call from Jack Bruce. Good Lord!" The other 'friend' in Jack's band was Mitch Mitchell. They'd jammed together with Jimi Hendrix in late '66, but now Mitch was at a loose end. He had stayed with Hendrix after Noel Redding was replaced by Billy Cox and was in the band for Woodstock, only to be replaced by Buddy Miles in Jimi's shortlived Band Of Gypsys.

Jack flew Mike, Larry, and Larry's wife and young son over to the UK first class and invited them all to stay with him and Janet. Jack brought Mike a gift – "a Fender Rhodes piano that was hauled around that I could play in the hotel room. That's the kind of guy he was."

The musicians rehearsed at different venues including The Lyceum in London where, as Mike recalls, "Jack handled it so that when the attendant left, the bar was still available". The first date of the tour was January 24 1970. It was only the second time Jack had played since the Slugs weekend, six months ago, prompting Nick Logan to ask if he was worried about being a bit rusty.

"No," Jack replied, "the only thing I may lack is the stamina to get adjusted to the physical side of touring again. When you're a bass player and you're not playing, your fingers get very soft. Mine have. Also my voice hasn't been used to singing very loud, but I'm looking forward to it very much." Jack was also asked if a week was enough for rehearsals. "With your average musician it wouldn't be," he said, "but with these guys it is enough."

As individuals they were certainly accomplished, but as it transpired a week really wasn't enough and they didn't quite gel as a working unit. Things got off to a rocky start at the Lanchester Arts Festival in Coventry. "That was hard," says Jack, "because Colosseum [the support act] were very powerful and together, and it was our first gig, so although I was top of the bill they were a hard act to follow." Reviewer Michael Watts noted that Larry's playing was "superb" and that Jack's basslines were "reminiscent of Bach", but that they just weren't playing as a band. They almost lost the audience with some longwinded improvisations, but won them back with 'Politician' and 'Sunshine Of Your Love', which Jack decided to keep in for the rest of the tour. They weren't helped that night by poor sound and balancing, which was only slightly improved the following night at the Lyceum, although the performance was much sharper, with an appreciative crowd clapping throughout the 90-minute set.

Then it was off the States. Most musicians have an ambivalent attitude to touring – they can't wait to get home while they're on the road, but get very restless once they're back. Jack had definitely been missing America and soon got into "living it up on the road", as he puts it. Texas-born Larry had come up through the creatively stimulating but less than lucrative New York jazz scene; Mike, accomplished as he was, hadn't progressed beyond playing in bars, and had until recently been focused on studying music theory at Boston's Berklee College Of Music. Now they were in Jack Bruce's first band after Cream, going to parties at Robert Stigwood's house, flying first class, ordering what they wanted from room service, and consuming unfeasible amounts of coke, hash, LSD, speed, and booze (leaving actual memories of this tour extremely hazy). In Chicago they were even visited by the Plaster Casters. They thought they had died and gone to heaven. Larry, now sober for 27 years, says simply: "It was insane."

The band arrived in New Orleans during Mardi Gras. "Booze flowed in the street and at the concert," Larry says. "I was so drunk I poured beer all over my guitar and Jack took it I was unhappy with something, but we were too loaded to have an argument." Mitch Mitchell got into the swing of things by nearly drowning at 4am in the swimming pool of their New Orleans hotel, the Royal Senesta, after swallowing a face full of downers. According to Jack, the quality of the gig "largely depended on how good or bad Mitch was, although in Texas he did the best drum solo I have ever heard".

They were a celebrity band. Jeff Beck and Noel Redding came to the Lyceum gig; Jimi Hendrix and John McLaughlin showed up to see their first Fillmore East show in New York. The audience went nuts and kept shouting for the band long after the support act Mountain took the stage – to the point where Leslie West went to the mic and shouted "shut the fuck up".

Considering the state they were all in, the musicianship was of a high order, and although Jack struggled with his vocals for the opening few gigs – as he had predicted – he soon grew stronger. Looking back now, however, Mike feels that "Jack, through us, did not achieve the vision of what those songs could be. I feel sad about that. His vision was achieved on the record, but not on the road with this band representing those songs. There were nights where it showed that we knew the songs better, we played them better, the songs had energy. But it didn't have a sense of permanence – we would have needed to sequester ourselves away and play together until our personalities revealed themselves. That sort of thing takes time."

What the musicians could not have imagined as they travelled from New York down to New Orleans was just how 'impermanent' Jack felt about the band. At that first Fillmore show, John McLaughlin introduced Jack to Tony Williams. Following their conversation, and only two gigs into his 'comeback' tour, Jack couldn't wait for it to be over.

once in a lifetime

CHAPTER 8

If you had to pick one year when the commercial power of rock first offered a serious challenge to the traditional pop business, it would be 1969. It was the year huge, open-air festivals first hit America, culminating in Woodstock and Altamont, and the year the Stones and Blind Faith played London's Hyde Park in front of the UK's largest ever rock audiences. Albums outsold singles for the first time, and rock bands were making the news everywhere: the death of Brian Jones; the break up of The Jimi Hendrix Experience; the end of The Beatles; the rise of Led Zeppelin. Although there was still a lingering doubt in the business about whether any of this would last, Cream had demonstrated in the most dramatic fashion that there was a massive pile of money to be made while it did.

By contrast, jazz was in a something of a crisis. Since the 20s it had gone through a number of major transitions, the most recent being the bebop revolution. Many of the Grand Masters were dead or in decline, however, and as new waves of free-form jazz drove the music even further from public attention and acceptance, the more visionary musicians looked across with envy at what was happening in rock and thought they absolutely deserved a piece of the action. In the vanguard of this realignment of jazz was Miles Davis and his young drummer, Tony Williams.

A precocious and scintillating talent, Tony Williams started playing drums when he was nine and sat in with Art Blakey's Messengers at 12. By 17 he had joined Miles Davis, whom he stayed with for six years, in the meantime also featuring on the seminal Eric Dolphy album *Out To Lunch*. At 18 he had the temerity to call his first solo album *Life Time*.

Tony's approach to the drums was nothing short of a sonic assault – hands and feet all capable of playing different rhythms, the expression of his style being the shimmering blur of cymbals, the crescendo of hi-hat, the syncopated battering of the snare drum. He could send a band off down any number of rhythmic pathways, and if you didn't go with him you'd be playing alone. He once said that asking a drummer not to play loud was like telling the bass player he could only use three of his four strings.

As well as being supremely confident, Tony was also disciplined, serious, and hungry. He could see how the music industry was being transformed, and as early as 1965 suggested to Miles that it would make good sense to support The Beatles. Miles eventually caught up and became enamoured of the new funk style of Sly Stone and the opportunity opened up by Cream to play extended improvisational music to a young, affluent rock audience. And as if to confirm Jack's belief that British jazz musicians could hold their heads up with the best the Americans could offer, Davis invited Dave Holland from England to play bass in his Quintet. Dave in turn recommended John McLaughlin; both played on *In A Silent Way* and the album on which jazz-rock came of age, *Bitches Brew*.

After recording *In A Silent Way*, however, Tony felt it was time to move on. Whatever came next, he told *Melody Maker*, "had to be something to hold my interest after playing with all the people I had done. Their level was so high ... it had to be an equal challenge ... and I couldn't do it with the traditional line-up of acoustic bass, piano, and two horns." So he recruited John McLaughlin (who also carried on doing sessions for Miles) and an enigmatic and underrated keyboard player, Larry Young, who had converted to Islam and now also went by the name Khalid Yasin.

Larry had been taught piano by Olga Bontill, a student of Bartok, and began recording as a leader for Prestige in 1960, releasing a number of soul-jazz albums including *Testifying*, *Young Blues*, and *Groove Street*. In 1964 he moved to Blue Note and recorded as part of a trio with guitarist Grant Green and drummer Elvin Jones, releasing two solo albums: *Into Somethin'* (with Sam Rivers on sax) and his best-known work, *Unity*. In May 1969 he recorded a track with Jimi Hendrix at the Record Plant in New York that would eventually be released on *Nine To The Universe* in 1980. (When Miles and

133

Tony were invited to record with Jimi they both tried to cash in, demanding $50,000 apiece just for turning up. It didn't happen.)

Tony, John, and Larry went into Manhattan's Olmstead Sound Studios for a two-day session to record *Emergency*, the debut album by the group Tony named Lifetime. The sound was quite unlike anything else on the music scene and set the tone for the live band to come: a maelstrom of fast licks and distortion from John; swirling curtains of gothic, dark sound from Larry; and a riptide of shattering percussion from Tony. The musical content and the way the compositions were organised were light years from modern jazz, which still based much of its repertoire on standards. The jazz community dismissed the double album out of hand, leaving Tony to look toward the rock world for validation of what he was trying to do. He also needed a bass player, but not just any bass player: somebody who could add yet more layers of savage power to the sound, who could sing and compose and bring with him the rock credibility Tony desperately sought.

He had already begun work on his next album, *Turn It Over*, when he went along to the Fillmore East with John McLaughlin to see Jack's band. Afterward John made the introductions; Tony invited Jack to come and record and to consider joining the band. "Most players are in a style I want to get away from," Tony told *Melody Maker*'s Chris Welch. "I met Jack and ... he was a bass player from another lifestyle. His singing really turned me on. It wasn't a bass player – it was like Jack himself."

Tony went back into Olmstead with Jack, who played and sang on three tracks: 'This Night This Song', 'Vuelta Abajo', and 'Turn It Over'. Jack's dynamic vocal range came in sharp contrast to Tony's. Tony insisted he could be a singer, but in truth all he could muster was a tuneless and virtually toneless sound; he knew he had 'limitations' but was outraged when one reviewer called his singing "experimentation at the listener's expense".

Better recorded than its predecessor, and with Jack's name on the cover, *Turn It Over* also sold more copies than *Emergency*. Jack and Tony grew close quite quickly. "He was my best friend at the time," Jack says. "I was closer to him than anybody else up to that point. He was a beautiful guy. He had some hang-ups like we all do, down to the extent of his talent. It was manifest so early on. His father was a tenor player and he came to one of our shows. Tony had just bought a brownstone in Harlem, which was quite rough at the time, and his father came along especially to give him a gun: 'Here you are, T.' I was quite impressed.

"Tony was very influenced by Miles, who was the coolest, most sophisticated guy – the snappiest dresser, he smoked Cuban cigars, he drove the Ferrari, had the best women. He tried to emulate Miles and liked my lifestyle – a few Ferraris, a nice town house, silver vial of cocaine, and an island. I introduced him to Monty Python, which he loved – he really got it. I'd drive Tony to the gigs in the Ferrari, while Bob [Adcock, who had elected to stay on as Jack's road manager rather than go off with Eric] took the other guys in my Bentley, so we weren't roughing it. What Tony really wanted was to be a rock star."

Tony was perfectly candid about this in an interview with Michael Walters. "This group is a money-making vehicle," he said. "I am tired of people looking at certain black artists, and saying, 'At last they are getting what they deserve after all these years.' I want twice what I deserve, because a whole lot of black people haven't got theirs ... I have this inbred thing that tells me that I'm good at what I do, and something else tells me that if I keep going and getting better, it is worth money."

Like Jack, Tony wasn't content with success at any cost. He would have to do it his way, on his terms, with *his* music and the musicians *he* wanted to work with. On stage he was ferocious and uncompromising; off stage he was often quite reserved but loved the thrill of racing cars and the good things in life – all of which goes a long way to explain his friendship with Jack.

The Lifetime tour started in the States and overall the reception was pretty positive. Some audiences were prepared to accept the musicians for what they were – a new band with a new approach, not too weighed down by the baggage of Cream and Miles Davis; others were not. Just over halfway through the tour, they played the Newport Jazz Festival. "We followed Buddy Rich," says Jack. "It was a bit drizzly. Then we went on and started with 'Dragon Song' and I've never seen an audience leave so fast – whoosh – three people were left at the front." There was often a stunned silence at the end of a gig, not necessarily because the audience didn't like the music, but because they were overwhelmed.

The best audiences were those in New York who were more used to hearing music that pushed into the outer reaches of jazz and rock and were more open to efforts at melding the two forms. Lifetime had a virtual residency at Ungano's, a hip industry basement club holding no more than 200 people on 210 West 70th Street between Amsterdam and West End Avenues – 13 nights, two shows a night. The repertoire majored on the compositions from the two Lifetime albums, but Jack contributed two new songs that hadn't been recorded yet, 'A Letter Of Thanks' and 'Smiles And Grins'. Snippets of 'Smiles

And Grins' could be heard as part of improvisations by Jack's previous band; now it had lyrics, although Jack was often reduced to shouting over the noise and distortion.

As good as the New York shows were, getting the US dates together was a struggle. As John McLaughlin would later say: "Everything except the music was incredibly bad – management, economics, administration, organisation … *incredibly* bad. The music was the only thing that kept us together." At least he and the others were living in the States. It was much more awkward for Jack, who would "go over at my own expense and stay at the St Regis Hotel, which was expensive, waiting and waiting for something to happen".

Monte Kay received a production credit on both Lifetime albums and was also comedian Flip Wilson's manager, which accounts for Lifetime's slot on *The Tonight Show* when Flip was the host. "We went into the rehearsal and played 'Dragon Song' – very dissonant, loud, and powerful," Jack recalls. "The guy came in and said, 'Do you know any Beatles songs?'" Kay was best known as the founder of the famous Birdland jazz club, and as manager, agent, and producer of various major jazz artists, from whom Miles Davis later said he "made millions".

The Charlie Parker/Monte Kay connection would explain Jack's recollection that Tony's road manager "used to be Charlie Parker's road manager, and also Frankie Lymon's; part of his job was to shoot Frankie up with heroin. So he'd had a checkered career. He was a nice guy, but he didn't get us any work." Intriguingly, Birdland was later taken over by Morris Levy, one of the most notorious music industry bosses ever, who had heavy links to the Mafia and who also ran Frankie Lymon's label, Roulette Records. So Tony might have had some dodgy characters lurking in the background, supposedly watching his back.

Sick and tired of Tony's hopeless management, Jack asked Robert Stigwood to set up a European tour. The band were pleased with the early dates in London at the Marquee and the Speakeasy. Watching the Marquee gig was Richard Williams from *Melody Maker*, an early champion of the band, who wrote: "You could tell something extraordinary was happening by the wide grins that flashed from McLaughlin to Williams to Bruce to Young and it was beautiful to behold." There was an ocean of applause after every number and an ovation at the end.

The Speakeasy was another great night. "Erupting with a furious storm of explosive energy, Lifetime left the Speakeasy audience appreciative, but slightly stunned," Williams wrote. "The sheer impact of such a relentless succession of shattering figures slammed off with such drive and verve set me chuckling with delight at times." There was a note of caution, however, in his suggestion that "Lifetime listeners are going to be baffled and bemused by it all".

European audiences seemed able to see past the pedigree and accept the music on it own terms. The band's two concerts in Scotland were also well received, but in England it was more difficult, especially outside London. They played the Dagenham Roundhouse in Essex to a crowd of drunks who could not have cared less about the music and who anyway were more used to seeing British blues-rock acts like Free, Rory Gallagher, and Blodwyn Pig. They also played a very small club in Plymouth with dreadful sound and an erratic power supply that caused a buzzing noise right through the set.

Another gig, in Wolverhampton, was cancelled entirely because the promoters ignored the contractual stipulation that the group be billed just as Lifetime with nobody's name bigger than anybody else's, none of the names more than half the size of the name of the band, and no mention of 'Cream' or 'Miles Davis'. "The clauses in Lifetime's contract make it impossible for us to advertise them properly," the promoter told *Melody Maker*, "and Stigwood's agency refused to alter them. This isn't London, it's way out in Wolverhampton and people just wouldn't realise who was in the band. It's a shame and we've had to book Deep Purple as replacements." "The group is going down remarkably well," Stigwood's office replied, "particularly in view of the type of music they play, and the days when you had to hype people like this are long gone."

Tony made clear in interviews at the time that the inefficiencies of his management were obvious to him right from the start, even before Jack joined the band. "I had to go rent the truck. *I* had to rent it, then *drive* it to New Jersey to get the organ at Larry's house, lift it – *I* had to help lift the organ into the truck, then the sound system, drive it all the way to Boston or somewhere, get it to the club, *set* it all up, play, *take* it all down, get it back into the truck, then drive it all the way back to New Jersey, then *I* had to take the truck back … that's no way to play."

When Jack joined it meant that, with RSO now involved too, "the finances shall we say were very unclear and they got out of hand. [Jack's] people naturally wanted to have control over it, so that would have meant me cancelling my people. Even though they weren't equipped and we were having problems because of them, I didn't think it was the right thing to do."

The various management figures appeared to be in a push-me-pull-you with the musicians involved. "One of the unfortunate things is that due to managerial type problems, the band isn't really a band," Jack told *Melody Maker*. "I'm just playing with them rather than being a full member. I have contractual obligations to fulfil." There were plans, never realised, to go into Electric Lady Studio to record an album. "I've got clearance to make one album with them, and we'll have to see how it goes after that."

There were issues inside the band as well – not the ego clashes you might expect between Jack, Tony, and John (pick any two from three), but rather more surprisingly between Tony and Larry. "In his autobiography, Miles slags off Coltrane because he wasn't a snappy dresser," Jack recalls. "Tony was very much in that way of thinking: a modern jazz musician should be so sharp and sophisticated, so that everyone would look up to them. Larry was almost like a cartoon character, very big and heavy. He wore a big dashiki and became a Muslim – a very amiable and quiet guy. And he was a genius – probably the one musician I have worked with who I could say without a shadow of a doubt was a genius, and I've worked with some great musicians. But Larry stands head and shoulders above all of them. He had this ability to make sounds and play notes that were completely unique. We played the Maryland in Glasgow and he played this organ solo where we would all stop and he would make sounds on a C3 using just the drawbars. I saw people crying. That was the power Larry had. It was astounding. But there was a friction between Larry and Tony that neither John nor I fully understood."

By Christmas 1970, Lifetime had gone supernova, but not before the band had a cosmic experience of its own. "We were driving to a gig at Manchester University," Jack remembers, "me, Bob, and Tony Williams in one car, Larry and John with the driver in the other. They went the wrong way up the A1 and across the Pennines. We were driving up the M1. As we were driving up the M6, I looked up and saw what looked like Mars because it was red, but it was much too big. It moved away ... and then it stopped. And we stopped, got out of the car, and watched it for about ten minutes. It got closer, then started doing all these erratic movements, and then accelerated away. As it moved away it changed shape and got a tail ... the actual movement of this thing was indescribable. It wasn't like anything I'd ever seen. So we watched it and then drove to Manchester in silence. We got to the gig just before the others and Larry Young came over and said, 'Hey man, we've just seen a flying saucer.' They were about fifty miles away in another place." (UFO sightings were noted on this date in Ministry Of Defence records for that period.)

At the time Jack acknowledged that the band pretty much played for themselves and hoped the audience would climb onboard. "That was a very heavy band," he said. "It was asking a lot of audiences to be willing to give as much of themselves as was necessary to get what there was emotionally out of that band ... especially in a baseball stadium in ... wherever it was." Looking back now he calls Lifetime "the most rewarding musical experience I've had. I wanted people to hear this music, but they just weren't ready for it. When it did work, like at the Speakeasy, it was amazing."

Unfortunately Lifetime were dogged even more than Cream had been by poor management and technology that couldn't even begin to cope with the demands of the music. It would be easy to say the band were ahead of their time, but maybe the music was just too full-on for it to sit comfortably with audiences (and the listening public, had they managed a whole album together). John McLaughlin pretty much took the same concept into The Mahavishnu Orchestra, which was backed by a proper management structure, label support, and an altogether less frantic, more melodic – some might say 'sanitised' – style. So too Weather Report and the bands led by Chick Corea and Herbie Hancock, each of whom followed more funky, mainstream paths to reap their rewards.

Having achieved so much so soon, and carrying with him such a sense of pride and self-belief, it was hard for Tony Williams to realise as time went on that his career was not going to pan out as he wished. He reunited with Jack for the occasional gig or recording and on John McLaughlin's *Electric Guitarist* but died of a heart attack following gallbladder surgery aged only 44.

Poor Larry Young seemed to drop off the radar entirely. He might have been dubbed the Coltrane of the organ, but his talent left his post-Lifetime achievements in the dust. He carried on with Tony for the drummer's next album, *Ego*, but then all but disappeared from view before dying aged 37 from undiagnosed pneumonia. Jack and John did play together again in a band later on – albeit one whose management took 'rip-off' to a whole new level.

○

Jack's mention of "contractual obligations" during his spell with Lifetime referred to the pressure on him to record a follow-up to *Songs For A Tailor*. But before that he got involved briefly yet intensely in a remarkable project that almost defied description – one that presented Jack with some of his most challenging work as a singer and caused further puzzlement in the rock world.

In 1967, jazz composer Carla Bley was working on a new composition called 'The Detective Writer's Daughter' when her poet friend Paul Haines, who had just moved to India, sent her something that seemed to fit the music

she was writing. They decided to collaborate on what might loosely be called
a jazz opera but which wasn't really an opera at all because there was no
discernible or consistent narrative thread.

After three years of bouncing lyrics and music between them, a sprawling
epic called *Escalator Over The Hill* emerged. It was labelled a
'chronotransduction', the name having been conjured up by Paul's scientist
friend Sue Speeth and apparently meaning 'a leading across time' – something
intangible that nevertheless echoes everywhere. "I never asked for an
explanation of what the phrase meant," says Carla. "I think it meant walking
through life without effort. Everything Haines wrote was a mystery to
everyone. I was not alone."

Escalator demanded an army of musicians and singers. Carla called up
Gato Barbieri, Don Cherry, and Charlie Haden, whom she had written for in
the past, but thought that it would be best if the vocalists didn't sound too
'trained'. For the lead parts, however, she knew she needed real professionals.
Carla's second husband, trumpet player and composer Mike Mantler,
suggested Jack Bruce. Carla had met Jack during his Cream days and had also
seen Lifetime at the Fillmore East; Jack was aware of Carla as "someone I
knew from when I was very young. We used to get printed music of Carla Bley
compositions around the time I was working at the Cell." After their second
meeting she sent Jack a letter, showing him the music and confirming how
many great musicians would be involved (among them John McLaughlin and
drummer Paul Motian). Carla had been thinking about Jack from early on in
the writing process, but as soon as he said he would do it, "everything was
now done with Jack in mind".

Apart from the appeal of something else that was new and different, Jack
was enthusiastic about the way the project was being financed: not by some
corporate label, but by Carla and Mike themselves. They had been part of the
Jazz Composers Guild, formed in 1964 in the belief that musicians working in
avant-garde and free jazz should take the business into their own hands. To
promote the music, the Guild put together a big band, The Jazz Composers
Orchestra Association (JCOA), for a series of concerts in 1964–65. The Guild
then dissolved in a flurry of philosophical differences, but Carla and her first
husband, Paul Bley, continued with the band while Mike Mantler set up the
New Music Distribution Service and the JCOA label.

"The whole thing is based on socialist principles," Jack remarked
approvingly to a journalist at the time. "They pay the top session rates and
employ the top guys – and not just those who are working all the time. They

also have people like Roswell Rudd, who doesn't work too much. In fact he couldn't make some of the sessions because he couldn't get time off from his day job as a cab driver – and you know how good *he* is."

Financing was always a problem, but Carla and Mike were able to use a donation of $15,000 from Sue Speeth and her husband (who had sold up and moved to India) to book RCA Studios in New York, which was capable of accommodating the 30 musicians required for the larger ensemble pieces. They set to work on November 30 1970 and hoped to start by recording 'Rawalpindi Blues' with Jack and Don Cherry playing together in The Eastern Band, but this proved impossible because Jack was still on tour with Lifetime. Instead the music was split into a dialogue between East and West: Don became the leader of The Desert Band, and when Jack arrived on December 7 his band with John McLaughlin became The Traveling Band.

The Traveling Band's recording of 'Rawalpindi Blues' was later described by Marcello Carlin of *Stylus Magazine* as "perhaps the most sublime 12 minutes of music ever created". Jack's opening blues lament prefaces some storming interplay between John and Jack backed by Paul Motian's subtle, supportive percussion. It certainly wasn't easy to capture, however. Everybody was up for two days and nights straight to nail the piece, and mixing it proved to be a nightmare. "We had indiscriminately filled up all 16 tracks right at the beginning and then crammed in other elements wherever there was the slightest space," Carla recalls. "So when we finally got down to mixing it, it was all hands on the board and it took two full days. One of the most unnerving and time-consuming parts was a process I used a few times called cross-fading, which involved mixing two 16-track tapes down to a two-track tape all at once. They used to flinch at RCA when we called in and told them how many machines we would need that day."

Jack stayed on in New York after the session expecting some more Lifetime gigs or maybe that mooted recording session at Electric Lady, but nothing materialised so he called Carla to say he was going back home. She quickly raised some cash to get him back in the studio to record some more of his vocal parts. Mike got the band together on February 16 1971 to record 'Detective Writer's Daughter' live with a band including John, Paul, Carla on organ, Charlie Haden, and Jimmy Knepper on trombone. They also recorded 'Little Pony Soldier', which Jack found "incredibly difficult to sing"; he found 'Businessmen' tricky too because "they were asking me to hit really high notes which I did with varying degrees of success. I was sight-reading it, so it was challenging stuff." Carla concedes that she wrote the piece "knowing his range, although I wrote a little bit too high". Filmmaker Steve Gebhardt shot footage of the RCA session, providing a fascinating glimpse of Jack tackling the songs under Carla's direction and persisting until he gets it right, although he ends one take with a frown and a terse "well, we'll leave that one for now".

Mike and Carla later needed further vocal contributions from Jack and the leading lady, Linda Ronstadt. But there was no money left for anyone to travel anywhere, so Carla took the risk of sending the completed backing tracks and her imitation of the vocals for the vocalists to overdub their parts. At one point they had to do a duet; Linda put down her part and sent it to Jack to add his contribution and send it back to Carla. Linda shared Jack's view about the challenge of the work; she told Carla she had never been confronted with music that was so difficult to sing.

Released as a three-LP set in 1971 (and a double CD in 1998), *Escalator Over The Hill* garnered much acclaim as a special musical event and won a French jazz award, even if nobody really knew what it was about. If there is a 'story' it centres on Cecil Clark's Old Hotel and the sleazy exploits of its clientele (as a metaphor for the state of the planet). The spine of the music is carried by three bands: The Hotel Lobby Band, designed to represent the crumbling façade of Western culture, as expressed through modern jazzers imprisoned in a senile Palm Court Orchestra; the drive and energy of the Traveling Band with Jack, John, Paul Motian, and Carla; and Don Cherry's Middle-Eastern influenced Desert Band. But the album is best appreciated for the individual performances, particularly those of Jack, John McLaughlin, Don Cherry, Paul Motian, Gato Barbieri, and Linda Ronstadt – and for Carla's heroic attempt to knit together pretty much every musical development of the 20th century. As one reviewer suggested, anybody who can cast themselves adrift in Alain Renais's cinematic Rubik's Cube *Last Year In Marienbad* would be right at home with *Escalator Over The Hill*.

O

Even before *Songs For A Tailor* was released in September 1969, Jack had a slew of new songs he wanted to record. Much of his next album emerged while he was at home one inspired afternoon: "It all came pouring out in the same order as it finished up on the record."

Together Jack and Pete created an album of intelligent, stimulating, and serious music about serious subjects. Even the more surreal songs have a psychological depth, and the overall effect is an album of real art, a powerful and cohesive combination of melodic and harmonic structure, lyrics, and voice.

Jack wanted an album that at least in part reflected his anger about the state Glasgow was in. "It was always neglected," he says. "I remember coming from Glasgow down to London to sing in the Socialist Sunday School Choir at the Albert Hall. I was about 12; I'd never seen such wealth and riches. It was paradise. I'd never even seen a zebra crossing. When I did the film with Tony Palmer, Glasgow still looked like it did in the war – bombsites and slums. So for the album I'd always had the title *Harmony Row*, because of the ambivalence of the name."

Jack decided on a more sparse approach this time around with no horn section, just Chris Spedding and John Marshall. "I'd sit at the piano and sing, have the guitar and drums going, which for me was really good because it meant there was space but also meant the other musicians had to be very careful [about] what they played. If there are a minimal number of instruments, you tend to play less, not more, because you can't really spread out – if you are playing live, you can see and hear everything that is going on. In the studio, you have to leave space for what might go on top."

This was "especially difficult for Chris", Jack says, but the musicians rose to the challenge. "It was a very different feel, pared down to three musicians," says John, "but the same kind of approach; he had the songs mapped out. He knew exactly what he wanted and it wasn't stressful in the way some sessions can be where you have no idea what's right and what's wrong. I had to go some to cop hold of what he really wanted – if you're just playing a backing track, you don't get the whole picture. Jack's an all-round musician; he can write parts. Not everybody likes that but I do because it gives me shape: I know what I'm supposed to be doing, then I can concentrate on him. Quite a few of the songs were done with Jack on acoustic guitar and me on drums.

"Jack's got a fantastic sense of time. I learnt a lot from Jack about how to deal with odd time signatures, how to groove at the same time. You can groove and be static, but to have moving lines and have that same kind of feel is more difficult. He's supreme at doing that. Chris was in his element too. Thanks to *Songs For A Tailor* he was flavour of the month studio-wise and he was extraordinarily busy."

The main *Harmony Row* sessions took place in January 1971 at Command Studios, although Jack had recorded a demo version of 'Escape To The Royal Wood (On Ice)' with Chris and John at Morgan Studios as early as October 1969. "There were written parts for 'Escape To The Royal Wood'," Jack recalls, "but they would just follow what I was doing on the piano. There would be a guide vocal – occasionally you'd end up with a finished vocal while

I was doing it live, but usually I'd record a guide vocal so I didn't have to concentrate so much on the vocals and then overdub the vocal later. As I got better on later records, I would deliberately do finished vocals." (For Jack, a guide vocal means when "you'd have the words and the melody, but you wouldn't have the best sound, so you'd only be using a live vocal mic because you can get really close to it. When you are using a proper vocal mic, it's quite a large area that's recorded, so you can't really use that because you're picking everything up. So you just have a close mic so people can hear you and you know where you are and the shape of the song is apparent.")

Having just two other musicians alongside him gave Jack scope as a multi-instrumentalist. He plays bass, cello, acoustic guitar, percussion, and harmonica on *Harmony Row*, but it was the strength of his piano and organ work that caught the attention of many reviewers.

Jack's vocals have an expressiveness that transcends the voice as instrument. There is a vulnerable innocence present as he reaches deep inside and confesses private feelings. *Harmony Row*'s 'Folk Song' is one of a number of outstanding ballads in the Bruce canon that best express the simple truth that you cannot be detached from your true self and still be a great musician. Listen to the beautiful choral orchestrations as Jack layers his vocals and hear how he soars at the end of the lines in the repeat of the fifth verse.

"I really thought ['Folk Song'] was something that already existed because I grew up on Robbie Burns and Scottish folk songs from my mother," Jack says. "So I hesitated about that one. The introduction using organ and piano is interesting because it was very much influenced by Messiaen, whose music I'd just started falling in love with."

'Can You Follow' started out as an instrumental called 'Green Hills', and that romantic, nostalgic rural theme from *Songs For A Tailor* carries through to 'There's A Forest'. Pete wrote 'Escape To The Royal Wood (On Ice)' and 'Folk Song' together as a kind of homage to Jack and Janet's marriage, which he says was "a good relationship to be around. I went with my girlfriend Sue to see *Babes In The Wood On Ice* and for some reason I felt very moved by it. Jack already had the music and it suggested something slightly archaic and showbiz."

'Morning Story', Pete says, "is Glasgow. I had written a poem called 'You, The Night And The Music' contrasting an industrial city where everyone is going to work while jazz musicians were leaving the clubs to go home to bed. A lot of that got into 'Morning Story'. Again it's the feeling of the landscape of Glasgow in which Jack invests a phenomenal sense of almost operatic drama. 'Smiles And Grins' is another city landscape: the personality, put a tiger in your tank [a slogan for Esso petrol back in the 70s], peeling off the layers of what lies beneath."

On 'Post-War' Jack says he was experimenting with "going between different feels in the same song". The lyrics were inspired by Pete's poet friend, Libby Houston. "Libby's poem is about her father, who was a bomber pilot," Pete says. "She wonders how he came to take a wrong turn in the blitz and never came back."

'Letter Of Thanks' and 'You Burned The Tables On Me' are both examples of Jack injecting compositional humour into his songs. In the first "every bar is a different length"; in the second "the sequence halves every time you play it. It starts off as eight bars, then four, then two, then one, then a beat." Each also recounts a recurring theme in Pete's life: failed relationships, expressed in the bizarre imagery of The Goons and another British poet, Spike Hawkins.

If you add Pete's glass-half-empty view of life to Jack's you get an empty glass and 'Victoria Sage', a song about the inevitability of death – "quite miserable that," Pete admits – although like other songs on the album it's deeply imbued with a sense of history. And there's life through the bottom of a glass in 'The Consul At Sunset', a lilting Latin throb inspired by Jack's love of *Under The Volcano*, Malcolm Lowry's novel about a British consul in Mexico drowning himself in booze (given to Jack as a wedding present by Dick Heckstall-Smith). The music was written for a proposed adaptation of the novel starring Richard Burton that was never made; a different version was later shot with Albert Finney as the consul.

○

Fortunately, when it came to touring to promote the album, both Chris and John were available. The money was a huge incentive, as John recalls: "[Jack said] he could only pay £50 a gig, which doesn't sound a lot now, but I couldn't believe it. I'd never been paid so much in my life. With Nucleus at Ronnie Scott's, we said we wanted £10 a gig and they said we were money-mad! I left Nucleus to do this." Who else would be involved wasn't clear, but Jack had the chance to road test some options when Larry Coryell invited him to do three nights at Ronnie Scott's. They played mostly as a trio but Chris came in to jam, as did Graham Bond and Mitch Mitchell.

There was a certain brashness and arrogance about Larry at the time, and on one occasion he managed to wind Jack up to a dangerous level. "I think on the Friday Larry made an announcement to the effect that it was great to be at Ronnie Scott's and 'nice to play with Jack and John, who in my opinion are the best UK rhythm section'," John recalls, "at which point Jack yelled 'bollocks'. The temperature went up amazingly and we started playing. It was toward the end of the second set and it may have been 'Powerhouse Sod', a full-on piece like that. It was coming to Jack's solo and he was playing the most amazing bass, he was so annoyed at what Larry had said, his adrenalin filled the club – then right at the climax the fuse went on his amp and it just cut out. He was just left hanging there and he picked up the amp and flung it in Coryell's direction. But it didn't hit him, it hit my hi-hat, and then there was a blazing row in the dressing room."

"To me that was a put-down," says Jack, "especially in a jazz context, and I hate being called a 'British blues player' because that's trad or John Mayall and I've never been that. I certainly don't feel like a 'British jazz musician'. I'm a musician who happens to be British." The trio were due to play a few gigs on the continent before Jack's tour started, but after the Ronnie Scott's incident he pulled out and was replaced by Roy Babbington.

Jack settled on a band of John, Chris, Graham Bond, and Art Themen, although because of his hospital duties Art couldn't commit to the whole tour, which began in August 1971 and ran (with breaks) until the following January. Art agrees with John that playing with Jack was a definite step up. "I was playing to a lot more people than I was used to with Mike Garrick and Stan Tracey," he says. "And playing with Jack bought me a car, a brand new Ford Cortina."

Early in the tour the band played two London club dates in aid of the Upper Clyde Shipbuilders. Shipbuilding was the lifeblood of the Clyde, but the industry had declined to the point where by the mid 60s only the Fairfield Yard was left within the boundary of Glasgow. It was merged with Upper Clyde Shipbuilders, but in June 1971 the yard went bust. The workforce, led by a group of Communist shop stewards headed by the charismatic Jimmy Reid, came up with the ingenious tactic of a 'work-in' so as to derail any media attempt to portray them as irresponsible strikers. Reid wanted to ensure that the workers projected the best image of the yard they possibly could and insisted on tight discipline. He famously instructed them that there should be "no hooliganism, no vandalism, and no bevvying [drinking]". These tactics won the shipbuilders much public sympathy and led to the campaign being broadened to include the whole trade union movement, the church, and other organisations. Reid announced at one rally that John Lennon had contributed £5,000 to the cause, prompting somebody to shout out, "I thought Lenin was deid!" When word was passed to the shop stewards by a journalist that Jack Bruce was playing a benefit gig, Communist Party HQ in Glasgow responded: "Oh aye, that's Charlie's boy, isn't it?"

Sandwiched between these two dates was a triumphant headline appearance at Hyde Park on September 4 1971. Support came from King Crimson and Roy Harper, who had almost died from an infection he acquired giving a sheep mouth-to-mouth resuscitation. "We followed him and I said, 'Thank you Roy Harper. Now we'd like to do a song of ours called 'Born Under A Baaad Sign'," Jack laughs, "I couldn't resist it. He took it very well, considering."

The band's set showcased many of the songs from the new album plus the obligatory Cream crowd-pleasers and gave Graham the opportunity to get his blues shout around songs like 'Have You Ever Loved A Woman?' Among the music-press headlines in praise of the concert were 'Beauty And The Bruce' and 'Sheer Magic From Bruce And Bond'. It was Jack's best live press since the breakup of Cream and provided an encouraging send off as the band hit the road.

As Chris recalls: "Jack is a very easygoing guy and very funny, but he did expect us to get it right, so we were pretty conscientious. It was fun but it wasn't straight rock. Jack was a pioneer of that – no one else was doing it then. This was before The Mahavishnu Orchestra had made a big impact. The band was way ahead of its time in that respect. The audiences loved Jack, but I suspect many of them were waiting for 'Sunshine Of Your Love', which we never played."

John remembers a bandleader of no compromise. "He has never coasted in his life. On a session we did for German TV, you'll see that his hands are damaged. He's got bandages. He came off this motorbike onto the gravel. But his hands healed amazingly fast, so I think he's got this really fast metabolism, and that is how he is and he always goes for it – although it doesn't always do him favours. Bob Adcock was stopped by the police once when we were on the way home and Jack started giving the policeman grief. And he gave this customs guy a terribly hard time – which just resulted in them taking the car apart. There was a gig in Norwich at the Lad's Club, where he chucked a mic stand into the audience and stormed off the stage. Years later I bumped into somebody in South America who said he'd been at the club that night when it happened. But that's part of the deal. He plays 110 per cent and I love it."

Most of the gigs passed without incident, but not the one at the Teatro Massimo in Milan, which marked Jack's first visit to Italy since his hurried departure in 1961. He remembers the venue being "a round building, like a circus. We drive to the gig and when we get there, there are thousands of people outside and smoke and flames everywhere. This was a time when anarchism was very big in Italy. The entire place is surrounded by police. We go through the police ring and they show us through this door – 'in there, in there' – and they put me in this room and throw teargas in after me!

"Teargas makes you panic, you have to get away, you can't just hold your breath, that's the point of it. I ran out of the room, down some stairs and went through a tiny door halfway down the staircase. I opened it, went through, and fell into this mad, anarchist audience. They lifted me up, passed me overhead and put me on the stage. Then the chief anarchist came up to the dressing room and said 'music should be free'. I said, 'Well, it's not up to me. I've got a living to make, just like you.' 'OK, so we will break the doors in.' They did, and they all poured in. We did play, came back for an encore, and in the time it took us to come off and go back on again, they'd stolen all the equipment!

"The next day was in Rome and that's when Graham wound me up so much that I ripped a sink out of the wall of the dressing room and threw it at him," Jack continues. "Art Themen wasn't there, and that was an important point because he was a great calming influence on everybody: highly intelligent, a surgeon, great player, and a great guy. My fuse was very short in those days, anyway, but Graham could be very tricky. I did have some mixed feelings about him being in the band simply because he had always been a leader, with me the sideman, much younger. I wondered how he might take to it. He did very well. But he did have a really bad drug problem at the time."

"Graham Bond was a bit of an intimidating figure to me," says Chris, "because as well as his amazing musical talent, he was also into magic and would turn up to shows in full regalia, robes with arcane symbols on them, smelling of incense and carrying an ornate wand. At the Hyde Park concert Graham put his wand down on the table backstage and I, in a vain attempt to lighten the mood, picked it up and said something lame like 'what a nice wand' when Graham came rushing over saying, 'You turned it upside down! Oh my spells, my spells!' Frightened the life out of me. At that point I thought the less said the better." Graham also managed to get them thrown out of a seedy dive in Hamburg's Reeperbahn – which, says Art, "takes some doing. All these geezers suddenly appeared from all four corners of the room, including this menacing dwarf." For Jack, having Graham in the band meant the music was quite intense but also that it was "a pretty good band. We did some good gigs and people actually liked it."

O

Harmony Row was released in July 1971 to consistently excellent reviews. The headline of *Melody Maker*'s review – 'Jack's Genius' – set the tone. Dave Gelly wrote an extremely insightful review for *Creem* which, given that he is that rare commodity, a respected critic *and* musician, bears reprinting in full.

I'm still digging little goodies out of Songs For A Tailor *and here comes another one. It's difficult to know where to begin. Let's start at the bottom and work up. Jack has always been a marvellous constructor of bass lines and in 'Sunshine Of Your Love' and 'Politician' the interest of the pieces lay in the insistent, growling under-melody as much as the tune on top. But with 'Tickets To Waterfalls' his preoccupation with the ambiguities of rhythm really begin to show so that the beat seemed at times to be moving in two directions at once.*

In this album, the bassline is so free and yet so solid that it is difficult to imagine anything more riveting or absorbing in the whole rock idiom. Listen, for example, to 'You Burned The Tables On Me' and you'll see what I mean. He sometimes adds the bass on after recording everything else and I just don't see how he does it; it's so perfectly integrated.

Perhaps it's as a result of listening to the first record so much, but to me Jack Bruce is an instantly recognisable composer. He has a great feeling for the melodic climax, the slow build-up to a key point in words and tune that makes everything that has gone before fall into place. Do you remember 'Theme For An Imaginary Western' on the first album? There's a kind of poised stateliness about the melody which defies description. Listen to 'Morning Story' on Harmony Row *and you will recognise the Bruce touch immediately. It sounds very simple, but it's very sophisticated in the best sense of the word. Similarly, 'Folk Song' with its clean open major-triad sound is the embodiment of the lyrics and a perfect piece of knowing restraint.*

There are things here that you wouldn't hear in any other context and there's not a single cliché to be heard anywhere. The textures are dense one minute and finely clear the next, but the transitions are so natural you'd hardly notice. And if you really want to hear something beautiful, hear 'There's A Forest'. This is just piano and voice with the piano going through extraordinarily tortuous chromatic paths while the melody almost (but not quite) follows. I don't know what Jack's vocal range is, but he seems to have developed a whole new falsetto register without sacrificing his own special, rather raw tone.

Harmony Row has only three people playing throughout – Jack, Chris

Spedding, and John Marshall. Who was the cloth-eared person who said that Jack needed a more 'pushing' drummer than John Marshall? It's not 'push' that matters (whatever that may be) but sympathetic rhythm. A piece properly played will develop its own momentum. You don't always need a Ginger Baker slogging it out in the background. And Chris Spedding, of course, is great. He manages to play everything in the right place with the right emphasis and without plastering the target. Any fool can rave away; it takes a real musician to go so far and no further.

I suppose this all sounds rather like a fan-club handout. I know what I value in Jack Bruce's music, but it's difficult to put into words. Perhaps it's enough to say that Harmony Row *contains everything I love in modern rock music without any of the usual tedious pretension. There is no fooling about here; the conception is realised and executed with extraordinary skill and sensitivity. You'll listen to this one (and the last) for a long time and still find new things to dig. And that is the best recommendation I know.*

Loyd Grossman of *Rolling Stone* ended his glowing review of the album in much the same vein: "Long after you've forgotten (Ginger Baker's) Air Force and Eric Clapton's latest, you'll be enjoying *Harmony Row.*" But despite all the accolades from respected magazines on both sides of the Atlantic, the album – Jack's favourite – failed to chart. Why? For once it wasn't entirely the fault of the record company: the album came out soon after its completion and was promoted with a tour very soon after its release.

In his review, Dave Gelly identified Jack's goal of achieving simplicity. As Jack explains: "What Messiaen was trying to do with other composers of that generation and possibly earlier generations of French musicians was to try and come up with music that in its realisation was very complex, with complex themes, but sounds very simple. You might be using birdsong as Messiaen did – some obscure Mexican thrush. Birds hear ten times faster than humans and their music is passed from generation to generation – it isn't the same as it was 100 years ago. But on the surface when you hear a nightingale or a thrush it sounds deceptively simple. And that's what I was trying to do in a pop or rock format – have fairly complicated structures and ideas, but that could communicate with people. But with this record, I didn't communicate with as many people as I had hoped or as many people as the first one did."

Musician and sound engineer turned neuroscientist Daniel Levitin recently wrote a fascinating book about understanding the human obsession with music, *This Is Your Brain On Music,* in which he explains that "music communicates to us emotionally through systematic violations of expectations". That's what Jack has done throughout his career, but in this case not enough people were listening.

It is likely that many Cream fans would have bought *Songs For A Tailor* without first hearing it or reading the reviews. It was enough that it was Jack's first solo album. Many of those fans would have been expecting Cream 2: The Sequel – Blind Faith had 'delivered' on Eric and Ginger solos, so why not Jack? Well, as we know, he didn't. Then came his first 'jazz-rock' band, followed by a stint in *Lifetime* and the release of *Things We Like*. This last project actually sold quite well: Jack was already a star, but all the other musicians were much better known by 1970 than they had been in 1968. Dick Heckstall-Smith and Jon Hiseman were leading Colosseum, one of the UK's top bands, and John McLaughlin was well known for his work with Miles Davis. The album would have been regarded (albeit incorrectly) as Jack's next 'solo' album. But it was unashamedly jazz and not what your average blooze-rawk fan wanted.

By the time *Harmony Row* was released Jack had left many Cream fans behind. He had been responsible for both strands of the Cream legacy – the idea of lengthy rock improvisation and soloing, and the creation of well-crafted songs brimming with musical innovation. He had taken that second legacy for his own but was in danger of being undone by the first. The concept of improvisation, a major driving force in musical developments for centuries, had been co-opted into rock as endless noodling, pointless jamming, and drum solos, most of which were crimes against humanity. So there was a sense for Jack that he was losing his audience. His growing despair over a faltering solo career into which he had poured his heart and soul was not helped by having to play penny-ante gigs at venues like The Lads Club in Norwich.

Then at the end of January 1972, with the tour almost over, he got a phone call and went for a jam at Island Records studios. And with The Imp Of The Perverse sitting on his shoulder, whispering in his ear, he decided to take the opportunity to have some fun back on the big US arena circuit, give the punters what they clearly wanted from him, and walk off with some big bucks. Jack made what remains his most controversial career move: West Bruce & Laing, a band with two priorities. The second was music, the first was heroin.

whatever turns you on

Felix Pappalardi had formed Mountain with guitarist Leslie West, formerly of The Vagrants, in 1969. American rock audiences saw Mountain as the natural successors to Cream. The riffs kept coming – 'Mississippi Queen', 'Never In My Life', 'Waiting To Take You Away' – but over time relations within the band soured. Drugs fuelled a rampant paranoia as it became clear that Leslie was the star of the show; Pete Townshend told Bud Prager he managed "the greatest guitar player in the world". Backstage arguments would ensue if, for example, Leslie was announced last by the MC rather than Felix. The combined aggression of Felix and his wife, Gail, drove the band closer to meltdown. To make matters worse the whole band started on heroin to take the edge off the mountains of coke they were consuming.

Felix quit the band in early 1972. The press were told he was exhausted and wanted to spend more time back home in Nantucket; in reality he was so strung out on heroin he could hardly function. He said he would see out the band's UK tour, which was scheduled to end on February 2 in Leeds, but Leslie and drummer Corky Laing wanted to carry on. They had heard that both Free and Mott The Hoople had broken up, so went to Island Studios hoping to recruit Paul Rodgers and Mott bassist Overend Watts. Instead they ended up calling Jack to come down for a jam. They played an 11-minute version of 'Play With Fire' and decided then and there to form a band. "Was I shy about asking Jack

Bruce to be in a band with me?" Leslie later mused. "Sure, but I'm a schmuck with huge balls. But it still shocked the crap out of me when he agreed."

It came as even more of a shock to Felix. "He was totally burnt out," Corky recalls, "but it did come as a big shock for him when West Bruce & Laing started. He and Jack were so very similar as people, wanting to lead from the front, always ahead, and I think it messed him up even more than he was already."

This was very typical of Jack. An idea comes up that appeals at that moment – perhaps because he's bored with whatever is going on at the time – and he goes for it. In this case there were also the underlying sense of getting back to basics, having more fun, and regaining a bigger public profile – so, from Jack's point of view, the right offer at the right time. "I just fancied doing those big gigs with a big noisy band, screaming into the mic," he says. "And maybe I felt I needed to make some money – except that bit never happened." His enthusiasm spun off into hyperbole when he told *Sounds*, in February: "It's the best thing that's ever happened to me – I'm more excited about this band that I've ever been about anything I've ever been in – including Cream and everything."

Jack had met Leslie and Corky through Felix, while Mountain had supported Jack's band with Larry Coryell in 1970. When Mountain came to the UK in May 1971 they all met up at the Intercontinental Hotel in London. It proved to be a fateful encounter. No stranger to cocaine, Jack eagerly snorted up two lines of a white powder on offer – except that "it turned out to be heroin". It was the first time Jack had tried the drug, and he was very lucky: both Robbie McIntosh (the drummer with The Average White Band) and Tim Buckley died on the spot after making the same mistake. Jack's relationship with drugs is discussed in more detail in the next chapter, but sufficed to say that this incident set him off on a chemical carousel that would keep rolling for the next 15 years.

○

Jack's studio jam with Leslie and Corky took place on January 26 1972. It was Corky's 24th birthday and, completely unbidden, Jack presented him with a very rare, experimental sports car: an Adams Probe, as used in the film *A Clockwork Orange*. The car sat only 16 inches off the ground; you had to drive it virtually on your back. The Adams brothers who designed it had one each, and there were only two others in existence: Jimmy Webb, who wrote 'MacArthur Park', had one; Jack had the other. Corky christened the car by vomiting his birthday booze all over it.

Jack BruceCOMPOSING HIMSELF

Jack still had a couple of dates left with his current band; after that he gave them all notice. Chris Spedding fired a pre-emptive strike by publicly announcing that he had quit the band because he thought the music was getting too complicated – something he still regrets. "There was a statement put out by Andrew King of Blackhill Enterprises, who were managing me at the time, which I had not approved the wording of, and which didn't reflect my thoughts – although I should admit accountability for it," he says. "I think Andrew was using the break-up of Jack's band to get some publicity for me. I think that made me the target for journalists hungry for a negative statement from me about Jack. Through my youthful naivety or just plain stupidity I think I gave them some satisfaction. This I deeply regret to this day."

Because of the confusion surrounding the break-up of Mountain and the rumours about Jack, the music press jumped to the conclusion that Jack was simply replacing Felix in Mountain, one singing bass-player for another. Jack quickly disabused the rock press of this in no uncertain terms, but behind the scenes the Mountain machine was very much involved in what Bud Prager described as "probably was one of the most complicated deals in the history of the record business".

In *Almost Famous*, gonzo journalist Lester Bangs (played by Phillip Seymour Hoffman) tells fledgling reporter William Miller (Patrick Fugit) that 1973, the year the film is set in, is "a dangerous time for rock'n'roll" because of the ever-encroaching power of the record industry. But in fact the danger point had long since passed. The rock scene in America was changing. The British Invasion of the early 60s was followed by a British rock invasion spearheaded by Cream in 1967–68 and carried on by Led Zeppelin, Deep Purple, and Black Sabbath, with The Who and The Rolling Stones still drawing massive crowds. Now, in the 'arena rock' era, American bands like The Grateful Dead and The Allman Brothers were crowd-pleasers, but on the heavy rock scene Blue Cheer, Iron Butterfly, Grand Funk Railroad, and Black Oak Arkansas just couldn't compete.

The audiences were changing too; the late 60s crowds were dominated by middle-class students on marijuana and acid who all sat on the floor nodding to the music. For many the music and the drugs merged into a communal, transcendental, consciousness-raising experience. But as rock audiences grew, drawing in kids from right across the social spectrum, the venues got bigger. The lesson of Altamont was 'proper security', so the vibe got heavier and more menacing, fuelled by a change in drugs toward violence-inducing alcohol and downers like Mandrax (known as Quaaludes in the States). Nobody was interested in the hippie dream; a sizeable chunk of the rock audience just wanted to get smashed and see some no-nonsense good ol' rock'n'roll. So when two thirds of Mountain and one third of Cream got together, the rock moguls correctly divined they had a license to print money.

Mountain were managed by Bud Prager, who had connections to Windfall and Felix. They were distributed by CBS in the USA and signed to Island in London alongside a slew of deals with Bell Records, Ampex, GRT, and others. Leslie West had two managers of his own: Gary Kurfirst, whom Bud recalled as "a 21-year-old stoned hippie", and Shelly Finkel, "a yentl, a mother-hen, complete opposite of Gary".

Jack was signed to Polydor through RSO. As soon as West Bruce & Laing were announced, Bud got a call from David Geffen, then manager of Crosby Stills & Nash, who told him: "I don't want to be presumptuous, and don't get offended, but the West Bruce & Laing thing is going to be huge. Putting together the contracts is going to involve 20 or 30 companies. I just did CSN&Y and I'm one of the few people who has dealt with all your principals, so I'm offering my services." Bud declined.

All the management people knew what was at stake. Leslie and Corky just signed what they were told to but Jack, being naturally suspicious of anybody connected to the rock business, put up some resistance. "There were a load of people who I didn't know or like," he recalls. "I remember having a meeting with Bud Prager and these other people and them wanting me to sign something that gave this guy a percentage of the tour. And I said 'no'. So they forcibly kept me in this room until I agreed to sign it."

With the flurry of paperwork out of the way, a 30-date tour of the USA was set up. There was no single, no album, and when the band played at Carnegie Hall on April 24 – with the tour virtually over – they still didn't have a record deal. Not that it seemed to matter, as the six-week tour had sold out in four days. Geffen was right: the band was huge, and now, when it came to negotiations with record companies, Bud Prager was in the driving seat. "There were only two companies for us to consider," he recalled. "There was Atlantic with RSO – getting West Bruce & Laing was huge for Stigwood. The other was CBS and Clive Davis."

In his book *Inside The Record Business*, Clive Davis confirms that the battle to sign the band "showed record-industry competition at its fiercest". "Clive and I met and decided that WBL was going to be his Led Zeppelin," Bud recalled, noting he had also decided that Robert Stigwood was "a very bright, clever, attractive man who was also just the worst person to do business with". As far as Bud was concerned he had already been screwed every which way by RSO over the royalties owed to Windfall for producing Cream, so he didn't want Stigwood controlling the destiny of WBL.

Clive Davis had spoken to Stigwood, who said he knew Bud wanted them on CBS, and he wasn't going to stand in the way so long as certain foreign deals were sorted out. Bud knew anyway; he had to come to some accommodation with Stigwood because he was Jack's manager, and because RSO had a distribution deal with Atlantic. "Stigwood and Ahmet Ertegun were joined at the hip," Bud said. So he agreed to meet with Stigwood in New York. What he didn't know was that Stigwood was planning a deal with Atlantic for a new subsidiary label for The Bee Gees and WBL. To help that process along, Ahmet Ertegun offered WBL a trip to Las Vegas on a Warner Brothers company plane to meet Elvis Presley. He also rented the band the entire penthouse floor at Caesar's Palace – and flew them back again.

Bud got a handshake from Clive Davis but knew he had to deal with Stigwood first – which is where the mind games began. Stigwood called Bud to say that he couldn't come to New York because he was recovering from a trip to Australia; could Bud come to London instead? Bud flew to London, but on the morning of the meeting got a call to reschedule for the afternoon ... then another call to move it to the following morning ... and then to the next day. He eventually met Stigwood at his mansion in Stanmore, North London.

"We sit down by the fireplace, dog sleeping between us," Bud recalled. "Stigwood says, 'Well, I suppose we have to resolve this?'

"'Yes.'

"'This is what I'm prepared to offer you. I'll give you the management of Eric Clapton.'

"'That's interesting – but he's a recluse. On heroin.'"

Instead of the usual conversation about advances and royalties, the meeting had turned into a series of offers to Bud personally to let WBL record for RSO. This wasn't what Bud had expected. Eventually he said: "Look, give me a million dollars and they're on RSO. Otherwise they're on CBS."

"They're on CBS," Stigwood replied. And that's what happened. West Bruce & Laing signed to CBS for an estimated one million dollars (about five million dollars today). So where was the band in all this? Jack remembers attending a ceremony for the presentation of a cheque for the first part of the advance. "It was one of those photos where they present you with a big cheque and I was feeling pretty good about it," he says. "Then someone who worked for Stigwood said, 'I'll have that.' And I never saw it again."

What WBL needed to do was get into a studio and record their first album. But unlike Mountain, the band had no leader. "The best rock'n'roll bands are not democracies," says Corky Laing. "Somebody has to be in charge." When it came to recording, he continues, "Leslie was not a big fan of studios. He just wanted to get in and out, whereas Jack relished going in and doing 150 voices as a choir. When you are a gut player like Leslie, the last thing you want to do is go over things again and again. Jack was comfortable in all the areas he'd been involved in; Leslie was only comfortable in hard-rock."

In Andy Johns the band had a producer who had been sharp and together during the making of *Songs For A Tailor*, but who since then had spent rather too much time in the company of The Rolling Stones and Led Zeppelin, with inevitable consequences. "I thought I needed some speed to get the album done, to mix the album quickly," he recalls. "Leslie hooked me up with this doctor who gave me these time-release speed capsules – I'm taking these things like candy and there's another guy bringing in a sack full of big rocks of coke into the studio; Jack and I are crawling after this guy like Hansel and Gretel as he's dropping lumps of coke out of this sack."

Andy was also a heroin user, and on one occasion fell asleep on his arm, causing nerve damage. Several days passed before he could work again, by which time he was on his own in the studio trying to finish the record. As Leslie West would later remark, archly: "The only tracks Andy Johns put down were in his arms."

While working on the album Jack stayed in a large New York apartment with Andy and his wife Paula, the younger sister of Patti Boyd. On the night they arrived Paula – who was also pretty strung out – dumped a plate of beans in Jack's lap, all over his black velvet suit with lace cuffs. The poor woman charged with cooking and looking after the place was from Poland and in her sixties; she spoke eight languages and had spent 40 years in Sub-Saharan Africa as a missionary. When she asked them what they wanted to eat, Andy recalls, "We told her roast beef, sprouts, mashed potatoes, and gravy, but were too out of it to ask for variations, so we had this every day for weeks."

In that time the band managed to come up with a few decent hard-rock songs for their first album, including the title track, 'Why Dontcha', and 'The Doctor'. There's also a stone classic from Jack and Pete, 'Out Into The Fields', which both regard as highly as 'Theme For An Imaginary Western', and which would later reappear, more appropriately, on Jack's 2001 solo album *Shadows In The Air*; and 'Pollution Woman', another strong Bruce-Brown composition that wouldn't have sounded out of place on a Cream album.

With Cream you could put 'Politician' or 'White Room' on the same album as 'As You Said' or 'Passing The Time' because the whole thing was properly structured and organised. There was a similar sense of cohesion about the first two Mountain albums, but *Why Dontcha* sounds like a ragbag of tracks thrown together. The band was so powerful, and had such a strong track record, that nobody interfered with the music – they were just left to get on with it. But given the antics in the studio, what else could be expected?

Bud Prager was tasked with taking the album to Clive Davis, who was waiting to hear the first recording from the band set to blow Led Zeppelin off the planet. "We went into a private office," he recalled. "[Clive] put it on, sat back, and I was supposed to be on a high like a manager rarely is. And I was sitting there – I did a transference, so I was not listening through my ears, but his. What I listened to was so bad I was in shock. I thought, 'Oh, please let him love it and not hear it the way I heard it.' But it was transparent and when he said, 'Well, they've done the album and we'll do the best we can with it' ... [I knew] it wasn't gonna happen."

Davis did take the trouble to phone Bud and tell him what he wanted as the single. The band refused and nominated a different track. When Davis got the call back from Bud, he could not have cared less – "whatever they want," he said, confirming that CBS, despite their massive investment, were not going to get behind the band (which itself is perhaps indicative of just how much money was floating around the industry in those days).

Clive Davis might not have got his 'Stairway To Heaven' but there was still plenty of money to be made out on the road. WBL embarked on two long tours of the USA in 1972, starting off in March at the Foster Auditorium at Tuscaloosa, Alabama. Road-managing once again was Bob Adcock; in the back of the car were Jack, Corky, and Leslie, all with big hair and packing ten sorts of drugs.

"We were driving near Birmingham, Alabama, and I think Bob was speeding a little bit," Jack recalls. "So we get pulled over by a cop. Me, Leslie, and Corky stayed in the car, just looking straight ahead. The cop stopped behind and Bob got out – which you aren't supposed to do. He walked away toward the cop to keep him away because of the drugs. Then he turns on the Liverpool accent: 'Y'right lad, how ya doing?' We can hear vague talking and then Bob comes back and we drive off. 'What was that all about?' Well, the cop said, 'If it wasn't for the three little ol' ladies in the back. I would have booked you.'"

WBL were a jam band; they spent little time in the studio and even less in rehearsals, so the main focus of their attention offstage was drugs. Bob was not impressed. "With that band, music was of no interest," he says. "I spent a lot of time with the band, on tour, in planes, in cars. Music was never an issue. It was something they had to do when they got there to get it out of the way. The whole thing revolved around scoring."

"We'd do mad things," says Jack, "like rent planes and fly to Montreal or Toronto and back in the dead of night and hope we didn't get busted. Or we'd fly in 'Balloon Man' – this famous guy who we'd get smack from. He had it in balloons and you can imagine where he kept them.

"We'd do those flights in rickety old planes like in *Almost Famous* that you wouldn't want to go in even if it was parked on the ground. We would take off whether it was foggy, snow, when everything else was grounded, whatever, to get to the gig. And I would sometimes fly the plane. If we weren't going so far we would go in a helicopter from a helipad in New York. The pilot was a Vietnam vet and completely mad, totally shell-shocked. We'd play some college and Bob Adcock would go ahead and arrange cars on the football field so we knew where to land. But quite often we'd get lost; and we were all out of our brains including the pilot. So we would actually go down and look at the road signs on the freeway, and all these motorists would go 'Arrggh!'"

Leslie and Jack on the road together were hard going; the dope wasn't enough to bind them. Leslie West was 300 pounds of uncultured New York chutzpah who gorged on doughnuts and burgers. "Jack didn't appreciate some of Leslie's attitude," Corky recalls. "Leslie was a bit intimidated by Jack's aloofness – and Jack could be a bad drunk, facetious and belligerent. Leslie has been through every drug there is, but didn't drink. Leslie had a problem with Jack when he drank and Jack would drink when he wasn't getting stoned."

From Jack's perspective, "Leslie was difficult to travel with. Most rockers are downmarket people; they don't read very much, their politics are quite right wing. Mostly they want to stand on a stage, make a big noise, be rich, and have lots of sex and drugs. You don't need to be Einstein to do that, but Weinstein was a different matter. Leslie was deliberately obnoxious on the road. He was huge – we would travel first class and he would take up two seats; he'd fart and belch and annoy everyone – in those days Leslie was pretty hard to take. Leslie never ate anything in public. He had such a bad eating disorder that eating was something I never really saw him do. He'd have a roadie simply to keep his secret food supply topped up. He also had some problems with the Mafia. He'd run up this huge limo bill. They wanted paying, but he couldn't pay, so the story goes that they made him work in a candy store to pay it off."

Even so, being as accomplished as they were – and with audiences just happy to see them together in the flesh – Leslie and Jack were able to keep it happening on stage time and again. Having sat behind Felix and Leslie in Mountain, Corky was in a good position to compare the two bands. "Jack's voice was like gospel," he says. "He sang from the heart, just screamed it out, sparks and fire. Felix was more lethargic and soothing, more ethereal, less of a chant. And there was a symbiotic relationship between Leslie and Jack; Leslie was not a fast, 'look at me' guitarist, he was a melodic player, and with Jack playing percussive bass behind it meant WBL was driven by the gut – erratic, a lot of fun, but difficult to keep up. Mountain was very consistent; with WBL you never knew what was going to happen. There would be a basic set, then Jack would go somewhere or Leslie would go somewhere else and I'd just try and keep up. Jack had more rhythm in one finger than most drummers have. I'd never seen anybody like that. Actually, Jack and Leslie didn't need a drummer. I happened to be there and had a lot of fun. My part in the band reflected that. Jack was very intense, Leslie looking down, pulling out the lyrical line. I could have left the stage, taken a dump, come back, had a beer – nobody would have missed me because the band was cooking. In Mountain, I had more of a function; there were parts I had to play. Felix was the dictator. In WBL we were on our own – and that was a problem. Jack had some visions, but he didn't have the patience to deal with Leslie. Jack was so on top of everything; Leslie was slower. WBL on stage was much more freeform than Mountain. When Jack stepped onto the stage he was *on*."

As a live band, WBL were savage, animalistic, and carnal; stripped of subtlety and nuance; raw and unforgiving. When it came to reviewing the live shows, most critics were equally unforgiving, as typified by a review of the band's April gig at the Hollywood Palladium in which the band was accused of being "loud, distorted, unpleasant" and "bor[ing] your dedicated Hollywood correspondent into acute alcoholism". The release of *Live Cream Volume II* shortly after the tour ended simply underlined for many that the band sometimes dubbed 'Why Bother Lads' were chasing the coattails of past glory.

West Bruce & Laing did receive some praise from an unexpected source: Lillian Roxon, one of the first mainstream journalists to take rock music seriously. Reporting on one of two sold-out shows at New York's Carnegie Hall, she wrote that heavy music was not usually her thing and that she had arrived at the gig with a bad headache; nonetheless Jack managed to make

Leslie sound so good that "the louder and coarser it got, the better it sounded". What started out as a rough, tough-looking audience was literally seduced into good vibes by the thick sound that enveloped the whole auditorium, she wrote, adding that while WBL were no Cream, the balance of power and texture in the band might help earn heavy music some newfound respect. She also warned against going to see WBL on a nostalgia trip – at least until the encore of 'Sunshine Of Your Love', "which gets a 17-minute standing ovation with balloons and streamers".

By the time they got to Radio City Music Hall on November 6, WBL were one of the biggest bands on the circuit; tickets for the 6,000-seater venue sold out in four hours. Realising he should have booked somewhere much bigger, promoter Ron Deisner was tearing his hair out, telling a reporter: "I think when I suggested them to the Music Hall, they thought because of the name [that] they were getting something like Crosby Stills & Nash. They weren't expecting the crowd they got out there. Those kids could really wreck the place."

Considering they were kept waiting until midnight, it's a miracle that the audience left the Hall intact. The reason for the delay was a reception thrown by Clive Davis on the 65th floor of the Rockefeller Plaza. It was a night out for the heavyweights of the rock business: America's most important promoter, Frank Barsalona, was there, and so were Dee Anthony, who managed Emerson Lake & Palmer; Johnny Winter's manager Steve Paul; and Nat Weiss, whose clients included James Taylor and John McLaughlin. All the sharks were circling each other, pumping hands, talking loudly, or brooding ostentatiously, too cool and important to talk to anybody. Leslie West spent the evening making guerrilla raids on the pastry table while being chased around by journalists and giving monosyllabic answers; Jack made an appearance at the head of the stairs to yell 'get fucked!' at the top of his voice. A business veteran moaned in a corner to anybody who'd listen: "Did you see what's standing in that line? Animals. I hate them. They've ruined the world. Rock used to be an elitist art form at one time and look what it's come to."

When the witching hour arrived the band rose out of the huge Radio City orchestra pit as geysers of smoke shot into the air through coloured stage lights and 6,000 people moaned with delight. The crowd went berserk, but for *Melody Maker*'s Michael Watts every step was an attempt to recreate Cream; when Jack got into 'Train Time' about halfway through the set, "the audience let out a howl that contained something other than affection and recognition; a sort of homesickness. And when the band encored with 'Sunshine Of Your Love' – albeit a draggy, vocally mediocre version – they lit up as if bulbs had been switched on in their mouths … It was depressing to see Bruce, after all his marvellous experimentation with Lifetime and his work with John Marshall, reduced to picking amongst the rubble of Cream."

If things were bad in the States they got a whole lot worse in Europe, as the band swirled around the plughole of addiction. Corky looks back on what was "a very, very dark time. New York meant coke, England meant heroin, because that's where the best quality was. I had this Hayman drumkit made that was going to be shipped back to the States. This heroin connection of Jack's said that her business connections would pay me $250,000 if they could put heroin in the drums. They were all metal so nobody would have noticed the extra weight. My wife chased her away with a knife and Jack and Andy went mad."

The European tour kicked off at the beginning of 1973; by then Bob Adcock had already decided that once the tour was done he would stop working with Jack. He didn't have a problem with Jack as a person but couldn't stand all the drug shenanigans and was especially pissed off with Leslie. "It really wasn't much fun," he says. "Nonstop aggravation. There's nothing worse than working with a band that thinks it knows it all when it doesn't. When you do a lot of gigs around the New York area, it's much better to stay in a hotel, base yourself there, and travel there and back to the gigs. We did that on charter planes out of Teterboro Airport, outside New Jersey. We were driving over the bridge out of New York on the way to the airport. And the weather was really terrible, really big thunderstorm. Leslie was off on one of his moods:

"'Has this plane got radar?'

"'It's a Beechcraft. We'll be lucky if it's got a propeller.'

"'Well, we may as well turn round now.'

"At that point I didn't give a shit whether the band did the gig or not. I could fly a plane and here's this fat musician with burgers hanging out of his mouth arguing with me about planes. Either shut up or talk about music. You're musicians: talk music!

"I did have respect for Jack's early bands," Bob continues. "Tony Williams, Larry Coryell – fabulous. And Jack was fabulous as well. But when you are talking about WBL, you are talking about gutter people. You are in a car, making sure they get to a gig, so they can earn a fortune, and they're not the slightest bit interested in being musicians. It is very de-motivating and I don't think Jack enjoyed it much either. Bands would have given their right arm for a tenth of their success – selling out 20,000-seater venues. And I thought the music was crap as well."

Although the band were set up for heroin in Britain, trying to smuggle drugs across European borders – where the very appearance of the band would draw police and customs like moths to a flame – was very risky. As long as they had supplies, they could get through the gigs; the mood would be reasonably stable and nobody would notice. But there were times when it just didn't work. Jack remembers playing "this beautiful theatre in Paris, but it was a terrible gig, because all three of us were in a lot of physical pain. We had this guy fly some supplies in." They were so sick that they could only play a short set; the crowd duly rioted, throwing chairs from the balcony.

There was another riot, naturally enough, in Italy. There had been some trouble with a previous band at the Palazzo Dello Sport in Rome so the military were out in force to prevent it happening again. The fact that they were all lined up with guns over their shoulders in front of the stage was provocative enough. Jack shouted at them from the stage and refused to do an encore, only to be told by the promoter that their safety couldn't be guaranteed if they left. The band played and fled, but when they got back to the car, all the tyres had been blown out. Corky says now that many of the European venues the band played were just not right for hard-rock. At the Circus Krone Halle in Munich "there were fuckin' lions in cages behind me. I reckoned they would let them out if they didn't like us."

WBL played two nights in London on April 20 and 21, the first of which wasn't too bad. "It was a tremendous gig," Jack says, "very exciting, the audience stormed the stage – more exciting than any Cream gig from an audience-reaction point of view. They just went bananas. I was very excited by this. Stigwood came on stage in his Savile Row suit and handed me a bottle of Dom Perignon wrapped in tin foil. I waved it about and then just threw it and as it flew, I thought, 'Oh no, I'm going to kill somebody.' I regretted it immediately. It went right to the back somewhere and smashed. Minutes later I'm back in the dressing room and Bud Prager came in with blood running down his face. 'That bottle. It got me.' It could have been some kid and I would never have forgiven myself." (Corky remembers another gift from Stigwood – a jar of caviar – ending up smashed against the dressing room wall.)

The second night was dreadful, however. Leslie started kicking the amps around and booted the mic stands into the front row; Jack spent most of the evening walking round and round in ever-decreasing circles, which he puts down to both the illicit heroin and "certain doctors who would shoot you up before a gig with whatever you want".

The band played four more gigs in England before starting work on that difficult second album – or in this case the impossible second album – with Andy Johns at Olympic. But there were some moments of black humour. One day Andy went over to where Jack was staying at a Holiday Inn because he knew Jack had been able to score some heroin. "He'd ordered some breakfast and I'm divvying this stuff up on a tape box," he recalls. "The door flies open and there's the waiter. I scurried off to the bathroom, but he clocked it. Then Jack dropped a piece of hash on the floor and it went under the bed. It was one of those beds with sackcloth underneath. Jack was looking under the bed; I offer him a lighter and the bed catches fire. The alarms go off, sprinklers start sprinkling, me and him on the floor, people being evacuated. The manager's at the door, 'What's going on in there?' Jack says, 'Oh, it's a good thing we were here. Your bed caught fire and we put it out. Imagine what would have happened if we hadn't been here.'"

The atmosphere in the studio "got really nasty because of the smack", Andy says. For some reason Leslie and Jack decided they weren't going to talk to Corky any more.

Leslie: "Andy, tell Corky to go to eighth notes on the hi-hat."
Andy: "You heard, Corky, right?"
Corky: "Well, yes, but tell Leslie he's an asshole."

In the end Corky and Leslie quit the band and went back to New York to start Leslie West & The Wild West Show with Mitch Ryder. WBL didn't formally break up; they just didn't get back together again. Andy and Jack were left to finish the album in London.

"We were in the men's room at Olympic and Jack starts blaming me for everything that was going wrong," Andy recalls. "'No, no,' I said, 'It's your band.' 'Fuck You!' We went back out into the studio and Jack's playing the piano and I dropped the lid on his fingers – not hard, but it must have hurt. The next thing I know I'm sitting at the mixing desk and there's this bottle of wine being poured over my head, which was fair enough."

Whatever Turns You On contains some serviceable rock songs and a couple of very good tracks: the stately 'November Song', which showcases some tasteful guitar from Leslie and 'Folk Song'-like touches from Jack; and 'Like A Plate', with its layers of vocal harmonies. 'Plate' came about after Jack was approached by one of The Plaster Casters, who ask Jack if he would "like a plate" after hearing that it meant a blowjob in English slang. "Andy Johns and

I had a big pile of plates that we wanted to record being pushed over and smashed," Jack recalls, "but we couldn't catch it in time so we kept sending out for more plates until Olympic was covered in bits of broken plates."

Andy winces at the thought of the "terrible evening when they were trying to do the cover for *Whatever Turns You On* – it was supposed to be a food fight. Leslie liked his cheeseburgers; he used to lie on his side in opium-smoking position. Jack and I turned him on his back, so he couldn't get up. We did have a food fight, and it ended up with this awful cartoon cover." The album limped out in July 1973, followed a year later by a forgettable live album taken mostly from an April '72 concert at the Aquarius Theatre in Boston – and that was it.

Bud Prager believed that "whatever they sold was absurd compared to what they could have sold. How big they were was absurd compared to how big they could have been. They were set up to be the biggest band in the world – the power, the money, the promotion was all there, waiting for the product. It was all undone by the music; they completely blew it."

Why Dontcha got to Number 26 on *Billboard* and stayed on the chart for 20 weeks; the second album barely scraped into the Top 100. In his memoir, Clive Davis wrote that although WBL were not as big as they could have been they "had important sales and chart albums … and Columbia certainly didn't lose any money". Given the amounts involved he probably had to make it sound like the whole thing wasn't a total car wreck. But if the music was undone by the drugs, what happened to the money?

Who better to ask than Bud? Did Jack, Leslie, and Corky get their just desserts in terms of the money? "Good question," Bud replied. "Probably no. They must have got something because cheques were exchanged. But they never got what they thought they would get." Corky remembers asking Bud directly: "Why did you burn me for all that money? You know you did" – to which Bud replied: "Yes, I know I did." But because WBL's songs were published by Windfall, Corky says, Felix Pappalardi probably earned more from the band than anyone else did.

Corky describes WBL as a "beast" – something they were able to hide inside as it rolled around the world. But while critics had few kind words about the concerts, opinion was very much divided about the recorded output. At one extreme, the band were deemed responsible "for some of the most nauseous music ever committed to plastic", but in the UK most reviews were very positive: there was a sense that British rock journalists were almost willing these albums to be good and trying to encourage people to go out and buy them. You honestly wonder if everybody was listening to the same music.

The controversy has continued among Jack's fans over the years. There are those for whom WBL were just a business-driven horror-show of mindless noise geared toward those who had only recently learnt to walk upright, made all the more gross and mystifying by the talent of the two main players. Yet there was also a generation of hard-rock fans who missed Cream and Mountain and who instead got their first fix of power-rock-blues headbanging with WBL. A scan through the comments left by Amazon customers reveals a revisionist view: that while they didn't work as a proper band, individually Leslie West and Jack Bruce were both at the top of their game. West Bruce & Laing epitomise either the best or the worst that heavy rock could offer in the early 70s. You pay your money and you take your choice. Whatever turns you on.

into the storm

J ack had come a long way from the little boy who nibbled chocolate from his dad's grocery van, sang at family socials, studiously learnt to play cello, and then as a teenager made his first tentative steps into the world of the professional musician. He was an international rock star: adored by fans, revered by critics, and moreover widely acknowledged by his peers as the best bass player in the world, with a voice and songwriting ability most musicians could only dream about. Yet by the time he turned 30 in May 1973 he'd been addicted to heroin for nearly two years.

"There was a romanticism about it," he says. "All the jazz musicians I idolised were almost without exception heroin users; even Mingus dabbled. I thought there must be something in it. It's buying into an idealistic lifestyle – being part of an elite, the outsider, deliberately cutting yourself off from society. I was fascinated by drugs before I'd even seen a drug and as soon as I could, I tried them."

Bebop was music of social and cultural isolation, born from a sense of outrage and frustration among a new generation of black musicians in the early 40s. They refused to play 'Uncle Tom' in white dance band orchestras and found themselves with no work during the Depression. The music they developed was angry and deliberately difficult, and the musicians who pioneered it – Charlie Parker, Dizzy Gillespie, Miles Davis, and Thelonious

Monk – adopted an arrogant stance. They were unapproachable and inward-looking, and turned their backs on a straight and blatantly racist white society. The barriers they threw up between themselves and the rest of the world created a romantic, tantalising image: the world-weary Gothic shadow, the Wandering Jew with a saxophone. Central to the creation of this tragic hero and the whole process of cultural isolation was an overpowering need to alter the distasteful reality of everyday consciousness. And like Zeus striding the pantheon of jazz gods, with all eyes turned to him, was Charlie Parker, whose shield against the outside world was heroin.

After the end of the Second World War, the Mafia resumed supplies of heroin into the USA through what became known as 'The French Connection' via Turkey and Marseille. The black districts of America's major cities were soon awash with the drug. There's a scene in *The Godfather* where the Dons of the five families meet to discuss the drug trade. Vito Corleone opposes the trade on moral grounds, but the Kansas City boss says they should sell only to "the dark people" because "they're animals anyway; let them lose their souls".

For those musicians who became hooked, the process of dependence was much more than the simple physical sensations of being stoned. Heroin served the symbolic, functional, psychological, and cultural needs of the cool, aloof, hipster jazz musician who could insulate himself still further from the world. There was an extra dimension for the black musicians – simply trying to operate in a world where you were a second-class citizen, whether in law or through tradition, and where a policemen or a Federal Narcotics Agent was just waiting for the chance to bust you. However famous you were, if you couldn't work in New York you were nobody. And to work in New York you had to have a cabaret card; if you got busted, the police took the card away, and it was down to largesse or bribes to get it back. The career of Thelonious Monk was one of many crippled for years because of this corrupt system.

But if for black musicians heroin symbolised the flight *away* from white society, for white musicians it symbolised the flight *toward* black society. They became, in Norman Mailer's words, 'White Negroes'. Their self-conscious aim was to "live with death as an immediate danger, to divorce oneself from society, to exist without roots, to set out on that unchartered journey into the rebellious imperatives of the self". Which is a pretty fair description of the heroin experience, and a good part of the reason why many of the biggest names among white jazz musicians – Chet Baker, Gerry Mulligan, Bill Evans, Art Pepper – all acquired heroin habits to match their reputations, alongside some of Jack's more direct influences, including Scott LaFaro and Charlie Haden.

Jack's introduction to drugs in the early 60s was typical of the times. Few ordinary people were aware of London's burgeoning drug culture. The bohemian literati and jazz community got their cannabis from dealers in Notting Hill and Brixton – and strong stuff it was, too. "There was Rangoon Red – the whole plant in newspaper – Congo Matadi, and kif, which you smoked in a pipe," Jack recalls. "And we'd do it deliberately. When I was with Graham, you'd ask a policeman for directions, wind down the window and they'd be this fug of pot smoke: 'Can you tell me where the Floral Hall is, officer?' Ironically Dick, who never touched any drug stronger than alcohol or tobacco, got banned from the Café Des Artistes for smoking herbal cigarettes."

Amphetamines weren't even regarded as 'drugs', in that loaded sense of the term, because they were legal, prescribed in their millions to depressed and overweight housewives. The young rock'n'rollers out on the package tours swallowed them like sweeties to stay awake. Possession of amphetamines was not made a criminal offence in the UK until 1964, following exposés in the tabloid press about drug use among young people on the London club scene and Mods and Rockers whacking each other senseless with deck chairs on Margate beach, eyes pinned and nerves jangling to the beat of speed.

The paradox of drug use in Britain was that while smoking cannabis was totally illegal, injecting heroin was not. In America it was a criminal offence simply to be a heroin user; track marks on your arms were enough to get you arrested, while the increasingly draconian laws of the 50s saw musicians sent to prison for years just for possessing small amounts of cannabis. It was very different in Britain. In the 20s a committee of doctors decided that as a last resort it was legitimate medical practice for a doctor to prescribe heroin or cocaine to a person in support of their habit. At the time, and for the next 40 years, there were very few heroin users around: most were middle-class, middle-aged women; some were doctors. It was actually a measure of 'first resort' because there was no treatment system, but it didn't matter; this handful of respectable people using morphine and heroin behind net curtains hardly posed a threat to society.

When Jack met up with Ginger, he found himself looking in on the secretive world of the heroin-ravaged jazz musician. Ginger had been a registered user since 1960. This didn't confer any special privileges like free heroin, it simply meant that your details were logged by the Home Office so they could keep track of the problem and check if you were getting prescriptions from more than one doctor. Ginger had been introduced to the drug by another jazz drummer, Dicky Devere, who had no compunction about turning other people on (unlike Ginger and Jack, who never did). Graham Bond's road manager Pete Bailey had a very straightforward view of Dicky: "What a bastard; what an evil little bastard."

Liz Baker remembers being at Dicky's place in the summer of 1960. "They went into the loo, Ginger came out and threw up," she says. "I had no idea what they were doing." Ginger had periods on and off heroin – and when he came off, he'd do it by himself. "It just became the backdrop to our lives," Liz says. Ginger's on-off relationship with heroin goes at least part of the way toward explaining his generally irascible nature. "Ginger had a tremendous ability to stop," says Jack, "but he was so grumpy when he was withdrawing. He would have a pint of Guinness with a triple vodka in it. That was his heroin substitute. Everyone has their own way of dealing with it. I got very close to Phil [Seaman] at one point, maybe closer than Ginger because he was married. I used to spend time with Phil, help him get a hit because he had no veins left. I was very curious to try it, but Ginger wouldn't let me and actually said he would kill me if I did, although I did persuade him to get me a gram of coke for my 21st birthday."

Until 1968 any doctor could prescribe heroin and cocaine; the only black market was in drugs over-supplied by doctors. Lady Isobel Frankau was the Florence Nightingale of heroin doctors; in 1962 alone she prescribed six kilos of heroin in tablet form. She would often write out prescriptions from the back of her Bentley. Ginger was one of her patients, and so too were American jazz musicians like Dexter Gordon and Chet Baker who would land in the UK en route to Europe to pick up supplies from Lady Isobel and a few other elderly doctors.

The law was changed because of the perceived cavalier prescribing practices of Frankau and John Petro, who took on Lady Isobel's patients after she died in 1967. From 1968 doctors had to apply for a special licence to prescribe heroin and cocaine to addicts. Most National Health doctors were only too happy to be able to turn drug users away and most of those licences were reserved for consultant psychiatrists working in the newly opened drug clinics. However, several private doctors obtained licences and carried on what was for them a very lucrative trade in supplying drugs to the rich and famous.

By 1968 the media was bursting with fake outrage about the hordes of students and hippies having sex while stoned on cannabis and LSD. As the Pied Pipers Of Doom, the new pop aristocracy were firmly in the crosshairs of an Establishment that was one part vengeful, one part jealous. What to do? It wasn't against the law to be a wealthy, young, long-haired pop star with a woman hanging off each limb, but drugs were another matter entirely. If you were going to write "So many fantastic colours / I feel in a wonderland / Many fantastic colours / Makes me feel so good / You've got that pure feel / Such good responses / Got that rainbow feel / But the rainbow has a beard" ('SWLABR') ... you might as well also write to the drug squad: "I'm using hallucinogenic drugs; please come and arrest me."

Donovan was among the first 'pop' stars to be busted in London, then a Rolling Stone whenever it was a slow day down at West End Central police station; and then there was John Lennon, where the police phoned the press first before they kicked the door in. One London policeman in particular, Sergeant Norman Pilcher, was on a mission to take musicians down a peg or two. He once famously broke into Eric's place in Chelsea, shouting "Where's Eric Clapton? Where's Eric Clapton?" – only to find that Eric had been tipped off (apparently by Ginger) and fled moments before. John Lennon immortalised Pilcher in 'I Am The Walrus' as "semolina pilchard".

These arrests were usually for small amounts of cannabis, resulting in an equally small fine, but it still counted as a drug conviction. The implications for a high-profile musician were enormous because a conviction meant you couldn't tour in the USA or Japan. By some miracle neither Jack nor Eric were ever caught with drugs in the UK, while Ginger was fireproof (at least when it came to heroin) because it was on prescription. And despite the clothes, the songs, and the times, Cream were not a heavyweight drug band. They smoked a lot of dope, but Jack had only had a few acid trips with Janet and Eric hardly even smoked cigarettes or drank much. Only Ginger had a serious habit and, apart from the odd incident, he kept that pretty much under control.

As the 60s drew to a close, however, an old favourite made a re-appearance in Hollywood. Cocaine had been a legitimate medicine: it was used as an anaesthetic and for various respiratory ailments up to end of the First World War but was then banned under international drug law before becoming notorious in the 20s among the first wave of Hollywood movie stars. Eventually the American factories producing cocaine from Peruvian coca leaves shut down and the stimulant drug of choice for medical and street use became the recently invented amphetamine.

By the 50s the coca farmers were having to look for a new outlet for their crops. Enter the Mafia once again. They had turned Cuba under Batista into a rich man's playground and now wanted to get into cocaine production, knowing they could sell it for a fortune to the high rollers for whom Cuba was a paradise of gambling and sex. The Mafia did deals with the growers and with

Colombian and Mexican gangsters to get the drug to Cuba. When Castro threw them all out in 1959, anti-Castro Cuban exiles began smuggling the drug into the USA – with the CIA looking the other way – where it found favour among the new generation of Hollywood film stars and their wealthy mates in the rock business.

Cocaine quickly spread through the rock hierarchy and became the ultimate status symbol. It was reassuringly expensive, pure, white, and sparkly, with no needles required. It came with its own designer accessory kit: silver mirror, razor blades, vials; you snorted it with $100 bills and felt like a million dollars for about 20 minutes. Then you needed some more, and then some more, and then some more. But hey, that's OK, I'm loaded, it's not addictive; what's the problem?

Because the effects of long-term coke use mirrored the nature of a business that thrived on the paranoia of fragile egos and being more aggressive and obnoxious than the next guy, nobody noticed that down the line somewhere there might be a problem with this drug. One of the problems was that some people were so completely wired, jittery, and jagged on coke that they needed something equally powerful to take them down the other side. Moving from sniffing one white powder to another was no step at all. Jack had been using coke quite heavily, shortening his fuse still further. "There was quite a lot of it around," Janet recalls of a trip to New York in early 1970. "I remember being offered it, but I was pregnant with Malcolm and was shocked to be offered cocaine."

There are many roads into addiction, and no doubt for the 60s generation of musicians the 'Charlie Parker death wish' was a powerful tug. Always an avid reader, Jack came across Evan Hunter's 1956 novel *Second Ending*, which tells the story of Andy Silvera, a young and highly talented trumpet player who succumbs to heroin. The book is the archetypal story of the white jazz guy who goes down the heroin trail, and certainly underscored Jack's belief in the romance of heroin. But the story is more complex than just the emulation of heroes; in fact, at no point in the story is there a reference to any big jazz artist, even though the plight of Charlie Parker, who died a year before the book was published, would have been well known.

Considering the potentially devastating outcomes, the genesis of heroin addiction can be almost banal. In *Second Ending*, the young Andy joins a band of much older guys. He is socially awkward and desperate to be part of their clique, but none of them are drug users. Andy's problems begin after the War but he has no real explanation of why. His career had moved up a gear, he was well dressed, and the woman of his dreams was now his girlfriend. "I didn't seem to need anything you know?" he says later in the book. "I had everything I could ever want I suppose?"

William Burroughs agreed. In 1953 he wrote: "You become a narcotics addict because you do not have strong motivations in any other direction. Junk wins by default. I tried it as a matter of curiosity. I drifted along taking shots when I could score. I ended up hooked. Most addicts I have talked to report a similar experience. You don't decide to be an addict. One morning you wake up sick and you are an addict." But that is too easy a rationalisation. If underneath you have anxieties and insecurities, or are prone to depression; if you are trying to bridge the gap between frustration and ambition; if your skin is wafer thin, life is too big, too small, or too painful and you need to escape, then some people look for the Big Something to ease the pain. It could be alcohol, chocolate, sex, work, or drugs.

"There are people like me, where as soon as you take it you like it – it's like you are complete, an instant feeling of completion," Jack says. "It's like there's a part of your personality and your physical being which has always been missing. You take it and there you are – complete. And that is obviously dangerous. I would say I was addicted from the very first time I tried it – mentally, not physically, of course. When I was an adolescent, I became quite religious for about six months. I was looking for something to complete myself. And I never found it until I found heroin.

"I have always been conscious of mental problems. I was always a bit of a lunatic from when I was a child. Was I schizophrenic? Was I bi-polar? Yes, you could say all those things about me. I don't need a diagnosis, but I've always had problems. I can remember as a child being extremely happy and overjoyed or being very down. During Cream, when that whole amazing thing was happening, it was like I wasn't really there. I was looking over my own shoulder at what was happening. I wasn't in the moment. Sometimes I was painfully shy, I would not be able to speak to people very well. When I was reading about Heath Ledger, I could see a lot of myself at that age – very, very similar – sensitive, but not in a good way, in a painful way. It was very difficult to get on stage and do those things. To have that self-belief was a big struggle for me.

"If I'm honest that's why I never tried heroin, because I knew if I did, I would like it too much. I think I was scared of it because I'd seen the effect on people like Phil Seaman and others who were around in the early 60s, poor guys who were ravaged by it. But it was more that I thought I would like it, so I stayed away from it until that fateful night at the Inter-Continental Hotel in Park Lane.

"To me heroin was like being with someone you love, very close, in front of a big roaring fire. But it doesn't last. The effects from that are very transitory. It's a limited honeymoon period and you think, 'I've cracked this' – and then it starts to take over literally every cell in your body."

By the time Jack started using heroin, the scene in London had moved on. The supply of legal heroin from doctors had dried up because of changes in the law, but now Chinese gangsters imported supplies from the Far East (the so-called Golden Triangle of Burma, Laos, and Thailand). Jack never registered himself as a user or tried to obtain drugs from doctors; instead the dealers were literally parked outside his house. Jack decided that the only option was to get out of London, so in September 1971 Janet found herself in a rock star's mansion in the Essex countryside.

Janet was devastated at having to leave their North London home. "It was a beautiful house," she says. "I loved that house, I put everything into it – and then Jack moved us out." Worse still, she was "plonked in the middle of the countryside – Jack drove back into London and just carried on. Malcolm was just a baby, I had Joey, my parents and friends had been close by. My life was in London." Although they had moved because dealers were stalking Jack, Janet thought that Jack was maybe only dabbling in heroin or that they were just coke dealers. She didn't really know he was addicted until 1972, when Jack rented a house in California during the first West Bruce & Laing tour.

"I brought Janet, Joey, and Malcolm over and rented a house in Belle Vue, Marin County," Jack recalls. "It was called the Organ House; this guy had built a whole house just to accommodate a full size pipe organ. It had a 16 or 32ft bass pipe. I would come back to the house at three or four in the morning and I would get to the organ and it was like *Phantom Of The Opera*. The neighbours got a petition up because they didn't want us to stay."

It was here that Janet says Jack told her about his heroin addiction. "He said, 'I give you the choice. I can cancel this tour and walk away from this situation.' But I knew [the big stadium tour] was what he had been looking for and legally he would be in serious trouble – we were literally right there with a gig the next day. So I asked him what difference it would make to the fact that he had this problem. And he said it wouldn't make much difference. And of course, I knew him inside out – there was no way I could say, 'Right, back on the plane.' It was ridiculous. And then West Bruce & Laing was just madness."

'Out Into The Fields' was in part a commentary on the flat and desolate landscape Jack had moved to out in the country, where animals were being shot by farmers and landowners, but also a reflection of his own inner landscape, empty and devoid of feeling, cold and isolated. One of those British middle-class, middle-aged addicts was the novelist Anna Kavan, a heroin user for 40 years until she died of an overdose in 1968. Her novel *Ice* was a similar metaphor for the frozen heart of the heroin-gripped soul. Her short story 'The Old Address' resonated strongly with Jack, particularly the pull of old drug haunts she inhabited in London, which for Jack too had become the most dangerous place to be.

As Charlie Parker famously said: "They can get it [heroin] out of your body, but they can't get it out of your mind." He was talking about the cravings. Actually detoxifying from heroin is not that difficult; even going cold turkey, while extremely unpleasant, is not life-threatening (unlike withdrawal from tranquilisers or alcohol). But it is only the start of the journey to recovery. If you remain in the same locale with the same connections, the chances of relapse are greatly increased. Simply walking past a place where you used to take drugs can induce an actual craving, so to that extent Jack was right to get away from London. But the underlying problems had not been resolved; the hour-and-a-half drive out of London was not far enough for Jack to cut his ties either with his connections or his new network of drug buddies.

Jack being Jack, there would be no half-measures. He was injecting heroin directly into his veins, not snorting it like Eric, Leslie West, or Corky Laing or skin-popping like Keith Richard. "It's better if you don't inject," he says, "because you don't get fixated on the whole business of getting high, which becomes an addiction in itself." It sounds strange, but despite all the chaos and misery of heroin addiction, there is a comfort for many users in the process of using – the ritual of preparing heroin for injecting; dissolving the drug in a spoon with some lemon juice; heating the spoon, tying off, injecting; then the physical sensations; then needing to score some more and beginning the process all over again. We all need rituals and habits in our lives to keep us grounded, but Jack did not have to concern himself with day-to-day realities. Janet looked after the family; Jack didn't have to fill in tax forms or go shopping, buy a TV licence, or any of that stuff. He could come and go as he pleased; out on tour, somebody else made all the arrangements.

Because of his status, all that was required of Jack was to be a creative artist. But his extreme sensitivity meant that when things were not going right for him – poor reviews, low sales, bad sound equipment, business people he didn't like, arguments with other musicians, tour hassles – and when life was just one huge dazzling light he needed to hide from, here was a way of retreating from pain using the best painkiller in the world, in the company of people who weren't that interested in JACK BRUCE – ROCK STAR. "There was a guy I used to score with called Eddie," he recalls. "He lived in Notting Hill. We used to sit in his flat and shoot up speedballs non-stop until the blood would coagulate in the syringe and you'd have to stop. Awful when I think about it."

In early 1973 Jack was invited to Morgan Studios by producer Bob Ezrin to lay down some tracks with drummer Aynsley Dunbar and a young guitarist, Steve Hunter, for what became Lou Reed's concept album *Berlin*, a happy-go-lucky tale of addiction, domestic violence, adultery, and prostitution. Jack recalls the sessions being "very basic. Lou Reed mumbling through a heroin haze; Bob Ezrin was doing a load of drugs as well. Then when I heard the finished product, it had an orchestra on it." Impressed with what he heard, Jack decided that he wanted Ezrin to produce his next solo album. He flew to Toronto and played Ezrin some new material. Unfortunately, Ezrin wasn't interested, so Jack had to think again.

Born of Jack's reflections on his desperate state of mind at the time, the new songs for what would become *Out Of The Storm* would be among the most personal of his collaborations with Pete Brown. Jack composed the music at home on his Blüthner piano; Pete thought the demos were "the best things I'd ever heard him do. In the lyrics I wrote, there is a fantastic amount of trying, keeping, hoping, and looking back. Things were really falling apart and I tried to make him sing positive things. I was trying to write things that Jack could relate to, that were going on in his life, so he totally influenced the mood of the songs. Sometimes he didn't like it when he sang things that he knew were about what was happening to him. But he sang with great conviction – art and life following each other around. I wanted to call this album *Into The Storm* because I knew there would be extremely rough weather ahead."

The word from RSO was that they wanted a commercial album. Jack had a set of songs to record, but no band. And so Andy Johns came up with a plan that admittedly took Jack a long way from London, but to just about the worse place he could go with a rock'n'roll drug habit in the mid 70s: Los Angeles.

O

Jack asked Pete to accompany him to LA. "With Jack, the music changes quite a lot as you go along, and by that time I'd become quite good at figuring out what was needed and making quick changes," Pete recalls. "So I guess he felt he could rely on me and took me with him. Some of it was written, some we were still working on. That was the first time I went to America, so that was a bit of a culture shock. We had some good times – and some strange times. It was the end of the hippie era and a lot of the hippie things were still around, funny drugs and weird people."

Andy Johns went with Jack and Pete as producer and suggested they use Jim Keltner on drums. Jack was much taken with Steve Hunter, whom he and Bob Ezrin had also heard playing with Alice Cooper in Toronto, so he too was brought in. The recording would be a re-run of *Harmony Row*: just Jack, a guitarist, and a drummer. They booked into Gary Kellgren's Record Plant in Los Angeles, one of the most prestigious and well-appointed studios on the West Coast.

Steve had been a huge Cream fan and with the trio set-up in place thought: "Great, we're gonna do another Cream record. But once I got out there and talked to Jack, I understood why he didn't want to do that. I wasn't disappointed, I just didn't know what to expect. But I learnt a huge amount about guitar playing from doing that record. Jack's construction of music was something I'd never been exposed to before as a professional musician – I was very young in the business; Jack's was only my third album. I was completely open. There were a lot of complex harmonies, and to inject a rock thing in amongst this was something I wasn't used to. It was a lot of fun. He had to tell me what the chords were – there were some I'd never heard of before. We worked together and I roughed out a chord chart, but he pretty much came up with stuff to play." Steve witnessed firsthand the instinctive rapport between Jack and Pete. "They had this incredible working relationship," he says. "Jack would say 'this line doesn't sing very well' and in five seconds Pete had fixed it. They hardly said anything to each other."

The working relationship with Jim Keltner was less productive. Andy wanted to use LA studio musicians because he expected them to work quickly and professionally, and get the basic tracks done in a week. It didn't quite work out like that. This was partly because, Andy says, he made the mistake of recommending someone who was "a wonderful drummer, but not right for Jack, who got so fed up with Keltner not being able to make the tracks while on triple rate that he fired him". (In his place Andy brought in Jim Gordon, whom Jack also played with on Frank Zappa's 1974 LP *Apostrophe*. The album, which featured Jack's growling bass on the title track, was Zappa's biggest commercial success.)

The other reason the sessions took longer than planned was drugs. For Steve Hunter, what was happening wasn't entirely obvious. "We were in Studio A, one of the big rooms, and I was expecting it to be crazy," he recalls. "I'd

177

done my drugs and didn't like them, and I couldn't drink because I'd get really sick. I smoked cigarettes and that was it. I wanted to be as good a guitar player as I could be and understand this whole recording process. I was trying to learn as much as possible. That's where my energies went."

So Steve can't have been around when Gary Kellgren, a heavy user, came into the studio one day with the new drug on the block: phencyclidine (also known as PCP or Angel Dust), a powerful anaesthetic with hallucinogenic properties. He laid out two huge lines for the band; not knowing what it was or how much to take, they all had hefty snorts of the stuff. As Pete, who was in the control booth, recalls: "They were all holding onto each other walking across the floor – Bobby Keys, Jim Keltner, Andy Johns, and Jack. Someone said, 'Don't let go of me or I'll float off into space.'"

At the end of that day's session they all went out, with Jack driving, still strung out on Angel Dust. "In theory we were taking Jim Keltner home," Jack says. "He lived in one of those funny bungalow-type Hollywood houses. There was a load of identical ones. On the way we went to a supermarket and had a shopping experience in slow motion. I remember seeing Jim crawling up this garden path. We drove away and it turned out it wasn't his house. He said we had abandoned him."

But Steve can't have missed what was going on in Studio C when Jack teamed up with John Lennon and Harry Nilsson during Lennon's 'lost' period away from Yoko. "They were so out of it," Jack recalls. "They were trying to figure out the chords to 'Stand By Me'. We left the studio at five in the morning, got back at two in the afternoon. They were still in there trying to work it out." This incident followed the recording of Mick Jagger's 'Too Many Cooks' – an all-star session featuring Lennon, Jack, Billy Preston, Jesse Ed Davis, Nilsson, Bobby Keys, and anybody else who happened to be hanging about. Jack went on several drunken binges with Lennon, Nilsson, and Ringo Starr and got thrown out of various clubs, but was less accommodating when "Mick came up to me at one point and said, "'ere Jack, got any drugs?' I told him to fuck off."

A drunken, violent, and suicidal Lennon was trying to work on *Rock 'n' Roll* with the equally demented Phil Spector while also producing Nilsson's *Pussy Cat*. Lennon and Spector were both thrown out of the studio while working on the album: Lennon for attacking guitarists Jesse Ed Davis and Danny Kortchmar, and Spector for pulling a gun on Stevie Wonder, who was down the corridor working on *Fulfillingness' First Finale*, because Wonder was using an engineer that Spector wanted.

With Stevie Wonder on the scene, Jack got to meet one of his heroes, James Jamerson. "He was looking for the Stevie Wonder session," Jack recalls. "I was recording 'Keep On Wondering', which was a tribute to Stevie. James came bursting into the control room, a bit out of his box, and I was doing a bass overdub. He took the bass out of my hands: 'That's not how it goes. It goes like this.' Then he realised it wasn't the Stevie Wonder session, but we did get to know each other quite well after that. He was an amazing guy, but not in the best of health or frame of mind. For him, being in LA was like being sent to Siberia. I was told that Tamla Motown had been taken over by the Mafia and they said they didn't want any junkies working there. They fired him basically and it finished him off."

The drug scene in Los Angeles was getting darker all the time, and the main reason was heroin. Coke still flurried around the town in blizzards. Everybody in the business seemed to be using it and offering it to somebody else – not just musicians, but accountants, DJs, promoters, lawyers, studio bosses, and record company executives. Joni Mitchell believed it had a direct impact on much of the music produced during this period by "sealing off the heart" and creating a cold, sterile, numb sound that West Coast rock people mistook for Californian sun-kissed cool.

The rise of cocaine reflected the speed at which the business had been moving since the late 60s. One minute a musician might be scuffling around Greenwich Village, the next he'd be on the cover of *Rolling Stone*. Bands were signed for huge advances and sent out on insanely long tours; ordinary kids growing up in ordinary families found themselves living in a goldfish bowl with more money than they knew what to do with, but still not able to believe they had a career that would last because everybody was telling them it wouldn't.

Heroin was a reaction on the part of musicians to slow everything down, to find a way to chill out, although they still needed coke to get on stage and be the biggest beast in the pack for 90 minutes. While coke was causing problems, nobody was actually dying from it yet. Heroin was different. LA became associated with the first spate of 70s rock deaths: Janis Joplin, Robbie McIntosh, Tim Buckley, and Danny Whitten from Crazy Horse overdosed there; the city's own lizard king Jim Morrison overdosed in Paris, while Cass Elliot died in London from a heart attack after years of intravenous drug use. When he was in LA in the late 60s, Graham Bond would go over to Cass's house and help her shoot up because she couldn't find the veins in her overweight arms. After Cass died, John Phillips got deeper into heroin.

Recalling a visit to Phillips's house in the company of Keith Richards, Corky Laing says: "We're not talking grams here or even ounces, but one or two pounds of heroin in the place."

There was no treatment yet for heroin addiction, no quick dash to celebrity rehab. You either had periods of sickness and health, like Ginger and Jack, where you found a way of cleaning yourself up so you could carry on working; or you became a recluse, like Eric Clapton; or, if you were unlucky, you died. But however prevalent the coke scene was in LA, heroin remained a world within a world. Jack, Andy Johns, and Johns's wife Paula were all heavy users, but whereas in London the dealers came looking for Jack, here he was little different to any other user on the street.

"Scoring is never easy," he says. "It doesn't matter how much money you've got. Somebody has got to score; you've got to make that connection with the person who has got the drugs. They get very popular when they don't come! They'll pretend that the drug supply has dried up in order to put the price up or make themselves more popular. It doesn't matter who you are." Jack says the only time when he didn't have to seek out dealers was in WBL, when the whole band was using. "But if you are the only one who is using then it's very difficult," he adds. "You end up either waiting for the connection or for somebody to go and score."

Amid the chaos of addiction, he was still quite careful. "I never got any infections," he says, "I never shared a syringe – I really had a thing about not doing that. I had it really organised. I had a little doctor's bag because I was really concerned about having clean needles – I didn't want to get infections. I had sterile water, lots of needles. I was very careful about that." He says he only overdosed once, "at Kit Lambert's place".

Hitting rock bottom in LA, Jack remembers "me and Paula being very sick and sending Andy out to score. Then he comes up in the elevator at the Riot House, comes in and says, 'You'll never guess what happened. I got mugged in the lift. They got all the money and all the drugs. It's all gone.' So that's what you are reduced to. When you're a junkie, it's all about waiting, waiting, waiting. And then the feeling when that guy walks in through the door – it's amazing. It's like all your ships coming in at once." Andy himself admits: "I think I fucked him over a few times, the only person I've done that to. It gets pretty naughty, things like, 'Oh, give me this money and I'll go and buy the drugs. Oh, no, I got robbed.'"

The Riot House was the nickname for the notorious Hyatt House Hotel, where British rock hooligans went crazy and simply paid for the damage. The

Who and the Stones sent TVs out of the window like falling rain while Zeppelin destroyed a whole floor with motorbikes. The idea of having your own room with walls and a door was simply an architectural affectation; you would go back to the room and find it filled with people you'd never seen before.

The Los Angeles Record Plant sessions carried on for ages – maybe as long as four or five months. The 'Too Many Cooks' session took place in December 1973, and Jack was there with his family for Christmas. Then around April or May they got kicked out, possibly for unpaid bills, and decamped to the Record Plant in Sausalito, another rock'n'roll madhouse with a jacuzzi, guesthouses, waterbed floors, laughing gas masks hanging from the ceiling, and two fake walls leading to an escape route in case of a drug bust. Sly Stone had all but taken up residence and had part of the place decorated to look like a human heart with all kinds of red, synthetic fur on the walls.

They stayed in the studio for a few weeks. Despite being very sick, Jack kept his problem well hidden from the musicians around him. Steve Hunter says Jack might arrive one day in a poor mood, but that he "took it that Jack was under a lot of pressure. This was his solo album and he had to keep it all together. I never had any trouble getting along with him – there was a nice mutual camaraderie between us. I really loved working with him, had enormous respect for him and wanted to do a good job on his record." And for all the time Jack spent alone with Pete, Pete says he never once saw Jack fixing.

O

In early May they flew back to London in time for a funeral that hit Jack very badly. Graham Bond had been suffering mental health problems for some while and spent time in a hospital in South London. He had become increasingly obsessed with magical rituals and firmly believed that dark forces were coming for him. On May 8 1974 he threw himself in front of a London Underground train. Jack was in an awful state and had to shoot up just to get himself through the ceremony.

It was a strange funeral. Graham had stipulated that he wanted no religious trappings, so everybody filed into South London Crematorium not quite knowing what would happen. Graham's wife and ex-wife were both there, so there was no real focus for mourning either – nobody quite knew who to offer condolences to (those who weren't stoned, that is). It took Jack to actually do something. He got up and started playing at the organ, and as folksinger Caroline Pegg recalls "it was the most fantastic experience – somehow it sounded like Graham, it seemed to take on Graham's life".

Afterward Jack simply retreated. Pete had to push him to finish the album. Andy Johns had taken the tapes into Olympic but was in no fit state to work on them properly, so Pete went around to Andy's flat to retrieve the tapes. As Andy remembers it, "Pete Brown showed up at my house one day. Jack had left one or two things like the top hat from *Goodbye*, which he'd given me in a fit of grandiose friendship. Pete was scurrying round my flat going, 'This is Jack's, this is Jack's' and 'I don't want you to see Jack any more. He nearly died and it's all your fault.'" (Pete says: "I had problems with Andy. He was a brilliant engineer, but he was fuckin' out of it and he was making mistakes.")

The man who saved the day, according to Jack, was Dennis Weinreich. He had a particular approach to his work. "The music business was changing," Dennis recalls, "and there was a tendency for the technology to start taking over. What I was doing was considering the essence of the music, the essence of a song, and trying to build around it. What a lot of engineers were doing was going for the perfect bass, the perfect guitar, and combining them – sometimes it will sound good and sometimes it will sound like a lot of instruments competing with one another. What I tried to do was to stack things, so the priorities were derived from the music and the song as opposed to the phonic picture" – or, as Jack puts it, "moving a cigarette packet round a snare for a month trying to get the perfect drum sound".

Dennis was known to RSO. "I'd done an album with Barbara Dickson and the cast album for *John, Paul, George, Ringo … & Bert* and everybody was happy with it. The record company were clearly concerned about getting any product from Jack. They'd said they'd invested a lot of money in the recording sessions but didn't have anything. Roger Forrester told me this is potentially a really great record, the rough mixes we'd heard from time to time sound great, and it would be wonderful if we could get that onto the record. Everyone was really impressed with what had come out of LA up to a point, but then it all seemed to go wrong. Everybody got lost. I was a 'drug-free' social smoker, didn't do anything in the studio. Pete wanted to look after his friend and felt that Jack would respond well to my energy."

Beyond working out what was on the tapes, Dennis had two very specific jobs to do. The first was to fix the vocals. "You push the faders and that voice comes back at you out of the speakers and you're thinking, my God, this is fabulous. The lead vocals were incredible, but there were mountains of backing vocals around everything, recorded in large clusters and mixed down. Some of those mix-downs were not done with the greatest care."

182

The other big fix involved the drum fill on 'Keep On Wondering', where Jim Keltner had gone out of time and slowed down. Dennis had to cut the tape exactly at the point where the drums had to stop. "I stuck leader in there so we could record all the way up to the point where the drums had to join the original drum track," he says. "And then we dropped it in on top of Jim's drums; we sort of matched the sound as best we could. I remember Jack sitting in the studio, staring into space, trying to work out how to play the thing."

"It was a combination of Jack's musicianship and Dennis's editing skills," Pete recalls with some awe. "You are actually talking about cutting bits of tape – and if you get it wrong, you've fucked up the whole tape. It was one of the most amazing things I saw Jack do in the studio. He said, 'OK, get me a crappy drum kit.' Jack dropped in this fill and you can't hear it, it's absolutely seamless."

Compared with the mayhem of the Record Plant, working with Pete and Dennis in Scorpio was so much better for Jack. He was now in the company of professional people who weren't stoned, had his interests at heart, and wanted to see the job done successfully. For Dennis, too, it was a very good experience. "Jack was really focused and healthy at this point," he says. "He was staying with Pete; we'd keep normal hours and come in around 11am. He quite liked it that we'd get to a certain point then step back and go and have dinner. The whole thing took about three weeks. It was a lot of fun and musically and artistically very satisfying."

With Jack back in London, however, the drug dealers started circling. He decided to get away to Scotland with Pete, but the omens were not good. On the way to the airport, a blackbird smashed into the car windscreen. "I was taking delivery of a boat," Jack says. "It had been taken up to Kip Marina at Inverkip, near Greenock on the west coast of Scotland. So we got the boat – I'd had some experience of sailing, but only on smaller boats. This was 40 foot, twin-screw, and headed for Sanda. Everything was going fine, but it was getting late so we decided to go to Arran for the night. We went to this little bay, set down the anchor, and then Pete said, 'I've got to phone my mum. I always have to phone her every day otherwise she gets upset.'

"We didn't have a radio, so I said we'd have to row to the shore. We got in this little tender and started rowing toward the shore and this squall hit us, just like that. I realised it was going to be very bad and I told Pete to forget the call, we had to get back to the boat. So now we are back to the boat, but by that time, the stern of the boat is right up in the air, where the ladder is, and then smacking down again with the swell. So I told Pete to carefully stand up and grab the ladder and climb on. But then he pulled down on the boat so hard, it smacked down on the tender and it capsized. So Pete's hanging onto the anchor chain and I'm in the water hanging onto the overturned tender with my fingertips. Now I'm thinking maybe this isn't such a bad way to go. I was withdrawing and feeling pretty shitty.

"We're about half a mile from the shore and there is the famous telephone box we'd been trying to reach. There's a couple going for a walk with their dog and we're going, 'Hey, hey' and they're saying 'Hello' and waving back. Finally the penny drops and they realise we're in trouble – not waving, but drowning. They go to the phone box and then after what seemed liked ages, this boat appears on the horizon coming toward us. There was one guy trying to get me on the boat; he realised he couldn't and started going away again! And so I'm waiting God knows how long and he comes back with a dinghy and a few people and they get us to the shore.

"They gave us these tartan blankets to wrap ourselves in and we were taken to this hotel. They were all very suspicious – the police were there and they thought we had stolen the boat. All these middle-class people are sitting there eating their fish and chips looking at us wrapped in blankets and Pete with his big beard. Meanwhile the storm has got worse and the boat has dragged its anchor toward the rocks. I realised I had to find someone experienced to help me out, to get back on the boat and save it.

"Someone said, 'Ah, Wee Dougie'll do it.' So we find Wee Dougie – a really old guy, but you could tell he knew everything there was to know about boats. 'Can you do it?' 'That's not a boat. It's a ship.' So we got a dinghy, set off again, got back on our boat and got to the marina." (Even then, according to Pete, they weren't quite 'out of the storm' as Wee Dougie and his mate were smashed out of their minds on whisky.)

O

For the album cover shot, Jack travelled around Scotland with a photographer trying to find a storm. You would have thought it would be easy to find bad weather in Scotland, but no luck. In the end they happened to find an old bike in the woods, propped it up against a tree, and that was it, with a very tiny shot of Jack in the background.

For RSO to allow an album cover where the star is hardly visible – a decision freighted on Jack's part with psychological significance – suggests that despite some initial enthusiasm, they didn't put any weight behind the record. At the time of its release in the autumn of 1974 they were no doubt focused instead on the much-heralded return of Eric Clapton, whose *461 Ocean Boulevard* and radio-friendly 'I Shot The Sheriff' were worldwide hits that year. Even so, there remained the underlying issue of how the label responded to Jack as an artist.

As Pete Brown observes, *Out Of The Storm* "was a good album, and an important one because it had a lot to say about what was going on. A lot of money was spent on the album, but it wasn't properly promoted. Jack was a complex character, and it became apparent that it wasn't just about wrestling with demons – the further he got into drugs, the more complex he got. At one point he was incredibly conscious and sensitive to what was going on in the world. When things were bad, I could see it was really hurting him. Most of the album is a serious record. Jack was developing as a very serious artist, but the structure just wasn't there to support him.

"Stigwood had no idea of the worth of an album like *Out Of The Storm*. Jack was doing serious work within the confines of the rock'n'roll industry and few people understood it. The business had no sense of his creativity. He was creating in 'pop' what Monk was creating in 'jazz'. He really was. It was to do with harmony, structure, and form, and he had that incredible individuality. You can recognise a Jack Bruce song anywhere – you hear the way the changes are running and it is as identifiable as anything in the better parts of popular music."

With Jack not having released a solo album for three years, *Out Of The Storm* was just as significant a 'comeback' album as *461 Ocean Boulevard*. But while Eric's drug problems were an open secret, Jack's were far less well known and certainly not discussed in print. A song like 'Keep It Down' could have been as big as Neil Young's 'The Needle And The Damage Done' but nobody knew what it was about. In fact so secret were Jack's troubles that one reviewer wrote that 'Golden Days' "reflects the new serenity Bruce seems to have found in his music and his life".

Most critics simply welcomed the latest offering from an artist whose true worth they recognised even if the label didn't. The headlines included 'Bruce Storms Back' and 'Bruce: Back On Top'; Barbara Charone called the album "a product of anguish and love" and "instantly appealing". Critic Karl Dallas praised "a truly superb album which manages to be realistic and inspiring at the same time in its vision of the world". He made special mention of Jack's keyboard work but, in keeping with most other reviewers, felt no need to remark on the exceptional bass lines – especially those on 'Keep It Down' and 'Timeslip' – because with Jack that kind of virtuosity was taken for granted.

Jack Bruce COMPOSING HIMSELF

And in *Melody Maker* Allan Jones closed his glowing review with the view that *Out Of The Storm* had re-established Jack as "one of the most important individuals currently working in rock".

In November 1974 Jack spoke to Steve Clarke of the *New Musical Express* about his thoughts on putting a band together to promote the album. Jack name-checked Steve Hunter and talked about a young drummer he had met in Los Angeles called Bruce Gary but was not "keen to say who exactly the other musicians in the band are other than the fact that there'll be a fairly large line-up with a keyboard player ... they should be on the road by the end of the year. He also hopes to get a band album done quickly and preferably record it live in the studio."

But as Robert Burns wrote:

> "The best-laid schemes o' mice an' men
> Gang aft agley,
> An' lea'e us nought but grief an' pain,
> For promis'd joy!"

songs
with
a
CHAPTER 11 tailor

Circumstances conspired to make the formation of Jack's next band a real struggle. It took at least six months, from the autumn of 1974 to April 1975, to finalise the line-up and rehearse the band for a tour. One of the first musicians Jack approached, during the American sessions for *Out Of The Storm*, was Steve Hunter. "Jack asked me if I'd be interested in touring," he recalls. "I said, 'Of course, just stay in touch.' I assumed there would be a tour maybe a couple of months after the album was released, but I never heard anything. Months went by and meanwhile I went to Canada to work on Alice Cooper's album *Welcome To My Nightmare* with Bob Ezrin. So I'm right in the middle of doing that and one night I get a call from Jack: 'OK Steve, are you ready to go on the road?' 'No, I'm doing other things now.' They were going to fly me out in a couple of weeks to start rehearsing. I felt terrible that I had to say no."

Andy Johns, who had been staying at Jack's country mansion since being fired from The Rolling Stones' sessions for *It's Only Rock'n'Roll* because he was "in a mess", suggested somebody else they might approach. "Mick Taylor was starting to bitch and moan – 'they never want to do any of my songs', 'they won't listen to me', and so on. So I called him up and told him that Jack and I wanted to do a project and that we needed somebody who was a major talent as well."

To Stones-watchers, Mick Taylor had always appeared to be an outsider in the band. He was never part of the Jagger-Richards inner sanctum and probably never wanted to be. He had begun a process of self-education during the band's 1972 US tour: he read Henry James and Joseph Conrad, wrote poetry and prose, and learnt to read music so that he could start composing. Easily the best technical musician ever to play with the Stones, he was never remotely stretched by the music of a band that had become slicker and more professional over time to the extent that it was impossible to make the same 15 songs sound fresh every night. "We only played for an hour and 15 minutes," he told a journalist at the time, "but quite honestly I used to feel bored on stage. It would seem like we were on stage for hours and hours."

Life was no better in the studio, where Mick's attempts to flex his creative muscles were ignored by Jagger and Richards, who just weren't interested in his compositions. He would subsequently express a certain bitterness that when he did make a more overt and identifiable contribution – on songs such as 'Time Waits For No One' and 'Till The Next Goodbye' – the credits simply and inevitably read 'Jagger–Richards'.

Mick had one other powerful reason for leaving the Stones, and one that was never spoken about in the press at the time: heroin. Even if he found churning through the same set boring, Mick was at least playing most nights while he was on tour. But the Stones weren't the Bluesbreakers. They could be off the road for several months, which sent Mick climbing the walls – especially as it was on stage that he felt he made his most significant contribution to the band. If you add to that the lifestyle that comes with being part of The Rolling Stones Circus, it was no surprise that a quiet, sensitive musician, feeling bored, frustrated, and unappreciated, might go off the rails.

Mick slipped into a narcotic reverie (topped off with a hefty side order of cocaine) during the chaotic *Exile On Main Street* sessions at Keith Richards's French mansion, Nellcôte. And as if being in the Stones wasn't enough, it was widely known that Mick's wife of the time was dealing drugs. There was nowhere to run; quitting the band was almost a matter of survival. Mick told Jagger he was leaving at a Stigwood party following Eric Clapton's concert at the Hammersmith Odeon on December 4 1974. Nobody had ever left the Stones before, so it came as something of a shock; Keith mumbled something about the timing being inconvenient as they had already started recording the next album.

In January 1975 Jack and Mick (looking fey and Byronic like a doomed aristocrat) appeared together on the BBC's *Old Grey Whistle Test* to discuss the new band. Jack said he had tried out lots of other musicians without success.

He didn't name names but it seems that Allan Holdsworth, Jon Hiseman, and possibly a young Clem Clempson were in the mix at the time.

Jack said specifically that he hadn't settled on a drummer yet, but back in November he had been planning to use a young drummer he had met in Los Angeles, Bruce Gary. Bruce wasn't Jack's first choice: that was Tony Williams. Jack didn't have Tony's number, so he phoned Carla Bley to see if she could help. Without missing a beat, Carla asked if she could be in the band. "I don't even think I asked him if he needed a keyboard player," she recalls. "I would have played anything." Jack thought it was a great idea. "It was unusual for a woman to be in a rock band and not be the singer," he says. "There was also this thing about promoting people to get them a wider audience and I really thought Carla was very special – still do – a very interesting composer, and I just wanted people to be aware of her. I didn't know what she'd be like in the band. But we had done things on *Escalator* where she had an interesting approach to keyboards, very simple. I didn't see her as a technical player, more of a composer who had a particular approach which appealed to me – very Kurt Weill and European."

In the meantime, Jack found that Tony was busy trying to put Lifetime back together, so Bruce Gary got the job. (Jack and Tony would however work together the following year on the unreleased *Wildfire* LP.)

"When I was at the Record Plant for all that time, there was a so-called Jim Keltner fan club," Jack recalls. "Every Sunday there would be this big jam session – that's when 'Too Many Cooks' was done. Bruce was at one of those sessions, hanging round the Record Plant, a wannabe drummer. He had toured with Albert Collins and he was really young. I was going back to the Hyatt House; he said, 'I'll give you a lift.' He had this pick-up truck and drove me and Pete to the hotel saying, 'I'm the drummer for your band, I'm your drummer. I know everything you've ever written better than you do.' He was really a full-on guy. So I said, half-jokingly, 'OK, come to my house.' After I got back to England, he showed up at my house with a suitcase – 'Here I am!' He moved in and was good for me. We played together a lot and I wrote some songs. He was really positive, just what I needed at the time."

Jack had in mind that they would record an album quite quickly and wanted to get into the studio with Mick and Bruce to see what would happen. Dennis Weinreich remembers getting a call "asking me if I was doing anything over the weekend. 'Nothing. Why?' 'Jack's got this drummer Bruce Gary ... we're thinking of going into Scorpio. Is it free?' Jack turned up with Andy Johns and Mick Taylor. We spent the weekend in the studio and it was just

189

fabulous, the music was unbelievable. I have no idea where those tapes are. Jack was great; Mick played as if he'd been released from a cage."

Back on *The Old Grey Whistle Test*, Jack mentioned Carla Bley as a definite member of the band alongside another keyboard player, Max Middleton, best known then for his work with Jeff Beck. But that didn't work out either. Jack turned instead to former Stone The Crows keyboardist Ronnie Leahy, who like Jack had grown up in Glasgow and attended the Royal Scottish Academy Of Music And Drama. Ronnie had started out as a bassist before switching to organ and playing in a number of 60s rhythm & blues bands. He worked as a session musician, played on various film soundtracks, and also featured in the ill-fated Stone The Crows, whose guitarist Les Harvey was electrocuted and died on stage. "I got a call out of the blue to come to a flat in the King's Road where Jack and Mick were," he recalls. "There was a piano in the flat, Jack stuck up some music, and we played. At the end, Mick said to Jack, 'Ronnie's the boy', and I was in."

Anyone watching the *Whistle Test* interview in January could be forgiven for thinking that the band was about to take off. But when Carla spoke to *Melody Maker* in March she said there was little she could reveal about the band that hadn't already been reported because she was "sworn to secrecy". It wasn't until April 9 that everything was ready for rehearsals. The band booked the Shepperton Film Studios and asked Dennis Weinreich to come down and sort out the sound. "Jack wasn't too happy with what he was hearing so I fixed that," he says. "Those rehearsals were really great; I feel terrible that we never recorded any of them."

Putting this band together was the biggest lift Jack had experienced for a long time. On the face of it he had a complete band of misfits: an ebullient Jewish drummer whose only prior experience was on the blues-bar circuit with Albert Collins; a female avant-garde jazz composer; an ex-Rolling Stones guitarist; and a rock pianist. And who had two keyboard players in a band together?

Jack hadn't toured for two years – the longest he'd been off the road since he left home in 1961. He was still battling heroin addiction and trying to find some positive way forward. "I didn't come down for three days after it all came together," he told journalist Barbara Charone. "I thought about all the possibilities of the band and it hit me. I'm not even sleeping well at night, it's that exciting." Even taking into account Jack's propensity to get incredibly enthusiastic about whatever he was doing at the time (only to tire of it quickly or as soon as something else came along), he had good reason to be optimistic.

The band looked and sounded exciting and experimental. Mick Taylor especially was a revelation. "I'd only known him as the guitarist in the Stones," Jack says, "but I couldn't believe it: his harmonic concepts, the direction he's going in, and his attitude to music are so similar to mine."

However, it quickly became obvious that despite being a band of composers, Jack and his cohorts would not be able to record a new album soon. They needed time to get to know each other. Only one new song was available: 'Without A Word', written by Jack and Pete and rehearsed at Scorpio with Mick and Bruce. The rest of the band's repertoire would come from Jack's existing material, with an emphasis on *Out Of The Storm*.

"At the beginning it was great fun," Jack says. "We rented an apartment in the King's Road – Carla and Bruce were living there, but we'd always hang out there. I took up the trumpet, Carla took up the saxophone, and we'd play really terrible versions of standards like 'My Funny Valentine'. The idea was that if we got good enough, we'd do something on stage. We never got good enough, but it was a lot of fun."

Before the rehearsals began they all went off to Jamaica as part of the 'bonding process'. The idea was that it would help Jack and Mick clean up before the tour started, but that plan was completely undermined by Mick's wife, who met them at Kingston Airport with a bag full of drugs. There were further portents ahead. Mick's house caught fire while the band were away; one of the very few items salvaged was a copy of *Out Of The Storm* given to him by Jack, who still has the burnt, upturned record. Then on the morning rehearsals were due to start Jack received some very unwelcome visitors.

"About 6am, these cars screeched up to the front door," he recalls. "It was the police. They forced their way in. They'd had a tip-off that I was the biggest dealer in the Eastern Counties. And they were absolutely vile. They had no search warrant. This dealer had given my name to take the pressure off himself. They searched the whole house, woke up the two boys. I said you can search anywhere, but don't disturb my two boys – so of course that's the first thing they did. They took a lot of private letters, which I never got back. They were a caricature of bad policing. It took me a long, long time to get a response from the Chief Constable Of Essex. All I got was 'we've decided to take no further action' – I never got an apology."

The band rehearsed from April 9–13 and then prepared for the first gig, in Barcelona on April 22, followed by dates in Madrid, San Sebastian, and three cities in France. It took time for the musicians to get to grips with the material. "Initially everything was written out, not every note, mainly chords, but you

191

really had to know the harmonic structure of the song quite closely to be able to play the correct chord, the correct way," Ronnie recalls. "It's all quite critical in Jack's music. Every note counts. That's the way he writes."

Ronnie was a highly competent musician, but he was way out of his comfort zone. Many of the songs were mini-epics in several parts with different tempos and time changes, two very active keyboard parts, and Jack's powerful lead bass lines. "The arrangements were quite complex and not easy to play," Ronnie says. "Carla did a lot of string sounds, a little bit of synthesiser work, and Hammond. I was playing more piano and so more percussive. I was playing hard with Jack and Mick; Carla was more atmospherics."

The interpersonal dynamics in the band were as complex as the music. Dennis Weinreich was perfectly placed to see what was going on. "You had a great drummer who was playing with the greatest musicians who were out there," he says of Bruce Gary. "He took a very good stance of sitting back and saying, 'I'm going to hold this thing together, but I'm not going to try and push it. I'm going to be a sideman in this.' So Bruce took the role that was needed – solid as a rock, reliable. But if Jack went off on a sort of rhythmic tangent, Bruce could follow him." (Ronnie saw Bruce as a "naive, All-American kid who stuffed himself with vitamin pills and ate steak every night".)

As far as Carla was concerned the band was an experiment in which Jack and Mick were the stars and "the rest of us were on a different level; we were just the hired help". As a jazz musician, like Larry Coryell in Jack's 1970 outfit, she had a whale of a time being in a rock band. The world of limos, first class flights, and smart hotels was something she'd previously only heard about. "I was thrilled with every bit of it," she says. "I always wanted to be as bad as possible, but I never knew anybody who would give me the opportunity until these people."

For Carla, however, being bad didn't quite mean cars in swimming pools or televisions out the window. "We would do things like change the breakfast menus on the notices hanging on the doors," she says. "An order for yoghurt and orange juice would become 17 bananas. Jack would do terrible things. He bought a stink bomb in a novelty shop and was throwing it back and forth on the airplane, but it didn't explode. When we got to the hotel in Hamburg he set it off and they had to close the entire floor."

Carla might also have mentioned the games of football using the global lampshades at the Hamburg Intercontinental Hotel with Chris Youle of RSO in goal, or the communal dowsing in water from vases of flowers. "In Denmark, outside the hotel all these young girls were waiting for Jack," she adds. "They mobbed him and he was having a good old time." Carla says she was utterly naïve on the substances front as well. "We went down to do a press conference in Madrid and Jack offered me my first gin and tonic – and it was only noon." Ronnie remembers Carla taking a brandy miniature from the hotel, knocking it back in the limo, and immediately throwing up. Rock'n'roll, eh?

In San Sebastian, Carla recalls, "we were staying at this old hotel which Jack absolutely loved; the rest of us were nervous because the doorknobs came off in your hand." Jack too has fond memories of that hotel. "I remember waking up in this amazing hotel and hearing this acoustic music, an acoustic version of 'Sunshine'," he says. "I went out on the balcony and there were all these Basque musicians playing for me. You don't forget things like that."

As far as drugs were concerned, the band had been relatively clean before the tour started. "Then we got to Barcelona," Dennis recalls, "and all of a sudden it seemed like 'oh, Jack Bruce and Mick Taylor are in town' and all the drug hangers-on turned up. You'd go back to the hotel and there would be 50 people hanging around." Carla says she had little idea about any of this, but confirms that Mick's wife kept showing up with drugs and that there were concerns about him hanging around with the wrong people.

The situation between Jack and Mick was yet more complex. Jack was clearly the bandleader, and on the surface Mick had no problem with that. But as Ronnie recalls: "Jack knows what he wants and if he doesn't get it, you'll know about it." While Mick and Jack got along reasonably well, Mick would not have responded positively to any criticisms from Jack and would find ways to wind him up. "Jack could be practising a part singing," says Ronnie, "and Mick would start tuning up in the middle of it, as loud as he possibly could, and of course Jack flew off the handle. Mick could be quite irritating at times."

The band could have broken up at any point during the early part of the tour. One particular flashpoint came in St Etienne on April 30. Dennis says there were problems even before the band got there. "The truck got stopped at the border coming up from Spain and there was a minibus with the road crew and I was with the band. The minibus was in a small accident; they were stranded with a broken-down vehicle and had to find another van. Me and the other guys [road manager Chris Cook and the driver] rigged the show but there was all this tension. There were no roadies, no backstage crew, a quasi-soundcheck that wasn't very successful. Something was going on in the band – there had been a big falling out, because after the soundcheck nobody was talking to each other." Jack said later: "We had this one crisis in France where Mick freaked out in his own quiet way and pointed out a lot of things, a lot of faults actually that I had. And it was kinda hard to take, but when I sat down and thought about it, I took it. And because of that I think I've become a better musician as part of a group than I was before the incident."

The following day's gig in Zurich was cancelled and the frustrations and tensions rumbled on, but as the tour progressed, this disparate band of musicians began to gel. Ronnie maintains these were "among the most memorable gigs I've ever played in my entire career". "When it was good, it was as good a band as I have ever heard," Dennis adds. "I remember a show in Munich: sitting there mixing the live sound, breathless at how good it is. I could not believe what I was hearing."

Jack could be a hard taskmaster, but he was also an inspiring bandleader. Ronnie says that by the time they got to Stockholm, the band were exhausted, "physically and mentally, on this whistle-stop tour. I remember Jack saying, 'when you're totally exhausted, you've got nowhere to go, musically, you just can't do it and that's when you do your best playing. You're under no pressure and you don't care.' And it's absolutely true, you lose all your inhibitions, you use energy you don't have, your mind is blank."

◯

On the night before Jack's 32nd birthday the band played in Hamburg. It was by common consent one of the better concerts of the tour. The evening opened with Jack, resplendent in a white suit, at the piano, pouring his heart into 'Can You Follow'. After an abrupt finish he slipped off his jacket, strapped on his bass, and introduced "a song about Glasgow", 'Morning Story'. While Mick stayed rooted to the spot and Carla was marooned behind a forest of keyboards, Jack hardly stopped moving, encouraging everybody to shine. At the back, Bruce Gary was demonic, curls flying as he bounced up and down on his stool to get as much purchase on his kit as possible, pulverising the drums and cymbals.

By now the band had worked sufficiently hard on the material that, although the songs spanned six years of Jack's solo work, the ensemble pieces were very fluid and well meshed. There was plenty of soloing, but it was integrated into each song instead of simply being an opportunity for grandstanding. And yet the musicians all still had their moment in the spotlight. Ronnie's came in the introduction to a medley of songs that varied on different nights but generally included 'Tickets To Waterfalls', 'Post-War', and 'Weird Of Hermiston'. A journalist told Ronnie after one gig that he never knew Ronnie play so well. Ronnie replied: "It's all down to who you are working with. I've never had the chance to play with people this good." Carla didn't play solos as such but cast a filigree web of textures across the songs. Her parts wove in and around Ronnie's; it was hard sometimes to work out who was playing what. And Mick fulfilled some of the promise of those early rehearsals, coming to the fore on 'Keep It Down' and showing how his playing had started to influence the Stones just before he left.

The band's only new song, 'Without A Word', and Jack's recent 'One' provided the calm before the storm of Tony Williams's 'Spirit', which Jack and Bruce built up with a blistering fury of power chords and funk. Jack put himself in the spotlight with a slowly building bass solo at the start of 'Smiles And Grins'. The only sop to the legacy of Cream was an encore of 'Sunshine Of Your Love'. One journalist called it "a laboured and unnecessary reference to 'the good old days'", noting that "this group is capable of running rings around Cream and don't need to hearken back to ancient triumphs"; another praised it for being neither a rehash "nor a sluggish rendition high on overkill like West Bruce & Laing".

By the time the band arrived back in the UK for the remaining six dates of the tour they seemed very upbeat. In front of journalists Jack and Mick seemed to empathise very strongly with their respective problems of forging a solo career, seeking the right people to play with, the frustrations of finding yourself isolated, and so on. As Barbara Charone wrote: "*This* Jack Bruce Band will last. It *has* to", urgently willing the band to succeed against expectation. There was some talk of a US tour, too, but Mick was firm in his belief that the band needed an album before they went. In interviews he said that the band needed a record to establish their identity – code for "we can't carry on just playing Jack's back catalogue" (a point on which everyone, including Jack, agreed).

The musicians were booked into Scorpio for a month from July 3 1975. Then on the day they were supposed to start, Jack took a call from RSO's Roger Forrester, who by now was effectively Jack's manager, to say that Mick wasn't coming to the studio, and had in fact left the band. So what happened?

The UK dates were the most difficult part of the tour. Jack's relationship with British audiences had been problematic because they were the least receptive to his post-Cream musical direction. All they really wanted was to hear Cream songs. There was a two-week gap between the last date in Holland and the first gig in Birmingham so the band went back to Shepperton for another day of rehearsals to make sure they were sharp and ready. But the first gig was a disaster: not because they played badly, but because hardly anyone came, and many of those who did left before the encore. Bands absolutely thrive on the vibe from the audience. In Germany and Scandinavia, the audiences knew the solo albums and really appreciated the music, but in Britain they just didn't care.

Jack and Mick both appreciated each other as musicians, and their public declarations of empathy about career challenges were genuine. "I know Mick really valued the music and adored Jack's singing and playing," says Carla. "But Mick was a low spark, sort of standing back there, enjoying himself musically, I think, but in a world of his own." Dennis thinks that part of the problem was that, while Carla might have thought they were all the hired help at the beginning, toward the end everybody wanted to get in on the act and have some fun. So Mick might have felt there was less room for him to play when, on some nights, they all travelled to different musical places, expending different energies and different intensities.

And then there was the heroin. Jack was trying his best to clean up but Mick wasn't prepared to – and, through his connections, was putting temptation in Jack's way at every turn. From Jack's point of view, Mick was doing nothing about his habit and nothing to keep the dealers away, but Ronnie is adamant that the drugs never got in the way of the music.

Watching the *Whistle Test* interview and the later recorded show, there's no way you would know there was a drug problem in the band. There wasn't a hint of rumour or speculation in the music press of the time, but this was true right through Jack's heroin addiction. He was never defined by his drug use. "Few people knew about it anyway," he says, "and music has always been a healing thing for me."

Even so, Ronnie says he was continually very annoyed by the drug situation. "I'd never experienced anything like it before and I'd get angry with Jack and Mick at times," he says. "In my naivety I thought they could just stop. It wasn't a problem musically; I only got a hint of it early on after a gig, in Jack's hotel room. He said it was 'fuckin' rubbish', but actually he was a bit strung out and was bad-tempered over that. It was definitely a Jekyll and Hyde thing."

If St Etienne had been a crisis point, the gig at the Apollo Theatre in Glasgow on June 3 was the band's Armageddon. It was an especially emotional evening for Jack: not only were his parents and other relatives present, but his father was dying of cancer. The diagnosis had come from a routine chest x-ray taken just before Charlie Bruce retired from working at Rolls Royce in East Kilbride. He subsequently spent some time in the Brompton Hospital in London during an extended stay with Jack and Janet before returning to Scotland. He died in 1976.

Robert Somerville was a senior shop steward with Charlie and recalls that he was "always a campaigner on behalf of the workers – he always talked about workers rights and how we should be campaigning to get a better living for everybody. He was very specific on how we should do this and he was always very passionate about it, I can assure you of that." Robert says Charlie was something of a role model for the younger activists coming up. "If he had a point of view, you would listen to him. I used to enjoy listening to him talk. He would talk about Jack, people would be interested in how Jack was getting on and he'd give us a wee résumé. He was very proud of Jack's achievements, he'd like to talk about him, but never in a boastful manner." Jack's mother found it almost impossible to cope with her husband's illness, but still had the energy to argue with Ronnie Leahy's mother, who was sitting next to her at the gig, about whose son was the better musician. Betty Bruce continued to find life an immense struggle after Charlie died. She passed away in May 1989, shortly after Jack's 46th birthday.

As it happens, one published review of the gig was very positive – even to the point of suggesting that the band went off with an energy they should have been building toward as the gig progressed. The exception was Mick, who turned his back on the audience and wouldn't play, only emerging for a solo on 'Third Degree' during the first encore. This was likely the result of a blazing row between Jack and Mick before the gig, apparently witnessed by Jack's family. Jack was beside himself at Mick's non-performance on that night of all nights; according to Carla he was "manic, almost suicidal" after the gig. Tempers cooled for the following night's show in Newcastle and a spirited, stripped-down performance for *The Old Grey Whistle Test* on June 6. But at the Crystal Palace Concert Bowl the next night the band were forced to reduce the sound levels by the local council, whose man-on-the-spot kept turning down the faders, and on the last night of the tour in Cambridge Mick almost dozed off on stage to the cat calls of the students.

Mick might well have found Jack too fierce and domineering, and perhaps felt that in spite of what Jack said about collaboration there would always be an issue about sharing the limelight and accepting other compositions. Mick also had some unresolved issues of his own: most fundamentally, he didn't know whether he wanted to be a guitarist in Jack Bruce's band or a solo artist. He may also have realised that, while he might aspire to be a singer and composer, he would struggle to get anywhere close to Jack, and so his contribution to any new material that would help forge the band's identity might be limited and substandard compared with what Jack would deliver.

Carla believes that writing in the studio, as Jack had envisaged, was always something of a dream. It was not anything she was used to, and Jack had never worked that way either. She also saw the limitations in what the others might contribute. "Mick wanted to do that as well, but I don't know how to write with other people," she says. "Jack would bring a song that he hadn't finished to a rehearsal, but nobody knew what to do next. Nobody offered anything; maybe Mick would offer a chord, but I didn't know how to do that and I still don't." This suggests that while Mick might have thought they could bring on new material quickly, when a new song was presented he couldn't engage with it – most likely because it was yet another song by Jack Bruce.

Mick has offered various reasons over the years for why he quit the band. "We got the band together quickly," he told *Guitar Player* in 1980, "and it was really like a promo tour for one of Jack's many solo albums. That was really different. I mean totally different. I had very high hopes and expectations of Jack and me being able to do something together. But it really didn't happen, you know. We just got a band together very quickly and went on the road playing Jack's songs. It didn't happen. I don't think it was a musical mismatch, I just think it was the wrong time. I'd left the Stones and I knew why I left but not where I wanted to go. Jack was in a bad patch too, and it was destined not to last. Some of these supergroups look good on paper, but … well, who knows what would have happened."

In 1990 Mick told *Downbeat* that Jack was "the most frustrating and musically interesting person I've played with". In 1999 he named Jack as a big inspiration in an interview with *Total Guitar*, adding, "Those three records he did after Cream folded are among the best solo albums any English [sic] musician has ever done. And Jack would show me some great open tunings, like the open Em7 tuning on 'Rope Ladder To The Moon'."

Back in 1975 Mick told *Rolling Stone* that he wasn't a solo artist, and in truth history has borne that out. While he has made quality contributions as a session musician and sideman, especially with Bob Dylan in the mid 80s, Mick's solo albums have had little impact. His original dilemma when he joined The Jack Bruce Band has continued to haunt him. But whatever his reasoning, his decision to quit the band on which Jack had pinned so much hope and expectation left Jack in pieces. Ronnie Leahy was living in Earl's Court at the time and remembers Jack coming round to tell him the news. "He was so upset. He asked me what we should do. I suggested we get another guitar player, go into the studio and carry on. But I remember feeling very angry because I felt this band could go places – fantastic possibilities."

The band still went into Scorpio with Dennis as planned. "We got basic drums, sounds, keyboards, and all that," Dennis recalls. "Carla was still around. Jack was not in good shape. He came in and hated the organ sound and everyone was saying 'What's wrong?' Ronnie was on my side on this and it became a real source of contention because up until then anything I did was great as far as Jack was concerned – and if it wasn't we'd be able to work together to get it right. But now I was 'another one who's deserting me', and that wasn't how I felt at all. I was there to do what I had always done, but that organ sound became a real line in the sand in my relationship with Jack.

"There was material around and there would be writing in the studio. Nobody wanted it to die. Bruce Gary was really upset that it fell apart; Ronnie's true ability as an anchor to hold it all together was just emerging. Maybe if Ronnie had been more assertive earlier on it might have survived because everybody respected him. Up until then he'd been more of a sideman."

Carla Bley had a particularly harrowing experience at the flat. "I remember sitting one evening playing the piano and Jack was incredibly out of it and the bathroom was full of blood," she recalls. "That was the most terrifying part for me. I thought, 'Oh no, he's shooting up.' Maybe I shouldn't have left."

They stuck it out for 11 days at Scorpio then cancelled the rest of the sessions. Compounding the misery for Jack, a week later Dennis flew to New York to do an album with Carla. She and Mick Taylor also tried to work together, first on a planned album by her husband Mike Mantler and then on some compositions originally sketched out for Jack's band, but nothing came of either project.

Jack was left in complete limbo. "What happened with that band was tragic," he says. "I had a lot of material for what subsequently became *How's Tricks* and we were going to write together as a band in the studio. I was going to try that approach and see what happened. I remember that Bruce had come up with a really good drum pattern and that could have been the jumping-off point for us writing something. Mick pulled quite a stroke, he really let me down. Then everybody got cold feet; Carl and Bruce split and we had no band. I had put a lot into the band and there were problems, but I saw a future for the band, I really did. But it was Mick's band as well. He could have changed things if he'd wanted to. It was such a shock. It took me quite a long while to get over that. To me that was my big chance solo-wise – playing big venues – and I had what I thought was a really good band, maybe a great band. I was heading in the right direction, and then for it all to happen in that way ... it was soul-destroying."

keep
it
CHAPTER 12 **down**

Jack spent the next year in retreat. The scars of betrayal and loss ran deep, and recovery was lengthy and painful. He needed to take stock, and could be forgiven for wondering if all the hassle was really worth it. Should he just give up trying to be a solo artist and bandleader and instead find a comfortable niche in somebody else's band or submerge himself in session work, or pack it in altogether?

All these thoughts crossed his mind, but in the spring of 1976 Jack emerged stronger and healthier than he had been for some time. That May he was invited to Germany to record with sax player and composer Charlie Mariano. Jack recommended drummer John Marshall while Charlie engaged Jan Hammer from The Mahavishnu Orchestra, Polish violin wizard Zbigniew Seifert, and Asian percussionist Nippy Noya.

Even by Charlie Mariano's standards of attracting the world's top musicians to join him, this very shortlived line-up was one of his finest, and the resulting *Helen 12 Trees* – a category-defying mix of jazz, rock, and Indian music released on the tiny but visionary label MPS – was one of the great lost recordings of the 70s, bursting with soul, kinetic energy, and improvisational surprise. Jack has played with many star drummers over the years, but his partnership with John Marshall is often underrated. On this album the pair provided an outstanding rhythm section of pulse and verve. One reviewer called it "the best example of post-Miles jazz-rock fusion ever recorded".

By the autumn, RSO was pushing Jack to try again with a new band and album. But the Charlie Mariano session and Jack's next attempt to forge ahead with a solo career were bookends to one of the more bizarre episodes in his colourful life. The general public see the musician's career in linear, logical terms – album followed by tour followed by album. That's how it is for longstanding, well-established acts like The Rolling Stones or The Who, but Jack has never been in that situation. He keeps coming together with different combinations of musicians to see if something might happen. Over the years there have been sessions with Jon Hiseman and Allan Holdsworth; Keith Emerson and Steve Hackett; Andy Summers and Dennis Chambers. These are often eagerly and prematurely reported in the music press, only to progress no further than studio try-outs and demos.

While Jack has always been up for a new idea, the proposition presented to him in the summer of 1976 turned out to be distinctly odd. He took a call from San Francisco from a guy we'll call 'B' who claimed to be promoting a singer with huge potential and keen to build an all-star band around him; the name of pianist Nicky Hopkins was mentioned. Andy Johns would be producing the sessions; it was Andy who suggested Jack. It would be an all-expenses-paid trip: was Jack interested? It sounded worth investigating, at least, and Jack had no other commitments, so he and Janet flew out to America.

They arrived in San Francisco and were met by one of B's assistants, who turned out to be the grandson of Jay Silverheels, the actor who played Tonto in *The Lone Ranger*. Janet was surprised that they weren't driven directly to see their host. "He didn't drive us to B's," she recalls, "but back to his place – and basically I've always thought we were kidnapped. That sounds very melodramatic but that's how I saw it. When we arrived at this place, Andy Johns and Paula were there. It was all a bit confusing and turned out to be complete madness. At one point I walked into Andy and Paula's bedroom just in time to see Andy waving a syringe around and Jack with his arm bared, having been really clean. So I had a tantrum and stopped it that time. Everyone was on another planet; I was horrified. We didn't know where we were or what was going on.

"It was decided we would all go out to dinner, but then the girlfriend of this assistant who had brought us here called me into her bedroom and said, 'I've just taken an overdose but you mustn't tell anybody.' I said, 'I'm sorry, I can't just say nothing.' 'No, no, you all go out and have dinner.' It was totally surreal. So I went up to this guy and said, 'Sorry to have to tell you this, but your girlfriend says she has taken an overdose.' And he just went berserk, screaming in my face that it was none of my business, saying we were going out anyway, so I just kept hitting him until he stopped shouting. I just lost it."

Janet is not sure how long they were at the house – a couple of days, maybe – but eventually she just told the guy to take them to B immediately. "I remember being driven at this reckless speed while Jack and I were both trying to keep calm and convince ourselves that everything would be all right because this guy was out of control and we were terrified."

They arrived at a mansion up a mountain road in Mill Valley, Marin Country, one of the richest areas in the country. It looked liked Tony Montana's villa in *Scarface*, covered in golden Buddhas with a 1936 Packard, a Maserati, various bikes, and a four-wheel truck out front – all of which was appropriate because B turned out to be one of the biggest drug dealers on the West Coast. He greeted them in person, striding around like the Lord of the Manor. "We were shown to our beautiful room, where there was laid out every type of hash and grass and, in a box, the purest cocaine with gold snorters," Janet recalls. "He had a very nice girlfriend, but she was messed up, everybody was doing coke. He had these very young girls around who were his 'cleaners' – actually 14-year-old wannabe somethings who he was having sex with. His girlfriend was accepting, but not very happy about it. He had this huge bed with controls that turned on TV screens, opened this and closed that. I remember being in there with this girl and I leaned on a pillow, felt something, lifted it up and there was a gun. She made a gesture to me as if to say 'you didn't see that, don't say anything'."

This was California, of course, where everybody 'does lunch' but nothing ever happens. But there were some half-hearted attempts at music. "Nicky Hopkins was carried in," says Janet. "He was in an absolutely dreadful state, didn't know his own name, didn't know if it was day or night. He had this weird girlfriend – who, along with B, was controlling him by keeping him in a state of absolute fear through black magic or something like that. They sat him down at the piano and he played brilliantly; then they poured alcohol down his throat and carried him out again."

Janet eventually left because she needed to get back to the children. Jack went with her but returned soon after with Pete. "Jack and I went out together," Pete recalls. "They paid first class PAN-AM and we were met by B and several of his mates. 'We've got a bit of a problem,' they said. 'There are these other people who have a studio and they've kidnapped Nicky Hopkins and they've got him locked in a studio to take part in some black mass ritual recording.' 'What are you going to do?' 'Well, we'll have to go and get the guns and get him out.' The vibe was incredibly heavy and frightening." B also had a private zoo, so the presence of crocodile pits and panther pens did nothing to lighten the mood.

Pete says the guy that B wanted to promote was very good-looking but couldn't sing. "They weren't able to rescue Nicky," he adds, "so we got Mark Naftalin instead. There was quite a good drummer and guitar player and we started doing some work." Jack says they did loads of rehearsals with crummy songs, but some good came out of it: he and Pete wrote 'Lost Inside A Song', which would appear on Jack's next album, and 'Madhouse', which requires no further analysis. Jack just wanted to get out of there as quickly as possible.

"B said this guy was coming from Chicago or Detroit and he's a really good guy," Jack remembers with a grimace. "'All you've got to do is be nice to this guy, shake his hand and give him a little dedication on the record. Your record will be double platinum.' And it probably would have been, but it was the Jewish Mafia. I had to meet this guy, shake his hand – and that's me giving my life to them. They would get a hit record and then own me. So I solved that dilemma by running away," he adds, although not before he'd managed to wrap B's Packard around a tree.

Jack had another reason for wanting to get out of there as quickly as possible. "They told me, 'Oh, you should have a check-up with our Chinese acupuncturist.' So I drove over there; he gave me an examination and told me I had skin cancer. The idea is this doctor would put you on a course of acupuncture and Chinese herbal medicine that would cost a fortune. People would pay up, live, and think what a great doctor he was." Jack phoned Janet, who told him to get back and see his own doctor. The check-up gave Jack the all clear. As far as Janet is concerned, people like B and Nicky Hopkins's girlfriend get off on being associated with famous musicians, but at the same time want to mess with their minds and exert control over them.

○

When it came to forming a new band, Jack was determined that it be more of a collaborative effort and was keen to avoid ego clashes and temperament by working with schooled musicians who would feel comfortable with his kind of material. His starting point was Hughie Burns, a Glasgow-born guitarist who had been developing a highly successful session career. Hughie in turn suggested a classically trained keyboard player, Tony Hymas, and between the two of them they brought in drummer Simon Phillips.

There were some similarities between this band and the previous one – both included a keyboardist who had never played in a rock band before and a young and unknown but highly talented drummer – but Jack was keen this time for all of the band-members to be equal partners in the album they were due to record and had contracts written to that effect. They also tried hard to come up with a name that wasn't The Jack Bruce Band but couldn't settle on one. "Jack loved this band; that's why he was prepared to give up solo artist status and give us a share of everything," Simon recalls. "He'd found some British musicians who got his music and could play it. He felt it could really grow."

RSO insisted that the new album should be more commercial than the sombre *Out Of The Storm* and so imposed a producer on the project. Bill Halverson was someone Jack knew from his Cream days, and who had since become a top-flight producer for acts such as Crosby Stills & Nash. Jack had previously only ever worked on solo projects with Felix Pappalardi, but he had no problems with Bill.

"He was the kind of producer I liked working with," Jack says. "He wasn't really full of musical ideas. It was more like suggesting little things. And the songs were already written. I think I was trying to be more commercial, more accessible, which is why I thought the band would be a really good influence." Jack's personal manager for a few months around this time was fashion photographer Justin de Villeneuve, best known for bringing the model Twiggy to public attention. He remembers Bill as "this Viking, about six foot five inches tall, blue eyes and long blonde hair, wearing a wolf coat".

Simon Phillips, just 20 years old at the time, says the band took off very quickly. "It worked instantly. What Jack loved was that we got the music very quickly. We went down to Jack's house a couple of times, then went into the Manor Studios and were there for about three weeks in October. We were very rock'n'roll about it; we just remembered everything in our heads. Jack rarely said anything. He trusted us to play what was right for the song." Simon was less happy with the drum sound – he prefers a brighter feel than the album's LA-style deadness – but remains immensely proud of an album he says contains "some of my best playing".

Of the album's ten tracks, five are straightforward Bruce-Brown songs. 'Waiting For The Call' is a natural successor to 'Politician' and 'Ministry Of Bag'; Jack says that, lyrically, it "sort of invented Margaret Thatcher before she became Prime Minister as she waited for the call like Winston Churchill". Hughie Burns was credited with Jack and Pete on two songs and wrote 'Baby Jane' on his own, while Pete and Tony co-wrote 'Something To Live For'.

The title of the album, *How's Tricks*, came from a poster Jack had at home of an Australian magician. Jack began a round of interviews to promote the album, his enthusiasm notably tempered by caution. But if his aspirations for the band were more low-key than usual, the reviews were, as ever, uniformly positive. While British fans had been largely intolerant of any movement by Jack away from his history, journalists continued to encourage his attempts to diversify and progress. The general consensus was that, without losing any individuality, *How's Tricks* managed to bridge the gap between public expectation and Jack's personal vision. The music was direct and grounded but never banal and simplistic, even while reaching for greater accessibility.

The album's release was delayed until March 1977 by a fire at the Polydor factory that also destroyed all the Cream multi-tracks. Despite solid music-press support and the services of a first rate producer, the album that was supposed to represent Jack's return to the commercial market failed to make the charts.

Tony Hymas had been under the impression that the track he wrote with Pete, 'Something To Live For', would be released as a single, and says cryptically that he was "very worried for about six hours" when he found out that this wasn't to be, during the second leg of the band's US tour. Pete also felt that 'Something To Live For' had commercial potential – The Hollies did a cover version – but whether it would have attracted enough airplay to push *How's Tricks* into the charts is another question.

The tour to promote the album began on March 5 1977 at Leeds University, where Tony noticed an immediate difference in the dynamics of the band. "I was really pleased with the album and looking forward to the tour – and suddenly everybody's ego is starting to surface," he recalls. "This was my first experience of Jack Bruce on stage and I was pretty startled. The gloves were off. It was much stronger, a boxing arena, gladiatorial."

The first gig was really a dress rehearsal. Tony and Hugh were a little hesitant at first, but Simon stormed through the set. They played for over three hours and by the end were brimming with confidence, leaving the stage to rapturous applause. The set was drawn largely from *Out Of The Storm* and *How's Tricks*; elsewhere around the country the audience reaction was quite muted until the encores of songs like 'Born Under A Bad Sign' and 'Sunshine' prompted a chorus of approval. Even so, Jack was almost overwhelmed by the response on the last night of the tour's first leg in London, the audience's spirits not dampened by the bomb alert that drove them all outside just as the musicians were getting into 'Something To Live For'.

Tony Hymas is neither the first musician in this story nor the last to declare that a particular gig with Jack was the pinnacle of his live experience. For Tony it came with the band's first US show, at the unprepossessing Shaboo Inn in Connecticut. It was, he says, "one of the greatest gigs I have ever been involved with. Everything we played made sense; there was common agreement. Simon and I were totally locked in rhythmically. Hugh was screaming. This was a small club and people afterward said they had seen something incredible. And it didn't happen again. I don't know why we couldn't do that again."

But with a musician like Jack, and the music he plays, no two gigs are ever going to be the same. The music itself is freeform and works from an expression of improvisation and flow, while the emotion and passion he brings to a performance transcends any technical expertise. At the same time, the elements that can leave audience and musicians breathless can be the undoing of a performance if the edifice is undermined by any number of factors, from bad mood to bad sound.

Jack felt very comfortable with this group of musicians on the road. "It was very much a 'British band'," he says. "Hughie's from Glasgow and Simon and Tony had this middle-class England thing going with cricket – they'd bowl to one another outside the gig. It makes a difference in the banter and the chat that you get in the car. With the Americans in those days you had to be a bit careful with the humour; they didn't do irony. I was healing; the tour was hard, but it was a really good tour and I was on best behaviour. I really liked playing with Simon. He picked up a lot from Billy Cobham – a lot of open-style energy in his drumming that suited my style."

"It was an apprenticeship," Simon himself says of playing with Jack. "He really helped shape my jazz roots. I grew up playing jazz, strictly mainstream, trad, and Dixieland in my dad's band." (Simon's father was the bandleader Sid Phillips, who died in 1973 after suffering a heart attack while playing cricket.) "I grew to hate that music," he continues. "As a 16-year-old, all I wanted to play was rock'n'roll. Jack introduced me to the idea that you could come from rock'n'roll and get into a jazz mentality. Jack got me to listen to Tony Williams in a different light; I realised you could play long notes, taking a single-stroke or double-stroke roll, but play it in a certain way and you can make the drums a sustaining instrument. It was so cool and individual. And when we were playing those songs, there was a beautiful looseness where anything could happen."

The band had to cancel two gigs at the aptly named Bijou Café in Philadelphia because the stage was too small – something that seemed to symbolise a problem Simon could see Jack having. "I think the tough thing for

Jack was when we went to the States. We were playing small clubs: he found that very hard to cope with. He'd been in the States playing large venues with Cream and West Bruce & Laing, and for him it was tough. He had a band he was very proud of but we are playing small clubs. I think it got to him."

Jack travelled with a minder to keep him away from drugs, which was just as well because Simon thinks some of the old drug connections Jack didn't want around any more were starting to show up. "Toward the end of the tour things got a bit tense, as it always does – the older you are the less you tolerate," he recalls. "For Tony it was a bit tough because he wasn't used to being in a rock band and being away from his family for so long. Hughie was self-contained and handled it very well. And I enjoyed it until the antics got started and Tony and Jack would butt heads." (Tony insists that Jack "has a great sense of humour", and that the two of them "had a lot of laughs".)

Despite these niggles, the feeling in the band was positive. As Tony recalls, they were all keen to get back in the studio and record a second album together – something Jack had not done with any of his other bands during his solo career. It took a while to sort out, but in August 1978, eight months after the end of the US tour, they finally went into Chipping Norton Studio in Oxfordshire. The producer this time was Dennis Mackay, who was only in his early twenties but had already worked with John McLaughlin, Pat Travers, and Phil Collins's Brand X.

This time, however, the atmosphere was very different from the *How's Tricks* sessions. "It was nothing like as much fun from the word go, that's for sure," Tony recalls. "Jack seemed a little edgy about it – I think he knew more what he wanted, he had more of a definite idea." There was a prevailing sense that Jack maybe regretted ceding control of the last album because he wasn't happy with some of the songs others had written, and that he now felt rather backed into a corner. The other problem, largely unnoticed in the band, was that Jack was using heroin quite heavily at the time, and if he was feeling sick it went into the mix of how he would react to what was going on in the studio. It seems also that heroin may have played its part in preventing Jack from hearing precisely what he wanted – or led to him hearing something different – and so the process took much longer.

Dennis Mackay's tale of getting the first track done gives the sense that recording *Jet Set Jewel* was far from routine. "I was working on two other projects as well and I only had a limited time and budget to get this album done," he says. "We spent a lot of time getting sounds. Then we were all ready to start tracking – and Jack disappears. When he comes back, he's different, his eyes aren't clear, but it really didn't click with me that he had gone off to take some stuff. We knew something was different, but nobody knew how to react. But you'd never know – he was so cool about it – never fucked up, never played out of time. He was just waiting for the vibe."

The vibe was a long time coming. Memories differ over this, but Dennis thinks it took days to get it done. The song was 'Mickey The Fiddler'. "We'd do a take and it sounded great, very professional," Dennis recalls. "Jack would come into the control booth, listen to it. 'No, it doesn't feel right.' This went on all day and into the night. We'd stop about 10pm or 11pm, come in the next day, have breakfast, off we go again, and the same thing is happening. The band would be saying to me, 'How long are we going to do this? What's he looking for?' 'Well, guys, he is looking for a certain feel.' Even Simon eventually starts looking at me while he is playing as if to say, 'I'm playing the same thing now as on all the other takes, and so is everybody else.' And they were getting quite upset about it. But Jack is just one of those guys. He's the main artist, he's the guy from Cream, world renowned, y'know?"

There was a lot of tension. Hughie Burns is a Buddhist, and according to Simon he was "doing an awful lot of chanting". The other musicians were fed up with Dennis for not being more forceful and taking control of the situation, and upset with Jack because they didn't know what he wanted and he couldn't explain it.

Then came the crunch moment. Every time the band came in to listen to yet another take, Tony picked up his charts, brought them into the control booth, and then took them back to the keyboards for the next attempt. Dennis was sitting next to Jack in the booth. "Tony says something to Jack who turns round to Tony – and I'll never forget this – and he says, 'Listen, man, where you play with notes, I play with feel.' In other words, you're playing exactly what's written and I'm not. I know the notes; I'm just trying to get the right feel. It was a profound moment for me as a producer and something I never forgot, but Tony threw all the sheets in the air, 'Right. That's fuckin' it. I'm outta here!'

"Jack leapt across the control booth to apologise, saying how sorry he was. But you know what? He was right! That very evening we went back in the studio after dinner to have another go. Simon starts clicking his sticks for the introduction, they start playing – and it's like magic. Thirty seconds into the track, *there* was the feel. I give Simon the thumbs up; he does the same with his stick. Jack comes into the booth, listens to it, and immediately says, 'That's the one.'"

If that wasn't trouble enough, Dennis then accidentally erased all 24 tracks of the song for about five bars. "I was doing a vocal overdub," Jack recalls, "and Dennis pushed the wrong button on the multi-track tape. So you had everything, then nothing, then everything again. In theory that would mean that you have to re-record the whole thing from scratch. But Simon said, 'We don't have to do that. Where it's erased, I'll keep playing along and then I'll stop.' And we thought nobody could do that just for five or six bars, but Simon did it perfectly first time."

With 'Mickey The Fiddler' finally put to bed it was a lot easier for Dennis to record the rest of the album. "After that everybody got it – learn the notes, put the music sheets away, let's go with the feel," he recalls. "This was Jack telling us what he wanted – you won't get it to start with, but eventually you will. That's the kind of perfectionist he is." Tony was upset at the time but says now that Jack's approach was to challenge his musicians to take risks. "You could say in those days I was a very correct player," he says, "and he probably wanted me to break out of that."

Dennis had problems of his own. Right at the start of the session his wife rang him in the studio and told him she was filing for divorce because he was working too much. (She later married the British radio DJ Nicky Horne.) Dennis would go off to a local pub every night to down several pints – "these were the drinking years," he says. But it was in the pub where this fraught recording session ended on a high note.

With their time at Chipping Norton coming to an end and the booze flowing freely, Dennis suggested that Jack might like to showcase some of the tracks for the locals – and Jack agreed. They talked it through with the landlord, who was very keen, but Dennis told him not to tell anybody: the band would just play for whoever was in the pub on the night. But when the band arrived at the pub it was heaving, with hundreds of people jammed in because, of course, the landlord had advertised it.

"We made a little space by the kitchen door so that Jack could come out and come up to the mic," Dennis recalls. "So he plays about half a dozen of these tracks and says 'that's it, that's it, thank you'. Jack goes off into the kitchen and the place erupts, thumping on the tables, stamping on the floor – 'Jack! Jack! Jack!' So I go into the kitchen. 'Hey Jack, they want an encore.' 'What am I going to do?' – because he is actually quite a shy guy. So I started singing the opening bars of 'Sunshine' … 'dadadada-da-da-da-dada-da?' 'All right!'

"The band is still out there, nobody knows what's going to happen. Jack and I come out of the kitchen and I am standing about four feet away from him on the same level – there is no band riser. He looks at me, looks at Simon, and starts the riff. Everyone goes berserk – it was such a moment, just in that little packed pub, an amazing and emotional moment."

There are only three Bruce-Brown compositions on *Jet Set Jewel* but Pete ranks one of them, the title track, among the very best songs he ever wrote with Jack. "It was about stupid and irresponsible pop people," he says. "It's got a lineage from the Stones, not the Stones themselves, but the people who hung around them. It's one of the few lyrics that's 'clever', and there is something rather chilling and cold about it. But it's clever in the way the best musical songs are – it came out by accident, very sharply focused. And the music is wonderful."

The best indication of Jack's mood at the time – and of why the recording was so troubled – came with 'The Best Is Still To Come'. Like *Out Of The Storm*, Pete was trying to write an encouraging song for Jack to sing. "That was a pain to write," he recalls. "Jack was in a dreadful state again. He wanted me to write something positive. In some ways Jack is a bit like Thelonious Monk – Jack understands Monk, and Monk used to write themes in his music, but they'd never quite be the same. So repeats weren't repeats; they sounded like repeats, but they actually weren't. Jack did that in spades in this song. Every line is different, every fuckin' line is different; the phrasing is different and there are millions of lines in it. Boy, I sweated over that one. It's an epic, you get wrung out, there were God knows how many drafts."

The album also includes three songs credited to another lyricist, David Hart. For Jack this association was as bewildering as it was brief. "He was quite an interesting individual," he recalls. "Extremely right wing, wealthy, upper class, Eton-educated. When I lived in the mansion, he had an estate not far away. This was in the period leading up to Thatcher – he was a speechwriter for her. I was fascinated because I'd never seen that level of British society – the sort of people who used to hang out at his place. I was just playing a part because I wanted to experience this. He was always trying to get girls, but he couldn't do it with all this power and money. He'd ask me what he was doing wrong. He wrote a play, which we performed at his house, called *Cream In Your Jeans*." The actress Stephanie Beacham took part in the play, which reunited Jack, Eric, and Ginger for probably the first time since 1968. Jack played Isaac Dogleash; Eric was the Mucous Kid; Ginger was Mr Draw Blood.

"David Hart was trying to be a creative guy," Jack recalls. "He played the flute and he said we should write some songs. I quite like the words he wrote for 'Mickey The Fiddler'. He claimed to have met this real guy in Primrose

Hill, a busker called Mickey. 'She's Moving On' was him bemoaning the fact that he couldn't get girls." Hart became Thatcher's closest political adviser, orchestrating the government campaign against the miners in the 80s by coordinating legal action against striking miners and bankrolling those who broke the strike. He went on to make and lose fortunes and was in the news again in 2004 when he was accused of being involved in a plot to overthrow the government of Equatorial Guinea.

In the end Jack was quite encouraged by how *Jet Set Jewel* turned out. "To me the album was a development of *How's Tricks*," he says. "I thought the songs were really good. I did have high hopes for that." Simon Phillips agrees that "there was some wonderful stuff on it – valid music that has stood the test of time and outlived all the other crap". Once the musicians got into the swing of recording, the songs came relatively easily, but as Simon recalls this caused problems with Jack's label, RSO. "First of all they brought in a new A&R guy and he tried to think of us as a pop band, but it wasn't a pop album. Then Jack would pull out a song – two takes – done, so we'd just jam. And I remember this guy coming into the rehearsals and wanting to listen to the material, and we'd say 'we've only done one song'. RSO did not take kindly to this and thought we were just messing about, but that's how the band was, a jazz approach."

However, RSO sent along more suits to hear the album, who gave it the thumbs down. Eventually RSO refused to release *Jet Set Jewel*, beginning the process which would see Jack being dropped from the label. And if that wasn't enough, Jack's marriage was running into trouble.

CHAPTER 13 new beginnings

Jack and Janet were both very young when they met – Janet was still at school, and Jack was barely out of his teens – and by 1978 they had been married for 14 years, during which time Jack had become one of the most famous rock musicians in the world. Together they were a strong couple; Janet would often accompany Jack on tour and they would talk long into the night, best friends as much as husband and wife. But although she didn't want to know any of the details, Janet knew that away from home Jack was unfaithful. He spent much of their marriage on the road, where the inevitable temptations would present themselves to a musician of his status.

There were three women who meant rather more to Jack than one-night stands. Jeanie 'The Tailor' Franklin was one; Jeni Dean, who gave Jack a fright while he and Janet were standing in the VIP section after his Hyde Park concert in September 1971, was another. "Jeni was a groupie, mixed race, tall and slim, Afro hair – a very typical 60s look," Jack recalls. "She was coming toward me holding a baby. I thought 'oh no', but it turned out not to be mine." The third woman had nothing to do with the music business. Sometime in the mid '70s, Jack went to score heroin from a guy who lived on a houseboat on the Thames, and who in turn suggested that he might also visit a woman named Carol who was holding more heroin than he was. "I went round to score," he says, "but I really fell for her and she fell for me. But you can't really call it an affair because it was all wrapped up in this drug thing." Jack would often stay at her flat when he was in London, right up to the early 80s.

Truth be told, women fancied Jack every bit as much as they had when he was a teenager. In her 1993 autobiography, *Backstage Passes*, Angie Bowie wrote: "Jack's a Scot, a wildfire Celt, exempt from the constrictions of Anglo-Saxon decorum. You know it as soon as you look in his eyes; his passion is all right there where you can see it, burning bright and ready to go ... Jack's an extraordinarily compelling person."

Angie went to Jack's house a few times in the company of other musicians. "Whenever I visited his house," she continues, "he'd sit down at the grand piano ... and play whatever he was working on – always wonderful music, very intense, often classical in form – and I'd get the peculiar feeling that everything he was doing, every note, every nuance was aimed directly at me. It was almost as if he were casting a spell, or seducing me somehow. It felt peculiar ... I'd lie down and die for that man, I really would."

Some women were apparently prepared to take inordinate risks to be with Jack. Bud Prager was sitting in his office one day at about 11am, "and who should come into my office but Gail Collins, who I had a real love-hate relationship with – the emphasis being on the hate. She says, 'I have to talk to you.' 'OK. What is it?' 'Well, you know, Felix and I ... I just came in to tell you ... I have royalties accumulated, right?'

"'Yes, you do,' I said.

"'I can have them?'

"'Yes, it's your money. But why?'

"'I'm in love. I've just had the most romantic, wonderful night of my life. I want to leave and we're gonna run off together. And if I tell you who it is, you must swear on your life not to tell anybody?'"

OK, Bud said, and Gail gave him the name: Jack Bruce.

"Now I don't know if this was true, if she was deluding herself, telling lies or what," Bud continued. "But I just looked at her and said, 'Gail. Think about this for a second. There are two guys in the world, that play bass, that were involved with Cream, that did a solo album together, one of them was the best man at your wedding. Of all the people in the world, why him?'

"Like I said, I didn't know what the truth of all this was, but I had a big decision to make here because of Felix's condition at the time with drugs. He'd actually come into my office, put a gun on the table, and told me to shoot him because he said his life was impossible. If Gail left him for Jack Bruce that would have been it, he would have killed himself. So I refused to give her the money."

'Other women' however were not the root cause of the problem between Jack and Janet – nor were the drugs. By her own admission, Janet had taken cocaine while on tour with Jack and was using prescription drugs to fight off depression. "Jack had his drugs," she says, "and I had mine." It was after Jo and Malcolm were born that Janet says their relationship began to change. Although they had help in the house, Janet had been brought up in a very working-class tradition that demanded mum be there for the children. But when Jack called her in distress when he was touring, or she took a call from the office to say that Jack needed her, she might spend days or sometimes even weeks away to be with him. This was always a troubling dilemma. And then when Jack *was* home she was often just too tired to be the same supportive friend she had been before. So Jack would go off to the local pub, where he could at some level be just an ordinary bloke having a pint and talking politics. But the locals were a bit in awe of Jack and his hard-earned status and wealth, so larking about was also tempered by a certain distance and respect.

Another fractious issue was the move out of London, which Jack admits was a mistake but says felt necessary "because of the access to drugs. It was very hard for Janet, and I'm a very difficult person to live with, let's face it."

Janet hated moving to the country, where she never really fitted in. Because of the mansion the Bruces were regarded as 'the rich folks up at the big house', and Janet was asked to open village fetes and the like. This was not her scene at all, and the general sense of isolation contributed to her depression. It wasn't so bad for the boys. Malcolm says he had a friend in the village he'd go off bike-riding with, and remembers there being "an annual fete – my parents let everybody use the garden; they used to have games and the whole village would descend on us".

There were flare-ups. Malcolm has a vivid memory of a chip pan flying across the kitchen in Jack's direction, while another row made the national press. According to a report in the *Daily Mail* in March 1978, Jack went out on a drinking spree after a dispute over money; on the way home he started racing a police car and clipped the side of a lawyer's house. Jack had already been disqualified from driving and this time refused to be breathalysed. The magistrate was informed of Jack's business problems by way of mitigation, but he still ended up being banned from driving for three-and-a-half years.

While it wasn't exactly the turning point, Janet feels that it dawned on her that Jack and she were pulling in different directions when they came to discuss which senior school the boys should attend. Although it went very much against the grain of their socialist principles, they decided to send the boys for private education at a boarding school. (As Janet recalls, the island of Sanda was sold to set up a trust fund for the boys' education; Jack had hardly been there since buying it.) Jo and Malcolm had felt a distance between themselves and the other children at the local school, so the idea was that they wouldn't be so out of place in a school where many of the children would come from privileged backgrounds. It didn't make much difference to Malcolm, however. "I still got called Little Lord Fauntleroy," he recalls, "even at boarding school, with all these wealthy kids there."

O

When John McLaughlin disbanded The Mahavishnu Orchestra in 1976 it caused a storm of decidedly non-spiritual bitterness and indignation. In the years since, John had made three poor-selling albums with the Indian group Shakti. The subsequent *Electric Guitarist* LP was meant to rescue his career from the doldrums. The album was in effect a jazz-fusion sampler co-starring many of John's contemporaries, including Chick Corea, Stanley Clarke, Jack DeJohnette, Billy Cobham, Narada Michael Walden, Carlos Santana, Jerry Goodman, and David Sanborn. But the most notable track was 'Are You The One? Are You The One?', which John had recorded with Jack and Tony Williams in California in January 1978. "It would be interesting to see McLaughlin tour with Williams and Bruce again," John Swenson wrote in his review of the album for *Rolling Stone*, "because together, these three musicians could put most conventional rock bands to shame."

That was the plan: John wanted to re-create Lifetime (without Larry Young, who died in March '78), except that this time it would in effect be his band. He played a gig with Tony and Jaco Pastorius in Cuba during the spring of 1979 for which they were billed as The Trio Of Doom, but Tony wouldn't do any more unless the band was called Tony Williams's Lifetime. John turned instead to Billy Cobham, who still felt aggrieved at the way the Orchestra ended and wasn't best pleased to be John's second choice for this new and exciting band ("I can laugh at myself now," he says).

John next called on keyboardist Stu Goldberg, who had been in one of the last manifestations of the Orchestra, and then contacted Jack. "I got a call from Cyril, John's manager," Jack recalls. "John was putting a band together with Billy and Stu Goldberg. At the time it was great for me because I wasn't doing much and I was pretty skint."

A European tour was arranged to start in October 1979, but the band were plagued with problems (not unlike those which derailed Lifetime). This was definitely John's band, but Jack was a bandleader too, while Billy had released a clutch of very successful solo albums and was an international star in his own right. Jack and Billy were both composers, and expected opportunities to play some of their own compositions. But as Jack recalls: "It looked like Billy and me were not going to be given time to rehearse our material until the last day of rehearsals." At times this creative tussle would play out on stage. "John wouldn't really let us 'take it out'," Jack says. "We would get black looks from him if we tried to."

When you get musicians of this calibre playing together there will naturally be plenty of magic moments. "Our first rehearsals in London were so electric and exciting," Stu recalls. "Everybody was up for it and we were very well prepared. And we played some wonderful concerts. Jack was very supportive on stage, it was a wonderful experience playing with him." Billy agrees. "It was a great musical experience," he says. "I was working with Jack for the first time and, I gotta tell you, there are very few voices like that one, if any."

Everything looked set. The problems didn't emerge until about halfway through the tour – and they were all to do with money. Billy Cobham was the smart one; he wouldn't leave home until the money was in an escrow account, ready for release when the tour was over. Jack and Stu were more trusting. "Money was promised into the accounts before we left home," Stu recalls. "Not there. We're getting ready to leave; still not there. You are starting to feel uncomfortable, the vibe is changing, and now you are on tour – and still the money is not there. Jack was extremely vocal about this."

All of this put John in a bad light because he was the leader. Worse still, the band's manager started playing mind games, which Stu says "took a huge psychological toll. Jack went to Cyril, who told him that John didn't want him paid. Then he would tell John that Jack had said John shouldn't be paid because Jack hadn't received any money." Relations in the band – especially between Jack and John – were fatally poisoned. Although Billy's money was safe, he had every sympathy for Jack and Stu.

Toward the end of the tour, the band's concert at the Rainbow Theatre in London in November almost didn't happen because the crew hadn't been paid either. Along with any creative tensions on stage, all this bad feeling inevitably impacted on the music – they ended up playing as individuals rather than a band. One reviewer of the Rainbow concert wrote that John was playing out the dying embers of a style of music now past its sell-by date, where the experience of jazz-rock was becoming a vacuous exercise in playing a lot while saying nothing. By the end the band-members were not communicating musically or socially.

After the Rainbow concert, Cyril invited Jack to dinner and told him he would pay him there and then. "But the cheque bounced," Jack says. "Eventually I got paid, but I also got the bill for the rehearsals and the band's stay at the Montcalm Hotel. Everybody was signing for everything but not paying the bills, and as I was the only British resident they sued me for the money. So I had to pay and then contact John and ask him to reimburse me because I couldn't get it from the manager. He did pay me eventually, but it did leave a very bad feeling."

Flash back to October 14 1979, when the tour reached the Liederhalle in Stuttgart. Margrit Seyffer, a 25-year-old graphic designer specialising in music books, had just returned home to Germany after a 13-month backpacking trip across the Americas from Vancouver down to Bolivia. She wanted to go to the concert but the queue closed while she was still in it. She tried to get a ticket through a friend, but that didn't work either. "I thought it wasn't to be and just gave up," she says. Instead she decided to work late to finish a job and then at around 1am took herself off to the local nightclub, the AT.

Meanwhile, Jack finished the gig and was invited to dinner by John's record company. "We went to this Italian restaurant," he says. "There was a guy with a beard and a dog and he was talking to me a lot while I was feeding the dog spaghetti. I was talking to this really nice woman as well and later in evening I said to her, 'Do you want to go somewhere?' She said she knew this club, the AT. So we went there and I saw this other woman dancing. She looked amazing and I immediately fell in love. But she didn't look German, she looked Peruvian or Turkish, so I wondered how I was going to talk to her. I know, I thought, I'll learn to dance in the next ten seconds. So I became John Travolta and did all these moves I'd never done before in order to get close to her."

Margrit invited Jack back to her place that night. When she turned on the engine of the car she'd borrowed, a Cream tape left in the machine blared from the sound system. It was the second coincidence of the night: the bearded guy with the dog Jack had met earlier turned out to be Margrit's ex-partner of the previous seven years. "In the end, when Margrit and I were together, we got custody of the dog, Mischa!"

The next morning Margrit drove Jack to the hotel he should have been staying in the night before to pick up his suitcase, which was still lying in the lobby. She said she'd take him to the next gig in Munich, but they hit a traffic jam and Jack literally had to run onto the stage at the last minute – much to the annoyance of John, who was also less than enamoured with Jack's Manny Schlepper t-shirt. ("He was so disapproving," Jack recalls with a giggle.)

Margrit went home after the gig but a week later Jack called to invite her to Milan. The trip pretty much cemented their relationship. "It was something I had never experienced before," she says.

Jack and Janet have differing views of their marriage during this period. As far as Jack is concerned, his relationship with Janet "had broken down some time before that, and although I hadn't actually left, I was spending a lot of time with Carol who was also using smack. It was definitely a time when I was looking for a new beginning, something to happen. But at the same time I was torn, as one always is. I'd been with Janet for a long time and I had the boys. Luckily for me, the depth and strength of the love Margrit and I had for each other just took over."

Even so, Margrit didn't hear anything from him for a while. "He just vanished," she says. "I knew he was using heroin, and I had known somebody who had died. When I was 19, I went to dance clubs and girls would just shoot up in the toilets." Margrit had no idea where Jack lived in England and no way of contacting him. Meanwhile Jack turned up at home stoned around the time of the Rainbow concert and Janet sent him away, not realising at the time that she had "pushed him away at a point when Margrit was there". There is no doubt that leaving his family was a huge step for Jack, and that all of the conflicting emotions and the hassles of the tour had sent him deep into the comfort zone of heroin.

Jack finally left home over Christmas 1979, just as Margrit arrived in London with a friend on the off chance of finding him. She happened to read an advertisement in *Time Out* magazine for a gig at Dingwalls on December 30 by Rocket 88, an occasional band led by blues pianists Bob Hall and Ian Stewart ('the sixth Rolling Stone'). Alexis Korner also played with them, as, when they were available, did Charlie Watts and Jack Bruce.

Rocket 88 had played a few dates in Europe straight after Jack's tour with John McLaughlin. Bob says Ian insisted Jack play acoustic bass. "One time Jack had gone and we were loading up after a gig and dropped Jack's bass off the back of the truck and it smashed," he recalls. "This was not just any bass, it was a very good instrument and we were terrified. 'Who's going to tell Jack we've smashed his bass up?' I think we had to play the next day or the day after, and Stu rang up a guy who restored instruments and this guy worked through the night to put this bass back together again. It must have cost a fortune, but by the time we got it back you couldn't tell – and we didn't tell Jack."

The Dingwalls gig had been arranged to celebrate 50 years of boogie-woogie. The queue stretched around the block and hundreds were turned away. "We were doing a soundcheck and somebody came up and said, 'There's a woman to see you'," Jack recalls. "I looked round, saw Margrit, and dropped my bass guitar. I was so stunned."

Although Jack had been living with Carol, he and Margrit quickly moved into Ronnie Leahy's flat in Earls Court. "We played Casino and drank a lot of Bailey's," Ronnie recalls. "Margrit stayed for about six weeks, then they both moved to Germany and back again to the UK to stay with Pete Brown."

Jack says he was looking for a new start, and as the new decade dawned he made the decision to move to Germany with Margrit. He also wanted to carry on playing with Billy Cobham. "We were friends, we had a good time together," he says. But he also had another very good reason for needing a new start – the repercussions of which would ripple through the 80s. Jack had been dropped by RSO Records, who then refused to represent him as a client and presented him with a set of what he describes as "Kafka-esque" accounts.

○

Robert Stigwood was never a hands-on artist manager. As the 70s wore on he lost interest in the music business, much preferring the world of film and theatre. He lavished attention on Eric Clapton and The Bee Gees because they were the most commercially successful of his acts, but in 1973 he began a run of huge successes as a film producer with *Jesus Christ Superstar*, which was followed by *Tommy* (1975), *Saturday Night Fever* (1977), and *Grease* (1978). The success of the accompanying soundtracks – combined with strong sales for Clapton and The Bee Gees – saw RSO become one of the most profitable independent labels in the world. The only blot on the landscape of unalloyed triumph was the awful *Sgt Pepper* film with Peter Frampton, which lost RSO millions of dollars.

By the late 70s Robert Stigwood had relocated to New York and the Bahamas, leaving RSO's London office as little more than a royalty-collecting agency, and certainly not a company concerned with promoting the career of Jack Bruce. The problem for Jack was compounded by the arrival of Al Coury, who came from Capitol Records to be President of RSO in America and had no interest in anything that wasn't Top 40.

Chris Youle worked for Polydor in Hamburg and was then brought in as MD of RSO Records in 1974. "Jack was a fantastic artist who didn't get the respect and support that somebody who had made the company vast amounts of money deserved," he says. "Robert wasn't interested at all. I had arguments with Robert that he had a duty of care, if you like. Jack Bruce and Cream had made him a lot of money." (Money that Cream suspected had been siphoned off to promote The Bee Gees when they arrived in the UK in 1967.)

After the disastrous Chuck Berry tour of 1965, Stigwood went cap in hand to Polygram, asking to be bailed out in exchange for a slice of RSO Records. But according to former RSO executive David English, Stigwood spent £50,000 promoting The Bee Gees in 1967. Where did the money come from? Stigwood revealed the truth in a very rare unguarded moment, captured on film, in *Rolling Hotel*, Reg Pyke's documentary about Eric's 1977 European tour. At one point everyone is sitting around drinking when Eric suddenly asks Stigwood to "talk about how you got started".

"Any other loony stories?" Stigwood replies. "I owe my life to Eric Clapton."

"I wasn't asking about your life. I was asking about your money. If it wasn't for me, Ginger, and Jack, you wouldn't have been able to bring The Bee Gees over from Australia, would you?"

"True," says Stigwood.

"Well, there you go then."

"After you finish filming this, I might strangle him," Stigwood says, although in a later outburst about money it's Eric who tries to strangle Stigwood. Not surprisingly, the film remains unreleased.

It is almost expected for a musician to claim that he or she has been ripped off by a combination of management, record company, agent, promoter, and publisher. But the truth is that they probably have. Contracts are designed by clever lawyers and accountants to put as much distance between the artist and a proper accounting of their earnings as possible, and to ensure that the artist is in hock to the company for as long as possible.

Add in the chicanery, 'creative accounting', and downright theft that goes on, and it is no wonder that even the biggest artists in the world – Elton John, The Who, The Beatles, the Stones, Pink Floyd, Sting, and George Michael – have been forced to turn to the courts for justice. But what all those artists have in common is the financial wherewithal to hire the brightest and the best to swim in the same sea as the sharks they were prosecuting – a luxury Jack could never afford.

If Jack's claims against RSO had come to court, the company would have been obliged to disclose far more accounting information than Jack could ever hope to secure by himself. But they didn't, so what follows is gleaned from interviews with a few key players and an attempt to analyse records held at Companies House.

There was no actual contract for Cream as a band. Jack, Ginger, and Eric were signed as individuals for recording, management, publishing, and agency representation – something that would never be allowed today because such an arrangement constitutes a potentially serious conflict of interest. The manager, for example, is supposed to negotiate the best deal for recording and publishing, but how can that be possible if it's all the same company? And just in case any of them had the bright idea to get a second opinion, Jack says there was a clause in the contract forbidding them to seek independent advice.

Instead of being paid directly by RSO, the members of Cream were each appointed directors of their own company – all subsidiaries of RSO – and could then draw tax-free loans from the companies (geared toward reducing their tax liability). Cream were also paid a 'wage' by the company (another way of paying less tax). These plans were devised by David Shaw, Stigwood's financial advisor. A former City banker, Shaw had earned the disapproval of his peers in the City – at a time when it still prided itself in having some moral standards – by continuing with a scheme called 'bond-washing' (which involved selling a bond as it was due to pay interest or its dividend and then buying it back at a lower price, resulting in a capital gain for the original seller) after the government had announced plans to outlaw the practice. While the idea of forming separate companies appeared to make some sense, Jack feels that this arrangement made it harder for Cream as a band to form a united front, and easier for RSO to "divide and rule".

Beginning in 1965, a complicated set of companies was established to deal with every aspect of the Robert Stigwood empire. According to the records, there were nearly 30 of them, including those set up individually for Cream and Dratleaf, which handled much of Cream's publishing. Again there's nothing inherently illegal here, just a bewildering array of companies and accounts – where money could be passed between one and the other, making it very difficult to keep track of income and expenditure except through expensive independent audits. One head-spinning item in the accounts shows that in August 1970, for example, RSO lent money to Polydor so that Polydor could lend money to Jack, Eric, and Ginger – enabling them to pay back loans from RSO.

As Bud Prager recalled: "RSO were screwing me every which way possible. I got accountings from Atlantic for the US [Cream] sales, but on International, I could never get a straight anything from Stigwood. In the end, they'd just say, 'We can't do the accounting, how much will you settle for?' One of Stigwood's senior vice-presidents actually said to me, 'I really have to thank you. We were going public, and if you'd sued us it would have blown us out the water.'" And if someone like Bud Prager – well versed in the black arts of rock management – couldn't trust the accounting, what hope was there for Jack?

What you had was a company prone to highly complex arrangements managing the affairs of one of the highest earning bands in the world – who had little option but to hope that everything was in order. It is true that if, for example, Jack wanted a car, the money was made available. But this would have been loose change compared to what the band was earning: the business of handing out money was indicative of how record labels treated their artists. In the late 60s, Billy Gaff (later Rod Stewart's manager) worked for RSO as a record plugger. Stigwood asked him if he would be Cream's tour manager. Gaff asked: "What would I have to do?" "Have you ever looked after children?" Stigwood replied. And that's what you do with children: you buy them toys as presents, but you don't reveal the extent of the family finances.

Jack never trusted Stigwood, and didn't want him as Cream's manager, but in some ways he needed to believe him. When he was offered shares in RSO, he took this as indicative that he was part of the 'family'. "I was told by Stigwood that I wouldn't have to worry for the rest of my life, that I was a major shareholder in RSO and that rather than taking the money, I was taking shares, that was the deal," he says. Unfortunately, having shares in RSO was not so good an idea as it might have seemed. Memories differ, but as Bud indicated above, the decision was taken around 1970 to float RSO on the London Stock Exchange.

Although the label would become immensely successful later on, it may well have been struggling at the start of the 70s. Cream were finished, Blind Faith had proven shortlived, Eric had gone into seclusion, and Stigwood wasn't getting the 'three Creams' he had hoped for. But the plan to turn RSO's red cow logo into a cash cow did not work; those close to the label at the time believe the City was still wary of any venture involving David Shaw. So RSO would have needed to buy the shares back, which would have depleted the share value – directly impacting on Jack's income.

Earnings from West Bruce & Laing should have made a substantial difference to Jack's bank balance, but as we have already seen most of that money finished up in other people's pockets. After the last WBL tour, Jack went into the RSO office to find out how much money he had earned. "Stigwood was sitting at his desk with David Shaw," he recalls. "I said, 'I must have done really well from that tour.' 'Yes,' he said, 'now you only owe us £40,000!' That was when I just wanted to die and retreat into smack. They really dragged me through the shit and I blame a lot of my drug problems on them. I thought if that's it, if that's what I've worked so hard for and got nothing, well, fuck it. The last power that you have is to kill yourself. That's the effect that it all had on me after WBL because it was so hard mentally and physically for me to do – and it was very successful."

O

Compared with what Jack must have earned in record sales, publishing, touring, and mechanical rights, Jack's actual outlay would have been relatively modest. Cream never travelled with a large entourage or stayed in top hotels, and spent little time in the studio – the songs were largely written and composed before they went in, and their touring schedule didn't allow for much recording time anyway. Jack had his North London townhouse, bought on a mortgage that would have been repaid when he bought the country mansion for roughly £30,000. The island of Sanda cost about the same, and there were a few luxury cars. But working on the same principle as Cream, Jack did not spend long recording his albums. The only time when there would have been significant studio costs was in 1974, when the main room at the Record Plant in LA was block-booked for weeks – and even then the studio manager would resell the studio space when Jack & co failed to turn up (which happened often), so RSO would have recouped some of the costs.

Interviewed by *Melody Maker* in February 1979, Jack tried to put on a brave face, suggesting in that time-honoured cliché of the music business that he and RSO had parted ways amicably, by mutual consent. "Obviously RSO has become such a huge concern that I just don't have the same feeling of being part of the family, the way it used to be," he said. "They've got more into films and shows, [and] because it's got so big, I don't see myself relating to it any more. So it's the end of my contract with RSO and I'll be going with another record company – which I can't divulge at the moment."

He was far less diplomatic when interviewed by the same publication in late 1980. When journalist Karl Dallas made mention of the unreleased album, Jack replied: "I'm one of the many people waiting in line to sort things out with Stigwood. There are about 15 people ahead of me in the queue."

Without mentioning it by name, Jack was referring to one of the largest lawsuits in the history of the music business. The Bee Gees had sued RSO for $75m, Polygram for another $75m, and were seeking a further $50m in punitive damages. RSO was accused of conflict of interest, fraud, "unfair enrichment" at the expense of the band, and "grossly inadequate" contracts, with royalty rates significantly lower than the industry norm. It was also alleged that Robert Stigwood had registered song copyrights in his name. Stigwood counter-sued for $310m on grounds of libel, extortion, and breach of contract, issuing furious press releases that caused the whole mess to be fought out very publicly.

In the end they all kissed and made up long before the matter reached the courts. But at the time when Jack piped up in the press, the suspicion is that Stigwood just took all his anger and frustrations out on him. "I was called into the office by Roger, who offered me a brandy and said, 'here, drink this, you're going to need it.' Then he told me that they would no longer represent me, but they weren't going to release me either. I said, 'Well, obviously, I'm going to sue.'"

Jack eventually secured an advance from Warner Chappell in 1989, which enabled him to go after some of his money. And for all the time this had been going on RSO were still collecting all of Jack's money (except the performing rights payments he had refused to sign over), effectively freezing his income.

About former manager Roger Forrester, Jack says: "I think he became a very good guy, especially for Eric, but back then he was certainly very unhelpful to me. I imagine he has regrets for some of the things he has done. I have mixed feelings about him; he wasn't like Stigwood, who has been so destructive in my life."

O

In January 1980 Jack appeared on television to promote an album he had played on, Cozy Powell's solo debut *Over The Top*. Among the other musicians on the album was guitarist Dave 'Clem' Clempson, whom Jack had met briefly in the early 70s when Clem was in Colosseum.

"Tony Reeves had left [Colosseum] and we hadn't come up with a replacement yet, but we had studio time booked," Clem recalls. "One of the tracks we wanted to record was 'Theme For An Imaginary Western'. It was decided I would play bass, so Dick took me round to Jack's place to borrow one." Clem also went out to Jack's country house around the time of the band with Mick Taylor and was friends with Ronnie Leahy, but he didn't see Jack again until the *Old Grey Whistle Test* recording. After the show Jack wanted to talk about forming a new band. "I couldn't believe it," Clem says. "I was so excited."

The new line-up was completed with the addition of drummer Billy Cobham and keyboardist David Sancious, who hailed from Asbury Park, New

Jersey, and had been in an early incarnation of Bruce Springsteen's E-Street Band. David started playing the piano at the age of six and studied classical music until he was well into his teens. He was also an outstanding guitarist. "Jack and I had so much in common," he says. "Once we met and had a chance to talk, we found we shared that common source of classical, blues, R&B, jazz, pop, and everything in between."

Jack and David were introduced by John Scher, an important East Coast promoter who was also briefly Jack's manager during the period after he was dropped by RSO but before his legal problems with the label started. Billy had produced David's first solo album, so between them all there was much common ground.

This latest Jack Bruce band was arguably a lot less stressful than any that had preceded it. The musicians were highly professional and competent; talking to them now, there is not the slightest hint of ego problems or tantrums, nor were there any hassles with the tour arrangements, venues, and the like. Clem in particular would become one of Jack's favourite guitarists.

As ever Jack was far from prescriptive about what his musicians should play. "I never remember Jack telling us what he wanted in terms of guitar parts," Clem recalls. "He'd just play us a song, say what the chords were, and we'd play it. It would just evolve, especially once we were playing it on stage."

David appreciated the fact that "everybody was asked to contribute something. Jack is a very schooled and knowledgeable musician, along with being very soulful and original. So he had charts for his songs, but there would be plenty of room for your own interpretation – a map with all the essentials there and blank spaces for you to fill.

"He might say 'this is the melody, and after 16 bars we move to this area where it is open, then back to the structure'. Clem was excellent at that, just fantastic." And Clem in turn had no problem with having another guitarist in the band. "On some songs David would play guitar, Jack would be on piano, and I'd play bass – it was great."

David really appreciated having Clem as the other guitarist. "Of all the ensembles I have played in where I've played with another guitarist, this band with Clem was the best because we became really close personal friends," he says. "The chemistry between the four of us was fantastic. We were in the same dimension, but Jack was down the road – he made everyone play better simply by being there. It was pure energy." Billy was just happy to be in a band situation where there was a clear leader and everybody knew what was going on. "We played Jack's music. That's what it was all about."

The band toured throughout 1980, a year which ended on a tragic note with the death of John Lennon on December 8. Five days later the band played a highly emotional show at New York's Palladium. Before that, they were in the USA in March, then took a break until July for six shows at the Venue in London before an appearance in October on the German television show *Rockpalast* and another stint in the States.

During the summer break they recorded an album, *I've Always Wanted To Do This*, at the House Of Music in New Jersey with Jack back in the saddle as producer. But before recording the album the whole band stayed at an idyllic spot called Lower East Lyn Farm in Devon. "That part was wonderful," Billy recalls. "That's where I wrote 'Wind And The Sea' for the album – a very special place."

The recording sessions were similarly calm. "In the studio [Jack] gives you all the freedom in the world," Billy adds. "It was clear how things were going to be and it just worked out nicely, very easy." It wasn't all quiet contemplation, however, as Clem took on Billy at racquetball. "I thought playing on stage with Billy was terrifying enough – this was even worse. He hit the ball and it pinged around the court for about 20 minutes while I chased around after it."

I've Always Wanted To Do This includes five Bruce-Brown songs as well as contributions from the other musicians. David wrote with Pete and with Clem, Billy contributed his song, and there was also a reprise of 'Mickey The Fiddler'. Although Jack was producing the album, his new label, CBS, made it clear that this should be an album of short songs with no extended playing. And with a very 80s sound at his disposal, Jack ended up with a rather thin and sterile ambience.

The best tracks are a pair of Bruce-Brown compositions. "There are bands with five people in it and it takes all of them to write a song, because they aren't strong enough as composers to do it individually," David says. "That's what separates Jack Bruce from all those others." For 'Bird Alone' Jack asked Pete to write a tribute to Thelonious Monk but got back a homage to Charlie Parker instead; even so, the result was a scintillating ensemble piece of starkly contrasting moods that Clem calls "absolutely stunning and very moving". The other highlight is 'Hit And Run', which Pete says is about the takeover of Motown by the Mafia.

With the album due out soon on CBS, the label sent over the head of its art department to discuss the cover. Jack had already come up with a name for the album and had an idea for the artwork, too. "The guys would all be sitting in the CBS office at Black Rock and I would jump in through a plate glass window," he says. "They said they couldn't get the insurance for that. But I didn't want to really do that, I thought you could just mock it up." Instead it went something like this:

> Art Dude: I've got a great idea.
> Band: OK ...
> Art Dude: Two white guys, two black guys, yeah?
> Band [uncertain]: Yeah ...
> Art Dude: OK – you strip off and we'll get a shot of your four asses and then put it out of focus so it looks like the surface of the moon!
> Billy Cobham: My momma told me never to do that.

Jack thinks that CBS pretty much pulled the plug on the record after that because the art director was quite high up the hierarchy. "They didn't promote the album," he says. "There were supposed to be flyers at every gig – that didn't happen. It was the same old story of wasted opportunities."

○

With his business problems still unresolved and his assets frozen, Jack was supported by Margrit, who had begun gradually taking over his business affairs and even bought him a synthesiser. Then in 1981 came a welcome chance for some extra income from an unexpected source. Guitarist Robin Trower was recording a new album at Konk Studios in North London. "In the 70s, I had a trio with James Dewar on bass and vocals and two different drummers," he recalls. "I felt after so many albums it was time to try something different, but I still wanted to keep the trio format. So you think, 'Bass? Vocals? Who's good?' And who do you come up with? Jack is the greatest. I met him in London and took him a cassette with a few song ideas. I had to see if he would be interested in working with me. That became BLT."

Jack says he found BLT very easy "because Robin had most of the tracks already recorded". The resulting *BLT* sold very well, breaking into the *Billboard* Top 40 without any touring to promote it, but Robin was not wholly satisfied with the album. "I wasn't completely knocked out by it," he says. "It was my input. I didn't feel I was getting anywhere. So I wasn't thinking about another album, but the record company and my manager were very keen that we did another. And because I wasn't happy with BLT, I came at it from a different viewpoint and it wasn't as successful musically."

Jack puts some of this down to the change of drummer, from Bill Lordan back to Reg Isidore. "He was a nice guy, but it didn't really work; the album took a long time and it got lost along the way, as records do if they take a long time. So it didn't have that freshness and spontaneity that the first one had. The essence of that kind of music is that it should sound and feel live without lots of backing vocals and so on. Usually the second take is the one. You do a run through, do another take, then you might think 'I can do it better' and spend the whole day doing takes. Then you go back to the second one and it's by far the best." Jack and Pete wrote some new songs for the album, *Truce*, but they didn't really gel with Robin's style – confirming in the eyes of some critics that Jack should resist the temptation to play in any more rock trios.

In the meantime Jack continued to play with Billy, Clem, and David over the next few years, with Bruce Gary coming in when Billy was unavailable. One tour that sticks in the mind of those who took part was the 15-date Midgie & Mackerel Tour of mainly tiny venues in Scotland in 1983, for which Jack was backed by Clem, Bruce, and Ronnie Leahy. Midges are the plague of the Scottish countryside during the summer: tiny, gnat-like insects against which there is no protection. And Jack, an excellent cook, would serve up the mackerel he and Margrit caught off the shore of the idyllic cottage they had bought together in Wester Ross. Jack remembers his time in the cottage as among the happiest of his life. He and Margrit hadn't even been looking for a place, but she just happened to catch sight of the cottage in an estate agent's window as they strolled through Inverness. They drove out west and bought it the next day using the proceeds from *BLT* and Margrit's own savings.

Jack and Janet were divorced in 1982, and after that Jack married Margrit, who was already pregnant with the couple's first child and loved spending time in the cottage, even when Jack was on tour. There was no shortage of visitors to Wester Ross. Jack's sons, Jo and Malcolm, came during the summer holidays, and there were visits from Jack's mum, Betty, and Margrit's parents, Robert and Lore, who drove all the way from southern Germany in their VW Camper van.

Natascha was born in 1982 and another daughter, Kyla, arrived in 1985, with son Corin born in 1992. Jack and Margrit would go off on two-day hikes, with Natascha on Jack's back and Kyla safely wrapped up in Margrit's South American shawl. "The two girls really gave me a positive outlook on life," Jack says. But in between the feral midges and the mouth-watering mackerel there was work to do. Jack recounts that "we played the Eden Court Theatre in Inverness, then we drove to Gairloch and on to Ullapool and the ferry to

Stornoway on the Isle Of Lewis. The gig was in a room at the back of the pub and people were coming in from all over the Western Isles. We got there for about 4pm, to play at 8 or 9. We were ready to play, but the guy said, 'Och, no, they're not nearly drunk enough yet." By the time they got on stage, the whole audience was totally trashed. "It was a lot of fun. It was really special to play those places."

The rest of the band had a laugh with Bruce Gary as well. On one occasion they were on the train up to Scotland and asked Bruce if he had his visa to cross the border. "A visa for Scotland?" "Oh, yes, they are very strict about that; if you haven't got one, you might get thrown off the train – or even sent to jail." Bruce went into a total panic, so they took off the top of the bench seat in the carriage and made him hide inside it – all six-foot-plus of him. After they crossed the border, they let him out, covered in dust and muck. He took it in good heart.

For his part Jack just enjoyed playing with his mates, dipping into his back catalogue, playing songs they all knew and loved. But it still felt incongruous for Jack Bruce to be playing little pubs in the middle of the Scottish countryside. That same year he also did a short, low-rent tour of Germany as part of the Jan Hammer Band. "That was bizarre," he says. "Jan really liked AC/DC and he wanted to be Angus Young, so he had a synthesiser on a strap. He had a German drummer who couldn't really cut the mustard and a 'troubled' keyboard player. We played small clubs, travelling in shitty buses, staying in cheap hotels for very little money."

One of Margrit's early business deals for Jack was a German-only release on Intercord recorded at Park Gates and Britannia Row Studios in 1983. Jack was talking to Ike Nossel, the engineer who owned the studio, "and Ike was getting a Fairlight [synthesizer]. I was fascinated by this – it was a wonder-machine that could do everything. You could have a whole orchestra, weird sounds. I wanted to call [the album] *One Man And His Box*, but it got called *Automatic*. It's just me, except 'Encore', which is a version of 'The Best Is Yet To Come'. Bruce Gary re-recorded the drums. I was experimenting with things in Germany using a synthesiser and sequencer I had. The Fairlight was fine, but the drum machine wasn't. In those days the only drum machine was the Linn Drum, which had a horrible sound – I think it was actually Billy who recorded the drum sounds for Linn!"

By and large, regardless of whoever else writes the songs for a Jack Bruce album, it is the Bruce-Brown songs that endure. But Pete wasn't getting on terribly well with Jack at that point. Jack was pretty sick – physically and psychologically – which explains why 'The Best Is Yet To Come' was reprised as 'Encore'. 'New World' was a further attempt to put a positive spin on life.

Pete says that the record company, Intercord, "were very dodgy and tried to claim the publishing, so we had to send them all sorts of funny letters". *Automatic* is often dismissed, probably because of the dated synthesizer technology used on it, but every song is a Bruce-Brown composition, so from that standpoint it is probably at least as strong as *How's Tricks* or *Jet Set Jewel*. It contains some first-rank compositions, notably the reggae-inflected 'Make Love', which is actually about the conflict in Northern Ireland but is every bit as infectious and commercial as the records The Police were making at the time.

Jack put together another band with David Sancious and Bruce Gary for a short European tour at the end of 1983. On November 1 1983 they appeared on *Rockpalast*, performing virtually the whole of *Automatic* and giving the songs a new warmth and colour. As this concert demonstrated, it doesn't have to be all *sturm und drang*, three egos battling for attention, using virtuosity just to be flash and being competitive instead of settling into the slipstream of the music. Jack was interested as much in the interaction between musicians and the spaces on the stage as he was in the intervals or space between the notes in his compositions. Jack, David, and Bruce were on electrifying form, intense but loose – a dramatic example of what musicians mean when they say playing with Jack brings out the best in them.

"That '83 tour stands out in my memory," David recalls. "It wasn't luxury touring but the shows were fantastic. There's something about three minds, three elements – harmonic, rhythmic, and the bass. It's more spiritual, a symmetry that happens when there are three of you. You can go deeper, be more spontaneous and do different things more quickly with three minds than with four or five – it's easier to create, perceive, and react. It happens so fast, and when it does, it's magic – and I was happy to get the chance to play the Cream material with one of the founders of the group because Cream was a very large part of my life when I was learning guitar. There was a time when I knew it all verbatim, note for note: the guitar parts, the solos, even the bass."

For the next few years the already serendipitous, unplanned nature of Jack's career was reinforced by the need to earn some hard cash, a journey that sent him traversing many pathways across the landscape of popular music.

In the early months of his legal wrangling with RSO, Jack was severely restricted in what he could do to earn money. Blues guitarist and bandleader Norman Beaker persuaded him to come and do a few low-key blues gigs in the north of England, really just to keep his hand in. Norman knew Dick Heckstall-Smith, "so that sealed the deal with Jack and all the gigs sold out. It just wasn't right that he couldn't play, and I think those gigs gave him a little boost when he was pretty down. Jack plays really hard and you play really hard back. It's not really competitive, more inspirational. When you play with Jack Bruce, the first song is like the encore. You come off at the end of the evening exhausted. You don't really know what you've done, except you've played everything you've ever learned."

There were one-off gigs with Nigerian drummer Fela Kuti (1983); Arlen Roth (1984); Tony Williams (1985); and Black Sabbath drummer Bill Ward (1986). And in November 1984 Jack took part in a performance of a mini-opera by Carla Bley based on Malcolm Lowry's *Under The Volcano*. As Dick introduced Jack to Lowry's writings, so Jack passed on the inspiration to Carla. "I played the snare drum and recited a bit," he says. "Very odd, very modern."

In 1986 Jack became a member of the aural action painting that was The Golden Palominos, founded by drummer Anton Fier and featuring at various times Carla, Michael Stipe, Richard Thompson, and John Lydon. "That was a mad band," he says. "Anton was completely drunk all the time. I remember Anton sitting in the first class lounge in Paris Airport with a bottle of brandy and drinking it in the 20 minutes we had between flights. In Budapest, he got so drunk he fell off the drum stool." That same year Jack put a band together for some gigs in Israel, where he had never played before. Conscious of his Jewish background, Bruce Gary refused to travel following a terrorist incident, so Jack hired Anton "because he was so drunk he wouldn't have noticed if somebody blew him up". (On another occasion in Israel, Jack had to replace Bruce with the Lebanese Mark Nauseef and took delight in emphasising Mark's heritage to the audience.)

Jack also played the Nice Jazz Festival with Ginger, saxophonist Courtney Pine, and French guitarist Bireli Lagrene during the summer of 1986. "It was a strange mix of players, but we just started to improvise," he says. "After the gig, Nesuhi Ertegun was there and said, 'You've got to help us out. There's a band called The New York All Stars and the rhythm section hasn't turned up.' So it was me and Bernard Purdie having a ball. I turned around and there was the whole of The Buddy Rich Big Band standing there, watching. When we finished, Buddy Rich came up to me and gave me this huge hug. Somebody told me later that he had told his bass player, 'That's what I want you to do.'"

The following year Jack was involved in concerts and recordings with Carla's husband Mike Mantler and a performance in Hamburg of *The*

Jack Bruce COMPOSING HIMSELF

Threepenny Opera with Sting and the Italian singer Gianna Nannini, for which Jack sang in German. But the most significant and enduring development for Jack started in 1983, when a cassette dropped through his letterbox and introduced him to an entirely new field of music.

O

The cassette came from Kip Hanrahan, who had been involved with Latino and jazz musicians for many years. Born in 1954 of Irish-Jewish descent (his grandfather was Russian and travelled with Leon Trotsky), Kip grew up in the Hispanic quarter of the Bronx. He heard Latino music on every street corner and hung out with guys he would later work with as musicians. He was one of very few white kids at a school where, he says, "you were defined by the music you listened to. We were the hip kids, carrying Mingus and Ornette Coleman records around. Even for the Hispanic kids, jazz was the cool thing."

Kip moved around the New York avant-garde jazz scene in the late 60s and early 70s and worked for Carla Bley and Mike Mantler in the Jazz Composers Orchestra Association and the New Music Distribution Service. He was becoming a skilled percussionist and learning as much as he could about record production at the feet of Teo Macero, the composer, musician, and producer who had a particularly long and fruitful relationship with Miles Davis at Columbia Records. He also dipped his toe in the movie world with experimental filmmaker Jonas Mekas and the New Film Cooperative and wrote scripts for some European projects, but became disillusioned with the industry because of the lack of artistic control and huge amounts of money being wasted. Through his work with Carla and Mike he could see that you could produce an album for a fraction of a film budget – and be in control right through production and distribution.

In 1979 Kip started his own label, American Clavé. Kip calls himself an auteur rather than a producer, contributing to the creation of his music by bringing musicians together, scoring charts, writing lyrics, gathering sounds, and generally creating that quintessential Kip feel: the Gauloise cool of the Parisian Left Bank at 3am, dark passions and smouldering eroticism etched in serpentine lyrics and throbbing with the subtleties and finesse of Latin rhythms, resulting in a sound that is diffuse yet all-embracing.

When Kip came to record his first album, *Coup De Tete*, he tried to do the vocals himself but couldn't get them to work. "I was going for a certain cadence," he says, "a melody in things that are spoken, very intimate, even uncomfortably so, but I don't have that strong a voice." For his next album he

232

worked with Carla Bley's partner, bassist Steve Swallow. "We were working on charts with more complex voicings," he recalls. "And I knew I couldn't do that. By then I had copies of *Songs For A Tailor* and *Harmony Row* as examples of how brilliant music could be. There was a restlessness in the music which is not always entirely comfortable – and that's what's in Jack. Nobody writes songs like those – it breaks the rules because, if you want to make that turbulence audible, then you have to break the rules. I sent Jack tapes with rough things, five drummers and maybe three basses."

Jack had an awareness of Latin music that went way back. "I always loved that kind of music even when I was a kid – The Dizzy Gillespie Big Band with Chano Pozo," he says. "That was my audition piece for The Murray Campbell Band, 'One Bass Hit'." Pete Brown could hear Jack's affinity for these rhythms even before he met Kip. "If you listen to the Latin fusion music of Airto Moreira or Hermeto Pascoal, there's actually a lot in common with Jack, some surprising musical parallels. It's like Jack was born into it."

When Jack first received the tapes he had no idea who Kip was. "But as soon as I heard the tracks," he says, "I thought, 'Yes, try and stop me.' Kip had a great vision of what my role would be within that line-up. I wasn't just going to be this rock'n'roll singer – he brought out this whole other side, more like talking than 'big' singing. I just loved the songs and the playing was a revelation to me. I needed a new direction and Kip really helped me. He found this other voice, which is lower and more intimate, and it meant in later years in my own writing I could rely on that voice. I felt I was part of this music. I can't stress enough how much of an influence he was on my music."

Before the invention of the microphone you had to have a big voice to fill the room. The trick with Bing Crosby and Frank Sinatra was the intimacy of the microphone: it sounded like they were singing to just one person in the room. "And if you are almost whispering," says Kip, "you can change the phrasing every time around, maybe clip the last note. Jack picked up on all of those ideas and ran with it in the shortest possible time, mastered it all and took it to a place I didn't even think it could get to."

Jack and Kip met at the Gramercy Park Hotel in New York and quickly found common cause in left-wing politics. "One of the first songs Kip wrote in the studio for *Desire Develops An Edge* was 'Working Class Boys'," Jack says, "because the night before that's what we'd been talking about." Kip soon found, as Carla Bley had when Jack agreed to work on *Escalator Over The Hill*, that with Jack on board all of his writing took on a new focus. "I would not have made the music I made without Jack, not just for his vocals, but for his emotions, his passions, what you see within him, making the light and dark of his character felt." The pair rewrote the songs Kip had initially sent Jack phrase by phrase.

Pete's assertion that Jack's soul was already imbued with Latin sensibilities before he met up with Kip is underscored by the inclusion on the album of the earlier 'Childsong', its Latin feel merging seamlessly with the pulse of conga player Milton Cardona. Jack says Milton was an important teacher. "There are certain things you have to understand about that music," he observes. "You can't just storm in there and be a rocker and play all over it. You have to approach it from the clavé point of view. The one thing you can't do is play against the clavé – that's almost considered blasphemous for someone like Milton, who is a Cuban Santeria priest. He taught me about clavé – if you get it wrong, you upset musicians beyond belief. It is the key, the heart of the music."

Cuban clavé rhythms have a religious significance because they form the basis of the songs used to communicate with the saints in Santeria, a blend of Catholicism and West African Yoruba culture. The percussion instruments are sacred, too. On 'The Life', a track from *Desire Develops An Edge*, Milton plays a checkere (or gourd), an instrument introduced to Cuba by slaves from Yoruba. The basic rhythms, on which all of the music rests, are forward and reversed rumba rhythms; a 'Cuban triplet'; and a 6/8 clavé based on the West African 12/8. Jack introduced his own rhythm to the musicians: "There's a whole thing they do in sevens, a very slow 7/4, which they call a 'Yak'."

Desire Develops An Edge was released in 1984 to great critical acclaim on both sides of the Atlantic. *Downbeat* gave it five stars and an early vote for album of the year. In *Musician*, Rabi Zabor called Jack "sensational" and "unforgettable", while *New York Beat* raved, "Bruce is a revelation … phrasing each song as if it were a personal monologue, shedding his arena-filling roar for a completely personal sound … Bruce emerges as a remarkably gifted singer." The French press were even more enthusiastic; *Le Monde* declared that Jack "gives one of the unforgettable vocal performances of the epoch".

With Jack clearly taking Kip's work to the next level, the pair decided to record a second album, but with a different approach: more commercial, with shorter tracks, more structure, and a less dense and cleaner sound. Kip even had his arm twisted to use a Synclavier ("at least it wasn't a drum machine," he says). 'Smiles And Grins' and 'Make Love' were both recorded for the new album; both, like 'Childsong', lent themselves to being melded into the style of the music. But despite the musicians' attempt to produce a more commercial record, *Vertical Currency* actually sold fewer copies than its predecessor. The reviews were no less fulsome, however: there was more praise for Jack's vocals, and Kip was hailed as "a vital force on the music scene". With the world drowning in robotic techno-pop, some music journalists were keen to celebrate music that was intelligent, passionate, and real.

Kip's albums often took some time to see the light of day because he was always short of funds. He went into the studio whenever he could, and whenever his cadre of musicians was available. His next album, *Days And Nights Of Blue Luck Inverted*, was recorded over two years and released in 1987; *Exotica* was recorded in 1992 and released in the USA a year later. There were two particularly fine performances from Jack on this album: a breathless, semi-devotional vocal on 'G-d Is Great', which he co-wrote with Kip, and 'The Last Song', a dark homily to the empty promise of a worker's paradise.

When Jack wasn't around to record, Kip often had problems with other singers. 'I would send a tape with some rough vocals," he says, "and they would memorise exactly what I did and just sing it back. After working with Jack you are spoilt, because you start out with your sketch and you finish up with a gorgeous painting." But with Kip, you never knew what divine madness was coming round the corner. Like Jack, he would want his musicians to transcend the notes on the charts, but he would take it right out there.

"He would have an arrangement very carefully written out, some esoteric piece of Venezuelan Big Band music something-or-other," Jack recalls. "Then he'd put all these beautifully written arrangements in front of you and then say, 'That's what I don't want.' He actually did that once." While recording *Exotica*, Kip told everybody to "memorise the parts and don't play a single note I wrote. I'm bored with this. This is what I meant two days ago, now let's surprise ourselves."

If there was one musician in Kip's community with whom Jack had a special affinity it was pianist Don Pullen. Spoken of in the same breath as McCoy Tyner and Cecil Taylor, Don was a strikingly individual player whose protean talents graced numerous recordings with Charles Mingus, his own Quartet with George Adams, and the stunning *New Beginnings*, recorded with Tony Williams and Gary Peacock and released in 1988.

In the years before his death from cancer in 1995 he became a devotee of Brazilian music and combined this with studio sessions and live performances with Kip and Jack. As Jack recalls, when Don was given only a short time to live, "Kip told me he wanted to play at his own memorial gig. He says, 'You're having the fun of the gig, why shouldn't I be there as well?' So we organised a gig at SOB's in New York and it was an amazing gig. He also said, to me, 'When I die, don't bother coming to the funeral, 'cos I won't be there either.' What a fantastic guy!"

Jack's appreciation of Don was both intuitive and visceral. "Of all the musicians I have ever played with, he really got what I was doing. Whether it was because he played with Mingus, I don't know. He always said I had elephant's ears and we used to do these improvisations together."

Because of the excellent reviews his work was receiving – and with Jack as a draw – Kip was able to book some one-off concerts and tours. The band's line-up varied, as did the studio sessions, according to who was around. *All Roads Are Made Of The Flesh* collects live performances from 1985–92 and includes a version of Jelly Roll Morton's 'Buddy Bolden's Blues' with Jack singing, accompanied by Don Pullen and Allen Toussaint. The album was released in 1995 and dedicated to Don's memory.

After recording *Desire Develops An Edge* the Haitian guys had asked Kip if Jack could join the band because they had never played with a white musician. Jack was the first musician from outside New York to join this circle of musicians; most of the others had known each other for years. They played live three times in 1984 – one gig at New York's Public Theater and a pair of radio broadcasts in France and Switzerland – before embarking on an eight-date tour of the USA and Europe the following year.

In Italy, Jack and Kip played a gig in the small town of Roccastrada that Jack says was "organised by nuns and the Communist Party". Ginger Baker was living in Italy at the time, tending an olive grove. He drove up to the village to join in – "Ginger actually liked that band, with Milton Cardona and Giovanni Hidalgo," Jack says – but Ignacio Berroa, the traps drummer, was less than happy and wouldn't play with Ginger because he thought his style was too primitive. Ignacio's background in macho Cuban percussion dictated that you exercised absolute technical control using just the wrists, not the arms. Kip says the gig finished up as more of a Bruce-Baker jam because the rest of the guys couldn't really follow what was going on.

One of the most significant concerts Jack and Kip played together was at New York's Carnegie Hall on October 26 1985, supporting Rubén Blades, in front of a Latino audience. Jack had another technical hitch of the sort he had encountered before: "Because of the Teamsters Union, you couldn't use your own stagehands," he recalls. "The roadies take the gear as far as the door and then it's taken by the guys who work at the venue, who don't know what they are doing. This happened at Madison Square Garden for the Cream gig, when this Mafia guy showed up and took two per cent of the gross as well. For that very important gig with Kip at Carnegie Hall, I didn't have my own technicians. This guy was setting up my gear and then gave me a guitar lead that was so short it wouldn't reach the mic. He gave me this look like 'go figure'."

There was another problem after the Carnegie Hall concert that resulted in Kip and Jack falling out for three years because Jack believed that Kip had fired him. "I didn't fire Jack," Kip says. "What happened was I was having trouble with two guys in the band. Ignacio, the drummer, wanted to be different from everybody else. Carnegie Hall was no big deal for this guy and he wasn't prepared to take it seriously. We were at the point where we were making noise and this was going to get us attention. Ignacio wouldn't do the rehearsals and instead said he had a wedding to play in the Bronx."

Kip decided to use Robby Ameen from Rubén Blades's band instead. When Ignacio turned up just before the gig, Kip was furious and started screaming at him. "So he said, 'OK if you didn't write any parts for me, I'll just keep fuckin' time.' And that's what he did right through the gig, just to spite me." (Robby eventually replaced Ignacio in Kip's band, and would later play with Jack, too.)

Kip also had an issue with conga player Jerry Gonzales, who had been out of the band for a while but wanted to come back. Kip said he could come back so long as he didn't get messed up on drugs and drag another conga player, Giovanni Hidalgo, into it as well. But it didn't work out like that. While Milton did his best to keep it all going, Jerry and Giovanni were stoned and Ignacio, the traps drummer, was just keeping time.

"I was livid," Kip says. "Everybody else was gorgeous – Jack, Steve Swallow, Charles Neville [tenor sax] – but all I could focus on was the drumming being so fucked up." Kip got into a fight backstage with Ignacio and chairs went flying. He then gave an interview to *Musician* while he was still wound up and said he would fire Ignacio, Jerry, and Giovanni, but it came out as if he was going to fire the whole band. "Steve called me from Europe and asked if I was firing him," Kip recalls. "Jack phoned and was really upset. I probably didn't really explain it properly, so that was it for about three years." Kip thinks Jack's reaction was so extreme because "he cared about everyone in that band, made a huge emotional commitment and expected the same thing back". Playing with Kip and the Latin guys was probably Jack's best experience since his band with Mick Taylor, yet here he was again with what seemed like more betrayal.

○

During his years in Germany, Jack returned to England several times for recording sessions, short tours with Bruce Gary, Ronnie Leahy, and Clem Clempson, and other one-off events such as memorial concerts for Alexis Korner and Ian Stewart. Although Germany was a necessary bolthole for Jack – especially if he wanted to establish a relationship with Margrit – he was homesick and missed Jo and Malcolm. Clem says if he was on tour with Jack in Germany, Jack was often quite upset that Clem would be flying back to England when he wasn't.

In 1986 it was decided that Jack and Margrit would move back to England, to a house in the country not far from his old mansion. But if Jack was returning to the UK – and to within striking distance of London – there was one prerequisite: he had to come off heroin for good.

Jack had not been using heroin constantly since 1971. "I wanted to work," he says, "and you can't be a user and work, especially when you are touring." Unless you were in a band like The Rolling Stones, where the dealers brought the drugs to you, there was no time to make connections with 'the man' while touring across Europe and America. "I would stop and replace heroin with alcohol and [heroin substitute] methadone." But there was still that pull of The Old Address. Margrit knew that if Jack went on his own to London, "it would be 100 per cent certain he would use. When he did the Robin Trower album [in 1981], he could be a month in London, then he would get back to Germany and have proper withdrawals. So he would want to go back to London and I would hide his passport. My family had a house in the Black Forest, and I literally locked all the doors so he couldn't leave the house. Then at four in the morning I had to take him to the hospital because he had such a bad asthma attack while he was withdrawing.

"Even if we went to London together, he would be so clever," she continues. "If we were in a hotel and it was raining, he would say, 'Oh, I'll go and get an umbrella so we can go out.' Instead he'd go and score. For me it was a long, long learning process."

Jack did try to seek professional help, but the help he sought was only geared toward detoxifying him from heroin and did nothing about his underlying reasons for using heroin in the first place. He tried a technique known as Rapid Opiate Detox, where he was sedated for about five days while withdrawing from heroin so that he wouldn't feel the worst effects of the withdrawals. At that point, Jack would have been detoxified, but that is only the beginning of the recovery journey – and he was not yet ready to take the next step.

Jack also tried neuroelectric therapy (NET), a technique pioneered by Dr Meg Patterson. The brain generates natural painkilling chemicals called endorphins, but when somebody uses heroin for a period of time, it pushes out or damps down the endorphins in the brain. When that person stops using heroin, the endorphins take a while to flood back in, and until they do there is a vacuum. That's what withdrawal is: the body reacts to the lack of endorphins and the person starts sweating, gets stomach cramps, feels sick, and has all the classic symptoms seen in films like *The French Connection*.

Much of the reason why people are afraid to stop using heroin is the fear of withdrawal, which is extremely unpleasant but not life-threatening. The idea behind NET is to excite those endorphins to start working quickly: to prevent the vacuum and so prevent withdrawal through the use of electrodes attached to the ears. NET has been touted as a 'cure' for heroin addiction but is no such thing because, like the sleep therapy, it only takes the person to the start of the journey. Eric Clapton also tried NET but was highly critical of it in his autobiography because of the lack of proper aftercare, which he felt was downright dangerous.

Dr Patterson did welcome Jack into her family, which he appreciated. He felt guilty on the one occasion he absconded to score, but was less enamoured by the efforts of Meg's husband, George, to ram Jesus down his throat. (It is not uncommon for ex-users to switch their dependence from drugs to religion or some form of cult – or as in Eric's case, to hit the bottle.)

Jack also tried a more conventional treatment, using the heroin substitute methadone on a reducing basis – the idea being that you start with a certain dose and day-by-day take a little bit less until you stop. He tried this himself and under medical supervision, but it never worked for very long. Sometimes he would try to get as far away from drugs as possible – he went to Barbados with Ronnie Leahy after the band with Mick Taylor broke up and later, again with Ronnie, to Scotland. They would ramble across the hills, with Ronnie there as friend and listener. "I had no will power, just a shell, a hollow person," Jack recalls. "Heroin completely destroyed my personality and my soul."

Then, around 1986, back in England, he went to see Dr Michael a'Brooke. Dr a'Brooke, who died in 1993, was something of a bon vivant with a liking for Cuban cigars and Savile Row suits. Most of his patients were rich and/or famous. An amateur calligrapher, he would present Jack with ornately written prescriptions that were well known to the local chemist near his clinic in Kent, but which caused a few raised eyebrows and hurried phone calls if Jack took them anywhere else. He was well thought of among his colleagues; when he died, a eulogy for him was read out by the Royal College Of Physicians.

Dr a'Brooke started Jack on a dose of methadone pills that was unusually high for the time and reduced them over a very gradual period. For the final reduction, Jack went into the clinic and was impressed with the doctor's manner, even if his services did not come cheaply. "I didn't have much money then, but enough for this," he says. "We just talked and he made you feel really worthwhile."

And this time it worked. Jack was still at the start of the recovery journey, and there was no lengthy therapy to resolve the reasons for Jack's initial pain, but things were different this time. There were other forces at work. By now Margrit had given Jack the ultimatum: "choose me and the family – or drugs". By 1986 Jack was 43 years old. There is a recognised pattern in clinical literature called 'maturing out', where some of those who have taken heroin for a long time just decide they've had enough, especially if there are other positive changes in their lives. Often these people do it by themselves, or with the help of family or friends, and never get anywhere near a drug treatment service.

So, by the mid 80s, Jack had stopped using heroin. He did carry on drinking, often quite heavily, and there was the odd relapse until 1994. But his regular, heavy drug using days were over.

a question of
of
time
CHAPTER 14

A nd now for something completely different: Jack Bruce, stage actor. In 1987, Jack was approached to appear in *The Tooth Of Crime*, a play by Sam Shepard. First performed in London in 1972, this intense and difficult play, full of surreal and existential dialogue and written in response to the rock deaths of the time, is set in a future dominated by a game that combines rock music with street violence. Hoss, played by Jack, is the ageing rock star facing the challenge of the younger Crow to be master of The Game. Hoss represents the old way of playing, and takes on various accents: a gunslinger, a 20s gangster, and a Delta blues singer. Crow is the upstart who looks like Keith Richards. They fight with knives; Hoss tries to get Crow to teach him the new ways of The Game but eventually kills himself.

"I had always liked Sam Shepard and the play was great," Jack says. "I didn't know if I was capable of this because, apart from one bit lasting a few minutes, Hoss is on stage all the time, talking a complete monologue. I become my father and have to talk in all kinds of American accents. I had to commit suicide every night, and that was hilarious because the instructions were that the actor had to shoot himself in the head and then, with as much bravery as possible, collapse on the floor. So I kept getting injured."

What the audience didn't know was the onstage rivalry was mirrored exactly by the sexual intrigue going on backstage. "It's quite a physical part,"

Jack continues, "but not having acted before I thought if somebody throws you across the stage, they are supposed to pretend. But the actor who played Crow was incredibly jealous of me because the producer was after me – she left her husband and everything. It was terrible, but I didn't want to know. So he was trying to hurt me on stage. I had to wear these high-heeled boots and he threw me and I dislocated my ankle. But I had to keep doing it for a month. Eventually she went off with this actor."

O

The 80s had so far been an experimental and transitional decade for Jack. He had a new family, new friends, and new musical associations, but there was still plenty or darkness and misery as well and no real opportunity to rebuild his career or put his life on a more stable financial footing. Fortunately, there was a glimmer of light ahead.

Since acquiring RSO in the mid 80s, Polygram had assumed control of the Cream back catalogue and had begun re-releasing the band's albums and Jack's solo work, first on vinyl and then on the new compact disc format. In 1988 Eric Clapton released *Crossroads*, a six-disc retrospective boxed set that included some Cream material and helped to further raise Jack's profile. Polygram then began to think about a producing a Jack Bruce retrospective. He was not consulted on what became *Willpower* (1989), but while the selection was pretty random, it did include two new tracks: the anti-heroin title song and 'Ships In The Night', which featured Eric and was originally recorded for the German label CMP.

CMP was a small experimental label run by Kurt Renker and Walter Quintus, whose countryside studio Jack used while he was living in Germany. Like Manfred Eicher's more famous ECM, CMP was born of a singular vision and provided an outlet for genres of jazz and other types of world and esoteric music that would never find a home on a major label. As a teenager, Kurt began by promoting jazz concerts by Jan Garbarek, Charles Mingus, and John Surman. He then produced his first album, a live recording of Nucleus, which was followed by a studio album with Charlie Mariano. "After five or six records," Kurt says, "I realised I enjoyed being in the studio and giving the artists the opportunity to really work there, do overdubs, and move away from straight jazz recordings." This stood in contrast to the way ECM worked: strict acoustic recordings, no overdubs; one day recording, one day mixing.

Kurt knew drummer Mark Nauseef, who in 1983 worked with Jack in the Eberhard Schoener Orchestra for a German television broadcast and as part of a one-off concert starring Fela Kuti. Mark, Kurt, Jack, and Margrit all met up in a Munich hotel bar and sat down and talked and drank together until six in the morning. Kurt and his engineer, Walter, were in the process of building a studio about an hour outside Cologne at Kurt's grandfather's house. Kurt offered Jack some studio time, but because of its isolation Ztudio Zerkall became a place where Jack just liked to hang out and relax.

Jack was still hoping to land a major record deal but eventually told Kurt he had some basic tracks he wanted to do with Clem Clempson and former Cockney Rebel drummer Stuart Elliott. This was in 1986; it took six years of occasional recording before the final album was released. "From the point where we started, it took about 18 months and we had about 80 per cent of the mixes done," Kurt recalls. "Jack tried to sell it to a major label for about two or three years, but nobody was interested. CMP wasn't really strong enough to handle it, but nobody else wanted it. By 1991, I actually felt we could do it; we had an office in New York and distribution was reasonably good. So we went back in and remixed some of the tunes and put it out."

Something Els (1992) was named after a foul-tasting German drink called Els and was the first of three albums Jack would record with CMP. Pete wrote some new songs with Jack and came out to see him in the studio in Germany. For Pete, it wasn't always relaxing – "one time there was some kind of NATO exercise going on; Panzers in the garden, truckloads of soldiers, jets flying over the studio. It was crazy, the last knockings of the Cold War" – so a good environment to write more political songs, including 'Peaces Of The East', about the Iran-Iraq war, and 'Criminality', which took aim at the British government under Thatcher.

'Criminality' was prompted by comments made by the British Home Secretary of the time, Douglas Hurd, about riots that had taken place within the black communities of London, Bristol, and Liverpool. These had been largely sparked by a build-up of tensions between the communities and racist elements within the police, who repeatedly 'stopped and searched' young black people. Hurd called the riots "criminality of the worst kind"; the song reflected Pete and Jack's view that the police and government were the real criminals.

There's a nice little interlude in 'Close Enough For Love': the sound of a party in the studio, with Margrit, Jo, and Malcolm in attendance. Jack plays piano and bass while somebody claps along on the onbeat instead of the offbeat, as people often do. Jack set himself a particular task for this track. "'Close Enough for Love' morphs from a love ballad, but hasn't got any cymbals or hi-hat – that was the challenge I set myself rhythmically. Then it goes into a jazz club bit at the end. I get very annoyed by certain aspects of pop or rock song recordings. For instance, there is a certain rhythm; you hear it all the time. Peter Sellers has a fantastic take-off of it when he does the 'Trumpet Volunteer' interview as Tommy Iron the rock'n'roll star. You still hear this terrible cod-rhythm that sounds like it swings but it doesn't. I also get annoyed that everything has to have a backbeat. Why?"

With Dick Heckstall-Smith on sax and a Flamingo Club feel, 'G.B. Dawn Blues' tries to capture the mood of driving back down south with The Graham Bond Organisation and hitting London just as rush-hour strikes. Everybody is bright and breezy, heading for work, and you feel like crap. The sessions also featured a German guitarist called Peter Weihe, whose lead parts were later overdubbed by Eric at a little studio near Shepherd's Bush in West London. Not surprisingly, two of the three songs featuring Eric were chosen by Polygram to add currency and profile to the *Willpower* compilation.

With all the white noise of Cream, solo reissues, and a retrospective album in the background, Jack was finally able to land the deal he was looking for. He found a businessman he could trust in Leslie Bider, head of music publishers Warner Chappell, and concluded a fair three-record deal. "It turned our lives around," Jack says, "because we got a serious chunk of money and it financed Margrit and me to go after other money that was owed."

In the meantime Jack set about recording his first major solo album for nearly ten years. *A Question Of Time* was produced by Jack and Joe Blaney for CBS's Epic label. The core of the band was guitarist Jimmy Ripp, who had played with Lou Reed, drummer Dougie Bound from The Lounge Lizards, and keyboardist Bernie Worrell from Funkadelic and Talking Heads. Jack and Bernie had first met in The Golden Palaminos and formed a strong bond. "I knew who Jack was and he was aware of P-Funk," Bernie recalls. "When we first played together, it was signed, sealed, and delivered because we were so close in the way we hear the same kind of thing, we feel each other's music. We have a lot in common – being beaten by record companies, owed monies – and we both have a classical music background."

Like David Sancious, Bernie was brought up in New Jersey. He started to learn music at the age of three when his mother taught him to play his first piano scale. Nobody else would teach him at first because they thought he was too young; eventually they found a teacher and Bernie started giving concerts aged only four. He wrote a piano concerto when he was eight and by ten was a member of the Plainfield Symphony and Washington Symphony Orchestras. He went to the New England Conservatory in Boston and had keyboard lessons at

Julliard, but moved away to Michigan after meeting George Clinton, who was then fronting a doo-wop group called Parliament (backed by The Funkadelics).

Bernie's affinity with Jack goes way beyond their classical lineage. Black funk players are locked in with Jack's music every bit as much as the Latin musicians. Here is a European musician who to their ears completely understands the emotional expression of another culture. They recognise the kindred soulfulness in his singing and playing, which Jack attributes strongly to his Scottish background.

Working with the core band on Jack's new album was an impressive array of guests: Allan Holdsworth, Vernon Reid, Paul Barrere from Little Feat, Tony Williams, Albert Collins, and Ginger Baker, with additional support from Mark Nauseef, Indian tabla player Zakir Hussain, and the singer from Parliament, Gary 'Mudbone' Cooper. Jack has an intuitive ability to pick the right musicians who can perform to their strengths and be emotionally compelling without overwhelming a piece. He knows who is 'out there' and what they can add by way of colours and textures.

Jack first saw Zakir Hussain performing with India's greatest sitar player, Vilayat Khan. They did one piece that was 70 minutes long; Zakir didn't come in for 45 minutes, but when he did the improvisation was perfect. Jack asked him afterward if he wanted to play on the album. Zakir features on two tracks, 'Kwela' and the title track, 'A Question Of Time'. "It's only got backward drums, Phil Spector kind of toms, instead of having a big backbeat," says Jack, who plays cello rather than bass on the track. "I wanted tabla there instead."

Jack's strength for reining musicians in was particularly important when it came to his choice of guitar players, with neither Allan Holdsworth nor Vernon Reid usually noted for their understated style. Although Jack's attempts at forming a band with Allan in the mid 70s hadn't worked out, he had remained a good friend. As Jack told *Guitar Player* in June 1990: "Before Allan recorded 'Obsession', I said, 'could you play, say, a hundred notes a minute instead of a thousand?' He proceeded to play the most beautiful solo, so structured and perfect. On 'Only Playing Games', I wanted a beautiful sound for the melody, and the way Allan plays the Synthaxe with the breath controller was absolutely perfect."

Jack had been introduced to Vernon Reid a few years earlier by Arto Lindsay, who worked with Kip. "We found that our roots were similar in that we were both influenced by free jazz and were both trying to take that into a rock format," Jack says. "We talked then about the possibility of playing together, so it was fantastic to finally get the chance."

Jack had originally wanted to get Albert King to play on the blues track, a version of Willie Dixon's 'Blues You Can't Lose'. "He was playing a club, Slims, near the studio," Jack recalls. "It was a converted shoe shop near the Bay Bridge and got badly damaged in the earthquake [in October 1989]. So I went to see Albert King at the soundcheck. He was sitting in the audience listening to his band, smoking his big meerschaum pipe. I went up to him, a bit nervous because of his reputation. 'I'm Jack Bruce. I was with Cream. We did "Born Under … "'

"'Where's my money?' 'What money?' He never wrote the song, but he'd been playing it for so long that it had become, for him, his song, even though it was written by Booker T. Jones and William Bell." Jack asked Albert if he wanted to play on the album, to which Albert replied that he wanted $40,000 and a contract with CBS. "The next week, Albert Collins was playing," Jack continues, "so I went down there and he was a completely different kind of person – a real live wire, a real entertainer. He showed up really late, really tired, and just sat down and played it in one take."

Jimmy Ripp was the least well known of the guitarists on the album, but Jack was ecstatic about his playing. Interviewed by *Guitar* in May 1990, he said: "He can play anything, make any sound, play any style, but I think he's taken for granted. On the 'Kwela' track, I wanted to get a Haitian arpeggio-style guitar thing and he pulled out this half-sized octave guitar, plugged it in, and played a mega version, beyond my wildest dreams of what I wanted."

In the context of all the reissues and Jack's absence from the limelight for nearly a decade, *A Question Of Time* was regarded very much as a The Return Of Jack Bruce. Some songs, such as 'Life On Earth' and 'Make Love', were reprised and updated from previous releases; 'Obsession' was a 'Sunshine' for the 90s, and one of several to restate key motifs from Jack's musical past. "I think every writer has about three ideas – it doesn't matter if you are Beethoven or me," Jack said at the time. "You get them when you are about 11 and you just rework them. The song 'A Question Of Time' is a statement of where I am now: it's got the classical bits, the jazz bits, the rock bits, and the blues bits."

Jack dreamt the words and music to 'Life On Earth': "I just woke up and wrote it all down." With a chord progression reminiscent of 'White Room' and 'Tales Of Brave Ulysses', the song had first appeared on *BLT* in 1981, but back then Jack was trying to fit it into the style of a Robin Trower album. Here he avoids the more obvious rock and blues clichés: the song is updated, but is still anchored by the melodic, rising-and-falling eighth-note-style bass runs that were so much a part of Cream improvisations. Eric would never have played a solo like Vernon Reid's, both distorted and out of tune, but it sounds completely right in the context of the notes around it – and not dissimilar to some of Jack's own wild bass work during the Cream era.

Jack has always liked the way Stax records would really start cooking in the fade-out, so when the opportunity arose he would employ a ferocious ride-out where everybody gets the chance to let rip – as he does on 'Flying'. The song is a tribute to several deceased musicians, so Paul Barrere's slide guitar salutes Duane Allman, and the horns are panned to the far left, as they were on Otis Redding's Stax recordings. "I tried to get some Roy Orbison in there too. It was written when he died, which is so sad. It sort of sums up life – he makes a great comeback, and all of a sudden he's gone."

When Jack and Pete get together to write, politics will never be far away. And so 'A Question Of Time' is about the Ayatollah; 'Let It Be' about Africa; 'Make Love' set against the background of the troubles in Northern Ireland. 'Only Playing Games' is an anti-war song; 'Life On Earth' shows concern for the planet; 'Grease The Wheels' revisits 'Politician' and 'Ministry Of Bag'. Even 'No Surrender' is a war cry for the Protestant hardliners in Northern Ireland, although it was more closely aligned to 'Keep It Down' – Jack and Pete's way of saying 'whatever you've got, bring it on'. And then there's 'Kwela', which is Zulu township slang for 'get up', a warning about approaching police vans and the name given to street music invented in the 50s by kids blowing penny whistles. The song itself was dedicated to two people sentenced to death in South Africa, with the vocals mixed very low to symbolise South Africa's unheard voices.

A Question Of Time was well received by the rock press, not least because it was shot through with full-on guitar solos, songs in the key of Cream – and one Ginger Baker, who featured on two tracks and was about to make a dramatic re-entry into Jack's life. The album's sales performance was underwhelming, however. Although it was not set up as a commercial exercise, Jack had done everything to ensure its success. It had everything rock fans could have wanted, but it ran up against the buffers of business politics. "CBS were due to be taken over by Sony, so Black Rock was in meltdown and nobody wanted to do anything," Jack recalls. "It had singles, radio songs, everything that would make it work, but it simply didn't get a proper release. I did all the right things, the right sort of album without selling out, spent a lot of time mixing it, and it just got lost." Jack and Pete fell out over business matters associated with the album and wouldn't speak again until Jack's 50th birthday concerts in 1993.

Jack Bruce COMPOSING HIMSELF

○

Despite the problems associated with its release, *A Question Of Time* still had to be promoted, so Jack needed a new touring band. Bernie Worrell and Gary 'Mudbone' Cooper were the first on board. When Bill Levenson was putting together *Willpower* he had discovered an old Cream reject, 'Hey Now Princess', which Jack re-recorded for his new album. Ginger came in and played some outstanding rhythmic melody lines, with the snare part on the bass drums and the hi-hat part on the toms. He recorded both this and 'Obsession' in one take and in the process rekindled Jack's enthusiasm for his old sparring partner. Whatever their differences, Jack felt that they were as natural together as Sly & Robbie or James Jamerson and Benny Benjamin, so he brought Ginger into his new band. "Of course, I had some trepidation about getting Ginger involved," he says, "but I thought maybe it would be all right this time, like I've always thought."

If Ginger was a blast from the past, Jack's choice of guitarist couldn't have been more contemporary. "We had these auditions, loads of people coming along – I've never done anything like that before," he says. "But there was nobody that was really doing it for me. We were just packing up when this kid bursts through the door with huge hair and everything in plaid, including the guitar, and shouts, 'You gotta let me play, you gotta let me play.' So he plugged in his amp and it blew up, and when we did play he didn't know any of my songs – and that was a kind of recommendation for me."

The kid in question was Blues Saraceno. He had only just turned 18 when he auditioned for Jack but was already something of a phenomenon, with a solo album to his name. He knew CBS A&R man Michael Caplan, who had helped assemble the musicians for *A Question Of Time*, and who suggested that Blues go along for the audition.

"On the day I got the call for the audition, I was out on Long Island doing a photo shoot for a promotion," Blues recalls. "I was told not to be late, so I jumped in my car and headed for New York City. I was doing fine until I got about two blocks away and the traffic came to a stop and I ended up being two hours late. I got there, tired, stressed out; I could not get it together. I still had make-up on from the photo shoot and my huge blue Mohawk.

"Jack asked me if I knew any of his songs and I said no, but he was fine with that. Then my amp blew up – Jack looked at me and said, 'You've got to be kidding.' Then we just played a song from the album, no more than five or ten minutes, Jack said thanks, and that was that. From my point of view it was

248

a disaster. But by the time I got home, there was a message on my machine calling me back on Monday."

Although Blues was of the Slash/Yngwie Malmsteen generation of rock guitarists, he was influenced by older players like Johnny Winter and Ritchie Blackmore. As a contrast to Ginger, and in an effort to update his image and attract new fans, Jack found the prospect of having this young guy in the band very exciting. Even so, he says, "I got a lot of stick for having Blues in the band. I thought he was just what I needed. Apparently the only type of guitarist I'm allowed is somebody trying to be a version of Eric Clapton."

Ginger's drum technician, Tom Goss, had done the auditions with Jack; it wasn't until about two weeks later that Ginger officially joined the band. And then the trouble started. They were about to begin rehearsals when they heard that Ginger had collapsed at JFK airport with a burst appendix and had to have an operation. With the tour still set to go ahead, they met up a few days later. "In walks Ginger in a long coat and he doesn't say a word," Blues recalls. "Jack looks at Ginger, Ginger looks at Jack. That was it: no introductions, no nothing. I was really taken aback. Ginger looked really tired and dishevelled. So I thought, OK, this is going to be interesting.

"We start the rehearsal and Ginger's playing really slowly, he looks like he's in pain. It gets faster and a little better, but we only rehearsed for a couple of days." Jack says Ginger didn't want to rehearse at all: "He'd had appendicitis and was just out of hospital. And anyway he thought it was only rock'n'roll, so he didn't need to rehearse."

Jack wasn't too concerned. "I said to Ginger, 'OK, here's a copy of the record. Just listen to that and I'm sure it will be fine.' So we're on the bus on the way to the first gig at the Bayou in Washington. I asked Ginger what he thought of the record and he hadn't even bothered to listen to it. 'I hate fuckin' rock'n'roll.' So I spent the whole journey writing out drum parts, thinking this is Ginger, he'll be able to handle it."

Meanwhile, Blues had fallen asleep on the bunk at the back of the bus. "I woke up about an hour and a half later and the bus is full of smoke," he recalls. "I jumped up thinking the bus was on fire and everybody's smoking, it was like Cheech and Chong in there, although the main culprit was Ginger and his pipe. Eventually Ginger followed the bus in a car rather than extinguish it."

When they arrived at the Bayou the place was sold out. Everything was set up and ready to go. Blues had never been on tour before, so was "anxious to get this first show started. One ... two ... three ... four ... I'm looking at Jack, Jack's looking at me. Something is not right: we're both checking, we both look at Bernie. We all turn our heads and Ginger is standing on his drum stool with a stick in each ear and he is screaming, howling. Ginger decided he wasn't going to play because it was too loud. So everything is going on, but there are no drums."

Jack remembers that opening song being 'Life On Earth', which starts with the bass, and says that Ginger wasn't playing because he hadn't learnt the songs from the album they were supposed to be promoting. "He was just holding the sheet music and shrugging his shoulders."

The crowd at the back of the balcony couldn't see what was going on and thought the drums were just too quiet, so started chanting, "Turn up the drums! Turn up the drums!" Jack was getting furious; Ginger was shouting to turn everything down. Blues had no idea what was going on. "The place is going nuts," he recalls, "and in the confusion the soundman has hit the talk-back button, where you talk to the musicians, and so everybody hears him say, 'If the drummer would play the fuckin' drums, I could turn them up.'"

Jack made a speech about how much he hated Ginger and then walked off. "That was the end of the gig," Jack recalls. "The roadie drove me around because I was in a real state." Ginger disappeared and had to be found by the police. Blues went back to the hotel. "Jack fired Ginger," he recalls. "Ginger quit, so I assumed the tour was off. I started getting my gear together, called my manager and told him I'm coming home. This is my introduction to touring with The Jack Bruce Band."

The following morning Jack and Ginger negotiated a cease-fire, but not before Jack slipped a letter of apology under Ginger's bedroom door. Yet it was obvious Ginger hadn't learnt the songs, so a compromise was reached. The show would be split into two halves: Tom Goss would play the new material and then there would be a Cream set with Ginger, although he did agree to play 'Obsession' and 'Hey Now Princess'. This wasn't entirely satisfactory from Jack's point of view because it meant the shows could run to as long as three hours. And then Ginger would be coming on for the second set just to play Cream numbers, where the crowd would go wild and undermine the first half of the show and Jack's new material. But it was that or cancelling the whole tour.

So the tour resumed, albeit with a stutter. Ginger was actually supposed to play the whole of the second gig, at the Chance in Poughkeepsie, New York, but never turned up. Tom Goss still didn't know all the songs for the first set, but the instruction was "No Ginger. Keep playing." So that first set was mainly a jam. They came off stage, the place was going crazy with anticipation, and then, suddenly, there he is in his long black coat, saying nothing to anybody, straight out on stage and into the second set.

The following night, at the Living Room in Providence, Rhode Island, wasn't much better. The band arrived an hour late, the promoter was pissed off, people were asking for their money back. But at that point the band could have cared less: they'd been on the bus for five hours, had no time to freshen up at the hotel, and instead were shown into a dirty, windowless, graffiti-scrawled dressing room – on the very same evening, incidentally, that Eric Clapton was finishing up 18 nights at the Royal Albert Hall.

Blues found the early gigs challenging. "There might or might not be a setlist," he says, "and there were no set starts or ends to any of the songs. I came from an era where you did three-and-a-half-minute songs; you start the same, you end the same. When Jack jumped up and landed – that's when the song stopped. And regardless of what was written on a setlist, you followed Jack. Looking back on it, that was the most amazing part, that's what I loved. It was wild, you never knew what was going to happen." In Boston, Blues took his guitar and threw it in the air. "Jack saw this and kicked over my stack. My guitar goes flying by him and the guitars get kicked across the stage."

In Baltimore, Maryland, the band played at Hammerjacks, one of the few venues in the city that could lure big-name acts. "The audience are drinking, they are rowdy, they haven't paid much to get in, and they are there just to hear the Cream stuff," Blues recalls. "Jack is doing some heartfelt piano ballads, so the dynamics are low. You can hear the bottles clinking and the people yelling and Jack was simply not having it. He starts yelling at the audience, then somebody says something back and Jack proceeds to topple the PA monitors into the audience. It was pandemonium. I've never seen anything like it. Then he kicks over his whole stage rig and it explodes across the stage. Meanwhile we are still playing – Ginger's not phased at all. Half the audience is being terrorised by flying equipment, the other half is loving it. I'm still soloing away; Jack climbs onto his rig, which is making sounds like King Kong, grabs his bass, shakes it at the audience, and walks off." The audience was in uproar; Blues just made a run for it and hid on the bus.

If Blues thought Jack and Ginger had settled their differences ... well, he still had a lot to learn. Chaos was the push-me-pull-you between Jack and Ginger, but the payoff was the show. "Jack and Ginger would be slagging each other off full-bore through the PA, flipping each other off. It was theatre on stage. But the moment they start playing together, there is a sound that you can't replicate."

Blues very much appreciated the fact that everybody got respect from Jack on stage. "Whoever you were, younger guys like me and Tom, you were judged on your merits," he says. "If you were on that stage, you were part of that team, part of that family, and you were given that respect." Not that Blues got much respect on stage from Ginger, who took to flicking matches at his Mohawk, which was made highly flammable by the amount of gel needed to hold it in place. By all accounts, Ginger didn't like Blues as a guitarist, and in particular didn't think he could handle the wah-wah sound of 'White Room' to save his life.

When the band got to San Diego just before Christmas 1989, Jack gave everybody presents. "He was very generous," Blues says. "He really took care of his musicians. He gave me a Rolex watch and he gave Mudbone a 24-carat gold necklace. He paid everybody well. He was very good about the money."

Bernie was the peacemaker, doing his best to stop Blues going off the rails and keeping Ginger well supplied with strong dope to chill him out. He agrees that Ginger definitely had Blues in his sights, and adds that he wasn't averse to reliving the old days by chucking a stick or two at Jack. "Anything could spark it off," Bernie says. "A tempo change, a missed cue, anything."

Blues decided he'd had enough after the first leg of the tour ended in Oakland, California. "I have a recollection of that tour being cancelled 14 times – and that was just on the first leg," he says. "I remember calling my management and saying, 'That's it, I can't do this any more. It's too crazy. They are at each other's throats every day.'" It took a call from Margrit to convince Blues to come back; she told him that Jack would cancel the tour otherwise. So the tour resumed with a large, prestigious gig at the Anaheim Conference Center. Blues and Jack both take the view that Ginger wouldn't really try that hard for some low-rent bar gig, but that he pulled out all the stops for bigger shows, and that night the band was on fire.

The 1,000-seater Arcadia Theater in Dallas was another roaring success. At the time Ginger was friends with Bill Laswell, who told Ginger he thought the band was really good. So when Bill and some of his friends were among the 3,000 people jammed into The Ritz in New York, it meant another evening with Ginger absolutely on top of his game.

As the tour moved into 1990 the band settled down, word got out and the venues increased in size, with industry heavy-hitters turning out in force. There was talk of a European tour but apparently Ginger didn't want to do it with Blues, so the band played together for the last time at Toad's Palace in Blues's home state, Connecticut. Then there was one last gig with Jack, Ginger, and

Blues as a trio at a huge open-air festival in Tel Aviv in 1991. "The whole city seemed to shut down," Blues recalls. "The more people there were, the more excited Jack became. He was absolutely in the zone here, almost oblivious – a wild man, shirt open, jumping around. The more out there it became, the more he loved it, and the crowd responded really well."

In 1992 Jack picked up where the old band had left off and took Blues on tour in a trio with Simon Phillips to Japan and Europe. Where Ginger was "crabby and dark", says Blues, "Simon was super polite, a very nice guy with great attention to detail and meticulous chops". The dynamic between Jack and Simon was very different. "Now we were getting into much more intricate drumming and my role changed," Blues recalls. "With Jack and Ginger, they were the dynamic and I played over the top of them. There was no holding it down with them because they were so freeform." With Simon the Cream songs sounded totally different. Blues had to be the hold-down guy because Jack and Simon would go right out of the box with odd time signatures. When they were in Japan, Blues recalls, the crowd would go crazy at the end of each song, but as soon as Simon clicked his sticks for the next song – total silence.

Blues joined Jack for one last tour in 1993 with yet another drummer, Gary Husband. Blues says that Gary was "more down the line and orthodox", while for Gary, Blues – now shorn of his Mohawk – "looked good, made a lot of noise, and provided a lot of the glue – he was also a pretty good rhythm guitarist – a very innocent, naked, and unsophisticated approach, a barebones player with a lot of attitude". In 1994 Blues was offered the chance to join the glam-metal band Poison. Jack was quite upset and offered him more money to stay, but for Blues it wasn't about that. Although he had never been a fan of Poison, he saw this "as a chance to play the big stadiums and festivals in front of 80,000 people".

Gary Husband had first met Jack with Allan Holdsworth down at Ronnie Scott's in 1979, during the time Jack, Allan, and Jon Hiseman were trying to put a band together and recorded what became known as the 'Sherwood Forest' demos. Gary was serving out his notice period with Barbara Thompson's Paraphernalia. "I was a bit wild in those days," he says. "I was having fun in the band – Barbara wasn't." Jon took Gary's place in the band, and there was a moment when it looked like Jack, Allan, and Gary would get it together. They played one freeform gig as a trio in a pub in South London – "a really wild night," Gary recalls -- but then Jack went off with John McLaughlin.

Gary's next meeting with Jack wasn't until 1992, when they were both involved in a benefit gig for Dick Heckstall-Smith, who was seriously ill at the

253

time. The gig took place at the Bull's Head pub in Barnes, West London. Jack, Gary, Ronnie Leahy, and Clem Clempson delivered a very eclectic mix of Jack's back catalogue, including 'Bird Alone' and rarely heard live performances of 'Weird Of Hermiston' (which Jack had played occasionally on his previous US tour) and 'Out Into The Fields'.

Gary then joined Jack and Blues on tour in 1993. Margrit wanted the band to play at an arts festival in Esslingen am Neckar, near her home in southern Germany. When Blues suddenly quit, Margrit picked up the phone and persuaded her all-time favourite guitarist to step in.

O

Jack had first met Gary Moore during the sessions for Cozy Powell's *Over The Top* in 1979; in 1984 Jack sang 'End Of The World' on Gary's album *We Want Moore*. Jack was looking for a new high-energy guitar partner, and after their very well received performance at Jack's 50th birthday they began to think about doing some kind of project together. At the time Gary was due to start work on another solo album. "I asked Jack whether he fancied doing some writing together," he recalls. "He came down to this little place I used to rent near Henley to work with me. I'd written some songs, but it was weird because they were going more his way – I was thinking of Jack singing them."

The idea was for the two of them to go into the studio with Gary Husband. But the recording kept getting delayed, and by the time the other two were ready Gary Husband had been booked into sessions with Billy Cobham. And then Gary Moore had the shock of his life: "Jack suggested we get Ginger over. I said, 'Are you sure about this?' But Jack said 'Yeah, yeah, it'll be fine. Don't worry, don't worry.' So Ginger came over to Hook End, a residential studio outside Henley owned by Trevor Horn. We tracked down his old drum kit from Cream at the London Rock Shop in Chalk Farm, but he didn't end up using it because it didn't sound as good as his modern kit.

"We started laying down tracks and it was very easy recording-wise, no problem at all, really fun. I got a real insight into the chemistry between those two, but it wasn't what I thought it would be at all. They weren't at each other's throats; I think Jack really looks up to Ginger, and Ginger knows it. So he will never tell Jack he is any good. It's like two brothers; Ginger really likes to wind Jack up. One day, I said to Jack, 'Can you ask Ginger to play a hi-hat pattern like 'Born Under A Bad Sign?' 'No way. You fuckin' ask him.' So I pressed the button in the control room and asked him. 'Yeah, sure man.' Jack looked at me, speechless."

Once Ginger got involved, of course, it was no longer a Gary Moore solo album – it had to be a band. Margrit went with Gary's manager, John Martin, to secure a deal for what was now BBM with Gary's label, Virgin. This caused some friction with the German label CMP because Jack still owed them an album. *Something Els* was followed in 1993 by *Cities Of The Heart*, a special CD of Jack's birthday concerts. According to Jack, a new businessman had come in to try to stem the losses on CMP and started to make trouble for Jack over the proposed album with Virgin. But Margrit sorted it all out eventually and the band set to work.

BBM's album *Around The Next Dream* was a substantial commercial success across Europe. It reached Number Nine in the UK on its release in 1994 but critics seized upon it because a number of the songs were very similar to Cream: 'Waiting In The Wings' ('White Room'); 'Where In The World' (a nod to both 'World Of Pain' and 'As You Said'); 'High Cost Of Loving' ('Born Under A Bad Sign'); 'Why Does Love Have To Go So Wrong' ('We're Going Wrong'). Even 'Cities Of Gold' was likened to 'Crossroads', although Jack had been performing it live since 1991.

Jack felt he could do no right. First he'd been dumped on by the business for albums that were 'not commercial enough'; now the critics were slating him for doing the exact opposite. Gary says Jack was upset further when they went to Spain and saw adverts for 'Gary Moore's new album' – a particularly sour point at the time as the recent spate of re-releases of Eric's material had failed to identify Jack as the composer of many of the Cream songs.

The familiar nature of some of *Around The Next Dream* appeared to confirm the industry view that BBM had formed because Jack and Ginger couldn't get Eric to agree to reform Cream after their brief reunion at their induction into the Rock & Roll Hall Of Fame. Bringing in their biggest fan on guitar, so the rumour went, was the next best option. This was simply not true, and as far as the songs were concerned – well, that was deliberate. "The idea was to draw on the influences of Cream to write the kind of songs that Gary and I imagined Cream would have been writing then," Jack says. "A lot of bands at the time, like Oasis, were being lauded for doing things that were very reminiscent of or even lifted from The Beatles. We got slagged off for doing something similar."

Gary felt that the band was under enormous pressure. "There was a lot of expectation because of the people involved," he recalls, "a lot of nitpicking, people looking for cracks in it" – although looking for cracks in BBM wasn't that difficult. In Cream, Eric had taken a back seat while Jack and Ginger slugged it out, but in BBM Gary was just as likely to get involved in spats. "Jack and I used to get feisty with each other," he admits, and this probably contributed as much to the demise of the band as anything to do with Ginger.

Even so, Ginger's reluctance to rehearse caused a great deal of bad feeling at the band's main practice session at London's Brixton Academy. The first two gigs of the tour were then cancelled because the band felt they weren't ready, while Gary was suffering from hearing problems. Jack also feels that Gary was very nervous about the whole venture: he was a major act in his own right, yet here he was about to tour with Ginger Baker and Jack Bruce in a trio with a set that would include 'Tales Of Brave Ulysses', 'I Feel Free', 'Spoonful', and 'Politician'. "I think Gary was very brave to do it at all," Jack says.

BBM got underway with a warm-up show at the Marquee, but the tensions were still there. Liz and Nettie Baker turned up and witnessed a shout-up going on between Jack and Ginger. Jack says that night "Ginger really unsettled me because he was in such a bad mood". But Gary played his part as well. "I said something to Jack afterward and he said, 'I don't like to discuss gigs after the gig'," he recalls. "And I said something really bad back and he got very upset. So it was me being highly strung as well."

The band had to cancel the following night's gig in Northern Ireland just to let tempers cool and moods lighten. But still nothing was going right. Gary describes their next gig, which was arranged to celebrate the 21st anniversary of Virgin Records, as "hideous. They kept changing the amount of time we were going to play, and when we went on stage nobody was even looking at us. They were all industry types, drinking with their backs to us. We were really angry."

When the tour got properly underway, most of the concerts went very well. BBM were going out for big money, selling out some of the largest venues in Europe, including three stadium shows in Spain that Gary says were "magic – we got into jamming and it was a very magical band". Jack remembers the band's gig at Glasgow's Barrowlands as "one of the trickiest gigs to do – if they don't like you there, they will let you know. But it was a massive success."

In the end, however, BBM were just overwhelmed by both internal and external pressures. Jack felt especially sorry for Margrit and John Martin. "They got a great deal with Virgin, and it was heartbreaking to see something that Margrit had made happen become a huge commercial success and then crumble away."

Gary took many positives from the experience. "I just loved playing with those guys," he says. "They helped me become a better player – changed my rhythmic feel and taught me to lay back a bit more and not be so frantic." He also grew very close to Jack. "He would just crack me up. It would be 4am, we'd have been drinking, and suddenly he'd say, 'I'm bored here. Let's get a flight home.' And we'd just do it spontaneously. Or we'd go to a club, get drunk, and a fight would break out. We'd be ducking all the flying glass. It was mayhem. Ginger never had anything to do with us socially. He wouldn't drink with us, he just thought we were idiots."

The pair have remained friends and played occasional gigs together in a trio with Gary Husband, including A Story Ended, a concert they performed at the London Astoria in June 2005 in memory of Dick Heckstall-Smith, who sadly died in December 2004 after a long illness.

○

In 1990 Jack fulfilled a dream by playing a solo concert in Germany and had in mind that he might do this again for his third CMP record. Label boss Kurt Renker was thinking the same way. "I wanted to make one that Jack might not be able to make for a while," he recalls. "Because I liked his singing and piano playing, there was a suggestion he should do a solo album." The idea also made practical sense because Jack thought the studio's isolated location might make recording with a full band at CMP difficult.

"I started to write with that in mind," he says, "and then decided to bring Bernie in because of that classic piano-Hammond gospel sound from the church." Bernie was "surprised and honoured to be asked to do it. It was different: there was more freedom for Jack and I would be the support system. I got his back." Together in the studio they produced an album of quiet beauty, combining the spiritual atmosphere derived from the instrumentation with the spare, ethereal inspiration of Thelonious Monk.

There were just two shows to promote the album, *Monkjack*: one in Edinburgh, and one in London. "Jack was a bit nervous and jittery about that London gig," Bernie recalls. "Just the two of us performing without a net, no drummer, no greatest hits, only new stuff." The *Times* review of the gig reminded readers that Jack was a "marketing department's nightmare, the restless, creative artist" but noted that the performance was full of "typically unpredictable [and] adventurous Bruce tunes packed with unexpected melodic twists and turns".

Kip Hanrahan did some early work on the album, co-writing 'The Food' and 'David's Harp', with its surprisingly religious overtones, but was then involved in a car accident. "Pete came in and finished [the songs] in my style better than I could have finished them," he recalls. "I was really taken aback." Jack and Pete also produced two new songs: 'Laughing On Music Street', a companion to 'Bird Alone'; and 'Time Repairs', more than a nod toward their attempt at rebuilding their relationship. Jack wrote two new instrumentals – the gothic-sounding 'Shouldn't We' and 'Know One Blues' – and recorded 'Immortal Ninth' for the first time. The rest of the album was made up of previously recorded songs, including 'The Boy' from the still unreleased *Jet Set Jewel*, about a boy who goes down on his own – a sentiment as horrible as it was prescient.

shadows in the air

CHAPTER 15

Once his sons became teenagers and Jack was in Germany, their relationship blossomed. "It was great," Malcolm says. "We would go on holiday to Germany, and when they moved back to England, Jo and I helped Margrit around the house. It was a very nice time. Jack was very supportive, warm and open. There was a real effort to be the dad."

By then both Malcolm and Jo were developing as musicians, but going down very different paths. "There were always instruments around," Malcolm says. "There were at least three pianos in the house when we were growing up, and basses and guitars. I had some formal piano lessons around seven or eight years of age. I played bass and guitar – Jack got me an Aria Pro for my tenth birthday. I played violin at school, joined choirs, did music O-level, then went to the Guildhall Junior Department at 16. Jo didn't take to formal music education; he went his own way as a keyboard player and songwriter. We both started writing songs and it got very competitive." On one of the boys' holidays in Germany, Jack had a four-track cassette recorder, and they all decided to record an album. "It got very 'oh, my song's got lyrics, so we'll do my song first'," Malcolm remembers fondly. "It was really lovely doing that."

Jack didn't really push the boys or demand they practise; as it became clear that they both wanted to pursue careers in music, he stayed very much in the background and let them go their own way. There were occasions when they took the stage with Jack: there was a concert in Budapest, recorded for television in 1991, with Ginger's son Kofi on drums and Norman Beaker there to keep tabs on the young 'uns, and for Jack's 50th birthday Malcolm transcribed the horn parts and also played alongside Jo. Jo was the first to strike out on his own when he went on the road with the sax player Bill Evans as drum technician for Dennis Chambers. He then became a founder member of Afro-Celt Sound System, a revolutionary fusion of modern dance rhythms with Celtic and African music. The band signed to Peter Gabriel's Real World and became the label's biggest act after Gabriel himself, embarking on sell-out world tours. Apparently unburdened by the weight of expectation, Jo was carving out a whole space for himself in the music business on his own considerable merits as a keyboard player and songwriter.

Then on October 8 1997 tragedy struck. Jo had been staying with a female friend in a flat in Mornington Crescent, North London. She went out in the morning; because Jo was alone after that, nobody knows the exact sequence of events, but he suffered a severe asthma attack. A neighbour found him at the bottom of the stairs and called an ambulance but it was too late. Jack heard what had happened from Janet; after the funeral, on October 18, he disappeared from view. He was already shocked by the untimely death, earlier in the year, of his good friend Tony Williams, aged only 44; now Jo's death drove Jack to the brink of insanity. He couldn't touch the piano keyboard for two years and has only quite recently been able to look at photos of his son. The mere mention of Jo's name often brings him to tears.

In the months preceding Jo's death, Jack had been on the road as a member of Ringo Starr's All-Stars. Jack did four tours of duty with the band, which over time included Peter Frampton, Simon Kirke, Gary Brooker, Todd Rundgren, Dave Edmunds, and Eric Carmen. These tours dominated Jack's schedule right through to 2000; it was surprising to see him as a sideman for this length of time. "It's not something I would normally do, but it was a good band, a lot of fun," he says. "And because I wasn't the leader, there wasn't so much pressure. It's nice to be a sideman now and again, and nice too that I could play a couple of my songs."

The All-Stars played first class venues and travelled around in private jets – and it was without doubt the cleanest tour Jack had ever undertaken. After those mad drinking days in Los Angeles with John Lennon, Harry Nilsson, and Jack, Ringo was now teetotal and banned alcohol in the rooms. He was joined in his sobriety by Peter Frampton and Simon Kirke. When the band played in Denver in May 1997, Ginger joined the band for 'White Room'; in New Jersey Jack brought on Bernie for 'Theme For An Imaginary Western', which he dedicated to Felix Pappalardi. But Jack was never going to be content simply tucked into the slipstream of somebody else's band. After the 1999 tour ended in March, he spent the rest of the year considering his next move.

Jack and Kip had sorted out their misunderstanding around 1989, and from 1991 onward Jack was a frequent guest in Kip's touring band, into which Kip had introduced what could best be described as an element of surprise. "My view of live performance had changed," he says. "I thought the only way it would sound legitimate with the many layers of rhythmic complexity, difficult vocals, impressive changes, was if we were locked. By the 90s I was thinking, I don't want to play the same thing every night, even if it was with different solos. So every night would be a different adventure." This caused a certain amount of consternation among the musicians. Kip might go to the horn section just before the gig, tell them to ditch all the horn parts, and then sing new ones to them. When the band played in Macedonia, Kip decided he was bored with the lyrics he had written and started writing new lyrics to a song Jack was already singing on stage. Jack looked at what Kip gave him and began to sing: "I have no fuckin' idea what you've written here, man – I can't read your writing." "What I did was outrageous," Kip admits. "You'd expect the person to freeze or freak or both, but Jack just went with it and announced, 'This just in, folks.'"

In keeping with the album covers, where Kip was always hidden in shadow, Jack found it difficult to get Kip to come out and take a bow. "When you're doing a gig with Kip," he says, "he would crouch behind me or the drums whispering instructions, but you couldn't hear what he's saying because of all the noise."

While Jack wouldn't go to Kip's extremes to keep the music fresh, Kip says he witnessed Jack becoming very annoyed with a sax player for playing the same solo on consecutive nights. The saxophonist's view was that the audience liked it the first night, so why not play it again. Jack was simply appalled that the guy would embarrass himself in front of the other musicians by repeating the solo.

Steve Swallow, who had been inspired by Jack to take up the electric bass in the first place, remembers a Jack who was more communal than scary. "As soon as the song was counted, Jack was the first guy off the cliff. That's a wonderful, exhilarating feeling. And if I was exhilarated by that, as the other bass player, imagine how the other soloists would have felt with that kind of attitude behind them ... he brings a wonderful sense of engagement to playing with other musicians." As far as Kip is concerned, if you don't pick up on that contagious energy, the light and dark that swirls around, you're not much of a musician. "You look like a piece of tissue paper on stage next to that immediate intensity and sincerity," he says. "If you are just reading lines, you look like an idiot."

The band last toured in 1994, but Jack had kept in touch with Kip and written songs with him. He was keen to play once again with the Latin musicians – so he simply commandeered the whole lot and formed The Cuicoland Express. He drafted in Bernie Worrell and Vernon Reid alongside Richie Flores on congas and two traps drummers: Robby Ameen and an explosive new talent, Horacio 'El Negro' Hernandez, who in his youth had gone to prison for playing 'White Room'.

Born in Havana in 1963, Horacio came from a very musical family. His grandfather played trumpet, as did his father, who was also a pianist and for 40 years hosted the only jazz programme on Cuban radio. But for young Horacio the traditional Cuban music of his grandfather was "old people's music", while his dad's modern jazz was just "for crazy people". He looked instead to his brother, who loved The Beatles, the Stones, and Cream. America was only 90 miles away, "so if you put up a coat hanger as an antenna you could capture the sounds. We used to hide in the bathroom, because it was very politically incorrect. It was more difficult for our parents, but we just liked the music, we had no idea what the songs were about."

Horacio was "always crazy about drums and percussion" and began playing in bands in his early teens. One evening he found out just how politically incorrect his music was while playing 'White Room' at the Patria O Muerte, a social club right on the beach. "The Special Forces arrived with searchlights and machine guns and told us all to lie on the floor," he recalls. "They said there was marijuana there and a topless girl, but it was all crap."

Despite being just 14 years old, Horacio spent two weeks in a maximum-security jail; some of his friends were in there for over a month. "My parents were terrified," he says, "but I wasn't scared at all." He was released without warning, and with no charges brought, at two o'clock in the morning, but not before all the instruments had been confiscated. "But no way was I going to give up playing," he continues. "I knew this was something I would do for the rest of my life. Music has made my life – and saved my life – saved it from being wasted, from Communism, and from just being on the island. It has been very crazy, but very nice."

Horacio first met Lebanese drummer Robby Ameen in the early 80s in Cuba, then later in Rome, and finally in New York, where Robby was recording for Kip on American Clavé. Robby made the introductions for Horacio to join the team.

Horacio's first proper encounter with Jack was during the recording sessions for *Shadows In The Air* in New York during late 1999 and early 2000. The product of a new deal with Sanctuary Records, the album was rich, intense, and beautifully produced and recorded, but was rejected by Warner Chappell as a 'new' Jack Bruce album because six of the 14 tracks had already been released. Three were Cream-era songs – 'Sunshine', 'White Room', and 'Dancing On Air' – but this was the first time that Jack had sought to re-interpret these songs on record with the Latin rhythm section. It worked superbly, freshening the sound three decades after their original release. Horacio believes the rhythmic structures were already in place from Jack's original compositions; he shared what Horacio calls "a common rhythmic language" with the Latin musicians, so the transition to an Afro-Cuban feel was easy.

Jack also reprised 'He The Richmond', 'Boston Ball Game 1967', and 'Out Into The Fields', which here feels properly integrated rather than submerged in the heavy-rock soup of a West Bruce & Laing album. But it's two of the new compositions written with Kip – 'Directions Home', dedicated to Tony Williams and Larry Young, and 'Milonga', named after a dance and music form related to the Argentinian tango – that provide proof, if it were needed, that after nearly 40 years of composing, Jack's creative glow was undimmed.

Kip says there were different methods of writing with Jack, and they were "all refreshing to me. Jack would play around on piano, creating melodies, discarding them. I would play them back, listening for lines to put lyrics to, and build songs from that." If there was an argument over a lyric, Kip will ask "what would Pete do?" but Jack "will never give a straight answer". (Kip says he adores Pete's lyrics, even though he knows the feeling isn't mutual.)

"We recorded *Shadows* very much as I would record my own records," Kip continues. "I don't feel it was *my* band; we were just a group of friends. We would write songs in the studio. So on 'Mr Flesh', for instance, we might decide to put a Cumbia rhythm [from Colombia] over a dancehall rhythm. So I'd call that out to Robby and El Negro. 'OK, Cumbia over Dancehall?' 'OK, what pace?' 'Bass line for that, Jack?' What about words ... let's see ..."

For Horacio, the recording sessions were a delight. "It was a pure joy to play those songs," he says, "especially 'White Room', because I was learning

this when I was 12 and it starts in 5/4 and I'm thinking 'Wow! What's that?'"
In the studio with Jack and Kip, he adds, "We all felt we were creating
something, that everybody was supporting each other. As soon as we started
playing, you knew that everybody there was the right person."

The Cuicoland Express went out on tour in 2001. "Man, we were really
cooking then," Horacio says with a gleam in his eye. With Robby Ameen as
the other drummer and Ritchie Flores on congas, "it was a total rhythmic
interaction, nothing to do with power, it was a rhythmic conversation. It was
a world-music band with our music, Bernie's funk, Vernon's jazz, and Jack's
background playing some classic songs, but in a totally different way. And Jack
is the best bandleader I have ever worked with, ever. But he also wants to be
part of the band – everything comes from respect; it was never 'you play this
and you play that'."

Bernie Worrell is adamant that The Cuicoland Express "was my favourite
line-up with Jack. You could take it anywhere. It was loose, warm, and
relaxed. Jack had fun with that. It was structured, but there were changes; you
put twists in it, colours, shades, accents, punctuation in the dialogue. It was a
cool thing, a healing thing."

The music actually evolved on the tour bus. Horacio says that everything
was recorded, and the musicians would listen to their parts and think about
how they might change or improve things the next night. It was unusual for
Jack to be involved in this kind of post-mortem, but it indicates the overall
sense of goodwill that existed between the musicians. That rapport shines out
in the DVD recording of their performance at the Cambridge Fayre in England
in July 2002 and also on the 'lost' recordings of the Melkweg concert in
Amsterdam in October 2001.

The Cuicoland Express were on the road in the wake of considerable
interest in Cuban music sparked by Ry Cooder's promotion of the Buena Vista
Social Club, but the tour was cut short by 9/11. They had a European tour
booked for October 2001, but a whole slew of dates for a US tour were blown
out, according to Horacio, who adds: "We couldn't even say 'hi, Jack' any
more. We had to say 'hello'."

The band did come together for Jack's next album for Sanctuary, however,
which was recorded in New York with mixing at Parkgate Studios during
2002–03 and co-produced by Kip. Gary Moore and Eric Clapton had
appeared on the previous album, but this time Jack confined the personnel to
his touring band plus his son Malcolm and Godfrey Townsend, a guitarist he
had met in 2002 on a Beatles tribute tour called Walk Down Abbey Road.

As with the Ringo tours, this was an all-star event in which each musician would be able to showcase his own material alongside the Beatles songs. The show toured in 2001 with John Entwistle, Alan Parsons, and Todd Rundgren as the main artists; for 2002, Parsons and Rundgren stayed, but the producers decided they needed a new big name and called on Jack. Godfrey was in the band, but was promoted to Musical Director on the grounds that "the stars were more likely to take orders from a nobody than one of their peers".

Godfrey says Jack was very helpful and supportive to him in his role as MD. Jack learnt everybody's songs as well as all the Beatles material and made sure Godfrey kept referring back to the 'Holy Bible' – a Beatles book containing all the tabs. One of Godfrey's jobs was to match the singers to the songs; Jack was allocated 'Eleanor Rigby'. For the very first concert, however, Jack committed the cardinal sin of making a mistake in front of hordes of rabid Beatles devotees, resulting in an audible groan from the audience. Unfazed, Jack picked up the lyric sheet, put on his glasses, and according to a local review of the concert delivered the most sublime rendition of the song anybody had ever heard.

Jack was up for a bit of showmanship as well. "When we played the Mohegan Sun Casino in Connecticut," Godfrey recalls, "there were some booths where people could sit right near the front of the stage. Jack stepped off the stage onto the backs of these booths – which were no more than six inches wide – still playing his bass, walked right to the end, and jumped a four-foot gap back onto the stage."

The line-up was subject to change depending on other commitments, so Christopher Cross joined instead of Eric Carmen. But unlike the Ringo tours, where it was clear and undisputed who was in charge, this tour became troubled and ill tempered. According to Godfrey, if Todd couldn't make a show, the others fell in behind Jack as the natural leader. But when Todd came back, he would want to take over, and started barking orders at the other musicians – so Jack would intervene on behalf of whoever was getting a tongue-lashing. Because he owned a copy of Eric's painted Gibson SG, Todd assumed he would be playing guitar on Jack's songs, to which Jack replied simply, "Godfrey's playing."

Godfrey also played on Jack's album *More Jack Than God*. Interviewers quizzed Jack on whether the title was a sly dig at Eric, but it wasn't. Godfrey had been playing acoustic guitar on a song called 'Kelly's Blues', written about a young girl Jack had read about who committed suicide after being subjected to constant bullying at school. Jack also played acoustic guitar on the track, and at one point engineer Jon Fausty asked him how the mix sounded through his headphones. "Do you need more Jack than God?"

The hypnotic and shimmering Latin sounds of these last two albums added new contours to Jack's sonic landscape. But one aspect of the music has remained constant – as the compositions are layered and textured in the studio and the lyrics go through repeated drafts, so it takes time to fully extract the essence of what is heard. Like a fine brandy, the music improves with age and should be savoured – and that applies no less to *Songs For A Tailor* than it does to *More Jack Than God*.

But Jack would not be promoting this new album. Kip says that he still had fights with Jack over the recording, the lyrics, or whatever, but that now "the fighting was not so intense, it was a different sort of awkward". Jack was seriously ill.

○

The first hint of a problem had come in 1997, when Jack underwent an insurance medical prior to the Ringo tour. He was told his blood pressure was on the high side, and after a series of tests it was revealed that Jack had serious liver damage, which he says was "no surprise really, after all the drinking, but I never went for medical check-ups. I always thought I was dying, so why bother?"

Fortunately, Jack was in no immediate danger, so the insurance was granted. He went on the tour, but further investigation and regular monitoring would now be essential. On his return to England, Jack saw his own doctor and was sent for a check-up at a local private hospital. For the next few years he went in every six months so that the doctors could keep an eye on his condition. The diagnosis was cirrhosis of the liver, which over time can mutate into liver cancer.

Jack felt fine and showed no symptoms, while the ultrasound scanning at the hospital revealed no tumours. The private hospital did not have a CT scanner (as many in the National Health Service do) but on the day of one of Jack's visits, a scanner was due to be set up in the car park for a short while so that certain patients could be screened. Jack was one of them.

The news was devastating. Not only did Jack have liver cancer, but because of the size and location of the tumours it was inoperable. The only option was a liver transplant. Jack was sent to the specialist unit at Addenbrooke's Hospital in Cambridge to undergo a battery of tests and assessments to see if he fitted the criteria for a transplant and ascertain if he would actually survive the operation. At first the doctors said nothing could be done; then they took a biopsy of the tumours and found that the largest one was benign, which meant they could operate.

In July 2003, Jack went on the waiting list for a liver transplant. "It was terrible really, because we would all be on this ward and the doctors would have their meetings and you would have to wait to find out if you were doomed or not. I was very lucky to be given a chance and eventually I went in during October. The Belgian surgeon who was doing the operation said, 'We've got a liver, but it's not the best. It's a bit fatty.' So I said, 'Let's wait for a better one then.' The reply was simple: 'You haven't got time to wait.'"

The operation itself went very well. Complex procedures such as these can take up to 12 hours, but Jack's took only six. There was no need for transfusions either, while the surgeon, knowing that Jack was a singer, decided against putting tubes down his throat (and risking damage to the vocal cords) and instead performed a tracheotomy.

The real horror of the operation was that Jack was conscious the whole time, experiencing what is known as 'anaesthesia awareness'. According to studies, this affects around 2,000 patients in the UK and over 20,000 patients in the USA every year. The patient is aware of what is going on but, because of the paralysing effects of the anaesthetics, cannot speak or signal to the medical staff. This can be extremely dangerous. There was every risk that Jack could have had a heart attack right there on the operating table, not because of his illness but simply through fear and shock – and nobody would ever have known. The psychological damage too can be devastating: one clinical psychologist from Leicester University was quoted as saying some of the worst cases of post-traumatic stress disorder he had ever seen were in patients who have survived this experience.

Jack was just terrified. "I went into a dream-like state; it was the only way I could handle it," he recalls. "I was lying on my tour bus during the '89 tour with Ginger and it was very, very cold. These three guys got on the bus, all wearing masks, and they wanted to steal something from me. Then suddenly Bernie Worrell was there and he looked after me. It all tied in with a night Bernie and me had in Minneapolis – quite a mad and frightening night together. We went to this club and there was a club within a club and you had to go down this trap door. And it got very scary 'cos I was the only white face; Bernie had to more or less protect me until we could actually escape." Jack was in danger of being stabbed that night; now here he was lying on an operating table while a surgeon with a scalpel took his liver.

Although the operation itself was a success, immediate complications arose as a result of an infection. Jack was taken to the Intensive Care Unit and administered an array of antibiotics to help deal with what the doctors thought was pneumonia, but this further weakened his immune system. His wound wouldn't heal and he had already lost a considerable amount of body weight and muscle tone. He was just about fit enough to be discharged for his son's 11th birthday. "Corin wanted a stretch limo to go to the Tower of London," he says. "I was in a terrible state but I held myself together."

Jack struggled through Christmas, but his health was going from bad to worse. The infection was no better; he had fluid on his lungs and was having difficulty breathing. Eventually the doctor was called. "I just started to die and the doctor was very concerned because he thought I wasn't going to make it. I wasn't that worried about dying. I felt sad about leaving everybody. The ambulance came and I remember waving goodbye to Margrit and my daughter Kyla and thinking, well, that's it."

Jack arrived at the hospital and was taken to the transplant ward. By now he was drifting in and out of consciousness and finally into a coma. One of the last senses to go is hearing, so Jack could hear what was going on around him even though he couldn't communicate. In the depths of his coma, the sounds of the real world merged in Jack's mind with the happenings of the strange and frightening parallel world he now found himself in.

What followed is best left to Jack to explain in his own words. It's just a snapshot of what happened over time as one scenario segued into the next. But it is worth pointing out that while Jack knew that the episode on the bus was some sort of dream or hallucination, as far as he was concerned what happened next was all too real.

O

"As soon as I got to the ward, it was a total nightmare. Suddenly I was in this French brothel where I saw the specialist, Graeme Alexander, and all the doctors, but they were trying to help me get out because I couldn't move.

"I thought I was in Belgium and then I thought I was in France. I was feeling really guilty that I had stolen some of my mother's drugs – she had some valium-type drugs, and somewhere in my crazy history I probably did borrow some. I'd gone on the ferry to Belgium and these drugs made me really ill, and because I was ill I spent the night in hospital. Then somehow I got to this hospital in Paris and I was looking out the window. I could see a Parisian skyline but actually it was Cambridge – and I did find that view of Cambridge later. On the sheets or blankets in the real hospital there was this French writing. Then I was wheeled into this lift and it went from France to Addenbrooke's. Then the Game started.

"There was this game that I was part of since I was a child, and there were all sorts of other characters, some of whom I had grown up with, like Jack Wild, who was the Artful Dodger in the film of *Oliver Twist*. It was really bizarre – why him? I've never even met him. Part of the game was that they could release this drug through the air-conditioning and then, depending on what drug they released, you could do the game slowly or quickly. It was a circular game – the whole floor was a circle, but you could only enter the game from a certain way, so that sometimes the nurse would join in, but she would have to get in through this door sideways. There was always this group of doctors and medical students. I would see these doctors in real life – but here there were three versions of them – all the same people, but they would look away as if embarrassed if they saw me looking at them, because the main group were fine but you weren't meant to see the other ones.

"I was in a small version of the ward – probably intensive care – and I was right at the door. I could hear everything: high heels click-clicking on the floor; that became part of an awful music going on. Margrit thought it would be a nice idea to have some music, so either they put earphones or a speaker near me so I could hear, but it was Cream, really loud, and it became Ginger and that became a whole history of the way Cream came about. Our car was in it, but a very bizarre version of the Austin Westminster. It was all to do with Neasden and getting a certain sort of bass rig, which was actually a tractor part. We had to go to this shed and get this tractor part. That developed into a very sexual dance involving ploughs and sugar – I think the plough was a bass guitar, and there was a female doing it as well, because then I became part of this Gypsy migration across Europe.

"Then there was this ward where they kept very famous people, but just kept them alive by transplanting their organs when they failed. There was Eva Peron – she walked past me in those high-heels and looked amazing. Admiral Yamamoto was there – he was given one or two boys a week and he played these insane computer games where if they lost they were executed; and we all thought that was a bit scandalous. It was like the Dennis Potter play, *The Singing Detective*.

"There was a French-Canadian guy in the bed opposite mine who had to blow his legs up because they would deflate – he had this pump, otherwise he would be flailing around. The hospital monitors became computer games. I got really jealous because this French guy had a better game than mine – a more deluxe version – and he had these special drinks that I couldn't have. He said to me, 'Eye don't zink ze way ze British treat zere 'eroes iz verry good' as he was inflating his legs. In the real ward there was a bed where they always put people who were about to die. They shuffled you around, and if you were in that bed you died. That was a true part of it. Some of the people who died, I don't know if it was real or not.

"I was in ICU – a glass door was open and there was a huddle of doctors and Pete Brown was among them. I was beckoning him but he wouldn't come into the room. Then I was moved to the criminal ward. Addenbrooke's had been bought by a consortium from Burma or Malaya (there were some Filipino workers on the ward); they were having a closing-down sale but I refused to move, so I had to be moved to this criminal ward and chained to the bed. I had all these tubes coming out, but the stand they went into – I thought it was a Mexican policeman. Why have they got a Mexican policeman guarding me so that I can't move? I had to get a suit and go to court – and there was this controversy over whether rock stars should get transplants – people outside with placards.

"I found a way of making everything all right by going back in time, which would also have protected all the children of the world. All I had to do was go to one of two spots – one was over Cuba and the other was over Scapa Flow – I had to go in a glider and do a back flip, and then time would reverse itself and it would all be fine. I was trying to get sponsorship for it. I did get to Cuba but didn't manage the back flip. I think that came from one of the last things I did before I went in for the transplant. In case this was my last chance, I went gliding, because I had always wanted to do that. I had won a trial lesson at a raffle at Corin's school and went with Natascha."

One of the more positive experiences Jack had involved music. "I was in charge of the radio and I was doing a BBC programme about the game and the music, produced by Corin, who was a darker, plumper version of himself but still my son. I've still got the music – I wrote it down because it was so intense and in such detail. One of the songs is 'My Heart Is A Guitar'." Overall, this parallel world was a hellish place, "full of darkness, about things happening in my life, but twisted – good things becoming malign and so full of poison".

○

One day the doctors told Margrit that they were planning to shut off the life-support machines in 24 hours. All of Jack's vital organs had failed and the machines were all that was keeping him alive. They had no idea what was wrong, why he wasn't responding to treatment, or why his whole body was shutting down. Margrit asked the family to come in to say their goodbyes. Then one of the doctors came into the family room with the news that there was a slight improvement in Jack's kidney function. He had another chance.

Nothing that had happened to Jack prior to this falls neatly into the typical near-death experience. He didn't travel down a tunnel or feel drawn toward a bright light, nor did he have any out-of-body experiences. But the next episode, when he says that "metaphorically, I could have turned my face to the wall", could be regarded as such.

"I was in Edinburgh, on the hill around Edinburgh Castle, and I was waiting for the result to see if I was going to be elected Thane Of Cawdor – in other words, die. There was this young girl, I don't know who she was, but someone who meant a lot to me. She had to go and find out the result. And it came back. No, you're not going to be elected this time. So that was when I decided I was going to live."

Then, in a scene reminiscent of the hospital drama *House*, the penny dropped. It turned out that Jack could not tolerate rapamycin, the drug being used to prevent organ rejection (something that affects one in a thousand patients, so one wonders why it wasn't considered earlier). Jack was switched to another immunosuppressant drug, tacrolimus, and within two days began to recover.

Jack's opinion of his treatment in hospital is mixed. Some of the nursing care was unimpressive, he says. "They knew who I was, and they would say things like, 'Huh, he doesn't look like much' – I was in a coma and they thought I couldn't hear them." They also managed to injure Jack's shoulders through rough handling. "Some of these nurses were in my dreams as well. There was one really scary nurse, and this thing happened where we had to move from one hospital to another because they were closing down and she had to get everything ready, but if she forgot one thing – that was it, I wouldn't make it. She had this mantra: 'If anything can go wrong, it will go wrong.'"

Needless to say, "the food was disgusting. The first meal they brought me after I was supposed to start eating was liver and onions. You couldn't make it up. I used to pretend I was eating or that Margrit was bringing me in some chicken soup, which she did often. I was on dialysis because my kidneys were failing and they had this machine that I think they were having problems with. In my mind, the food would come down this machine. It would somehow be broadcast from the kitchen through the air and then go down the tubes, and you could pick what you wanted to have: 'Would you like curry or mash potato; what flavour would you like?' Completely hilarious. They sent the nutritionist round to get me to eat this food and I'd have an apple or a yoghurt."

But Jack is full of praise for the surgeon who conducted the operation and the rest of the transplant team, and says there were some "wonderful nurses and an amazing physiotherapist who got me breathing properly and eventually walking. I was so determined. I didn't know how weak I was; the first time I tried to get out of bed on my own, I just fell straight on the floor – I was just laughing, it was crazy. But then you start on the Zimmer frame, and I remember going down the corridor feeling very proud of myself. Then I was on the crutches, and you can get quite stuck on those, but you've got to stop using them and try and walk on your own. I remember doing this for the first time and this doctor who hadn't seen me for a while came toward me. It was like he'd seen a ghost; he couldn't believe it."

Jack was finally discharged on April 1 2004, almost a shadow of his former self, to begin the long, arduous physical and psychological road to recovery. There was a powerful incentive, however. Maybe the ultimate goal to reach for. Cream were reforming.

CHAPTER 16 **reunion**

When Jack led Cream out on stage at the Royal Albert Hall on May 2 2005, as nervous as he was, he knew he had proved his mother wrong in the most dramatic way. As far as she was concerned, he was not like the other tough little Gorbals boys; he was frail, fragile, and needed to be wrapped up. But Jack knew different and now, barely a year after the doctors were suggesting his life-support machine be switched off, he was stepping up to the mic to start the most anticipated concert in the history of rock.

"I had already agreed to do it while I was still in hospital," he says. "I remember Margrit telling me about it. I couldn't walk or even talk, but I said I'd do it. It gave me the incentive – that was my goal. But I didn't think I would make it really."

Jack's priority was getting his voice back. He had been to a hospital close to home to get his vocal cords checked out, where it was confirmed that no damage had been done by the tracheotomies. So he went to see Mary Hammond, a world famous voice coach who lived in North London. The train and taxi ride to her house was slow and painful. When he arrived he showed her a photo of his vocal cords and, with masterful understatement, told her he had a gig coming up. "She told me 'no problem'," he recalls. "But she said I had to be brave and realise that I had to build my voice up while overcoming the fear that I would try too hard at the start and somehow 'break' it." Over the months, Jack gradually gained the physical and mental strength required and listened to everything that Cream had ever played. By the start of rehearsals at Bray Film Studios in April 2005 he was as ready as he ever would be.

○

From the moment Cream left the stage at Madison Square Garden in November 1968, journalists trotted out one stock question at any opportunity: would Cream ever reform? Jack was usually warmest toward the idea and would never rule it out. Eric was more wary; Ginger dismissed any such notion out of hand, and was adamant in the years directly following the breakup that he would never play with Jack again.

For the best part of 30 years, their paths rarely crossed. Eric and Jack pursued very different musical careers, while Ginger seemed unsure as to whether he wanted to be a musician at all. After the collapse of Airforce, he invested – and lost – heavily in business ventures in Nigeria. Then followed a few desultory bands under his own name and some frankly bizarre associations with John Lydon's Public Image Ltd and Hawkwind. It wasn't until the late 90s that he released jazz material worthy of his talent. His main – and rather unlikely – passion was polo; he had a polo business in Colorado until he relocated to South Africa following problems with the US immigration authorities.

In 1987 Eric agreed to play on the extra tracks on *Willpower*, the same year Jack appeared with Eric on the British television arts programme *The South Bank Show*. In October 1988, at the end of a tour, Eric turned up on stage with The Jack Bruce Band (then featuring Anton Fier, Pat Thrall, and Dave Bravo) and tore into a 20-minute trip down memory lane, split just about equally between 'Spoonful' and 'Sunshine Of Your Love'. So excited was Jack at that point that in 1989 he told *Guitar World* that a reunion was very much on the cards for the following year. But, as we know, something equally unlikely happened instead: Ginger joined Jack's band. Financial reasons would have been pressing, but nonetheless, for all his declarations, there he was playing Cream songs on tour with Jack.

The wires really began to hum about a reunion when Cream were inducted into the Rock & Roll Hall Of Fame in January 1993. They were initially reticent about taking part; certainly Jack was never comfortable with the glitzy, self-congratulatory side of the music business. But they played 'Born

Under A Bad Sign', 'Crossroads', and 'Sunshine', with Eric later admitting that this was a major catalyst toward him believing that they could play together again. At the Hall Of Fame ceremony, he recalled, "We were supposed to make acceptance speeches, and I found myself overwhelmed. As I was talking I could feel the tears coming into my eyes and I hadn't realised how much that whole thing had meant to me – it was the early part of my musical experience and it was very powerful. And we played so well, so quickly. It always kept coming back to me; if we can, why shouldn't we?"

Jack believes that Eric's manager at the time, Roger Forrester, held Eric back from taking the idea any further. Eric and Forrester parted company around 1998, but it was a letter from Margrit to Eric's lawyer, Michael Eaton, about the severity of Jack's illness that prompted Eric to make the first move. Ginger too had been experiencing physical problems that could have ended his career. Realising that they were the only major 60s band with all of the original members still living, and "feeling a little more generous to my own past and wanting to get in touch with that again", Eric contacted Margrit and also personally contacted Ginger, whose response to an earlier approach from Eric's office had been firmly in the negative.

○

Jack was the last to arrive on the first day of rehearsals and went in rather nervously, expecting all the old aggravation to kick in. But everything went well. There was just one musical disagreement between Jack and Ginger, about the rhythmic phrasing of 'Spoonful', "but Ginger was right and I quickly apologised". They were booked for about three weeks of rehearsals, but found they didn't need that much. They started with a few basic songs and over time built up the final setlist. It was relaxed and friendly; one time they sat around talking politics and foxhunting before running through 'Politician'. But it didn't stop them feeling very shaky as they walked out on stage.

The *Daily Telegraph* broke the news of the reunion in November 2004; anticipation grew to fever pitch from the moment it was officially confirmed. All three had agreed they wouldn't give any interviews in the run-up to the concerts: five nights at the Royal Albert Hall. Alongside the hysteria went the rumours, the best one being that, because of back and arm problems, Ginger would be replaced by Phil Collins. When tickets eventually went on sale the Royal Albert Hall website simply melted. Fans came from America and Japan, some paying over $2,000 on eBay for the privilege of seeing the band. The rock world had never seen anything like it. This was not just a concert; not just a reunion. For Cream fans it was the Second Coming. And contrary to a few of the more sniffy and patronising reviews, the Albert Hall was not just stuffed with balding, middle-aged blokes reliving their youth. The under-30s were well represented, including one 18-year-old from New York who changed his mind about a huge birthday party and asked for a Cream ticket instead.

Things began a little tentatively. Eric was suffering from a bout of 'flu for the first three nights, and Jack took rests on a stool. But they relaxed into the music and gained in strength and confidence as the week progressed. There were many in the audience who would have been happy just to see Eric, Jack, and Ginger standing on a stage together playing 'My Old Man's A Dustman' on spoons and kazoo, but the truth was this was never going to be a nostalgia trip.

If the rehearsals had gone badly, the shows would have been cancelled. The Cream bar had been raised too high for the standard to be any less than excellent. They all played magnificently well: Ginger was tight and precise, updating many of the polyrhythms from his back catalogue; Eric showed just how much the blues is his heart-music; and Jack was in miraculously good voice on incredibly testing songs like 'We're Going Wrong'. And even though they were not going hell for leather, like the old days, Eric was still working harder than he was used to, conscious that the other guys on the stage would offer respect but no deference. Jack made it slightly easier for Eric, tending toward rhythm-guitar lines on the bass and making the whole thing less competitive, and feeling that "our time and feel is better and we've matured; we're not trying to prove anything to anyone or to each other".

There were many highlights across the five nights: the loping renditions of 'Spoonful'; the almost freeform-jazz style of the improvisations in 'Sweet Wine'; seeing Jack and Ginger smiling and nodding to each other as they got right into the pocket together song after song. As if to emphasise the timelessness of the compositions, 'Politician' seemed even more relevant now than in 1968, when hardly a day goes by without another exposé of British political sleaze and spin. And when Jack wrote 'We're Going Wrong', he couldn't have known the desperate days that all three would face over the years. They came off the stage elated at what they had achieved. And as Eric subsequently wrote in his autobiography, they should have left it at that.

○

There were no immediate plans for more gigs, but then Cream were made an offer they really could not refuse to play three nights at Madison Square

Garden. It turned out to be a big mistake. Interviewed later amid reports of an even bigger payday in Japan, Ginger was adamant Cream would never play again. "The Albert Hall was great, but not the shows we did at Madison Square Garden," he said. "That was a fucking disaster."

Yet the response in New York was as appreciative and excited as it had been in London. Ginger's daughter Nettie was there and says that everybody was dancing and having a great time. But there were some missed cues and fluffed lyrics, a reflection of how little they had rehearsed for these shows. You might ask, after the Albert Hall gigs, how much rehearsal was really needed to play songs that were part of their very being. But a band with their reputation needs to be pin-sharp, and for MSG they were not.

Jack was fighting a private battle with his health. His hands were cramping up and he was having fluid drained from his lungs, fearful that the cancer was returning. What did resurface was the classic sublimation of whatever was bothering Ginger: the accusation that Jack was playing too loud. Eric apparently stormed off the stage after the first night, raging about it being 1968 all over again. The camera carried on running after an interview shot for a Cream DVD and caught Ginger declaring that he wasn't going out for the second night. You hear the producer gently remind Ginger how much money is at stake, how his five-year plan for a polo enterprise in South Africa could be realised literally overnight. Eventually Ginger appeared with Perspex screens around the kit. But as Jack explains, he really couldn't understand what the problem was.

"Overall I don't really agree with this idea that MSG was a bad gig," he says. "On the first night it sounded great. I was having a blast – just at the point where I switched from the EB1 (the Gibson violin bass) to the fretless, I felt so joyous and I turned round to smile at Ginger and he pulled this face, and my heart sank and it was so difficult to carry on. And in between leaving the stage and coming back for the encore I apologised to him. I said, 'I'm really sorry if I've done anything to upset you, if I inadvertently had my bass up too loud, it wasn't deliberate.'

"We should have put the screens up first off. I realised afterward that the amps had been set up so that the fretless bass amps were closer to Ginger than those for the EB1 – when I switched [basses], it sounded as if I had turned it up, but it was just that the amps were nearer. The other way round and he might not have noticed anything. But I just play the bass at the volume required. I never had a problem with Ringo, who would have been the first to say 'turn it down' if it was too loud. So I don't really understand this."

Likewise, Malcolm Bruce is mystified by the apparent volume issue at MSG. "There is so much echo in the place," he says, "and the sound dissipates, so I don't see how it could be that loud on stage unless the amp is literally turned round in your face. Ginger wants there to be a problem."

Despite everything, Jack turned up at the Shepherd's Bush Empire in London in December 2008 for a Zildjian cymbals event in honour of Ginger. Jack played, and there is a photo of the two of them embracing. So you can never say never when it comes to Jack and Ginger, but as for Cream ever playing again – it seems very unlikely.

O

Jack's public profile has never been higher since Cream disbanded in 1968. His contribution to popular music was recognised in 2005 with a *Bass Player* Lifetime Achievement Award, while in 2007 the Royal Scottish Academy Of Music & Drama opened a Jack Bruce Zone for the performing arts, for which Jack played a short set with Clem Clempson, Gary Husband, and daughter Natascha. Cream received a Lifetime Achievement Grammy in 2006; Jack and Pete Brown picked up a BMI Award in London for two million plays of 'White Room'.

Jack's performances for the BBC from 1971–78 were collected on a special three-CD release that was followed by a long overdue six-CD retrospective, *Can You Follow?* On stage, Jack boosted the income of some local children's charities by taking part in a Rock'n'Roll Fantasy Camp in Las Vegas and has trodden the nostalgia boards for an American package tour called HippieFest backed by Godfrey Townsend and Steve Murphy and starring whoever survived the torrent of Owsley acid.

He has also performed his songs with two big-bands in Germany and Britain, and in December 2008 flew to Japan for a set of concerts in tribute to Tony Williams with Vernon Reid, organist John Medeski, and the extraordinary percussionist Cindy Blackman.

Jack's plans to record a third album with his Latino musicians ran aground when Sanctuary Records collapsed, but he reunited with Robin Trower after nearly 30 years to record the well-received *Seven Moons* in 2008. According to Robin, there had always been talk of the pair getting together again. "A few years ago, I started to think about doing a remix of the best of the two albums, because whenever I listened to them I would think that the mixes were not very good, very lumpy and 80s," he says. "So I went over to Jack's place, listened to the albums, and he agreed they could be better, but he said we ought to write a couple of new things for the package – and that's how *Seven Moons* started. Within a couple of days we had four strong ideas so we knew it wouldn't be that difficult to carry on and put an album together. Since we worked together before, I think I know more about trying to put something together that works for Jack as well."

Jack suggested they use Gary Husband on drums. Surprisingly, Gary says that after all of his years playing with Jack, only now was he happy with his performance. "There's a very special thing that Jack had with Ginger and Tony Williams, to do with time relationships and rhythm correspondence, it's both antagonistic and complimentary," he says. "Jack would throw things at me like I was a hound he was trying to shake off his ankle, musical practical jokes. My natural tendency is to play on top of the beat or even a little ahead, but Jack would always tell me to wait a bit. It took a long time for me to be able to go on stage and not have all this stuff in my head. On that album with Robin Trower, I finally found a way to play with Jack successfully; I learnt Jack's sense of rhythm." The band successfully toured the album in 2009, a year marked by live CD and DVD releases.

○

Very little of Jack's career has ever been planned, so he is unlikely to start planning now. But however serendipitous his choices, they have left him very comfortably off. Over the years, he has very much enjoyed the fruits of his success: houses at home and abroad, a boat, an island; prestige cars, the best hotels, the first class travel. But the most important thing in his life is his family. He has been with Margrit now for over 30 years and it gives them both great satisfaction to see how well their children are doing.

Music, of course, is in the blood; when the children were young, Natascha played cello, Kyla piano and violin, and they would perform with Jack at their local Suffolk church. For Kyla's school, Jack wrote an 'alternative' nativity called *Little Stars*, since commercially published, about the legends of the constellations, starring Kyla as Orion.

Approaching his 18th birthday, Corin shows great promise as a drummer and would love to be in a professional band. "That would be perfect for me," he says. "I don't want anything else, although living in the real world, that might not happen." Kyla also had dreams of a life in the music business when she was younger but, mindful of how difficult a road that could be, she turned her creative skills elsewhere. After graduating from the famous Glasgow School Of Art she is now making her way in the world of film.

It is Natascha, performing as Aruba Red, who has followed most firmly in Jack's footsteps. Her evocative mix of reggae, dub, and acoustic music demonstrates an eclecticism inherited from her dad. Her musical journey has also been influenced by some of the musicians she has met through him, especially the Puerto Rican and Cuban guys she recorded with in New York. She released her debut album in 2008, with songs featuring a socio-political conscience very reminiscent of Jack's, and demonstrates a similar wariness of the music business. "I'm at a bit of a crossroads really. The album did really well for what it set out to do and now there is some mainstream interest, so the decision is whether to go that way or remain independent."

How much of a disconnect is there for the family between Jack Bruce the famous rock star and Jack Bruce the dad? Although they are well used to his status, Natascha says she gets "really nervous for him before a gig and really emotional when he's up there – and very protective. So we are really connected. And it's always interesting watching how other people react to the music when they don't know who you are. Weird, but good." Kyla adds, "When you realise the number of people who have been affected by his music, it just blows you away. Shit, that's my dad!"

As many times as they have seen Jack perform, they all agree that the Cream reunion gigs were something very special. Natascha speaks for them all when she says: "We'd all grown up with Cream, we'd seen the pictures and read the articles, and everybody's dads would always be talking about them. But to see it for real was amazing, momentous."

As a family, they have not suffered too much from Jack's celebrity status. Jack keeps himself quite private and out of the spotlight, rarely attending the many celebrity functions to which he and the family are regularly invited. "We've never been in an environment with other rock stars' kids," says Natascha. "I've met people at events and along the way and there seems to be this clique who know each other and go to the same clubs. But dad stays out of that, and has kept his creative process pure – he hasn't let the media or the industry affect what he does, and I really respect him for that."

O

Jack will never rest easy. He retains the ethos of the working musician: if an opportunity arises – if it sounds interesting and the pay is OK – he'll go for it. He continues to harbour thoughts about completing his trilogy of Latin albums, and the guys from The Cuicoland Express would be overjoyed to play with Jack again. He would also like to play for the first time in South America.

But whatever he chooses to do, his place in the history of popular music is secure. Gustav Mahler asked himself if a man could win fame in his own time while remaining a true artist. If you go looking for the man in the music, there you will surely discover that Jack has done just that by creating a body of work that is intense and powerful, lyrical and emotional, articulate and questioning.

As a solo artist for more than 40 years, cocooned within his own privacy and reticence, Jack has been on a lonely road of exploration. He realised very early on that if he wanted to play music of craft and intelligence, he would have to write it himself. But while the ripples of unease still flow, the quest for challenge continues. He acknowledges that nowadays his health has to be a determining factor in what he can achieve, but also that "I need to do more to make up for all the time I missed". Or in the words of a famous song:

I've been in and out, I've been up and down,
I don't want to go until I've been all around.

APPENDIX I
Bass-ic Instincts

"He plays the bass like a composer. There are lots of bass players out there who can play the instrument to death but are blissfully unaware of what's going on around them. Jack is always playing with a composer's view of the music, able to strike a remarkable balance between freedom and fluidity and still perfectly serve the needs of the song."

STEVE SWALLOW

"Irrefutably and undeniably, Jack was the first electric bass virtuoso in history, the first bass player to distinguish himself with a sound that was original, and the only player, other than Jaco, to sound like himself on a fretless bass. His influence over me as a youth was life-changing."

JEFF BERLIN

Although he could well afford it, Jack Bruce is no bass guitar collector. He regards the bass as a working instrument, not something you simply gaze upon lying in its case or leaning on a stand. Nor is he a slave to gadgets and gizmos.

"In the 70s I used a lot of effects like digital delay," he says, "then I gave it all up. But I've got back to using chorus, Octivider, flanger, and so on with Robin Trower and it seems to work well." As for amplification, he told *Guitar Magazine* in 1992 that "going through lots of gear alters the power and intensity of the sound and you lose the character of the bass itself. Amps should do just that: amplify the sound of the bass, nothing else."

That said, Jack has been at the forefront of various sonic developments. "I was a pioneer in using a mixture of valve and transistor amps," he says. "I used to do it for myself using a combination of Crown amps for the valve [tube] and Gallien-Krueger for the transistor, and various collections of speakers. [Amplifier maker] Larry Hartke liked that approach and they came up with amps that combined both. I'm still using Hartke gear."

Some of Jack's earlier experiments were rather less successful. At the 100 Club on April 1 1964 he tried hooking up an old WEM Pick-A-Back bass amp to an ancient Grampian. The results were explosive and blew Jack ten feet across the stage.

Jack's bass sound is so distinctive that he is often asked for his secret. "I always say that it's in the fingers. There is no magic box of tricks you can plug into for that Jack Bruce Sound." He mainly uses his index and middle fingers, with his thumb resting on the string to dampen it in the style of James Jamerson (who he says "did a lot of not playing strings but just damping them"). There's no special Jack Bruce technique, either. "Technique is often misunderstood," he says. "It's useful, but technique on its own is useless. I'm a vocalist and a keyboard player, so the bass itself is just another means of getting the message across. But I think there is something special about using a stringed instrument, the whole physicality of the thing. The movement from brain to finger to string is one I've grown attached to."

Which takes us to the instrument itself. Jack first encountered the electric bass when he had to hire a Guild to play with Ernest Ranglin. The first bass he owned was a Japanese Top Twenty (which melted in the incident at the 100 Club). He then bought a Fender VI six-string bass with The Graham Bond Organisation to compensate for the departure of guitarist John McLaughlin. He has rarely used anything other than a four-stringed instrument since, but does own "five-string fretted and fretless basses for particular songs if I want to get to low C". He next added a Danelectro to his arsenal before acquiring the bass he is most associated with, the Gibson EB3. It would be wrong to think that the EB3 totally dominated Jack's work with Cream, however. Both the Fender and the Danelectro were regularly used in the studio.

"A lot of the distortion of the EB3 was to do with the volume, but also to do with the fingers," he says. "Because I play acoustic bass, I play very hard, the opposite of somebody like Duck Dunn, who turns the volume up very high but plays very lightly." The EB3 was a short-scale bass with a biting tone allied to light gauge La Bella strings that were easy to bend, making it the perfect choice for Jack to demonstrate that basslines can be melodic and contrapuntal as well as supportive. Jack has owned three EB3s over the years. His main instrument was stolen during West Bruce & Laing and not recovered for nearly ten years. According to Bruce Gary, when the guitar resurfaced in New York the first thing Jack did was to open the back plate to reveal the diode that Dan Armstrong had installed to maintain that special overdriven sound when Jack was not playing through Marshall amps.

Jack eventually tired of that sound, however, and began the long search for a bass that would be as perfect as possible for the sound he wanted: a bass full of depth, warmth, and expression. He tried a Hohner fretless (which he then lost in the fire at Mick Taylor's house in 1975), then a Dan Armstrong Perspex fretless bass in around 1976–77, followed by a Spector bass. He also road-tested a Wal and a Music Man, and for a time settled on the Aria SB1000 ("I guess because they had a good deal for me").

It was while living in Germany in the early 80s that Jack discovered the Warwick fretless bass. "I was working in Kurt Renker's studio and I was still searching for a bass that I really loved," he recalls. "I went into a music shop in a small town and they had a Warwick. I tried it, liked it, and bought it. Warwick found out, got in touch, and asked me what I thought of it. I said it was a good bass, but that it needed improvements – the balance was very bad. It was a very heavy bass made of wenge/bubinga, much heavier than a Fender. You need the weight to get the sound, but the balance was all wrong, and that's where the Warwick Thumb comes from."

The Warwick remains Jack's favourite bass. He uses SIT strings: "It stands for Stay In Tune," he says, "and if you stretch them initially, they do." But for the Cream reunion concerts, Jack gave an airing to the classic violin-shaped Gibson EB1. "There's an authenticity about the sound," he says. "It's got so much heft, an unmistakable sound like nothing else – and it limits me technically. If I'm playing in a band, like the one at the moment with Robin, where I don't want to be playing lots of notes, the EB1 is great – it is not a bass where you can play lots of notes."

Was he tempted to play the EB3 for the 2005 shows? "Eric and I did try using the gear we had in the 60s," he says. "I think Eric had a Les Paul and we both had Marshalls. But it sounded terrible, so we had some fun and went back to our modern gear."

APPENDIX II
Discography COMPILED BY Bob Elliott

1. SOLO WORK

Jack's first solo release was a single released in the UK on December 3 1965, 'I'm Gettin' Tired (Of drinkin' And gamblin' Etcetera)' / 'Rootin' Tootin'' (Polydor BM 56036). The single featured Don Rendell on saxophone and John Stevens on drums and was included on *Rare Tracks* (Polydor Special 2482 274) in 1976. It can also be found on *The Anthology: Can You Follow?* (Esoteric Recordings ECLECBOX 1).

Songs For A Tailor

1. Never Tell Your Mother She's Out Of Tune
2. Theme For An Imaginary Western
3. Tickets To Waterfalls
4. Weird Of Hermiston
5. Rope Ladder To The Moon
6. The Ministry Of Bag
7. He The Richmond
8. Boston Ball Game, 1967
9. To Isengard
10. The Clearout
11. The Ministry Of Bag* (demo)
12. Weird Of Hermiston* (alternate mix)
13. The Clearout* (alternate mix)
14. The Ministry Of Bag* (alternate mix)

Recorded at Morgan Studios, Willesden, London, UK, April–June 1969. Released in 1969 (Polydor 583 058). Remastered and reissued in 2003 (Polydor 065 603-2) with bonus tracks marked *. Jack Bruce: bass, organ, piano, electric piano, guitar, cello, vocals; Chris Spedding: guitar; George Harrison: guitar (1); Jon Hiseman: drums (all tracks except 5,7); John Marshall: drums (5,7); Harry Beckett: trumpet; Henry Lowther: trumpet; Dick Heckstall-Smith: tenor and soprano saxophones; Art Themen: tenor and soprano saxophones; John Mumford: trombone (8); Felix Pappalardi: vocals (5,9), guitar (9), percussion (7).

Things We Like

1. Over The Cliff
2. Statues
3. Sam Enchanted Dick (Medley): Sam's Sack/Rill's Thrills
4. Born To Be Blue
5. HCKHH Blues (Hayseed Country Kicking Ho Ho Blues)
6. Ballad For Arthur
7. Things We Like
8. Ageing Jack Bruce, Three, From Scotland, England*

Recorded at IBC Studios, London, UK, August 1968. Released in 1970 (Polydor 2343 033). Remastered and reissued in 2003 (Polydor 065 604-2) with bonus track marked *. Jack Bruce: double bass; Dick Heckstall-Smith: saxophones; Jon Hiseman: drums; John McLaughlin: guitar (3–8).

Harmony Row

1. Can You Follow?
2. Escape To The Royal Wood (On Ice)
3. You Burned The Tables On Me
4. There's A Forest
5. Morning Story
6. Folk Song
7. Smiles And Grins
8. Post War
9. A Letter Of Thanks
10. Victoria Sage
11. The Consul At Sunset
12. Green Hills (Can You Follow?)* (instrumental version)
13. You Burned The Tables On Me* (electric piano version)
14. There's A Forest* (first take)
15. Escape To The Royal Wood (On Ice)* (instrumental demo)
16. Can You Follow?* (first take)

Recorded at Command Studios, London, UK, January 1971, except track 13, recorded at Morgan Studios, Willesden, London, UK, October 6 1969. Released in 1971 (Polydor 2310 107). Remastered and reissued in 2003 (Polydor 065 605-2) with bonus tracks marked *. Jack Bruce:

bass, organ, piano, electric piano, acoustic guitar, vocals; Chris Spedding: guitar; John Marshall: drums, percussion.

Jack Bruce: At His Best

A1. Never Tell Your Mother She's Out Of Tune
A2. Morning Story
A3. Theme For An Imaginary Western
A4. Post War
A5. Tickets To Waterfalls
A6. Folk Song
A7. You Burned The Tables On Me
A8. He The Richmond
A9. Victoria Sage
B1. A Letter Of Thanks
B2. The Clearout
B3. HCKHH Blues (Hayseed Country Kicking Ho Ho Blues)
B4. Boston Ball Game, 1967
B5. Rope Ladder To The Moon
B6. Weird Of Hermiston
B7. Smiles And Grins
B8. To Isengard
B9. The Consul At Sunset
B10. Can You Follow?

Released in 1972 (RSO Records 2659 024), the first of many 'best of' compilations. Includes material from *Songs For A Tailor*, *Things We Like*, and *Harmony Row*.

BBC Live In Concert Jack Bruce & Friends

1. You Burned The Tables On Me
2. Folk Song
3. A Letter Of Thanks
4. Smiles And Grins
5. We're Going Wrong
6. The Clearout
7. Have You Ever Loved A Woman
8. Powerhouse Sod
9. You Sure Look Good To Me

Recorded for BBC Radio 1's *In Concert* at the BBC Paris Theatre, London, UK, on August 18 1971. Broadcast on August 29 1971. Released in 1995 (Windsong WIND076). Jack Bruce:

bass, piano, vocals; Graham Bond: keyboards, alto saxophone, vocals (7); Chris Spedding: guitar; Art Themen: tenor saxophone; John Marshall: drums, percussion.

Out Of The Storm
1. Peaces Of Mind
2. Golden Days
3. Running Through Our Hands
4. Keep On Wondering
5. Keep It Down
6. Into The Storm
7. One
8. Timeslip
9. Peaces Of Mind* (first mix)
10. Keep On Wondering* (first mix)
11. Keep It Down* (first mix)
12. Into The Storm* (first mix)
13. One* (first mix)

Recorded at Record Plant Studios in Los Angeles and San Francisco, California, November 1973–May 1974. Released in 1974 (RSO Records RSO 2394 143). Remastered and reissued in 2003 (Polydor 065 606-2) with bonus tracks marked *. Jack Bruce: bass, organ, piano, electric piano, clavinet, harmonium, harmonica, vocals; Steve Hunter: lead, rhythm and acoustic guitars; Jim Keltner: drums (2,3,4,5,6,10,11, 12); Jim Gordon: drums (1,7,8,9,13).

Live On The Old Grey Whistle Test
1. Can You Follow?
2. Morning Story
3. Keep It Down
4. Peaces Of Mind
5. One
6. Spirit
7. Smiles And Grins
8. White Room
9. Hit And Run
10. Slow Blues
11. Livin' Without Ja
12. Dancing On Air
13. In This Way
14. Theme For An Imaginary Western
15. Politician

Tracks 1–7 recorded by The Jack Bruce Band at BBC TV Centre, London, UK, June 6 1975. Tracks 8–15 recorded by Jack Bruce & Friends at the University Of Surrey in Guildford, UK, May 11 1981. Released

in 1998 (Strange Fruit WHISCD 010). Jack Bruce: bass, piano, vocals; Mick Taylor: guitar (1–7); Carla Bley: organ, synthesizer, clavinet, mellotron, electric piano (1–7); Ronnie Leahy: piano, electric piano, synthesizer (1–7); Bruce Gary: drums (1–7); Clem Clempson: guitars, vocals (8–15); Billy Cobham: drums (8–15); David Sancious: keyboards, guitar (8–15).

Live '75 Jack Bruce Band
A1. Can You Follow?
A2. Morning Story
A3. Keep It Down
A4. Peaces Of Mind
A5. Tickets To Waterfalls/Weird Of Hermiston/Post War
A6. Spirit
B1. One
B2. You Burned The Tables On Me
B3. Smiles And Grins
B4. Sunshine Of Your Love

Recorded at the Free Trade Hall, Manchester, UK, June 1 1975. Released in 2003 (Polydor 065 607-2). Jack Bruce: bass, piano, vocals; Mick Taylor: guitar; Carla Bley: organ, synthesizer, clavinet, mellotron, electric piano; Ronnie Leahy: piano, electric piano, synthesizer; Bruce Gary: drums.

How's Tricks
1. Without A Word
2. Johnny B 77
3. Times
4. Baby Jane
5. Lost Inside A Song
6. How's Tricks
7. Madhouse
8. Waiting For The Call
9. Outsiders
10. Something To Live For
11. Without A Word*
12. Something To Love For* (single edit)

Recorded at Manor Studios, Oxfordshire, UK, October–December 1976, except track 11, recorded at Scorpio Sound, London, UK, November 28 1974. Released in 1977 (RSO Records RSO 2394 180). Remastered and reissued in 2003 (Polydor 065 608-2) with bonus tracks marked *. Jack Bruce: bass, harmonica, lead vocals; Hughie

Burns: guitar, vocals, lead vocal on (4); Tony Hymas: keyboards, vibraphone, vocals; Simon Phillips: drums, glockenspiel, vocals; Mick Taylor: guitar (11); Carla Bley: organ, synthesizer, clavinet, electric piano (11); Ronnie Leahy: piano, electric piano, synthesizer (11); Bruce Gary: drums (11).

Jet Set Jewel
1. The Boy
2. Head In The Sun
3. Neighbour, Neighbour
4. Childsong
5. Jet Set Jewel
6. Please
7. Maybe It's Dawn
8. Mickey The Fiddler
9. She's Moving On
10. The Best Is Still To Come

Recorded at Chipping Norton Studios, Oxfordshire, UK, and Trident Studios, London, UK, August–October 1978. Released in 2003 (Polydor 065 609-2) 2003. Jack Bruce: bass, piano, cello, lead vocals; Hughie Burns: guitar, vocals; Tony Hymas: keyboards, vocals; Simon Phillips: drums, percussion, vocals; Dick Heckstall-Smith: saxophones (1,3).

I've Always Wanted To Do This
1. Hit And Run
2. Running Back
3. Facelift 318
4. In This Way
5. Mickey The Fiddler
6. Dancing On Air
7. Livin' Without Ja
8. Wind And The Sea
9. Out To Lunch
10. Bird Alone

Recorded and mixed at the House Of Music, West Orange, New Jersey, August 1980. Released in 1980 (Epic EPC 84672). Jack Bruce: bass, harmonica, lead vocals; Clem Clempson: guitars, vocals; Billy Cobham: drums, vocals; David Sancious: keyboards, guitar (7,9).

Jack Bruce: The Collection
1. Tales Of Brave Ulysses
2. SWLABR
3. White Room

4. Politician
5. As You Said
6. Never Tell Your Mother She's Out Of Tune
7. Theme For An Imaginary Western
8. Tickets To Waterfalls
9. Spoonful
10. Weird Of Hermiston
11. Rope Ladder To The Moon
12. He The Richmond
13. The Clearout
14. I Feel Free
15. Folk Song
16. Golden Days
17. Running Through Our Hands
18. Keep It Down
19. Keep On Wondering
20. Sunshine Of Your Love

Released in 1992 (Castle Communications CCSCD 326), another 'best of', featuring Cream material and tracks from *Songs For A Tailor*, *Harmony Row*, and *Out Of The Storm*.

Concert Classics Volume 9
1. White Room
2. Hit And Run
3. Clem's Blues
4. Born Under A Bad Sign
5. Livin' Without Ja
6. Dancing On Air
7. Post War
8. Theme For An Imaginary Western
9. Facelift 318
10. Morning Story
11. Tightrope
12. Traintime
13. Politician

Recorded live at the Rainbow Music Hall, Denver, Colorado, November 20 1980. Released in 1999 (Concert Classic RRCC00709). (Single CD release of *Doing This … On Ice!*) Jack Bruce: bass, piano, harmonica, lead vocals; Clem Clempson: guitars, vocals; Billy Cobham: drums, vocals; David Sancious: keyboards, guitar.

Doing This … On Ice!
A1. White Room
A2. Hit And Run
A3. Clem's Blues
A4. Born Under A Bad Sign
A5. Livin' Without Ja
A6. Dancing On Air

A7. Post War
A8. Theme For An Imaginary Western
B1. Facelift 318
B2. Morning Story
B3. Tightrope
B4. Traintime
B5. Politician
B6. Sunshine Of Your Love
B7. Bird Alone

Recorded live at the Rainbow Music Hall, Denver, Colorado, November 20 1980. Released in 2001 (Pilot 125). Also released as *Bird Alone* in 2005 (Neptune TUNECD114). Jack Bruce: bass, piano, harmonica, lead vocals; Clem Clempson: guitars, vocals; Billy Cobham: drums, vocals; David Sancious: keyboards, guitar.

Automatic
1. A Boogie
2. Uptown Breakdown
3. Travlin' Child
4. New World
5. Make Love (Part II)
6. Green & Blue
7. The Swarm
8. Encore
9. Automatic Pilot

Recorded at the Britannia Row Recording Studios in London, UK. Released in 1983 (Intercord 145069). Jack Bruce: bass, keyboards, programmed drums, piano, harmonica, cello, acoustic guitar, vocals; Bruce Gary: percussion programming assistance, drums (8).

'I Feel Free' / 'Make Love (Part II)'
1. I Feel Free
2. Make Love (Part II)

Released in 1986 (Virgin 108 325-100), featuring two new studio recordings not available on any other release. Jack Bruce: bass, vocals; Clem Clempson: guitar; Ronnie Leahy: keyboards; Bruce Gary: drums.

Willpower: A Twenty Year Retrospective
1. Willpower
2. As You Said
3. White Room
4. Rope Ladder To The Moon
5. Theme For An Imaginary Western

6. Never Tell Your Mother She's Out Of Tune
7. Can You Follow?
8. Morning Story
9. Folk Song
10. Keep It Down
11. Peaces Of Mind
12. Without A Word
13. How's Tricks
14. Jet Set Jewel
15. Mickey The Fiddler
16. The Best Is Still To Come
17. Ships In The Night

Released in 1989 (Polydor 837 806-2), a 'best of' release with two new songs recorded with Eric Clapton and three songs from the then-unreleased *Jet Set Jewel*. Jack Bruce: bass, piano, organ, acoustic guitar, harmonium (11), cellos, vocals; Eric Clapton: lead guitar (1,17); Clem Clempson: guitar (1); Maggie Reilly: vocals (17); Stuart Elliot: drums (1,17); Peter Weihe: acoustic guitars (17).

A Question Of Time
1. Life On Earth
2. Make Love
3. No Surrender
4. Flying
5. Hey Now Princess
6. Blues You Can't Lose
7. Obsession
8. Kwela
9. Let Me Be
10. Only Playing Games
11. A Question Of Time
12. Greasin' The Wheels

Recorded at Savage and Alpha-Omega Studios, San Francisco, California, and Electric Lady and Greene Street Recording Studios, New York City. Released in 1989 (Epic 465 629 2). Jack Bruce: bass, piano, keyboards, synthesizer, acoustic guitar, cello, vocals; with guests Eric Clapton, Ginger Baker, Tony Williams, Vernon Reid, Bernie Worrell, Gary 'Mudbone' Cooper, Allan Holdsworth, Albert Collins, and many others.

Something Els
1. Waiting On A Word
2. Willpower
3. Ships In The Night
4. Peaces Of The East

287

Jack Bruce COMPOSING HIMSELF

5. Close Enough For Love
6. G.B. Dawn Blues
7. Criminality
8. Childsong
9. FM

Recorded at Ztudio, Zerkall, Germany, 1986–92. Released in 1993 (CMP Records CMP CD 1001). Jack Bruce: bass, keyboards, vocals; with guests Eric Clapton, Maggie Reilly, Clem Clempson, Peter Weihe, Stuart Elliot, Trilock Gurtu, Dave Liebman, Dick Heckstall-Smith, and many others.

Cities Of The Heart
A1. Can You Follow?
A2. Running Through Our Hands
A3. Over The Cliff
A4. Statues
A5. First Time I Met The Blues
A6. Smiles And Grins
A7. Bird Alone
A8. Neighbour, Neighbour
A9. Born Under A Bad Sign
B1. Ships In The Night
B2. Never Tell Your Mother She's Out Of Tune
B3. Theme For An Imaginary Western
B4. Golden Days
B5. Life On Earth
B6. N.S.U.
B7. Sitting On Top Of The World
B8. Politician
B9. Spoonful
B10. Sunshine Of Your Love

Recorded live at E-Werk, Cologne, Germany November 2–3 1993. Released in 1994 (CMP Records CMP CD 1005). Jack Bruce: bass, piano, vocals; with guests Maggie Reilly, Gary 'Mudbone' Cooper, Gary Moore, Clem Clempson, Dick Heckstall-Smith, Art Themen, Henry Lowther, John Mumford, Bernie Worrell, Jonas Bruce, Malcolm Bruce, Francois Garny, Ginger Baker, Simon Phillips, Gary Husband, Pete Brown, and Kip Hanrahan.

Sitting On Top Of The World
1. Can You Follow?
2. Over The Cliff
3. First Time I Met The Blues
4. Neighbour, Neighbour
5. Ships In The Night
6. Born Under A Bad Sign

7. Theme For An Imaginary Western
8. N.S.U.
9. Sitting On Top Of The World
10. Politician
11. Spoonful
12. Sunshine Of Your Love

Recorded live at E-Werk, Cologne, Germany November 2–3 1993. Released in 1997 (Times Square 9003); compiled from *Cities Of The Heart*.

Monkjack
1. The Food
2. The Boy
3. Shouldn't We
4. David's Harp
5. Time Repairs
6. Laughing On Music Street
7. Know One Blues
8. Folk Song
9. Weird of Hermiston
10. Tightrope
11. Third Degree
12. Immortal Ninth

Recorded at Ztudio, Zerkall, Germany, May 1995. Released in 1995 (CMP Records CMP CD 1010). Jack Bruce: piano, vocals; Bernie Worrell: Hammond B3 organ.

The Jack Bruce Collector's Edition
1. Waiting On A Word
2. Ships In The Night
3. Theme For An Imaginary Western
4. Sitting On Top Of The World
5. Life On Earth
6. N.S.U.
7. Folk Song
8. The Wind Cries Mary
9. Politician
10. Rope Ladder To The Moon
11. Childsong
12. Time Repairs
13. Third Degree
14. Colotomix II

Recorded at Ztudio, Zerkall, Germany 1986–1995 and live at E-Werk, Cologne, Germany, November 2–3 1993. Released in 1996 (CMP Records CMP CD 1013). A 'best of' comprising material Jack recorded for CMP Records, plus new recordings of 'Sitting On Top Of The World' and 'Politician'.

Shadows In The Air
1. Out Into The Fields
2. 52nd Street
3. Heart Quake
4. Boston Ball Game, 1967
5. This Anger's A Liar
6. Sunshine Of Your Love
7. Directions Home (For Tony Williams And Larry Young)
8. Milonga
9. Windowless Rooms
10. Dark Heart
11. Mr Flesh
12. He The Richmond
13. White Room
14. Surge

Recorded at Sorcerer Sound, Soundtrack, and RPM Studios, New York City, and Olympic Studios, London, UK, November 1999– December 2000. Released in 2001 (Sanctuary SANCD 084). Jack Bruce: bass, piano, acoustic guitar, vocals; Vernon Reid: guitar; Horacio 'El Negro' Hernandez: drums; Robby Ameen: drums; Richie Flores: congas; Alfredo Triff: violin; with guests Eric Clapton, Dr John, Gary Moore, Chanquito Luis Quintana, Malcolm Bruce, Andy Gonzalez, and others.

More Jack Than God
1. So They Invented Race
2. Follow The Fire
3. Kelly's Blues
4. We're Going Wrong
5. Bizniz
6. Progress
7. I Feel Free
8. Ricin (Daylight Gathering)
9. The Night That Once Was Mine
10. Milonga Too
11. Cold Island (For Cozy Powell)
12. Politician
13. Lost In The City (Jam Mix)

Recorded at Sorcerer Sound and RPM Studios, New York City, and Parkgate Studios, Battle, UK, 2002– 2003. Released in 2003 (Sanctuary SANCD 211). Jack Bruce: bass, acoustic guitar, piano, organ, synthesizer, digital drums, vocals; Vernon Reid: guitar; Godfrey Townsend: guitar; Malcolm Bruce: guitar, piano; Bernie Worrell: Hammond B3 organ; Robby

Ameen: drums; Horacio 'El Negro' Hernandez: drums; Richie Flores: congas.

Rope Ladder To The Moon: An Introduction To Jack Bruce
1. Never Tell Your Mother She's Out Of Tune
2. Rope Ladder To The Moon
3. Weird Of Hermiston
4. Theme For An Imaginary Western
5. Tickets To Waterfalls
6. Things We Like
7. Folk Song
8. You Burned The Tables On Me
9. Can You Follow?
10. Morning Story
11. Running Through Our Hands
12. Timeslip
13. One
14. Keep It Down
15. How's Tricks
16. Without A Word
17. Jet Set Jewel

Released 2003 (Polydor 065 610-2).

HR Big Band Featuring Jack Bruce
1. Never Tell Your Mother She's Out Of Tune
2. Rope Ladder To The Moon
3. Spoonful
4. Smiles And Grins
5. Born Under A Bad Sign
6. Theme For An Imaginary Western
7. Milonga
8. The Consul At Sunset
9. We're Going Wrong
10. Deserted Cities Of The Heart
11. Sunshine Of Your Love

Recorded live with the Hessischer Rundfunk Big Band, conducted by Jörg Achim Keller, at the 37th Deutsches Jazzfestival in Frankfurt, Germany, October 26 2006. Released in 2007 (HR Musik HRMJ 03807). Jack Bruce: bass, piano, acoustic guitar, vocals; Jörg Achim Keller: conductor, arranger; Tobias Weidinger: trumpet, flugelhorn; Martin Auer: trumpet, flugelhorn; Thomas Vogel: trumpet, flugelhorn; Axel Schlosser: trumpet, flugelhorn; Günter Bollmann: trombone; Peter Feil: trombone; Christian Jaksjø: trombone; Manfred Honetschläger: bass trombone; Heinz-Dieter

Sauerborn: alto, soprano saxophone, flute; Oliver Leicht: alto, soprano saxophone, flute; Steffen Weber: tenor, soprano saxophone, flute; Andreas Maile: tenor, soprano saxophone, flute; Rainer Heute: baritone saxophone, bass clarinet; Peter Reiter: piano, electric piano, keyboards; Martin Scales: guitar; Thomas Heidepriem: bass; Danny Gottlieb: drums; Farouk Gomati: percussion; Corin Bruce: cowbell.

Spirit: Live At The BBC 1971–1978
A1. You Burned The Tables On Me
A2. Folk Song
A3. A Letter of Thanks
A4. Smiles and Grins
A5. We're Going Wromg
A6. The Clearout
A7. Have You Ever Loved A Woman
A8. Powerhouse Sod
A9. You Sure Look Good To Me
A10. Jack's Gone
A11. Clearway
A12. Powerhouse Sod
B1. Can You Follow?
B2. Morning Story
B3. Keep It Down
B4. Peaces Of Mind
B5. One
B6. Spirit
B7. Without A Word
B8. Smiles And Grins
B9. Fifteen Minutes Past Three
B10. Ten To Four
C1. Madhouse
C2. Without A Word
C3. Times
C4. Baby Jane
C5. Born Under A Bad Sign
C6. Lost Inside A Song
C7. Something To Live For
C8. How's Tricks
C9. Spirit
C10. Out Into The Fields
C11. You Burned The Tables On Me
C12. Twenty Past Four

A1–A9: Jack Bruce & Friends, recorded for BBC Radio 1's *In Concert* at the BBC Paris Theatre, London, UK, August 18 1971. A10–A12: Jack Bruce, Jon Hiseman, and John Surman, recorded for BBC Radio 3's *Jazz In Britain*, London, UK, August 10 1971. B1–B8: The Jack Bruce Band, recorded for *The Old Grey Whistle*

Test at BBC TV Centre, London, UK, June 6, 1975. B9–B10: Jack Bruce, Jon Hiseman, and John Surman, recorded for BBC Radio 3's *Jazz In Britain: At The Third Stroke*, London, UK, June 26 1978. C1–C11: The Jack Bruce Band, recorded for BBC Radio 1's *In Concert* at the BBC Paris Theatre, London, UK, April 14 1977. C12: Jack Bruce, Jon Hiseman, and John Surman recorded for BBC Radio 3's *Jazz In Britain: At The Third Stroke*, London, UK, June 26 1978. Released in 2008 (Polydor 5305568). Jack Bruce: bass, piano, vocals; Graham Bond: keyboards, alto saxophone, vocals (A1–A9); Chris Spedding: guitar (A1–A9); Art Themen: tenor saxophone (A1–A9); John Marshall: drums, percussion (A1–A9); Jon Hiseman: drums (A10–A12, B9–B10, C12); John Surman: baritone and soprano saxophone, bass clarinet, celeste (A10–A12, B9–B10, C12); Mick Taylor: guitar (B1–B8); Carla Bley: organ, synthesizer, clavinet, mellotron, electric piano (B1–B8); Ronnie Leahy: piano, electric piano, synthesizer (B1–B8); Bruce Gary: drums (B1–B8); Hughie Burns: guitar, vocals (C1–C11); Tony Hymas: keyboards, vocals (C1–C11); Simon Phillips: drums, vocals (C1–C11).

The Anthology: Can You Follow?
A1. Hoochie Coochie Man (live)
A2. Early In The Morning (instrumental)
A3. Night Time Is The Right Time
A4. Rockin' (live)
A5. Doxy (live)
A6. I Saw Her Standing There (original version)
A7. Long Tall Shorty
A8. Little Girl
A9. High Heeled Sneakers
A10. Strut Around
A11. Wade In The Water
A12. Traintime
A13. Baby Make Love To Me
A14. Spanish Blues
A15. Baby Be Good To Me
A16. Last Night
A17. Hear Me Calling Your Name
A18. Stormy Monday (live)
A19. I'm Getting Tired (Of Drinkin' And Gamblin' Etcetera)

A20. Rootin' Tootin'
B1. Spirit Feel
B2. (I Can't Get No) Satisfaction
B3. Steppin' Out
B4. I Want To Know
B5. Crossroads
B6. Wrapping Paper
B7. I Feel Free (mono mix)
B8. Spoonful (mono mix)
B9. N.S.U. (mono mix)
B10. We're Going Wrong
B11. Dance The Night Away
B12. Sunshine Of Your Love
B13. SWLABR
B14. Traintime (live)
B15. As You Said
B16. White Room
B17. Deserted Cities Of The Heart
B18. Politician (live)
B19. Doing That Scrapyard Thing
B20. Ageing Jack Bruce, Three, From
Scotland, England
C1. Things We Like
C2. The Ministry Of Bag (demo
version)
C3. Never Tell Your Mother She's Out
Of Tune
C4. Boston Ball Game, 1967
C5. To Isengard
C6. Rope Ladder To The Moon
C7. Theme For An Imaginary Western
C8. Weird Of Hermiston
C9. Tickets To Waterfalls
C10. The Clearout
C11. To Whom It May Concern: Them
C12. To Whom It May Concern: Us
C13. One Word
C14. Two Worlds
C15. Can You Follow?
C16. Escape To The Royal Wood
(On Ice)
C17. Folk Song
C18. You Burned The Tables On Me
C19. There's A Forest
C20. Morning Story
C21. Out Into The Fields
C22. Pollution Woman
D1. Scotch Krotch
D2. Like A Plate
D3. Powerhouse Sod (live)
D4. Apostrophe
D5. Peaces of Mind
D6. Keep It Down
D7. One
D8. Timeslip
D9. Without A Word
D10. Spirit (live)
D11. How's Tricks

D12. Something To Live For
D13. Childsong
D14. The Best Is Still To Come
E1. Jet Set Jewel
E2. She's Moving On
E3. Waiting For The Call (live)
E4. Hit and Run
E5. Livin' Without Ja
E6. Dancing On Air
E7. Bird Alone
E8. Carmen
E9. Automatic Pilot
E10. Green & Blue
E11. Willpower
E12. Ships In The Night
E13. Waiting On A Word
E14. No Surrender
E15. A Question of Time
E16. Kwela
F1. Make Love
F2. Obsession
F3. Running Through Our Hands (live)
F4. Life On Earth (live)
F5. Waiting In The Wings
F6. City Of Gold
F7. The Wind Cries Mary
F8. David's Harp
F9. The Boy
F10. Time Repairs
F11. 52nd Street
F12. Directions Home (For Tony
Williams And Larry Young)
F13. Surge
F14. Heart Quake
F15. Milonga
F16. The Night That Once Was Mine
F17. Progress
F18. So They Invented Race

Released in 2008 (Esoteric
Recordings ECLECBOX 1), a deluxe
anthology featuring selections from
throughout Jack's career, including
work in various bands: A1–A4 Alexis
Korner's Blues Incorporated; A5 The
Graham Bond Quartet; A6 Duffy
Power & The Graham Bond Trio With
John McLaughlin; A7–A17 The
Graham Bond Organisation; A18 John
Mayall's Bluesbreakers; B1–B2
Manfred Mann; B3–B5 Eric Clapton &
The Powerhouse; B6–B19 Cream;
C11–14 The Tony Williams Lifetime;
C21–C22, D1–D3 West Bruce &
Laing; D4 Frank Zappa; E3 Rocket 81;
E8 Robin Trower & Bill Lordan; F5–F6
BBM; F7 Mark Nauseef & Miroslav
Tadic; F8–10 Bernie Worrell.

2. BANDS
Alexis Korner's Blues Incorporated
Jack plays on 'Everything She Needs',
'Hoochie Coochie Man' (live), 'Early In
The Morning' (instrumental), 'The
Night Time Is The Right Time', and
'Rockin'' (live).

Selected discography:
Rhythm & Blues (Decca LK 4616)
1964
Bootleg Him! (RAK Records SRAKSP
51) 1972
Broken Dreams Vol. 7 (Line OLLP
5398 AS) 1984
British R'n'B Explosion Vol. 1 (See For
Miles SEE CD 224) 1988
BBC Radio Sessions (Music Club
MCCD 179) 1994
The Blues Scene (Deram 844 801-2)
1999
*Kornerstoned: The Alexis Korner
Anthology 1954–1983* (Castle
Music CMEDD 1026) 2006

The Graham Bond Quartet
*Rhythm & Blues (With A Little Soul):
At Abbey Road 1963–67* (EMI 7243 4
93453 2 4) 1998. Jack plays on
'Wade In The Water', a demo
recorded for EMI on May 16 1963.
Solid Bond (Warner Bros. WS 3001)
1970. Jack plays on 'Ho Ho Country
Kicking Blues', 'The Grass Is Greener',
and 'Doxy', all recorded live at Klooks
Kleek R&B Club, West Hampstead,
London, UK, June 26 1963.

The Graham Bond Organisation
'Long Tall Shorty' / 'Long Legged
Baby' (Decca F 11909) May 15
1964
Hoochie Coochie Man EP (Decca DFE
4616) August 1964
Blues Now (Decca LK 4681) and
Broken Dreams Vol. 7 (Line OLLP
5398 AS): Jack plays on an
alternate version of 'Wade In The
Water', recorded in 1964.
Gonks Go Beat soundtrack LP (Decca
LK 4673): Jack plays on
'Harmonica', recorded in 1964.
'Tammy' / 'Wade In The Water'
(Columbia DB 7471) January 29
1965
'Tell Me (I'm Gonna Love Again)' /
'Love Come Shining Through'
(Columbia DB 7528) April 2 1965

'Lease On Love' / 'My Heart's In Little Pieces' (Columbia DB 7647) July 23 1965

Some of these early recordings can be found on *The Anthology: Can You Follow?*, and on:
Rhythm & Blues (Decca LK 4616) 1964
Hard-Up Heroes (Decca DPA 3009/10) 1974
Sixties Lost and Found Vol. 2 (See For Miles CM 123) 1983
Sixties Lost and Found Vol. 3 (See For Miles CM 126) 1983
Broken Dreams Vol. 7 (Line OLLP 5398 AS) 1984
The Soul Of British R'n'B 1962–68 (See For Miles SEE 67) 1986
R&B Scene Vol. 2 1963–1969 (See For Miles SEE 73) 1986
British R'n'B Explosion Vol. 1 (See For Miles SEE CD 224) 1988
Sixties Explosion 62–69 Vol. 1 (See For Miles SEE CD 223) 1988
Pop Inside The 60's Vol. 2 (See For Miles SEE CD 399) 1994
The Mod Scene (Deram 844 549-2) 1998
The R&B Scene (Deram 844 798-2) 1998
The Mod Scene Vol. 2 (Decca 844 924-2) 1999

Jack also appears on the following LPs by The GBO:
At The Beginning (Charly Records/Bellophone CR 3060) 1980
The Sound Of '65 (Columbia 33 SX 1711) 1965
There's A Bond Between Us (Columbia 33 SX 1750) 1965
The Sound Of '65/There's A Bond Between Us (Edsel Records DED 254) 1988

John Mayall's Bluesbreakers
Jack plays on the following six songs, recorded live at the Flamingo Club, London, UK, November 7 1965:
'Maudie', 'It Hurts To Be In Love', 'Have You Ever Loved A Woman', 'Bye Bye Bird', 'Hoochie Coochie Man', and 'Stormy Monday'.

Jack can be heard on:
Looking Back (Decca SKL 5010) 1969
Primal Solos (London LAX 146) 1977

Blues Breakers (With Eric Clapton) (Deluxe Edition) (Decca 984 180-1) 2006

Manfred Mann
Jack plays on 'That's All I Ever Want From You Baby', 'Spirit Feel', 'Tennessee Waltz', 'Tengo Tango', 'She Needs Company', 'When Will I Be Loved', 'Still I'm Sad', 'I Got You Babe', 'My Generation', '(I Can't Get No) Satisfaction', 'You're Standing By', 'Machines', 'Driva Man', 'It's Getting Late', 'Come Home Baby', 'Pretty Flamingo', and 'Let It Be Me'.

Selected discography:
Instrumental Asylum EP (HMV 7EG 8949) 1966
Soul Of Mann (HMV CLP 3594) 1967
EP Collection (See For Miles SEE CD 252) 1989
Best Of The EMI Years (EMI E2 0777 89490 2 2) 1993
The Singles Album (EMI EMS 1121) 1995
Manfred Mann At Abbey Road: 1963–1966 (EMI 7243 821136 2 1) 1998
Manfred Mann: BBC Sessions (EMI 7243 4 977720 2 6) 1998
The Best of Manfred Mann (Ascot CDP-596096) 1999
All Manner of Menn: 1963–1969 (Raven RVCD 102) 2000
Down The Road Apiece (Caroline CROL97215) 2007

Cream
'Sweet Wine', 'Sleepy Time Time', and 'Cat's Squirrel'. Alternate versions with different guitar overdubs released 1996 on a rare French EP.
'Wrapping Paper' / 'Cat's Squirrel' (Reaction 591007) UK October 7 1966
'I Feel Free' / 'N.S.U.' (Reaction 591011) UK December 9 1966
'I Feel Free' / 'N.S.U.' (Atco 6462) USA January 1967
'Strange Brew' / 'Tales Of Brave Ulysses' (Reaction 591015) UK May 27 1967
'Strange Brew' / 'Tales Of Brave Ulysses' (Atco 6488) USA July 1967
'Spoonful Pt. 1' / 'Spoonful Pt. 2' (Atco 6522) USA October 1967

'Sunshine Of Your Love' / 'SWLABR' (Atco 6544) USA February 1968
'Anyone For Tennis' / 'Pressed Rat And Warthog' (Polydor 56 258) UK May 1968
'Anyone For Tennis' / 'Pressed Rat And Warthog' (Atco 6575) USA May 1968
'Sunshine Of Your Love' / 'SWLABR' (Polydor 56 286) UK September 6 1968
'White Room' / 'Those Were The Days' (Atco 6617) USA October 1968
'White Room' / 'Those Were The Days' (Polydor 56 300) USA January 1969
'Crossroads' / 'Passing The Time' (Atco 6646) USA February 1969
'Badge' / 'What A Bringdown' (Polydor 56 315) UK April 1969
'Badge' / 'What A Bringdown' (Atco 6668) USA April 1969
'Sweet Wine' / 'Lawdy Mama' (Atco 6708) USA August 1969

Selected discography of LPs, CDs, boxed sets, and rare tracks:
Fresh Cream (Reaction 593 001 mono) (Reaction 594 001 stereo) UK 1966
Fresh Cream (Atco 33-206 mono) (Atco SD 33-206 stereo) USA 1967
Disraeli Gears (Reaction 593 003 mono) (Reaction 594 003 stereo) UK 1967
Disraeli Gears (Atco 33-232 mono) (Atco SD 33-232 stereo) USA 1967
Wheels Of Fire (Polydor 582 031/2 mono) (583 031/2 stereo) UK 1968
Wheels Of Fire (Atco SD 2-700) USA 1968
Wheels Of Fire: In The Studio (Polydor 582 033 mono) (Polydor 583 033 stereo) UK 1968
Wheels of Fire: Live At The Fillmore (Polydor 582 040 mono)(Polydor 583 040 stereo) UK 1968
Goodbye (Polydor 583 053) UK 1969
Goodbye (Atco SD 7001) USA 1969
Best Of Cream (Polydor 583 060) UK 1969
Best Of Cream (Atco SD 33-291) USA 1969
Live Cream (Polydor 2383 016) UK 1970
Live Cream (Atco SD 33-328) USA 1970

Jack Bruce COMPOSING HIMSELF

Live Cream Volume II (Polydor 2383 119) UK 1972
Live Cream Volume II (Atco SD 7005) USA 1972
Cream: Pop History Vol. 1 (Polydor 2475 014) Germany 1971
Heavy Cream (PD 3502) USA 1972
Heavy Cream (Polydor 2959 022) UK 1973
Best Of Cream (Polydor 2675 087) France 1973
The Best Of Cream (RSO MW 8663 / 8664) Japan 1978
The Best Of Cream Live (RSO MW 8665 / 8666) Japan 1978
Rock Legends: Cream (RSO 2475 219) Australia 1980
Cream (six LP boxed set)(RSO Records 2658 142) Germany 1981
Strange Brew: The Best Of Cream (RSO Deluxe RSO 5021) UK 1983
Eric Clapton: After Midnight EP (Polydor PZCD8) 1988; includes a live performance of 'Sunshine Of Your Love' recorded at the Fillmore Auditorium in San Francisco, California, on March 7 1968
The Very Best Of Cream (Polydor/Chronicles 523752) 1995
Those Were The Days (Polydor 539 000-2) UK/US 1997
Clapton, Bruce & Baker: First U.S. Tour (Classic Interview Series rscd 1002) 2000
The Best Of Cream: The Millennium Collection (Polydor/UMGD 000782302) 2000
BBC Sessions (Polydor 000006902) 2003
Disraeli Gears (Deluxe Edition) (Polydor 000331-02) 2004
Cream Gold (Polydor 4193) 2005
I Feel Free: Ultimate Cream (Polydor 987110) 2005
Royal Albert Hall: London May 2–3–5–6 2005 (Reprise WTVD 49416) 2005

Audiophile recordings on LP and CD:
Fresh Cream CD (DCC GZS 1022) 1992
Fresh Cream LP (DCC 2015) 1996
Disraeli Gears CD (MFSL UDCD 562 mono/stereo) 1992
Wheels Of Fire 2LP (MFSL-2-066) 1992
Wheels Of Fire 2CD (DCC GZS(2)

1020) 1992 (the second repress from the USA includes alternate mixes of 'Sitting On Top Of The World', 'As You Said', and 'Passing The Time' on disc 1, but these bonus tracks are not identified on the CD or in the liner notes).
Goodbye CD (MFSL UDCD 681) 1996
Live Cream / Live Cream Volume II 2CD (MFSL UDCD 2-625) 1995

Tony Williams Lifetime
'One Word' / 'Two Worlds' (Polydor 2066 050) 1970
Turn It Over (Polydor 2425 019) 1970; 1997 remaster includes a bonus track
Ego (Polydor 2425 065) 1971
Lifetime (Polydor Special 2482 179) 1976
Spectrum: The Anthology (Verve 537 075-2) 1997

West Bruce & Laing
Why Dontcha (CBS Records 65314) 1972
Whatever Turns You On (RSO Records RSO 2394 107) 1973
Live 'n' Kickin' (RSO Records RSO 2394 128) 1974
Why Dontcha (Columbia CQ-31929) quad mix LP 1976
Whatever Turns You On (Columbia CQ-32216) quad mix LP 1977
(The two quadrophonic LPs are totally different mixes: most of the tracks have additional or new guitar and bass parts, and in some cases new vocal tracks.)

BBM
Around The Next Dream (Virgin CDV 2745) 1994
Where In The World EP (Virgin VSCDG1495) 1994
Where In The World EP (Virgin VSCDX1495) 1994

3. SESSIONS
Nancy Spain with Alexis Korner's Blues Incorporated 'Blaydon Races' / 'Up Town (instrumental)' (Lyntone LYN 298) – both tracks also available on Kornerstoned: The Alexis Korner Anthology 1954-1983.

Duffy Power with The Graham Bond Quartet 'I Saw Her Standing There'

(alternate version) / 'Farewell Baby' (Parlophone R 5024) 1963

Jack also features on various Duffy Power tracks on the albums Rare 60's Beat Treasures Vol. 1 (Gone Beat BT-CD 77010), Rhythm & Blues (With A Little Soul): At Abbey Road 1963–67 (EMI 7243 4 93453 2 4), Innovations (Transatlantic TRA 229), Little Boy Blue (Edsel EDCD356), Just Stay Blue (Retro 802), Leapers and Sleepers (RPM D 240), and Vampers And Champers (RPM D 320).

Ernest Ranglin & The GBs 'Just A Little Walk Parts I and II' / 'Swing-A-Ling Parts I and II' and 'So-Ho' (Black Swan 1EP704) 1964 – Jack's first session on electric bass.

P.J. Proby 'Hold Me' / 'The Tips Of My Fingers' (Decca F11904) 1964

Winston G With The Graham Bond Organisation 'Please Don't Say' / 'Like A Baby' (Parlophone R5266) 1965

Eric Clapton & The Powerhouse What's Shakin' (Elektra EKS 74002) 1966

The Hollies 'After The Fox' / 'The Fox Trot' (United Artists UP 1152) 1966 – Jack plays on the A-side.

Paul Jones 'I've Been A Bad Boy' / 'Sonny Boy Williamson' (HMV POP 1576) 1966 – Jack plays on the B-side.

The Mike Taylor Trio Trio (Columbia SCX 6137) 1966

The Merseys Unearthed Merseybeat Volume 1 (Viper CD 016) 2006 – Jack plays the bowed bass intro on 'Sorrow', recorded in 1966.

Donovan A Gift From A Flower To A Garden (Epic B2N 171) 1967 – Jack plays on 'Someone's Singing'.

Crazy Blue (aka The Aynsley Dunbar Retaliation) History Of Bitish Blues Volume 1 (Sire SAS 3701) 1973 – Jack plays on 'Stone Crazy', recorded in August 1967.

Martha Velez *Fiends And Angels* (London SHK 8395) 1968

Martha Velez *Angels Of The Future/Past* (Sire 9 25962 2) 1989

The Scaffold 'Thank U Very Much' / 'Ide Be The First' (Parlophone R 5643) 1967 – Jack plays on the A-side.

The Scaffold 'Lily The Pink' / 'Buttons Of Your Mind' (Parlophone 5734) 1968 – Jack plays on the A-side.

The New Jazz Orchestra *Le Dejeuner Sur l'Herbe* (Verve SVLP 9236) 1968

Michael Gibbs *Michael Gibbs* (Deram SML 1063) 1969

Neil Ardley, Ian Carr & Don Rendell *Greek Variations* (Columbia SCX 6414) 1969

Carla Bley & Paul Haines *Escalator Over The Hill* (JCOA 3LP-EOTH) 1971

Lulu 'Everybody Clap' / 'After The Feeling Is Gone' (Atlantic 2091-083) 1971 – Jack plays on the A-side.

Bobby Keys *Bobby Keys* (Warner Bros WB 46 141) 1972

Michael Mantler *No Answer* (WATT/2) 1973

Lou Reed *Berlin* (RCA NL 84388) 1973

Frank Zappa *Apostrophe* (Discreet Records K59201) 1974 – Jack plays on the title track.

John McLaughlin *In Retrospect* (Polydor 2675 091) 1974 – double LP release of the Tony Williams Lifetime's *Emergency* and *Turn It Over.*

Locomotive GT *Locomotive GT* (Epic EPC 80229) 1974 – Jack plays harmonica on 'She's Just 14'.

Mick Jagger *The Very Best Of Mick Jagger* (Atlantic 8122-79961-0) 2007 – Jack plays on 'Too Many Cooks', recorded in 1974.

Pete Brown *Before Singing Lessons 1969–1977* (Decal LIK D7) 1977 – Jack plays on 'Spend My Nights In Armour', recorded in 1974.

Charlie Mariano *Helen 12 Trees* (MPS G22941) 1976

John McLaughlin *Electric Guitarist* (CBS 82702) 1978

John McLaughlin *This Is Jazz, Vol. 17* (Columbia/Legacy CK 64971) 1996 – Jack plays on 'Are You The One? Are You The One?'.

Les Dudek *Ghost Town Parade* (Wounded Bird WOU 5088) 1978

Cozy Powell *Over The Top* (Ariola 201 178-320) 1979

Bernie Marsden *And About Time Too* (Trash TRSH-2001) 1979

Rocket 88 *Rocket 88* (Atlantic K 50776) 1981

Jon Anderson *Songs Of Seven* (Atlantic ATL 50 756) 1980

Jon Anderson *Animation* (Polydor 2383 624) 1982

Bob Hall & Friends *It's Boogie Time* (JETON 600 6605) 1981

Bob Hall & Friends *Blues & Boogie Explosion* (JETON 100 3320) 1981

Soft Machine *Land Of Cockayne* (EMI 1C 0381575811) 1981

Trevor Rabin *Wolf* (Chrysalis 202 847-320) 1981

Cozy Powell *Tilt* (Polydor 2391 527) 1981 – Jack plays on 'Cat Moves'.

Jack Bruce, Robin Trower, Bill Lordan *B.L.T.* (Chrysalis CHR 1324) 1981

Jack Bruce, Robin Trower, Bill Lordan *Truce* (Chrysalis CHR 1352) 1982

Jack Bruce, Robin Trower, Bill Lordan *No Stopping Anytime* (Chrysalis VK 41704) 1989

Gary Moore *Corridors Of Power* (Virgin CDV 2245) 1982 – Jack provides vocals on 'End Of The World'.

Mose Allison *Lessons In Living* (Elektra/Musician 60237) 1982

Ellen McIlwaine *Everybody Needs It* (Blind Pig BP-1081) 1982

Allan Holdsworth *Road Games* (Warner Bros. 92-3959-1) 1983

Kip Hanrahan *Desire Develops An Edge* (American Clave AMCL 1009/1008) 1983

Kip Hanrahan *Vertical's Currency* (American Clave AMCL 1010) 1985

Kip Hanrahan *A Few Short Notes From The End Run* EP (American Clave AMCL 1011) 1986

Kip Hanrahan *Days And Nights Of Blue Luck Inverted* (American Clave AMCL 1012) 1987

Kip Hanrahan *Anthology* (American Clave AMCL 1020/1026) 1993

Kip Hanrahan *Exotica* (American Clave AMCL 1027) 1994

Kip Hanrahan *All Roads Are Made Of The Flesh* (American Clave AMCL 1029) 1995

Kip Hanrahan *A Thousand Nights And A Night (1-Red Nights)* (American Clave AMCL 1036) 1996

Kip Hanrahan *I Was Born, But …* (American Clave AMCL 1034) 2001

Kip Hanrahan *Drawn From Memory (Greatest Hits, Or Whatever …)* (American Clave AMCL 1032) 2001

Mark Nauseef *Wun-Wun* (CMP Records CMP 25 ST) 1984

Carla Bley, Steve Swallow, Reiner Brüninghaus *Lyrics: Texte Und Musik Live* (Cosmus Records NSV 1412) 1984 – recorded live at Spiegelzelt aud der Domplatte in Cologne, Germany, on November 22–24 1984.

Jack plays bass and a small drum and sings on 'For Under The Volcano'.

The Golden Palominos *Visions Of Excess* (Celluloid CELL 6118) 1985 – Jack sings and plays harmonica on 'Silver Bullet'.

The Golden Palominos *Blast Of Silence* (Celluloid CELL 6127) 1986 – Jack sings on '(Something Else Is) Working Harder'.

The Golden Palominos 'The Animal Speaks (1)' / 'The Animal Speaks (2)' (Celluloid CELL 190) 1986 – Jack sings on the B-side.

Charlie Watts *Live At Fulham Town Hall* (Columbia FC 45070) 1986 – Jack plays cello.

Inazuma Super Session *Absolute Live!* (Epic/Sony 32.8H-132) 1987

Michael Mantler *Michael Mantler: Live* (WATT/18 833 384-2) 1987

Michael Mantler *Many Have No Speech* (WATT/19 835 580-2) 1988

Leslie West *Theme* (Passport PBCD 6061) 1988

Standing In The Shadows Of Motown: The Life And Music Of Legendary Bassist James Jamerson (Hal Leonard Publications HL 00698960) 1989. On the CD that comes with the book, Jack talks about James Jamerson and plays on '(Come 'Round Here) I'm The One You Need'.

Bill Ward *Ward One: Along The Way* (Chameleon Records 02-74816) 1990

Links *Links* (Musikerhof ST9201) 1992

Michael Mantler *Folly Seeing All This* (ECM 1485 / 517 363-2) 1992 – Jack sings on 'What Is The Word'.

Paul Haines *Darn It!* (American Clave AMCL 1014/18) 1993 – Jack plays on 'Rawalpindi Blues'.

People *People* (RCA/BMG 74321 18240 2) 1993

People *Hold Onto Your Dreams* (RCA/BMG 74321 17585 2) 1993

Mark Nauseef / Miroslav Tadic *The Snake Music* (CMP Records CMP CD 1006) 1994

Dick Heckstall-Smith, Jack Bruce, John Stevens *This That* (Antonal Records ACD 3017) 1994

Gary Moore *Ballads And Blues 1982–1994* (Virgin CDV 2768) 1994

Various Artists *Alexis Korner Memorial Concert Vol. 1* (Indigo IGOCD 2050) 1995

Michael Mantler *The School Of Understanding* (ECM 1648/49 537 963-2) 1996

Leslie Mandoki *People In Room No. 8* (Polystar Plus 537 213-2) 1997

Leslie Mandoki *People In Room No. 8* EP (Polydor 571 003-2) 1997

Leslie Mandoki *Talalkozasok* (Warner Music Hungary 3984-21250-2) 1997

Various Artists: *A Tribute To Cyril Davies: Knights Of The Blues Table* (Viceroy/Lightyear 54189-2) 1997 – Jack plays on 'Send For Me'.

The Slab Boys: Original Soundtrack (Oceandeep Soundtracks OCD 06) 1997 – arranged by Jack.

Anthony Hindson & Friends *It's A Curious Life* (Wind In Hare WIHM CD 1001) 1999

Bruce Cameron *Midnight Daydream* (Brain Cell Records BC001) 1999

The New Gary Husband Trio *From The Heart* (Jazzizit JITCD 9918) 1999 – Jack sings on 'Once I Loved'.

Ringo Starr & His All Starr Band *The Anthology … So Far* (KOCH Records KOC-CD-8312) 2001

Dick Heckstall-Smith & Friends *Blues And Beyond* (Blue Storm Music 3004-2) 2001 – Jack sings on 'Hidden Agenda'.

Network (featuring Larry Coryell) *Highly Committed Media Players* (Wenlock Records WEN 017) 2001 – Jack plays on 'Manic Depression', also released as a single (Wenlock Records WEN 025).

Gov't Mule *The Deep End Volume 1* (ATO/BMG 79102-21502-2) 2001 – Jack plays on 'Fool's Moon'.

Crazy Chris Kramer *Vol. 1: Guarantee For The Blues* (Blow Til Midnight BTM0007) 2001

Various Artists: *From Clarksdale To Heaven: Remembering John Lee Hooker* (Eagle Records EAGCD228) 2002

Leslie Mandoki *Soulmates* (Paroli/Sony 509522 2) 2002

Leslie Mandoki *Is There A Dream Left* EP (Paroli/Sony 673539 2) 2002

Leslie Mandoki *Soulmates: Jazz Cuts* (Paroli/Sony 511120 2) 2003

Leslie Mandoki *Soulmates Allstars: Legends Of Rock* (Paroli/Sony 519021 2) 2005

John Cage *The Works For Piano 5* (Mode 123) 2003

Crazy Chris Kramer *Vol. 3: Guarantee For The Blues II* (Blow Til Midnight BTM0009) 2003

Vargas Blues Band *Love, Union, Peace* (DRO East West EW 851) 2005 – Jack plays on 'Pretty Blue'.

Jack Bruce, Robin Trower, Gary Husband *Seven Moons* (V-12 / Big Daddy Records 501112) 2008

Vibe Tribe *Views* (SVR 5003-2) 2008 – Jack sings on 'Here I Am' and 'Speak To Me'.

Jack Bruce, Robin Trower, Gary Husband *Seven Moons Live* (RUF 1151) 2009

4. UNRELEASED STUDIO RECORDINGS

The Graham Bond Quartet (Graham Bond, Jack Bruce, Ginger Baker, John McLaughlin), recorded at Abbey Road Studios, Studio 2, London, UK, May 16 1963.

1. Spanish Blues
2. It's Happening
3. Slippin' & Slidin'
4. Cabbage Greens
5. Wade In The Water (officially released)

The Graham Bond Organisation (Graham Bond, Jack Bruce, Ginger Baker, Dick Heckstall-Smith), recorded for Decca Records in 1964.

1. Cabbage Greens
2. Long Legged Baby
3. Hoochie Coochie Man
4. Wade In The Water
5. Green Onions
6. High Heeled Sneakers
7. [Untitled]

Cream *Disraeli Gears* demos recorded at Ryemuse Studio/Mayfair Productions, London, UK, March 15 1967. Includes false starts, out-takes, and studio chat that has never been officially released.

1. Take It Back
2. The Clearout (demo officially released)
3. Weird of Hermiston (demo officially released)
4. We're Going Wrong (demo officially released)
5. Blue Condition
6. Hey Now Princess (demo officially released)
7. SWLABR (demo officially released)

Jack Bruce, Tony Williams, Allan Holdsworth, Laura 'Tequila' Logan, and Webster Lewis, recorded at Europafilmstudion in Stockholm, Sweden, 1975, for the unreleased *Wildlife* LP.

1. Little Zorro
2. Happy Tears
3. Hot & Sticky
4. Scirocco
5. The Spirit

Jack Bruce, Jon Hiseman, and Allan Holdsworth, recorded at Townhouse Studio, London, UK, 2001 (the 'Sherwood Forest' demos).

1. White Line
2. Bird Alone
3. Where Is One
4. Tightrope

Hot Flash with Jack Bruce, Andy Summers, and Bruce Gary, recorded Los Angeles, California, 2001.

1. Blind World
2. Yet The Bird
3. Holy Terror
4. Laughter In The Rain

5. VIDEO AND DVD

Gonks Go Beat (Warner Home Video PES 38203) – bizarre 60s comedy; includes The Graham Bond Organisation performing 'Harmonica'.

Shindig Goes To London, Part 2 – broadcast December 9 1965; includes rare live footage of The Graham Bond Organisation playing 'Hoochie Coochie Man' at the 1965 National Jazz & Blues Festival at Richmond Athletic Grounds in Richmond, Surrey, UK, on August 7 1965.

Supershow (Eagle Rock) 2003 – filmed over a two-day period in March 1969 in Staines, Surrey, UK; includes footage of Jack performing with Eric Clapton, Buddy Guy, Roland Kirk, Dick Heckstall-Smith, Stephen Stills, Buddy Miles, and many others. Also features Colosseum and The Modern Jazz Quartet.

Rope Ladder To The Moon (Isolde Films) 1969 – 50-minute documentary of Jack performing in the studio, walking the streets of Glasgow, and at home on Sanda Island in Scotland. Produced by Tony Palmer; broadcast in Europe and USA in early 70s but never officially released on video or DVD.

Jack Bruce & Friends Live (Classic Pictures) 2002 – filmed at the Grugahalle in Essen, Germany, on October 19 1980 for Rockpalast TV;

also features Billy Cobham, Clem Clempson, and David Sancious.

Eco Rock (Umbrella Entertainment) 2004 – filmed at the Eco Rock Festival in St Andrews, Scotland, in July 1988; features The Jack Bruce Blues Band, Van Morrison, and others.

The Music Of Jimi Hendrix (TDK UK) 1995 – tribute concert featuring Jack, Vernon Reid, Terry Bozio, and many others; filmed at the Liederhalle in Stuttgart, Germany, on July 23 1995.

Ringo Starr & His Fourth All-Starr Band (MPI Home Video)1998 – filmed at the Pine Knob Amphitheatre in Detroit, Michigan, May 30 1997.

Jack Bruce: The Cream Of Cream (Rittor/Warner Bros) 1998 – instructional video for electric bass featuring Jack, Gary Moore, and Gary Husband.

Gary Husband: Interplay And Improvisations On The Drums (Rittor/Warner Bros) 1998 – instructional video for drums featuring Jack, Gary Moore, and Gary Husband.

Legends Of Rock: Live At Castle Donington (SPV Recordings) 2002 – filmed at the Castle Donington in Donington Park, UK, on June 23 2001; features performances by Uli Jon Roth and Michael Schenker with guests Jack Bruce, Clive Bunker, Don Airey, and others.

Gov't Mule: Rising Low (A Film By Mike Gordon) (ATO Records) 2002 – documentary about what happened when 25 bass players, including Jack Bruce, came together to record *The Deep End* with Gov't Mule.

Live At The Canterbury Fayre (Classic Rock Productions) 2003 – Jack Bruce & The Cuicoland Express at the Canterbury Fayre 2002 in Kent, UK, August 24 2002; includes material from *Shadows In The Air*.

Jack Bruce At Rockpalast (Weiner World Ltd) 2005 – two-disc set of performances from the three concerts

Jack performed at Rockpalast in Germany in 1980, 1983, and 1990.

Seven Moons Live (RUF 3018) 2009 – Jack Bruce, Robin Trower, and Gary Husband at the Concertgebouw De Vereeniging in Nijmegen, Holland, February 28 2009.

With Cream
The Story Of Beat-Club Vol. 1 1965–1968 (ARD-Video) 2008 – includes performances of 'I Feel Free' (from show 17; broadcast February 25 1967) and 'Strange Brew' (from Show 20; broadcast May 20 1967).

Det Var En Lordag Aften (Nordisk Films) 1968 – obscure film made in Copenhagen, Denmark, in early February 1968; includes performances of 'World Of Pain' and 'We're Going Wrong'.

All My Loving (Voiceprint) 2007 – documentary produced by Tony Palmer for the BBC; includes previously unseen footage of Cream, Hendrix, The Who, Pink Floyd, and others.

Cream: Farewell Concert (Image Entertainment) 2005 – documentary about Cream's concert at the Royal Albert Hall on November 26 1968; includes interviews conducted in March 1968 in San Francisco, California. Produced by Tony Palmer.

Strange Brew (A*Vision Entertainment/Time Warner) 1991 – includes footage of Cream's TV peformances on Beat-Club from Bremen, Germany, in 1967; the farewell concert at the Royal Albert Hall; and interviews from 1991.

Fresh Live Cream (Image Entertainment) 1993 – includes footage of Cream from the Revolution Club in London, January 1968; the farewell concert at Royal Albert Hall; and interviews from 1993.

Classic Albums: Cream: Disraeli Gears (Eagle Rock) 2006 – includes archival live footage and a solo performance of 'We're Going Wrong' by Jack, plus 2005 interviews with Jack, Eric Clapton, Ginger Baker, Pete Brown,

Ahmet Ertegun, John Mayall, Manfred Mann, Ben Palmer, and others.
Cream: Classic Artists (Image Entertainment) 2006 – authorised two-disc set; includes previously unreleased archival footage, interviews with Jack, Eric, and Ginger, performance footage, rare and unseen photographs and memorabilia, and a live recording of Cream at the Konserthuset in Stockholm, Sweden, March 7 1967.

Royal Albert Hall London May 2–3–5–6 2005 (Rhino) 2005 – two-disc set; includes alternate takes and interviews.

Inside Cream: 1966–1969 (Music Video Distributors) 2005 – critical review; includes archive footage. One to avoid.

Cream: Total Rock Review (Navarre Corporation) 2006 – critical review; includes interviews with leading rock critics and musicologists, rare live footage, and musical clips of 'Sunshine Of Your Love' and 'White Room'.

APPENDIX III
Live Performances 1965–2009
COMPILED BY Bob Elliott

John Mayall's Bluesbreakers
Oct 23 1965: *Saturday Club*, BBC Light Programme Radio 1, London, England (broadcast Oct 30)
Nov 6 1965: unknown venue, London Airport, Heathrow, London, England
Nov 7 1965: Flamingo Club, London, England (recorded by John Mayall)
Nov 11 1965: Klooks Kleek R&B Club, Railway Hotel, West Hampstead, London, England
Nov 12 1965: Bluesville R&B Club, Manor House, Finsbury Park, London, England
Nov 13 1965: Blue Moon Club, Cheltenham, England
Nov 14 1965: Ricky Tick Club, Plaza Ballroom, Guildford, England
Nov 17 1965: Scaffold Club, Northampton, England
Nov 19 1965: Zambesi Club, Hounslow, London, England
Nov 20 1965: University, Leicester, England
Nov 21 1965: Red Cross Hall, Sutton, England
Nov 21 1965: Blue Moon Club, Hayes, England

Manfred Mann
Nov 22 1965: Gaumont Cinema, Bradford, England
Nov 23 1965: Ritz Cinema, Luton, England
Nov 24 1965: Ritz Theatre, Chatham, England
Nov 25 1965: ABC Cinema, Cambridge, England
Nov 26 1965: ABC Cinema, Southampton, England
Nov 27 1965: Granada Cinema, East Ham, London, England
Nov 28 1965: Coventry Theatre, Coventry, England
Nov 29 1965: ABC Cinema, Northampton, England
Nov 30 1965: Guildhall, Portsmouth, England
Dec 2 1965: Granada Cinema, Bedford, England
Dec 3 1965: Colston Hall, Bristol, England
Dec 4 1965: ABC Cinema, Plymouth, England
Dec 5 1965: ABC Cinema, Exeter, England
Dec 6 1965: Adelphi Cinema, Slough, England
Dec 7 1965: *Saturday Club*, BBC Light Programme Radio 1, London, England
Dec 10 1965: *Ready, Steady, Go!*, ITV TV Studios, Wembley, England

Dec 12 1965: *Thank Your Lucky Stars*, ITV Rediffusion Studios, London, England
Dec 16 1965: City Hall, Salisbury, England
Dec 18 1965: Bridlington Spa, Bridlington, England
Dec 28 1965: Marquee Club, London, England (with The Mark Leeman Five)
Dec 29 1965: Locarno Ballroom, Stevenage, England
Dec 21 1965: *Radio Luxembourg's Old Years Night Spectacular*, London, England
Jan 7 1966: Matrix Hall, Coventry, England
Jan 8 1966: Baths Hall, Scunthorpe, England
Jan 13 1966: University, Hull, England (the band were involved in a car accident after this show and several dates had to be cancelled)
Jan 15 1966: University, Leeds, England (cancelled)
Jan 18 1966: *Pop Profile*, BBC Radio Light Programme, London, England (cancelled)
Jan 21 1966: *The Joe Loss Pop Show*, London, England (cancelled)
Jan 21 1966: Hornsey Town Hall, London, England
Jan 22 1966: Imperial Ballroom, Nelson, England (cancelled)
Jan 23 1966: Jigsaw Club, Manchester, England (cancelled)
Jan 24 1966: Marquee Club, London, England (Eric Burdon joined in on vocals with Paul Jones still ailing from the effects of the car accident)
Jan 28 1966: Civic Hall, Wolverhampton, England
Jan 29 1966: University, Manchester, England
Jan 30 1966: Redcar Jazz Club, Coatham Hotel, Redcar, England
Feb 15 1966: Sherwood Rooms, Nottingham, England
Feb 16 1966: *Jazz Club*, BBC Light Programme
Mar 1 1966: Marquee Club, London, England
Mar 7 1966: Pavilion, Bath, England
Mar 8 1966: Big Beat Session, Winter Gardens, Malvern, England

Manfred Mann
Mar 19 1966: Regent Street Polytechnic, London, England
Mar 21 1966: Tiles Club, London, England
Mar 25 1966: University, Canterbury, England
Mar 26 1966: Guildhall, Southampton, England
Mar 27 1966: Agincourt Ballroom, Camberley, England
Mar 28 1966: Co-ed Eva Youth Centre, Newport, Wales
Mar 30 1966: unknown venue, Dudley, England
Apr 3 1966: Daily Express Record Star Show, Empire Pool, Wembley, England (with Cliff Richard & The Shadows, The Spencer Davis Group, Georgie Fame)
Apr 6 1966: Corn Exchange, Bristol, England
Apr 7 1966: Town Hall, Kidderminster, England
Apr 8 1966: Agincourt Ballroom, Camberley, England
Apr 9 1966: Gliderdrome, Boston, England
Apr 12 1966: Marquee Club, London, England (with Bluesology)
Apr 13 1966: Spring Festival, Mid Herts College Of Further Education, Welwyn Garden City, England

Apr 14 1966: Ritz, Skewan, Wales
Apr 14 1966: Aspen Lido, Port Talbot, Wales
Apr 15 1966: Regal Ballroom, Ammanford, Wales
Apr 16 1966: Imperial Ballroom, Nelson, England
Apr 19 1966: *Pop Inn*, BBC Light Programme
Apr 19 1966: *Saturday Club*, BBC Light Programme Radio 1, London, England (broadcast Apr 30)
Apr 21 1966: *Top Of The Pops*, BBC TV Studios, London, England
Apr 22 1966: *Now!*, ITV Rediffusion Studios, London, England
Apr 22 1966: *Ready, Steady, Go!*, ITV TV Studios, Wembley, England
Apr 23 1966: Memorial Hall, Norwich, England
Apr 25 1966: 99 Club, Barrow-In-Furness, England
Apr 26 1966: Locarno, Glasgow, Scotland
Apr 28 1966: *Top Of The Pops*, BBC TV Studios, London, England
Apr 29 1966: Scene At 6:30, Granada TV (TV)
Apr 29 1966: Faculty of Technology, Manchester, England
Apr 30 1966: University, Leeds, England
May 3 1966: Barry Training Centre, Glamorgan, Wales
May 4 1966: Top Rank Ballroom, Cardiff, Wales
May 5 1966: *Top Of The Pops*, BBC TV Studios, London, England
May 5 1966: City Hall, Salisburg, England
May 6 1966: Coronation Ballroom, Ramsgate, England
May 7 1966: Floral Hall, Southport, England
May 8 1966: Phoenix Theatre, London, England (benefit for *Private Eye* magazine)
May 12 1966: *Top Of The Pops*, BBC TV Studios, London, England
May 13 1966: University, Birmingham, England
May 14 1966: Pavilion Ballroom, Buxton, England
May 15 1966: Redcar Jazz Club, Coatham Hotel, Redcar, England
May 20 1966: Raith Ballroom, Kirkaldy, Scotland
May 20 1966: Dobie Hall, Labert, Scotland
May 21 1966: Olympia Ballroom, East Kilbride, Scotland
May 22 1966: Lido, Balloch (near Inverness), Scotland
May 28 1966: *The Joe Loss Pop Show*, BBC Light Programme
May 28 1966: Pembroke College, Oxford, England
May 29 1966: Supreme Ballroom, Ramsgate, England
June 8 1966: Marquee Club, London, England
June 9 1966: Pier Ballroom, Worthing, England
June 10 1966: *Ready, Steady, Go!*, ITV TV Studios, Wembley, England
June 10 1966: Civic Hall, Wolverhampton, England
June 11 1966: Queen's Hall, Leeds, England
June 12 1966: Mojo Club, Sheffield, England

Group Sounds Four
June 13 1966: *The Jazz Scene*, BBC Light Programme (broadcast June 19)

Manfred Mann
June 17 1966: Silver Blades, Birmingham, England

June 18 1966: Uxbridge Blues Festival, Hillingdon, Uxbridge, England (with The Alan Walker Group, The Action, The Good Goods, The Steam Packet)
June 20 1966: Christchurch College, Oxford, England
June 23 1966: University, York, England
June 24 1966: University, Southampton, England
June 25 1966: Keswick Training College, Norwich, England
June 26 1966: St Luke's College, Exeter, England

Cream
July 18–28 1966: Rehearsals in a church hall, Kensal Rise, England
July 29 1966: Twisted Wheel, Manchester, England (debut gig; may have taken place on July 30)
July 31 1966: Sixth National Jazz & Blues Festival, Windsor, England
Aug 1 1966: Cooks Ferry Inn, Edmonton, England
Aug 2 1966: Klooks Kleek R&B Club, Railway Hotel, West Hampstead, London, England
Aug 6 1966: Beat & Blues Festival, Town Hall, Torquay, England (with The Drifters, The Package Deal)
Aug 9 1966: Fishmongers Arms, Wood Green, England
Aug 12 1966: Bromel Club, Bromley Court Hotel, Bromley, England
Aug 13 1966: Blue Moon Club, Cheltenham, England
Aug 16 1966: Marquee Club, London, England (with The Clayton Squares)
Aug 17 1966: Orford Cellar, Norwich, England
Aug 19 1966: Cellar Club, Kingston-Upon-Thames, England
Aug 20 1966: Mojo Club, Sheffield, England
Aug 21 1966: unknown venue, Warrington, England
Aug 24 1966: Eel Pie Hotel, Eel Pie Island, Twickenham, England
Aug 26 1966: Il Rondo Club, Leicester, England
Aug 27 1966: Ram Jam Club, Brixton, London, England
Aug 27 1966: All Night Rave, Flamingo Club, London, England (early hours of Aug 28)
Aug 28 1966: Beachcomber Club, Nottingham, England
Aug 29 1966: Community Centre, Welwyn Garden City, England (with Chicken Shack)
Sep 1 1966: Concorde Club, Southampton, England
Sep 2 1966: Bluesville 66, Manor House, Finsbury Park, North London, England
Sep 4 1966: Ricky Tick, Thames Hotel, Windsor, England
Sep 5 1966: Garston, Liverpool, England (cancelled)
Sep 7 1966: Town Hall, Farnborough, England
Sep 9 1966: unknown venue, Folkestone, England
Sep 10 1966: Marquee Club, Birmingham, England (moved from the Penthouse Club)
Sep 11 1966: Skyline Ballroom, Kingston-Upon-Hull, England
Sep 12 1966: Bluesville Club, St Matthew's Baths Hall, Ipswich, England
Sep 15 1966: Ricky Tick, Corn Exchange, Bedford, England
Sep 16 1966: Hermitage Halls, Hitchin, England
Sep 17 1966: Drill Hall, Grantham, England
Sep 18 1966: Blue Moon Club, Hayes, England
Sep 19 1966: Atlanta Ballroom, Woking, England

Sep 20 1966: *Saturday Club*, BBC Light Programme, Radio 1, London, England (cancelled)
Sep 23 1966: Ricky Tick, Corn Exchange, Newbury, England
Sep 26 1966: Starlite Club, Star Hotel, West Croydon, England
Sep 27 1966: Marquee Club, London, England (with The Herd)
Sep 29 1966: unknown venue, Newcastle, England
Sep 30 1966: Ricky Tick, Hounslow, England
Oct 1 1966: Regent Street Polytechnic, London, England (with The Washington DCs; Jimi Hendrix jammed with Cream on 'Killing Floor')
Oct 2 1966: Country Club, Kirklevington, England (cancelled; Jack ill)
Oct 3 1966: Wall City Jazz Club, Chester, England (presumably cancelled)
Oct 4 1966: Fishmongers Arms, Wood Green, London, England (presumably cancelled)
Oct 5 1966: Reading University, Reading, England (presumably cancelled)
Oct 6 1966: York University, York, England (cancelled)
Oct 7 1966: Kings College, Strand, London, England
Oct 8 1966: University Of Sussex, Brighton, England (Ginger collapsed at this gig)
Oct 9 1966: Birdcage, Kimbells Ballroom, Portsmouth, England (probably cancelled)
Oct 11 1966: Flamingo Club, London, England (probably cancelled)
Oct 12 1966: Orford Cellar Club, Norwich, England
Oct 13 1966: Club A Go Go, Newcastle Upon Tyne, England (moved from the New Yorker Discotheque at McIlroy's Ballroom in Swindon)
Oct 14 1966: unknown venue, Newark, England
Oct 15 1966: unknown venue, Sheffield, England
Oct 15 1966: Jigsaw Club, Manchester, England (early hours of Aug 16)
Oct 16 1966: unknown venue, Coventry, England
Oct 17 1966: Majestic Ballroom, Reading, England
Oct 20 1966: Carnival Dance, St Gile's Youth Club, Willenhall Baths Assembly Hall, Wolverhampton, England (with The N'Betweens, Listen [with Robert Plant], and The Factotums)
Oct 21 1966: *Bandbeat*, BBC Radio 1, London, England
Oct 21 1966: Bluesville 66, Manor House, Finsbury Park, North London, England
Oct 22 1966: Union Hop, Leeds University, Leeds, England
Oct 23 1966: Beachcomber Club, Nottingham, England
Oct 24 1966: Bluesville Club, St Matthews Baths Hall, Ipswich, England
Oct 27 1966: New Yorker Discotheque, Swindon, England
Oct 28 1966: Il Rondo Club, Leicester, England
Oct 29 1966: University, Bristol, England (probably cancelled)
Oct 29 1966: All Night Rave, Midnight City Club, Birmingham, England (early hours of Oct 30)
Oct 30 1966: Agincourt Ballroom, Camberly, England
Oct 31 1966: Atalanta Ballroom, Woking, England

Nov 1 1966: *Ready, Steady, Go!*, ITV TV Studios, Wembley, England (broadcast Nov 4)

Nov 2 1966: unknown venue, Hemel Hempstead, England

Nov 3 1966: Ram Jam Club, Brixton, London, England

Nov 4 1966: University, Coventry, England

Nov 5 1966: Town Hall, East Ham, London, England

Nov 7 1966: New Spot Club, Thorngate Ballroom, Gosport, England

Nov 8 1966: *Saturday Club*, BBC Light Programme, Radio 1, London, England (broadcast Nov 12)

Nov 8 1966: Marquee Club, London, England (with The Race)

Nov 11 1966: Public Baths, Sutton, England

Nov 12 1966: University, Liverpool, England

Nov 13 1966: Redcar Jazz Club, Coatham Hotel, Redcar, England

Nov 15 1966: Klooks Kleek R&B Club, Railway Hotel, West Hampstead, London, England

Nov 17 1966: University, Norwich, England (moved from Burkes in London, England)

Nov 18 1966: Hoveton Village Hall, Wroxham, England (wih The News)

Nov 19 1966: Blue Moon Club, Cheltenham, England

Nov 21 1966: *Monday Monday*, BBC Light Programme, Radio 2 London, England

Nov 21 1966: The Pavilion, Bath, England

Nov 22 1966: Chinese R&B Jazz Club, Corn Exchange, Bristol, England

Nov 25 1966: California Ballroom, Dunstable, England

Nov 26 1966: Corn Exchange, Chelmsford, England

Nov 27 1966: Agincourt Ballroom, Camberly, England

Nov 28 1966: *Guitar Club*, BBC Radio 1, London, England (broadcast Dec 30)

Nov 28 1966: Atalanta Ballroom, Woking, England

Dec 2 1966: Hornsey College Of Art, Hornsey, London, England (with The In Crowd, The Wrong Direction)

Dec 3 1966: Birdcage, Kimbells Ballroom, Portsmouth, England (second show cancelled after Ginger collapsed during first)

Dec 4 1966: Starlite Ballroom, Greenford, England (cancelled; Ginger ill)

Dec 5 1966: Bluesville 66, The Baths Hall, Ipswich, England (cancelled; Ginger ill)

Dec 7 1966: Skyline Ballroom, Kingston-Upon-Hull, England (cancelled; Ginger ill)

Dec 9 1966: *Rhythm & Blues World Service*, BBC Radio 1, London, England (broadcast Jan 9 1967)

Dec 9 1966: Bluesville 66, Manor House, Finsbury Park, North London, England

Dec 10 1966: Isleworth Polytechnic, Isleworth, London, England

Dec 12 1966: Cooks Ferry Inn, Edmonton, London, England

Dec 13 1966: University of Exeter, Exeter, England (with Screaming Lord Sutch)

Dec 14 1966: Bromel Club, Bromley Court Hotel, Bromley, England

Dec 15 1966: University Of Sussex, Brighton, England

Dec 16–18 1966: Paris, France (various TV/radio)

Dec 17 1966: La Locomotive Club, Place Blanche, Paris, France

Dec 18 1966: Agincourt Ballroom, Camberly, England (probably cancelled)

Dec 19 1966: Atalanta Ballroom, Woking, England

Dec 20 1966: Tuesday Beat Session, Winter Gardens, Malvern, England

Dec 21 1966: *Top Of The Pops*, BBC Radio London, England (broadcast Dec 29)

Dec 21 1966: Bromel Club, Bromley Court Hotel, Bromley, England

Dec 22 1966: Pier Pavilion, Worthing, England

Dec 23 1966: Odeon Cinema, Birmingham, England

Dec 24 1966: Midnight City Club, Birmingham, England (with Family and others)

Dec 30 1966: Double Giant Freak-Out Ball, The Roundhouse, Chalk Farm, London, England (with The Alan Brown Set)

Jan 7 1967: Ricky Tick, Thames Hotel, Windsor, England

Jan 10 1967: *Saturday Club*, BBC Light Programme, Radio 1, London, England (broadcast Jan 14)

Jan 10 1967: Marquee Club, London, England (with Catch 22)

Jan 11 1967: *Top Of The Pops*, BBC TV Studios, London, England (broadcast Jan 12)

Jan 13 1967: Ricky Tick, Guildhall, Southampton, England

Jan 14 1967: Lanchester Arts Festival, Polytechnic College, Coventry, England

Jan 15 1967: Ricky Tick, Hounslow, England

Jan 16 1967: *Monday Monday*, BBC Light Programme, Radio 2, London, England

Jan 18 1967: Town Hall, Stourbridge, England

Jan 19 1967: Arts Ball, Leicester College of Art, Granby Hall, Leicester, England (with Zoot Money, The Birds, Shotgun Express)

Jan 20 1967: Club A Go Go, Newcastle-Upon-Tyne, England

Jan 21 1967: Floral Hall, Southport, England

Jan 24 1967: Chinese R&B Jazz Club, Corn Exchange, Bristol, England

Jan 25 1967: *Parade Of The Pops*, BBC Radio, London, England

Jan 26 1967: *Top Of The Pops*, BBC TV, London, England

Jan 27 1967: Adelphi Ballroom, West Bromwich, England

Jan 28 1967: Ram Jam Club, Brixton, London, England

Feb 3 1967: All Night Rave, Queens Hall, Leeds, England

Feb 4 1967: Technical College, Ewell, Epsom, England

Feb 5 1967: Sunday At The Saville, Saville Theatre, London, England (with Sands, Edwin Starr)

Feb 9 1967: City Hall, Salisbury, England

Feb 10 1967: Bluesville 67, Manor House, Stockport, England

Feb 11 1967: Bath Pavilion, Matlock, England

Feb 15 1967: Assembly Hall, Aylesbury, England

Feb 17 1967: Woodlands Youth Centre, Basildon, England (with The Riot Squad)

Feb 18 1967: Tofts Club, Folkstone, England

Feb 19 1967: Starlite Ballroom, Greenford, London, England (with The Gods, featuring Mick Taylor)

Feb 22 1967: Bromel Club, Bromley Court Hotel, Bromley, England

Feb 24 1967: *Beat-Club*, TV Bremen, Germany

Feb 25 1967: Star-Club, Hamburg, Germany

Feb 26 1967: Star-Club, Kiel, Germany

Feb 27 1967: Manchester & Salford Students Rag Ball '67, Salford, Manchester, England (with 15 other groups, including The Graham Bond Organisation)

Mar 1 1967: Ulster Hall, Belfast, Northern Ireland (with The Interns, The Group, The Few, The Styx)

Mar 2 1967: Queens University Students Hall, Belfast, Northern Ireland (with The Interns, The Green Angels, The Faculty)

Mar 5 1967: Copenhagen, Denmark (press conference; cancelled)

Mar 6 1967: Ekstra Bladets Pop Pool, Falkoner Centret, Copenhagen, Denmark (with Defenders, Hitmakers, Sir Hendry & His Butlers, Lollipops, Peter Belli & Seven Sounds)

Mar 7 1967: Onkel Thores Stuga, Stockholm, Sweden

Mar 7 1967: Konserthuset, Stockholm, Sweden (radio)

Mar 8 1967: Cue Club, Liseberg Cirkus, Gothenburg, Sweden (with Steam Packet, The Gonks, Annabeenox, The Jackpots)

Mar 11 1967: St George's Ballroom, Hinkley, England

Mar 12 1967: Tavern Club, East Dereham, England (with The Feel For Soul)

Mar 14 1967: Central Sound, London, England

Mar 14 1967: Beachcomber Club, Nottingham, England

Mar 16 1967: Regent Street Polytechnic, London, England

Mar 18 1967: Bristol University Students Union, Bristol, England

Mar 20 1967: *Monday Monday*, BBC Light Programme, Radio 2, London, England (broadcast Mar 27)

Mar 21 1967: Marquee Club, London, England (with Family)

Mar 22 1967: Locarno, Stevenage, England

Mar 25–Apr 2 1967: Murray The K's 'Music In the Fifth Dimension' Show, RKO Paramount Theatre, New York, NY, USA (one or two songs performed during several shows each day)

Apr 7 1967: Municipal Hall, Pontypridd, Wales (cancelled)

Apr 9 1967: Redcar Jazz Club, Coatham Hotel, Redcar, England

Apr 14 1967: Ricky Tick, Newbury, England

Apr 15 1967: Rhodes Centre, Bishop's Stortford, England (with The Teapots)

Apr 16 1967: Daily Express Record Star Show, Empire Pool, Wembley, England (with various acts including Paul Jones, The Kinks, The Troggs)

Apr 18 1967: Chinese R&B Jazz Club, Corn Exchange, Bristol, England

Apr 19 1967: Beachcomber Club, Nottingham, England

Apr 21 1967: Brighton Arts Festival, The Dome, Brighton, England (with The Who, The Merseys)

Apr 22 1967: Ricky Tick, Hounslow, England

Apr 26 1967: Birdcage, Southampton, England

Apr 28 1967: University, Edgbaston, Birmingham, England (with Victor Brox)

Apr 29 1967: University, Leeds, England (with Midnight Train, The Moss Chapeltown Band)

May 1 1967: Starpalast, Kiel, Germany (probably cancelled)

May 2–3 1967: *Hor Hin-Schau Zu*, Berlin, Germany (TV; probably cancelled)

May 5 1967: Municipal Hall, Pontypridd, Glamorgan, Wales

May 6 1967: *Sound & Picture City*, BBC TV (three songs mimed using borrowed equipment)

May 6 1967: RAF Station, Royal Agriculture College Charity Appeal, Chippenham, England

May 7 1967: *NME* Poll Winners Concert, Empire Pool, Wembley, England (with various acts including The Beach Boys, Spencer Davis Group, Cliff Richard)

May 7 1967: Swan Hotel, Yardley, Birmingham, England

May 19 1967: *Beat-Club*, Bremen, Germany (TV)

May 20 1967: Stadion, Berlin, Germany

May 21 1967: Jaguar-Club, Scala, Herford, Germany (with The Tonics)

May 23 1967: Marquee Club, London, England (with Family)

May 26 1967: Goldsmiths College Summer Ball, New Cross, London, England

May 27 1967: Pembroke College May Ball, Grand Marquee, Oxford, England (with The Who)

May 27 1967: Exeter Eights Week Ball, Exeter College, Oxford, England (with The Tribe, The Other Extreme, The Cabinet)

May 29 1967: Barbecue 67, Tulip Bulb Auction Hall, Spalding, England (with The Jimi Hendrix Experience, Pink Floyd, The Move, Geno Washington & The Ram Jam Band, Zoot Money & His Big Roll Band, Sounds Force Five)

May 30 1967: *Saturday Club*, BBC Light Programme, Radio 1, London, England (broadcast Jun 3)

June 1 1967: Palais des Sports, Paris, France

June 3 1967: Ram Jam Club, Brixton, London, England (with Impact Blues)

June 8 1967: Locarno, Bristol, England

June 9 1967: Civic Hall, Wolverhampton, England (with The N'Betweens)

June 10 1967: Wellington Club, East Dereham, England (with Boz Burrell, Feel For Soul)

June 11 1967: Starlite Ballroom, Greenford, England (with The Triads)

June 12 1967: Trinity Hall, Cambridge, England (with The New Vaudeville Band)

June 15 1967: *Top Of The Pops*, BBC Light Programme, London, England

June 16 1967: University Of Sussex, Brighton, England (late replacement for The Who)

June 22 1967: *Dee Time*, BBC TV, London, England

June 23 1967: University, Durham, England

June 24 1967: Carlton Ballroom, Eardington, Birmingham, England

June 25 1967: Wheels Discotheque, Reading, England (with The Iveys)

June 27 1967: Tuesday Beat Session, Winter Gardens, Malvern, England

June 28 1967: Floral Hall, Gorleston-on-Sea, England (with Feel For Soul; the equipment van arrived late so Cream only performed only two songs using borrowed gear)

June 29 1967: *Top Of The Pops*, BBC Light Programme, London, England

June 30 1967: Bluesville 67, Manor House, Finsbury Park, North London, England

July 1 1967: Upper Cut, Forest Gate, London, England

July 2 1967: Saville Theatre, London, England (with Jimmy Powell & The Dimensions, The Jeff Beck Group, John Mayall's Bluesbreakers)

July 7 1967: Ballerina Ballroom, Nairn, Scotland (postponed after equipment van broke down)

July 8 1967: Cream climb Ben Nevis with photographer Robert Whitaker

July 8 1967: Beach Ballroom, Aberdeen, Scotland

July 9 1967: Kinema Ballroom, Dunfermline, Scotland (with The Shadettes)

July 10 1967: Ballerina Ballroom, Nairn, Scotland (rescheduled from July 7)

July 12 1967: Floral Hall, Great Yarmouth, England

July 14 1967: *Joe Loss Show*, BBC Light Programme, Radio 1, London, England

July 15 1967: Supreme Ballroom, Ramsgate, England

Aug 4 1967: City Hall, Perth, Scotland

Aug 5 1967: Market Hall, Carlisle, England

Aug 6 1967: McGoos, Edinburgh, Scotland (with the Jury)

Aug 7 1967: Locarno Ballroom, Glasgow, Scotland

Aug 8 1967: Palace Ballroom, Douglas, Isle of Man, England (with Sounds Incorporated)

Aug 12 1967: Floral Hall, Corleston-on-Sea, England (make-up date for June 28)

Aug 13 1967: Seventh National Jazz & Blues Festival, Windsor, England (first photographic evidence of Jack playing an EB-3)

Aug 15 1967: Explosion '67, Town Hall, Torquay, England

Aug 17 1967: Speakeasy, London, England (introduced by Frank Zappa as a "dandy little combo")

Aug 19 1967: unknown venue, Southport, England

Aug 20 1967: Redcar Jazz Club, Coatham Hotel, Redcar, England

Aug 22–27 1967: Fillmore Auditorium, San Francisco, CA, USA (with The Paul Butterfield Blues Band)

Aug 29–Sep 2 1967: Fillmore Auditorium, San Francisco, CA, USA (with Gary Burton, The Electric Flag)

Sep 4–6 1967: Whisky A Go-Go, West Hollywood, CA, USA (with The Rich Kids)

Sep 8 1967: Cross Town Bus Club, Brighton, MA, USA (cancelled)

Sep 10–16 1967: Psychedelic Supermarket, Boston, MA, USA

Sep 22 1967: Action House, Long Beach, Long Island, NY, USA (with Moby Grape)

Sep 23 1967: Village Theatre, New York, NY, USA (according to a fan review, Moby Grape cancelled and were replaced by Canned Heat)

Sep 24 1967: Action House, Long Beach, Long Island, NY, USA (with The Neons)

Sep 26–29 1967: Cafe Au Go Go, New York, NY, USA (with The Paupers)

Sep 30 1967: Village Theatre, New York, NY, USA (early show with The Soul Survivors, Richie Havens)

Sep 30–Oct 1 1967: Cafe Au Go Go, New York, NY, USA (with The Paupers)

Oct 3–8 1967: Cafe Au Go Go, New York, NY, USA (with Richie Havens)

Oct 11–12 1967: Fifth Dimension Club, Ann Arbor, MI, USA

Oct 13–15 1967: Grande Ballroom, Detroit, MI, USA (with MC5, The Thyme; The Rationals; The Apostles)

Oct 19 1967: Romanos Ballroom, Belfast, Northern Ireland (postponed)

Oct 24 1967: *Top Gear*, BBC Radio 1, London, England (broadcast Oct 29)

Oct 28 1967: Union Dance, University, Southampton, England (with Nelson's Column, The Quik)

Oct 29 1967: *Top Gear*, BBC Radio 1, London, England (with DJs John Peel and Pete Drummond)

Oct 29 1967: Sundays At The Saville, Saville Theatre, London, England (with The Bonzo Dog Doo-Dah Band, The Action; compered by John Peel)

Nov 1 1967: Bal Tabarin, Bromley, England

Nov 2 1967: Romanos Ballroom, Belfast, Northern Ireland (rescheduled from Oct 19)

Nov 3 1967: Strand Ballroom, Portstewart, Northern Ireland (with The Playboys Showband)

Nov 6 1967: Bush House, BBC Russian Service, London, England (interview with Eric and Jack; broadcast Nov 14)

Nov 6 1967: Silver Blades Ice Rink, Streatham High Road, England

Nov 10 1967: Toppot, Ny Adelgade, Copenhagen, Denmark (press conference)

Nov 11 1967: *TV-Byen* (TV Village), Studio A, Gladsaxe, Denmark

Nov 11 1967: Hit-Club, Vejgaard Hallen, Aalborg, Denmark (with The Defenders, Parrots, Go-Go)

Nov 12 1967: Falkoner Centret, Copenhagen, Denmark (with Steppeulvene, The Defenders)

Nov 13 1967: Pasila TV, Helsinki, Finland

Nov 13 1967: Kulttuuritalo, Helsinki, Finland

Nov 14 1967: Konserthuset, Stockholm, Sweden (with Hansson & Karlsson, The Young Flowers)

Nov 15 1967: Lorensbergs Cirkus, Liseberg, Gothenburg, Sweden (with The Young Flowers plus a couple of local groups)

Nov 17 1967: Rigoletto, Jonkoping, Sweden (with The Ramblers, The Piccadillys)

Nov 18 1967: Idrottshuset, Orebro, Sweden (with King George & The Harlem Kiddies)

Nov 23 1967: Club A Go Go, Newcastle-Upon-Tyne, England

Nov 24 1967: Central Pier, Marine Ballroom, Morecambe, England (with The Doodlebugs, The Top Katz, DJ Lord Byron)

Nov 26 1967: *Twice A Fortnight*, BBC TV, Lime Grove Studios, London, England (broadcast Dec 2)

Nov 28 1967: Marquee Club, London, England (cancelled; Ginger ill)

Dec 1 1967: Top Rank, Brighton, England (cancelled; Ginger ill)

Dec 2 1967: Owens Union Building, University, Manchester, England (cancelled; Ginger ill; replaced by The Moody Blues)

Dec 3 1967: *Happening Sunday*, BBC Radio 1, London, England

Dec 9 1967: Union Dance, University, Bristol, England

Dec 18 1967: *Rhythm & Blues World Service*, BBC Radio, London, England (hosted by Alexis Korner)

Dec 20 1967: Debutante's Ball, Chicago, IL (private party for wealthy family)

Dec 22–23 1967: Grande Ballroom, Detroit, MI, USA (with Billy C. & The Sunshine, MC5, Soap)

Jan 5 1968: Industrial Club, Norwich, England (with The Healers)

Jan 9 1968: *Top Gear*, BBC Radio 1, London, England (broadcast on Jan 14)

Jan 10 1968: Revolution Club, London, England (rehearsal; filmed for French TV)

Jan 13 1968: *Fenklup (VARA)*, Amsterdam, Holland (broadcast Jan 19)

Jan 14 1968: Redcar Jazz Club, Coatham Hotel, Redcar, Cleveland, England (cancelled)

Jan 19 1968: Top Rank Suite, Brighton, England (with The Mike Stuart Span; rescheduled)

Jan 20 1968: University Union, Leeds, England

Jan 27 1968: St Mary's College, Twickenham, England (with Alan Brown, The Chris Ian Dreamboat Show)

Feb 2 1968: Technical College, Nottingham, England (with Thatch)

Feb 3 1968: Carnival '68, University College, London, England (with Two Of Each, The Millionaires, The Soundtrekkers)

Feb 5 1968: *Vognmandsmarken*, Osterbro, Copenhagen, Denmark (shot on the back of a flatbed truck for the movie *Det Var En Lordag Aften*)

Feb 6 1968: unknown venue, Osterbro, Copenhagen, Denmark (filmed for the movie *Det Var En Lordag Aften*)

Feb 7 1968: Tivolis Koncertsal, Copenhagen, Denmark (with Hansson & Karlsson, The Young Flowers)

Feb 9 1968: Arts Ball Goes Hollywood, University, Leicester, England (with The Crazy World Of Arthur Brown, Family, Wynder K. Frogg, The Freddie Mack Show)

Feb 10 1968: University, Manchester, England

Feb 23 1968: Santa Monica Civic Auditorium, Santa Monica, CA, USA (with Steppenwolf, Penny Nichols, The Electric Prunes)

Feb 24 1968: Earl Warren Showgrounds, Santa Barbara, CA, USA (with Taj Mahal, The James Cotton Blues Band)

Feb 25 1968: Swing Auditorium, San Bernadino, CA, USA (with The Caretakers)

Feb 29–Mar 2 1968: Winterland Arena, San Francisco, CA, USA (with Big Black, Loading Zone)

Mar 3 1968: Fillmore Auditorium, San Francisco, CA, USA (with Big Black, Loading Zone)

Mar 7 1968: Fillmore Auditorium, San Francisco, CA, USA (with Jeremy & The Satyrs, Blood Sweat & Tears, The James Cotton Blues Band)

Mar 8–10 1968: Winterland Arena, San Francisco, CA, USA (with Jeremy & The Satyrs, Blood Sweat & Tears, The James Cotton Blues Band)

Mar 11 1968: Memorial Auditorium, Sacramento, CA, USA (with The Grateful Dead)

Mar 13 1968: Selland Arena, Fresno, CA (with Blue Cheer)

Mar 15 1968: San Fernando Valley State College, Northridge, CA, USA (early show with Canned Heat)

Mar 15–16 1968: Shrine Exposition Hall, Los Angeles, CA, USA (with The James Cotton Blues Band, Mint Tattoo)

Mar 17 1968: Star Theatre, Phoenix, AZ, USA

Mar 19 1968: Family Dog, Denver, CO, USA (cancelled)

Mar 21 1968: Beloit College, Beloit, WI, USA

Mar 22 1968: Clowes Memorial Hall, Butler University, Indianapolis, IN, USA (with American Breed)

Mar 23 1968: Shapiro Athletic Center, Brandeis University, Waltham, MA, USA (2:15am performance; with Orpheus)

Mar 24 1968: State University Of New York Gymnasium, Stony Brook, NY, USA (with The Vagrants; cancelled; Jack ill)

Mar 26 1968: Union Catholic High School, Scotch Plains, NJ, USA

Mar 27 1968: Staples High School, Westport, CT, USA

Mar 29 1968: Hunter College Auditorium, New York, NY, USA (with The Apostles)

Mar 30 1968: State Fair Music Hall, Dallas, TX, USA (with Vanilla Fudge)

Mar 31 1968: Music Hall, Houston, TX, USA (with Vanilla Fudge)

Apr 2 1968: State University Of New York Gymnasium, Stony Brook, NY, USA (rescheduled)

Apr 3 1968: Morris Civic Auditorium, South Bend, IN, USA

Apr 5 1968: Back Bay Theatre, Boston, MA, USA

Apr 6 1968: Commodore Ballroom, Lowell, MA, USA

Apr 7 1968: Eastman College Theatre, Rochester, NY, USA (with Vanilla Fudge; Cream cancelled as their equipment failed to arrive on time)

Apr 8 1968: Capitol Theatre, Ottawa, Ontario, Canada (with Olivus, The Heart; Jack fled to the airport after the gig but was convinced to stay by road manager Bob Adcock)

Apr 10 1968: Yale University, Woolsey Hall, New Haven, CT, USA (with Randy Burns)

Apr 11 1968: Thee Image Club, Miami, FL, USA (with Blues Image)

Apr 12–14 1968: Electric Factory, Philadelphia, PA, USA (with Woody's Truck Stop; The Nazz; Friends Of The Family)

Cream returned to the UK here for a ten-day break, with several shows postponed until June. It had long been thought that the gigs at the Electric Factory in Philadelphia were moved to April 19–21, but this is not the case, since the April 27 Melody Maker *reports that Eric attended an Ike & Tina Turner show at London's Revolution Club on April 19.*

Apr 21 1968: *Romp*, ABC TV (broadcast today but possibly filmed on Mar 14)

Apr 26 1968: The Cellar, Arlington Heights, IL, USA

Apr 27 1968: Coliseum, Chicago, IL, USA (with The Mothers Of Invention)

Apr 28 1968: Kiel Opera House, St Louis, MO, USA (with Spur)

May 2 1968: The Factory, Wisconsin State University Fieldhouse, Madison, WI (cancelled because the club had closed down)

May 3–4 1968: The Scene, Milwaukee, WI, USA (with The Invasion, The Corporation)

May 5 1968: Magoo's & New City Opera House, Minneapolis, MN, USA (early show with The Litter)

May 6 1968: Family Dog, Denver, CO, USA (originally scheduled for March 19)

May 10 1968: Toledo Sports Arena, Toldeo, OH, USA

May 11 1968: Akron Civic Centre, Akron, OH, USA

May 12 1968: Music Hall, Cleveland, OH, USA (afternoon show with Canned Heat)

May 14 1968: Veterans Memorial Auditorium, Columbus, OH, USA

May 15 1968: Veterans Memorial Field House, Huntington, WV, USA (with The The Grass Roots, The Kickin, Mustangs, The Purple Reign)

May 17–18 1968: Convention Center, Anaheim, CA, USA (with Spirit)

May 18 1968: Ice Palace, Las Vegas, NV, USA (with Hunger; advertised but cancelled)

May 19 1968: Community Concourse, Exhibit Hall, San Diego, CA, USA (with The Brain Police)

May 20 1968: *The Summer Brothers Smothers Show*, CBS Television Studios, Los Angeles, CA USA (broadcast July 14; hosted by Glen Campbell)

May 24 1968: University Of Southern California, Robertson Gym, Santa Barbara, CA, USA (with The Electric Flag)

May 25 1968: Civic Auditorium, San Jose, CA, USA (with Orphan Egg)

May 27 1968: Swing Auditorium, San Bernadino, CA, USA

May 28 1968: Pacific Center, Long Beach, CA, USA

May 29–30 1968: Eagles Auditorium, Seattle, WA, USA (with The Easy Chairs, Calliope)

May 31 1968: Stampede Corral, Calgary, Alberta, Canada

June 1 1968: Pavillion Sales Annex, Edmonton, Alberta, Canada (with The Grass Roots)

June 2 1968: Pacific Coliseum, Vancouver, British Columbia, Canada (with The United Empire Loyalists)

June 5 1968: Massey Hall, Toronto, Ontario, Canada (with Duke Edwards & The Young Ones)

June 7–9 1968: Grande Ballroom, Detroit, MI, USA (with MC5, The Carousel; Nickel Plate Express; St Louis Union; The James Gang, The Thyme)

June 11 1968: Paul Sauve Arena, Montreal, Quebec, Canada (with Duke Edwards & The Young Ones)

June 14 1968: Island Gardens, West Hempstead, Long Island, NY, USA (band arrived late and played only three songs)

June 15 1968: Oakdale Music Theatre, Wallingford, CT, USA (two shows)

June 16 1968: Camden County Music Fair, Cherry Hill, NJ, USA

Jack Bruce, Dick Heckstall-Smith, Jon Hiseman
July ? 1968: 100 Club, London, England (the impetus for *Things We Like*)

Cream
Oct 4 1968: Alameda County Coliseum Arena, Oakland, CA, USA (with It's A Beautiful Day, The Collectors)

Oct 5 1968: University Of New Mexico, Albuquerque, NM, USA

Oct 6 1968: Auditorium Arena, Denver, CO, USA (with a hypnotist)

Oct 11 1968: New Haven Arena, New Haven, CT, USA

Oct 12 1968: Olympia Arena, Detroit, MI, USA (with Friend & Lover, The Siegel-Schwall Blues Band)

Oct 13 1968: Coliseum, Chicago, IL, USA (afternoon show with Conqueror Worm)

Oct 14 1968: Veterans Memorial Auditorium, Des Moines, IA, USA (with Conqueror Worm)

Oct 16? 1968: TTG Studios, Hollywood, CA (Jack jams with Jimi Hendrix, Buddy Miles, and Jim McCarty)

Oct 18–19 1968: The Forum, Inglewood, CA, USA (with Deep Purple)

Oct 20 1968: Sports Arena, San Diego, CA, USA (with Deep Purple, The Buddy Miles Express)

Oct 24 1968: Sam Houston Coliseum, Houston, TX, USA

Oct 25 1968: Dallas Memorial Auditorium, Dallas, TX, USA (with Vanilla Fudge, The Young Rascals)

Oct 26 1968: Miami Stadium, Miami, FL, USA (afternoon show with Terry Reid)

Oct 27 1968: Chastain Park Amphitheatre, Atlanta, GA, USA (afternoon show with Terry Reid)

Oct 31 1968: Boston Garden, Boston, MA, USA (cancelled)

Nov 1 1968: The Spectrum, Philadelphia, PA, USA (with Terry Reid, Sweet Stavin Chain; revolving stage)

Nov 2 1968: Madison Square Garden, New York, NY, USA (with The Buddy Miles Express, Terry Reid)

Nov 3 1968: Civic Center Arena, Baltimore, MD, USA (with headliners The Moody Blues, Terry Reid)

Nov 4 1968: Rhode Island Auditorium, Providence, RI, USA (with Terry Reid; second show cut short by time restrictions)

Nov 26 1968: Royal Albert Hall, London, England (with Taste, Yes)

Mike Gibbs Orchestra
Feb 22 1969: Nuffield Theatre Studio, University, Lancaster, England (recorded for BBC Radio 3; broadcast Feb 24)

Supershow with *Eric Clapton, Buddy Guy, Stephen Stills, Colosseum, and others*
Mar 17–18 1969: Staines, England (filmed in a factory)

Mike Gibbs Orchestra
Apr 11 1969: *Jazz Workshop*, BBC Radio, London, England (broadcast Apr 30)

Dave Gelly Sextet: A Tribute To Mike Taylor
May 17 1969: *Jazz Workshop*, BBC Radio, London, England (broadcast June 4)

Jack Bruce, Larry Coryell, Mike Mandel, plus drummers Steve Haas and Bob Moses
July 11–12 1969: Slug's, New York, NY, USA

Mike Gibbs Orchestra
Oct ? 1969: University, Coventry, England
Jan 15 1970: London School Of Economics, London, England

Jack Bruce & Friends *with Larry Coryell, Mitch Mitchell, Mike Mandel*
Jan 24 1970: Arts Festival, University, Coventry, England (with Colosseum, New Jazz Orchestra)
Jan 25 1970: Lyceum, Strand, England
Jan 30–31 1970: Fillmore East, New York, NY, USA (with Mountain)
Feb 6–7, 9 1970: The Warehouse, New Orleans, LA, USA (openers include Zephyr, White Clover, Darkhorse, Pacific Gas & Electric)
Feb 13–14 1970: Eastown Theatre, Detroit, MI, USA (openers include Savage Grace, The Tea, Steve Booker, Teegarden & Van Winkle)
Feb 20–21 1970: Kinetic Playground, Chicago, IL, USA (with James Gang, Siegal-Schwall, Mason Proffit, Soft, Truth)
Feb 22 1970: Electric Factory, Philadelphia, PA, USA (with Albert King, Edison Electric Band)
Feb 25 1970: Music Hall, Houston, TX, USA (with Mountain)
Feb 26 1970: Fillmore West, San Francisco, CA, USA
Feb 27–28 1970: Winterland, San Francisco, CA, USA
Mar 1 1970: Fillmore West, San Francisco, CA, USA (openers include Johnny Winter, Mountain, Eric Mercury, Birthrite)

The Tony Williams Lifetime
Apr 7–12 1970: Slug's, New York, NY, USA
Apr 12 1970: unknown venue, Toronto, Ontario, Canada (advertised in *Billboard* but probably cancelled)
Apr 16 1970: University Of Toledo Student Union Multi-Purpose Room, Toledo, OH, USA
Apr 17–18 1970: Capitol Theatre, Port Chester, NY, USA (with Lee Michaels, Charlie Brown)
Apr 19 1970: Tufts University, Medford, MA, USA (with Mountain)
Apr 24–25 1970: unknown venue, Pittsburgh, PA, USA (advertised in *Billboard* but probably cancelled)
Apr 24 1970: The Birmingham Palladium, Detroit, MI, USA (with The Rationals)
Apr 25 1970: The Birmingham Palladium, Detroit, MI, USA (with The Rationals)
Apr 26 1970: unknown venue, Minneapolis, MO, USA (advertised in *Billboard* but probably cancelled)
Apr 27 1970: *Tonight Show*, New York, NY, USA (probably cancelled)

May 1–2 1970: Ludlow's Garage, Cincinnati, OH, USA
May 6 1970: Stores, CT, USA (advertised in *Billboard* but probably cancelled)
May 8–9 1970: Action House, Island Park, Long Island, NY, USA
May 15 1970: unknown venue, Chicago, IL, USA
May 31 1970: unknown venue, Atlanta, GA, USA
June 13 1970: unknown venue, San Francisco, CA, USA
June 19 1970: unknown venue, Portland, OR, USA
June 25–28 1970: unknown venue, Los Angeles, CA, USA (previous eight shows advertised in *Billboard* but probably cancelled)
July 7 1970: New York, NY, USA
July 11 1970: Newport Jazz Festival, Newport, RI, USA
July 18 1970: New York Pop, Randall's Island, NY, USA (cancelled)
July 28–31 1970: Ungano's, New York, NY, USA
Aug 1 1970: Powder Ridge Festival, Middlefield, CT (cancelled)
Aug 4 1970: Harmonyville, NJ, USA
Aug 7–15 1970: Ungano's, New York, NY, USA
Aug 16 1970: Ohio Valley Jazz Festivial, Crosley Field, OH, USA
Aug 28 1970: Action House, Island Park, Long Island, NY, USA

Nucleus
Sep 11 1970: Notre Dame Hall, London, England

The Tony Williams Lifetime
Oct 2 1970: University, Lancaster, England
Oct 3 1970: Roundhouse, Dagenham, England
Oct 6 1970: Marquee Club, London, England
Oct 7 1970: Speakeasy, London, England
Oct 9 1970: Chez Club, Leytonstone, England
Oct 10 1970: Belfry, Sutton Coldfield, England
Oct 16 1970: Sisters, Tottenham, London, England
Oct 18 1970: Kinema Ballroom, Dunfermline, Scotland
Oct ? 1970: Ronnie Scotts Jazz Club, London, England
Oct ? 1970: *Beat-Club*, Bremen, Germany (recorded for TV but not broadcast)
Oct 23 1970: Essener Pop & Blues Festival, Essen, Germany
Oct 25 1970: Hampstead Country Club, Haverstock Hill, London, England
Oct 26 1970: Albert Hall, Nottingham, England
Oct 29 1970: Basel, Switzerland
Oct 30 1970: Zurich, Switzerland
Nov 1 1970: Royal Court Theatre, London, England
Nov 2 1970: Colston Hall, Bristol, England
Nov 3 1970: Town Hall, Oxford, England
Nov 4 1970: City Hall, Sheffield, England
Nov 6 1970: City Hall, Newcastle-upon-Tyne, England
Nov 7 1970: University, Hull, England
Nov 8 1970: Caley Cinema, Edinburgh, Scotland
Nov 9 1970: Maryland, Glasgow, Scotland
Nov 10 1970: Town Hall, Birmingham, England
Nov 12 1970: California Ballroom, Dunstable, England

Nov 13 1970: Chesford Grange, Kenilworth, England
Nov 14 1970: Starlight Ballroom, Boston, England
Nov 15 1970: Winter Gardens, Bournemouth, England
Nov 20 1970: Knufflesplunk Community Center, Welwyn Garden City, England
Nov 21 1970: Umist College, Manchester, England
Nov 22 1970: Redcar Jazz Club, Coatham Hotel, Redcar, England
Nov 23 1970: Civic Hall, Wolverhampton, England (cancelled)
Nov 26 1970: Revolution Club, London, England
Nov 27 1970: Van Dyke Club, Davenport, Plymouth, England
Nov 29 1970: Fairfield Hall, Croydon, England
Dec 2 1970: The Dome, Brighton, England
Dec 3 1970: St Georges Hall, Liverpool, England
Dec 5 1970: Chelsea College, Chelsea, England
Dec 10 1970: Rebecca's, Birmingham, England (cancelled; band never showed up)
Dec 18 1970: East Berks College, Windsor, England (probably cancelled)
Feb 19 1971: Rock Palace, Brooklyn, NY, USA (cancelled)
Feb ? 1971: Electric Banana, Brooklyn, NY, USA (cancelled)
Feb ? 1971: The Main Point, Ardmore, PA, USA (cancelled)

Nucleus
Apr 24 1971: Torrington, London, England

Larry Coryell Band
July 18 1971: Nice Festival, Nice, France (radio broadcast)

Jack Bruce Trio with John Marshall, Chris Spedding
July 20 1971: Sounds Of The Seventies, BBC Radio, London, England (broadcast Aug 6)

Jack Bruce & Friends with Larry Coryell, Graham Bond, John Marshall, Chris Spedding
July 29 1971: Campus TV, Park Toorenvliet, Middelburg, Holland

Larry Coryell with Jack Bruce, John Marshall
Aug 5–7 1971: Ronnie Scott's Jazz Club, London, England

Jack Bruce, Jon Hiseman, John Surman
Aug 10 1971: Jazz In Britain, BBC Radio 3, London, England (broadcast Aug 31)

Nucleus
Aug ? 1971: Summer Review, BBC TV, London, England (broadcast Aug 27)

Jack Bruce & Friends with Graham Bond, John Marshall, Chris Spedding, Art Themen
Aug ? 1971: Out Front, Granada TV, Manchester, England
Aug 19 1971: BBC In Concert, Paris Theatre, London, England (broadcast Aug 29)
Aug 26 1971: Country Club, Hampstead, England (UCS Benefit; Dick Heckstall-Smith replaced Art Themen)

Sep 4 1971: Hyde Park, London, England (with King Crimson, Formerly Fat Harry, Roy Harper)
Sep 26 1971: Bumpers Club, London, England (UCS Benefit)
Sep 27 1971: Swing In, TV recording, Germany (interview and solo tracks; rehearsal tracks filmed on a different date)
Oct 5 1971: Old Grey Whistle Test, BBC TV, London, England
Oct 8 1971: Queens Hall, Leeds, England
Oct 9 1971: Winter Gardens, Great Malvern, England
Oct 23 1971: Polytechnic, Bristol, England
Oct 28 1971: Music Hall, Aberdeen, England
Oct 29 1971: University, Stirling, England
Oct 30 1971: Queen Margaret's Union, Glasgow, Scotland
Oct 31 1971: Kinema Ballroom, Dunfermline, Scotland (with The Change)
Nov 4 1971: Central London Polytechnic Festival, London, England
Nov 6 1971: Essex University, Colchester, England
Nov 7 1971: Greyhound, Croydon, England
Nov 10 1971: Top Rank, Cardiff, England
Nov 11 1971: Umist, Manchester, England
Nov 12 1971: University, Newcastle, England
Nov 13 1971: University, Sheffield, England
Nov 16 1971: Teatro Massimo, Milan, Italy (without Art Themen)
Nov 18 1971: Teatro Broncaccio, Rome, Italy (without Art Themen; Graham leaves the band again)
Nov 19 1971: Goldsmiths' College, London, England
Nov 20 1971: University, Exeter, England (Graham Bond leaves the band around this time)
Nov 22 1971: Watford Town Hall, Watford, England
Nov 25 1971: University, Aberystwyth, England
Nov 26 1971: University, Oxford, England
Nov 27 1971: Polytechnic, Leicester, England (without Art Themen)
Dec 3 1971: South Bank Polytechnic Student Union, London, England
Dec 4 1971: Lads' Club, Norwich, England
Dec 5 1971: Chelsea College, London, England
Dec ? 1971: The Stadium, Liverpool, England
Jan 11 1972: Rheinhalle, Dusseldorf, Germany
Jan 12 1972: Musikhalle, Hamburg, Germany
Jan 13 1972: Kongresshalle, Frankfurt, Germany
Jan 14 1972: Deutsches Museum, Munich, Germany
Jan 15 1972: Deutschlandhalle, Berlin, Germany
Jan ? 1972: Polytechnic Annual Ball, Wolverhampton, England
Jan 29 1972: Borough Rd. College, Isleworth, England
Feb 12 1972: Imperial College, London, England

West Bruce & Laing
Mar 17 1972: Foster Auditorium, Tuscaloosa, AL, USA
Mar 18 1972: Pirate's World Amusement Park, Dania, FL, USA (with Country Joe McDonald)
Mar 19 1972: Fort Homer Hesterly Armory, Tampa, FL, USA (with Black Oak Arkansas)

Mar ? 1972: unknown venue, Key West, FL, USA
Mar 23 1972: Kemp's Coliseum, Orlando, FL, USA
Mar 24 1972: Convention Hall, Miami, FL, USA
Mar 25 1972: The Warehouse, New Orleans, LA, USA
Mar ? 1972: Pershing Auditorium, Lincoln, NE, USA
Mar ? 1972: East Carolina University, Greenville, NC, USA
(with Brass Park)
Mar 29 1972: Music Hall, Houston, TX, USA
Mar 30 1972: Terrace Ballroom, Salt Lake City, UT, USA
(with Malo)
Mar 31 1972: Community Concourse, San Diego, CA, USA
(with Cold Blood)
Apr 2 1972: Winterland, San Francisco, CA, USA (with Cold
Blood, Jackie Lomax)
Apr 4 1972: Center Arena, Seattle, WA, USA (with Cold
Blood)
Apr 7 1972: Hollywood Palladium, Hollywood, CA, USA
(with Dr Hook & The Medicine Show, Free)
Apr 8 1972: Denver, CO, USA
Apr 9 1972: University of Colorado Fieldhouse, Boulder, CO,
USA (with Free)
Apr 10 1972: Fort Collins, KY, USA
Apr 12 1972: Kiel Opera House, St Louis, MO, USA (with
Free)
Apr 13 1972: Oklahoma City, OK, USA
Apr 14 1972: State Fairgrounds, Springfield, IL, USA
Apr 15 1972: Northwestern University, McGraw Hall,
Evanston, IL, USA
Apr 16 1972: Cinderella Ballroom, Detroit, MI, USA (with
Cradle)
Apr 18 1972: Veterans Memorial Auditorium, Columbus,
OH, USA (with Jeremy Clay)
Apr 20 1972: Ohio University Convocation Center, Athens,
OH, USA (with Emerson Lake & Palmer)
Apr 21 1972: Public Hall, Cleveland, OH, USA (with
Mahavishnu Orchestra, Procol Harum, David Rea)
Apr 23 1972: Stony Brook University Gymnasium, Stony
Brook, NY, USA
Apr 24 1972: Carnegie Hall, New York, NY, USA (two shows
with David Rea)
Apr 27 1972: Aquarius Theatre, Boston, MA, USA (with
Spencer Davis)
Apr 28 1972: The Spectrum, Philadelphia, PA, USA (with
Spirit, Fleetwood Mac)
Apr 29 1972: Capitol Theatre, Passaic, NJ, USA (with Uncle
Bucks)
Apr 30 1972: Fairfield University Gym, Fairfield, CT, USA

Jack Bruce, Jan Akkerman, Pierre van der Linden
Sep 30 1972: Oval Festival, London, England ('Powerhouse
Sod' jam)

West Bruce & Laing
Sep 30 1972: Penn State University Recreation Bldg, State
College, PA, USA (cancelled)
Oct 19 1972: Auditorium Theatre, Chicago, IL, USA
Oct 20 1972: Michigan State University, East Lansing, MI,
USA (with Country Joe McDonald)

Oct 22 1972: SUNY Cortland Lusk Field House, Cortland,
NY, USA (with Grin)
Oct 23 1972: Ford Auditorium, Detroit, MI, USA
Oct 26 1972: Alexander Memorial Coliseum, Atlanta, GA,
USA (with Edgar Winter Group, Stonehenge)
Oct 28 1972: Wake Forest University Union, Winston-
Salem, NC, USA
Nov 4 1972: Capitol Theatre, Passaic, NJ, USA
Nov 6 1972: Radio City Music Hall, New York, NY, USA
Nov 7 1972: DAR Constitution Hall, Washington DC, USA
(with Wild Turkey)
Nov 9 1972: Palace Theatre, Waterbury, CT, USA
Nov 10 1972: Aquarius Theatre, Boston, MA, USA (with
Grin)
Nov 11 1972: Penn State University Recreation Hall, State
College, PA, USA (with Elephant's Memory)
Nov 22 1972: Winterland, San Francisco, CA, USA (with
Crazy Horse, Snail)
Nov 24 1972: Palladium, Hollywood, CA, USA (with Mott
The Hoople, Flash Cadillac, The Continental Kids)
Nov 25 1972: Convention Center, Anaheim, CA, USA (with
John Mayall, Delbert & Glen)
Nov 26 1972: Community Concourse, San Diego, CA, USA
(with Foghat)
Nov 29 1972: Memorial Auditorium, Dallas, TX, USA (with
Edgar Winter Group, Foghat)
Nov 30 1972: Oklahoma City, OK, USA
Dec 2 1972: Sports Stadium, Orlando, FL, USA
Dec 3 1972: Memorial Hall, Kansas City, KS, USA (with
Edgar Winter Group)
Dec 5 1972: Corpus Christi, TX, USA
Dec 7 1972: Houston, TX, USA
Dec 8 1972: Wichita, TX, USA
Dec 9 1972: Pershing Auditorium, Lincoln, NE, USA (with
Edgar Winter Group)
Dec 10 1972: Coliseum, Denver, CO, USA (with J. Geils
Band)
Dec 12 1972: Fox Theatre, St Louis, MO, USA (with J. Geils
Band)
Dec 13 1972: Auditorium Theatre, Memphis, TN, USA (with
J. Geils Band)
Dec 15 1972: The Spectrum, Philadelphia, PA, USA (with
James Gang, Foghat)
Dec 17 1972: Orpehum, Boston, MA, USA
Mar 26 1973: Chateau Neuf, Oslo, Norway
Mar 27 1973: Concert Hall, Gothenburg, Sweden
Mar 28 1973: Falkoner Center, Copenhagen, Denmark
Mar 31 1973: De Doelen, Rotterdam, Holland
Apr 1 1973: Concertgebouw, Amsterdam, Holland
Apr 2 1973: National Theatre, Brussels, Belgium
Apr 4 1973: Stadthalle, Vienna, Austria
Apr 5 1973: Theatre du Chatelet, Paris, France (radio
broadcast)
Apr 6 1973: Festival Hall, Berne, Switzerland
Apr 8–9 1973: Palazzo dello Sport, Rome, Italy
Apr 10 1973: Palazzo dello Sport, Bologna, Italy (cancelled)
Apr 11 1973: Palalide, Milan, Italy (cancelled)
Apr 13 1973: Cirkus Krone Halle, Munich, Germany

Apr 14 1973: Landwirtschaftshalle, Kaiserslautern, Germany

Apr 15 1973: Musikhalle, Hamburg, Germany

Apr 16 1973: Jahrhunderthalle, Frankfurt, Germany

Apr 20–21 1973: Rainbow Theatre, London, England (with Jimmy Stevens)

Apr 22–23 1973: Free Trade Hall, Manchester, England (with Jimmy Stevens)

Apr 24 1973: City Hall, Newcastle-upon-Tyne, England (with Jimmy Stevens)

Apr 25 1973: Green's Playhouse, Glasgow, Scotland (with Jimmy Stevens)

Apr 26 1973: Leeds University, Leeds, England (with Jimmy Stevens)

Jack Bruce Band with Mick Taylor, Carla Bley, Bruce Gary, Ronnie Leahy

Apr 22 1975: Badalona Hall, Barcelona, Spain

Apr 24 1975: Real Madrid Hall, Madrid, Spain

Apr 26 1975: Velodromo Hall, San Sebastian, Spain

Apr 28 1975: Salle Des Sports, Bordeaux, France

Apr 29 1975: Salle Vallier, Marseille, France

Apr 30 1975: Palais Des Sports, St Etienne, France

May 2 1975: Rheinhalle, Bregenz, Austria

May 3 1975: Cirkus Krone Halle, Munich, Germany

May 4 1975: Stadthalle, Offenbach, Germany

May 5 1975: Rosengarten Halle, Mannheim, Germany

May 7 1975: P.E. Jansson Hall, Brussels, Belgium

May 8 1975: De Vliegermolen, Voorburg, Holland

May 10 1975: Westfalen Halle, Dortmund, Germany

May 11 1975: Philipshalle, Dusseldorf, Germany

May 13 1975: Musikhalle, Hamburg, Germany

May 14 1975: K.B. Hallen, Copenhagen, Denmark

May 15 1975: Scandinavium Hall, Gothenburg, Sweden

May 16 1975: Grona Lund, Stockholm, Sweden

May 19 1975: Pinkpop 75, Geleen, Holland

May 30 1975: Birmingham Odeon, Birmingham, England

June 1 1975: Free Trade Hall, Manchester, England

June 3 1975: Apollo Theatre, Glasgow, Scotland

June 4 1975: City Hall, Newcastle-upon-Tyne, England

June 6 1975: Old Grey Whistle Test, BBC TV, London, England

June 7 1975: Crystal Palace Concert Bowl, London, England

June 9 1975: May Ball, University, Cambridge, England

Jack Bruce Band with Simon Phillips, Hughie Burns, Tony Hymas

Mar 5 1977: Leeds University, Leeds, England

Mar 7 1977: Birmingham Aston University, Birmingham, England

Mar 8 1977: University, Lancaster, England

Mar 10 1977: Polytechnic, Oxford, England

Mar 11 1977: University Of East Anglia, Norwich, England

Mar 12 1977: University, Sheffield, England

Mar 14 1977: University, Salford, England

Mar 15 1977: Strathclyde University, Glasgow, Scotland

Mar ? 1977: Chateau Neuf, Oslo, Norway (cancelled)

Mar 21 1977: Jarlateatern, Stockholm, Sweden

Mar 22 1977: Tivolis Koncertsal, Copenhagen, Denmark

Mar 23 1977: Stakladen, Aarhus, Denmark

Mar 25 1977: Hochschule der Kunste, Berlin, Germany

Mar 26 1977: Musikhalle, Hamburg, Germany

Mar 27 1977: Philipshalle, Dusseldorf, Germany

Mar 29 1977: Congresgebouw, The Hague, Holland

Mar 30 1977: Hassalt, Belgium

Apr 1 1977: Pavillion De Paris, Paris, France

Apr 2 1977: Stadthalle, Offenbach, Germany

Apr 3 1977: Deutsches Museum, Munich, Germany

Apr 4 1977: Konzerthaus, Vienna, Austria

Apr 6 1977: Volkhaus, Zurich, Switzerland

Apr 12 1977: Pavilion, Hemel Hempstead, England

Apr 14 1977: BBC In Concert, Paris Theatre, London, England (broadcast Apr 30)

Apr 15 1977: New Victoria Apollo, London, England

July 2 1977: Roskilde Festival, Roskilde, Denmark

Oct 27 1977: The Other Side, Wilmington, DE, USA

Oct 28 1977: Shaboo Inn, Willimantic, CT, USA

Oct 29 1977: Shaboo Inn, Willimantic, CT, USA

Oct 30 1977: D'Place, Dover, NJ, USA

Nov 1–2 1977: My Fathers Place, Roslyn, NY, USA

Nov 7 1977: Agora Ballroom, Cleveland, OH, USA

Nov 11 1977: Paul's Mall, Jazz Workshop, Boston, MA, USA

Nov 16–17 1977: Bottom Line, New York, NY, USA

Nov ? 1977: Bijou Cafe, Philadelphia, PA, USA (two shows; cancelled)

Nov 21 1977: The Great Southeast Music Hall, Atlanta, GA, USA

Nov 28 1977: Ivanhoe Theatre, Chicago, IL, USA (two shows)

Nov 30 1977: Blue Note, Boulder, CO, USA

Dec 2–4 1977: Roxy Theatre, Los Angeles, CA, USA (two shows)

Dec 8 1977: The Catalyst, Santa Cruz, CA, USA

Dec 9–10 1977: Old Waldorf, San Francisco, CA, USA

Jack Bruce, Jon Hiseman, John Surman

June 26 1978: At The Third Stroke, BBC Radio London, England (broadcast Sep 4)

Norman Beaker & No Mystery

Apr ? 1979: Band On the Wall, Manchester, England

Apr ? 1979: Bradford Hotel, Liverpool, England

Apr ? 1979: Broadfield Hotel, Sheffield, England

May ? 1979: Manchester Factory, Manchester, England

Head

June 5 1979: College Of Art, Glasgow, Scotland (broadcast on Radio Scotland's Jazz And That)

The All-Star Rock Band

July ? 1979: Live Music Show, London, England

Rocket 88

July 8 1979: Bracknell Jazz Festival, Bracknell, England

July 14 1979: North Sea Jazz Festival, The Hague, Holland

Head
July 17 1979: College Of Art, Glasgow, Scotland (broadcast
on Radio Scotland's *Jazz And That*)

John McLaughlin, Jack Bruce, Billy Cobham, Stu Goldberg
Oct 7 1979: Chateau Neuf, Oslo, Norway
Oct 8 1979: Konserthuset, Stockholm, Sweden
Oct 9 1979: Olympen, Lund, Sweden
Oct 11 1979: Tivolis Koncertsal, Copenhagen, Denmark
Oct 12 1979: Neue Welt, Berlin, Germany
Oct 13 1979: Rudolf-Oetker-Halle, Bielefeld, Germany
Oct 14 1979: Liederhalie, Stuttgart, Germany
Oct 15 1979: Deutsches Museum, Munich, Germany
Oct 16 1979: Stadthalle, Vienna, Austria
Oct 18 1979: Stadthalle, Kassel, Germany
Oct 19 1979: Jahrhunderthalle, Frankfurt, Germany
Oct 20 1979: Stadthalle, Bremen, Germany
Oct 21 1979: Philipshalle, Dusseldorf, Germany
Oct 22 1979: Congress-Centrum Halle, Saal 1, Hamburg, Germany
Oct 23 1979: Stadthalle, Braunschweig, Germany
Oct 24 1979: Stadthalle, Erlangen, Germany
Oct 25 1979: Salle Tivoli, Strasbourg, France
Oct 26 1979: unknown venue, Nancy, France
Oct 27 1979: unknown venue, Roubaix, France
Oct 29 1979: Pavillion de Paris, Paris, France
Oct 30 1979: unknown venue, Reims, France
Oct 31 1979: unknown venue, Annecy, France
Nov 1 1979: Theatre De Verdure, Nice, France
Nov 6 1979: Rotterdam, Holland (cancelled)
Nov 7 1979: Amsterdam, Holland (cancelled)
Nov 8 1979: Palilido Theatre, Milan, Italy
Nov 9 1979: Palasport, Turin, Italy
Nov 12 1979: Rainbow Theatre, London, England

Rocket 88
Nov 16 1979: Congress-Centrum Halle, Hamburg, Germany
Nov ? 1979: Hamburg Jazz Festival, Hamburg, Germany
Nov ? 1979: Rotation Club, Hanover, Germany (*Rocket 88* LP recorded here)
Dec 15 1979: The Venue, London, England (broadcast on BBC radio on Jan 19 1980)
Dec 30 1979: Dingwalls, London, England

Cozy Powell & Friends
Jan 8 1980: *The Old Grey Whistle Test*, BBC TV, London, England
Jan 9 1980: *BBC In Concert*, Paris Theatre, London, England (broadcast Jan 12)

Jack Bruce & Friends with *Billy Cobham, Clem Clempson, David Sancious*
Mar 13 1980: The Bayou, Washington DC, USA
Mar 14 1980: Triangle Theatre, Rochester, NY, USA
Mar 16–19 1980: Bottom Line, New York, NY, USA (Mar 19 show broadcast live on WNEW-FM)
Mar 20 1980: Fast Lane, Asbury Park, NJ, USA
Mar 22 1980: Irvine Auditorium, Philadelphia, PA, USA
Mar 23 1980: Stony Brook University Gymnasium, Stony Brook, NY, USA
Mar 24 1980: Main Act, Lynn, MA, USA
Mar 25 1980: Rutgers University, New Brunswick, NJ, USA

Rocket 88
June ? 1980: 100 Club, London, England

Jack Bruce & Friends *as above*
July 28–30 1980: The Venue, London, England
Oct 19 1980: Grugahalle, Essen, Germany (broadcast on *Rockpalast*)
Nov 14 1980: San Diego University, San Diego, CA, USA
Nov 15 1980: Santa Monica Civic Auditorium, Santa Monica, CA, USA
Nov 16 1980: Dooley's, Tempe, AZ, USA
Nov 18 1980: Zellerbach, Berkeley, CA, USA
Nov 20 1980: Rainbow Music Hall, Denver, CO, USA
Nov 22 1980: Uptown Theatre, Kansas City, MO, USA
Nov 28–29 1980: Park West, Chicago, IL, USA
Dec 2 1980: Agora Ballroom, Cleveland, OH, USA
Dec 3 1980: Harpo's Hanger, Detroit, MI, USA
Dec 5 1980: Triangle Theatre, Rochester, NY, USA
Dec 6 1980: J. B. Scott's, Albany, NY, USA
Dec 7 1980: State University Of New York, New Paltz, NY, USA
Dec 9 1980: Hofstra University, Long Island, NY, USA
Dec 10 1980: Center Stage Theatre, East Providence, RI, USA
Dec 11 1980: Harvard Square Theatre, Cambridge, MA, USA
Dec 13 1980: Palladium, New York, NY, USA (with The Michael Stanley Band)
Dec ? 1980: Ramapo College, Mahwah, NJ, USA
Dec 26 1980: Capitol Theatre, Passaic, NJ, USA
Dec 27 1980: Nassau Coliseum, Uniondale, NY, USA
Dec 29 1980: Toads Place, New Haven, CT, USA
Dec 30 1980: Civic Centre, Springfield, MA, USA
Dec 31 1980: Tower Theatre, Upper Darby, PA, USA
Jan 6 1981: Agora Ballroom, Atlanta, GA, USA
Jan 10 1981: *Saturday Night Live*, NBC TV, New York, NY, USA

Rocket 88
Jan ? 1981: The Half Moon, Putney, London, England

Alexis Korner, Jack Bruce, Ginger Baker
Feb 17 1981: *Lieder & Leute*, Baden-Baden, Germany

Jack Bruce & Friends *as above*
May 11 1981: University Of Surrey, Guildford, England
May 12 1981: New Victoria Apollo, London, England
May 13 1981: New Victoria Apollo, London, England
May 21 1981: Mogadur Theatre, Paris, France
May 24 1981: Tivolis Koncertsal, Copenhagen, Denmark
May 25 1981: Grota Lejon, Stockholm, Sweden
May 28 1981: Kulttuuritalo, Helsinki, Finland

Jack Bruce & Friends *with Clem Clempson, David Sancious, Bruce Gary*
Dec 16 1981: Capitol Theatre, Passaic, NJ, USA (radio)

Mose Allison
July 21 1982: Casino De Montreux, Switzerland (TV)

A Gathering Of Minds
July 23 1982: Casino De Montreux, Switzerland (radio)

Jan Hammer Band
Jan 26 1983: Fabrik, Hamburg, Germany
Jan 31 1983: Capitol, Mannheim, Germany
Feb 1 1983: Metropol, Berlin, Germany
Feb 2 1983: Ear Musichall, Kuhstedt, Germany
Feb 3 1983: Bebop, Hildesheim, Germany
Feb 4 1983: Leinedomicil, Hannover, Germany
Feb 5 1983: Dejavu, Lubeck, Germany
Feb 6 1983: Dochdu, Bocholt, Germany

Jack Bruce Band *with Clem Clempson, Bruce Gary, Ronnie Leahy*
May 14 1983: Bonar Hall, Dundee, Scotland
July 27 1983: Tamdhu, Bannockburn, Scotland
July 28 1983: Plough Inn, Perth, Scotland
July 29 1983: The Venue, Aberdeen, Scotland
July 30 1983: Eden Court Theatre, Inverness, Scotland
Aug 1 1983: Cabarfeidh, Stornaway, Scotland
Aug 3 1983: Tam Dhui, Blairgowrie, Scotland
Aug 4 1983: Abbotts Hall, Kirkcaldy, Scotland
Aug 5 1983: Rock At The Park, Bathgate, Scotland
Aug 6 1983: Heathery Bar, Wishaw, Scotland
Aug 7 1983: Mayfair, Glasgow, Scotland
Aug 8 1983: Micks Club, Carlisle, England
Aug 9 1983: Pavilion, Ayr, Scotland
Aug 10 1983: Chequers, Falkirk, Scotland
Aug 11 1983: Queens Hall, Edinburgh, Scotland

Jack Bruce Band *with David Sancious, Bruce Gary*
Oct 6 1983: *Lieder & Leute*, Baden-Baden, Germany (TV)
Oct 7 1983: Stadthalle, Vienna, Austria
Oct 8 1983: unknown venue, Pinkerfeld, Germany
Oct 10 1983: unknown venue, Munich, Germany
Oct 12 1983: Capitol, Mannheim, Germany
Oct 13 1983: unknown venue, Koblenz, Germany
Oct 14 1983: unknown venue, Basel, Switzerland
Oct 15 1983: unknown venue, Zurich, Switzerland
Oct 17 1983: unknown venue, Genf, Germany
Oct ? 1983: Kongresshalle, Freiburg, Germany
Oct 21 1983: unknown venue, Lengede, Germany
Oct 22 1983: unknown venue, Beverungen, Germany
Oct 24 1983: Schauburg, Bremen, Germany
Oct 25 1983: Fabrik, Hamburg, Germany
Oct 28 1983: unknown venue, Bremerhaven, Germany
Oct 31 1983: Wesel Festival, Wesel, Germany
Nov 1 1983: Zeche, Bochum, Germany (broadcast on *Rockpalast*)
Nov 2 1983: Quartier Latin, Berlin, Germany

Fela Kuti Group
Nov 15 1983: *Klassik Rocknacht*, Circus Atlas, Munich, Germany (orchestra conducted by Eberhard Schoener)

Jack Bruce *with Rainer Baumann, Zabba Lindner*
Dec 16 1983: Fabrik, Hamburg, Germany

Jack Bruce & Friends *with Clem Clempson, Mark Nauseef, Ronnie Leahy*
May 31 1984: Lochem Festival, Lochem, Holland (radio)
May 31 1984: Paradiso, Amsterdam, Holland
June 2 1984: Parkzicht, Rotterdam, Holland

Alexis Korner Tribute
June 5 1984: Palais Ballroom, Nottingham, England (BBC radio)

Kip Hanrahan
July 2 1984: Public Theatre, New York, NY, USA

Jack Bruce & Friends *with Clem Clempson, Bruce Gary, Ronnie Leahy*
July 10 1984: Jonathan Swift's, Cambridge, MA, USA
July 12 1984: Lupos Heartbreak Hotel, Providence, RI, USA
July 13 1984: Pier 84, New York, NY, USA
July 14 1984: The Joyous Lake, Woodstock, NY, USA (two shows)
July 17 1984: The Bayou, Washington DC, USA (two shows)
July ? 1984: Stage West, Hartford, CT, USA
July 20 1984: My Fathers Place, Roslyn, NY, USA (two shows)
July 24 1984: Bottom Line, New York, NY, USA (two shows)
July 25 1984: Bottom Line, New York, NY, USA (two shows)
July 28 1984: Golden Bear, Huntington Beach, CA, USA (cancelled)

Jack Bruce *with Rainer Baumann, Zabba Lindner*
Aug 18 1984: Open Air Stadtpark, Hamburg, Germany

Jack Bruce & Friends *as above*
Aug 24 1984: Pavilion, Ayr, Scotland
Aug 25 1984: Star Club, Glasgow, Scotland
Aug 26 1984: Mayfair, Glasgow, Scotland (Radio Clyde)
Aug 27 1984: Queens Hall, Edinburgh, Scotland
Aug 28 1984: Queens Hall, Edinburgh, Scotland
Aug 29 1984: The Venue, Aberdeen, Scotland
Aug 31 1984: Albert Hall, Stirling, Scotland
Sep 1 1984: Whitehall Theatre, Dundee, Scotland

Kip Hanrahan
Oct 21 1984: Nancy Jazz Festival, Nancy, France (radio)
Oct 25 1984: unknown venue, Zurich, Switzerland (radio)

Jack Bruce & Friends *as above*
Nov 1 1984: Zeche, Bochum, Germany
Nov 2 1984: Kreuz Saal, Fulda, Germany
Nov 5 1984: Stadthalle, Koln, Germany
Nov 9 1984: Maxim, Stuttgart, Germany
Nov 14 1984: Metropol, Berlin, Germany

Nov 16 1984: Alexandra, Copenhagen, Denmark
Nov 19 1984: Batschkapp, Frankfurt, Germany

For _Under The Volcano_
Nov 20–22 1984: _Spiegelzelt Auf Der Domplatte_, Cologne,
Germany (TV)

Arlen Roth
Nov 28 1984: Ohne Filter, Baden-Baden, Germany (TV)

Jack Bruce & Friends with _Dick Heckstall-Smith, Tim Franks, and others_
Dec 1 1984: Band On the Wall, Manchester, England
Dec 2 1984: Broadfield Hotel, Sheffield, England

Concert For Ethiopia
Dec 9 1984: Usher Hall, Edinburgh, Scotland

Jack Bruce & Friends with _Tony Williams, David Sancious_
Dec ? 1984: unknown venue, Leverkusen, Germany

Kip Hanrahan
Feb 24 1985: Shakespeare Theatre, Boston, MA, USA
Feb 27 1985: Sounds Of Brazil, New York, NY, USA
Mar 1 1985: 9:30 Club, Washington DC, USA
July 4 1985: Theatre Antique De Vienne, Paris, France
July 6 1985: First Pendley International Jazz Festival,
Pendley Manor, Tring, England
July 13 1985: North Sea Jazz Festival, The Hague, Holland
July 16 1985: Roccastrada, Italy (with Ginger Baker)
July 18 1985: Antibes Jazz Festival, Antibes, France (radio)

The Golden Palominos
July 20 1985: Womad Festival, Kenn Pier Farm, Clevedon,
England (cancelled)

Jack Bruce & Friends with _Clem Clempson, Bruce Gary, Ronnie Leahy_
Aug 25 1985: Queens Hall, Edinburgh, Scotland

Kip Hanrahan
Oct 26 1985: Carnegie Hall, New York, NY, USA (with Ruben
Blades)

For _Under The Volcano_
Nov 8 1985: Mark Taper Forum, New Music America
Festival, Los Angeles, CA

Jack Bruce Band with _Clem Clempson, Anton Fier, Ronnie Leahy_
Jan 13–14 1986: Liquid Club, Tel Aviv, Israel
Jan 18 1986: Bin Yanei Ha-ooma National House Theatre,
Jerusalem

Jack Bruce Band with _Clem Clempson, Bruce Gary, Ronnie Leahy_
Jan 20 1986: Stadthalle, Kassel, Germany
Jan 21 1986: Stadthalle, Offenbach, Germany

Jan 22 1986: Jazzgalerie, Bonn, Germany
Jan 23 1986: Stadthalle, Erlangen, Germany
Jan 24 1986: Philipshalle, Dusseldorf, Germany
Jan 26 1986: Schutzenhaus Albisguetki, Zurich,
Switzerland
Jan 27 1986: Kongresshalle, Saarbrucken, Germany
Jan 28 1986: Metropol, Aachen, Germany
Jan 29 1986: Metropol, Berlin, Germany
Jan 30 1986: Grosse Freiheit 36, Hamburg, Germany
Jan 31 1986: Jovel Cinema, Munich, Germany
Feb 1 1986: Kulturzentrum, Mainz, Germany
Feb 2 1986: Maxim, Stuttgart, Germany
Feb 3 1986: Steinbruch-Theatre, Nieder-Ramstadt,
Germany

Ian Stewart Tribute
Feb 23 1986: 100 Club, London, England

Bernd Konrad Project
Mar ? 1986: Theaterhaus, Stuttgart, Germany (TV)

The Golden Palominos
Mar ? 1986: unknown venue, Ann Arbor, MI, USA
Mar ? 1986: unknown venue, Washington DC, USA
Mar ? 1986: Student Union Ballroom, University Of
Massachusetts, Amherst, MA, USA
Mar 7 1986: Paradise, Boston, MA, USA
Mar 13 1986: Peabody's Down Under, Cleveland, OH, USA

Charlie Watts's All-Star Jazz Orchestra
Mar 23 1986: Fulham Town Hall, London, England
July 4 1986: Bracknell Jazz Festival, Bracknell, England

Jack Bruce, Ginger Baker, Bireli Lagrene, Courtney Pine
July 10 1986: Nice Jazz Festival, Nice, France (Jack and
Bernard Purdie also perform with the New York All Stars)

The Golden Palominos
July 19 1986: Casino de Montreux, Switzerland (TV)
July 20 1986: unknown venue, Milan, Italy (TV)

Mike Mantler/Nick Mason Project
Feb 8 1987: Kongresshalle, Frankfurt, Germany (radio & TV)

Jack Bruce, John Entwistle, Nick Mason, Rick Fenn, and others
Feb 9 1987: Fachblatt Messeparty, Dorian Gray, Frankfurt,
Germany

The Threepenny Opera
May 1 1987: _Deutsches Schauspielhaus_, Hamburg,
Germany (TV; orchestra conducted by Eberhard
Schoener)

Inazuma Supersession with _Anton Fier, Kenji Suzuki_
May 10–11 1987: Ink Stick Shibaura Factory, Tokyo,
Japan (radio)

Tooth Of Crime
June 5–July 11 1987: Bridge Lane Theatre, Bridge Lane, Battersea, London, England (a play by Sam Shepard; Jack played Hoss)

Mike Mantler
Aug 25 1987: Astoria, London, England
Aug 28 1987: Saalfelden Jazz Festival, Saalfelden, Austria

Norman Beaker Band
Dec 1 1987: Band On The Wall, Manchester, England
Dec ? 1987: Community Centre, Poynton, Stockport, England
Dec 9 1987: The Old Vic, Nottingham, England
Dec 10 1987: Park Hotel, Tynemouth, Newcastle, England
Dec 11 1987: Blackpool, England

Leslie West, Jack Bruce, Joe Franco
Dec 19 1987: The Chance, Poughkeepsie, NY, USA

Norman Beaker Band
June 23 1988: Fife Aid, Craigtown Park, Fife, Scotland
Aug 28 1988: Preservation Hall, Edinburgh, Scotland

The Jack Bruce Blues Band with Dick Heckstall-Smith, Norman Beaker, Tim Franks, David Bainbridge
July 24 1988: Eco Rock, St Andrews, Scotland

Jack Bruce Band with Anton Fier, Pat Thrall, David Bravo
Sep 29 1988: Kenwood Tavern, Levittown, PA, USA
Sep 30 1988: War Memorial, Trenton, NJ, USA
Oct 1 1988: Sundance Saloon, Bay Shore, Long Island, NY, USA
Oct 5 1988: El Mocambo, Toronto, Ontario, Canada
Oct 8 1988: Stone Pony, Asbury Park, NJ, USA
Oct 9 1988: Toads Place, New Haven, CT, USA
Oct 10–11 1988: Bottom Line, New York, NY, USA (Eric Clapton guested on Oct 10, Mick Taylor on Oct 11)
Oct 12 1988: The Bayou, Washington DC, USA
Oct 14 1988: Theatre Of The Living Arts, Philadelphia, PA, USA
Oct 25 1988: The Spectrum, Philadelphia, PA, USA
Oct 26 1988: The Centrum, Worcester, MA, USA (opening for The Moody Blues)
Oct 28 1988: Madison Square Garden, New York, NY, USA (opening for The Moody Blues)

Dickie Betts Band
Nov 1 1988: Lone Star Cafe, New York, NY, USA (radio)

Jack Bruce Band as above
Nov 9 1988: Central City, Gainesville, FL, USA
Nov 11 1988: Late Night With David Letterman, NBC TV, New York, NY, USA (Jack sits in with Paul Shaffer)
Nov 12 1988: Center Stage Theatre, Atlanta, GA, USA
Nov 13 1988: Storyville Music Club, New Orleans, LA, USA
Nov 14 1988: Rockefeller's, Houston, TX, USA
Nov 15 1988: San Antonio, TX, USA

Nov 16 1988: Hard Rock Cafe, Dallas, TX, USA
Nov 18 1988: The Shark Club, Austin, TX, USA
Nov 21 1988: Mississippi Nights, St Louis, MO, USA
Nov 22 1988: Vogue Theatre, Indianapolis, IN, USA
Nov 23 1988: Royal Oak Theatre, Detroit, MI, USA (with Ian Hunter)
Nov 25 1988: Agora Ballroom, Cleveland, OH, USA (with Ian Hunter)
Nov 26 1988: Riviera Theatre, Chicago, IL, USA (with Ian Hunter)
Dec 4 1988: Night Music, NBC TV, New York, NY, USA (other guests: Joe Walsh, Al Green, Highway 101, Nat Hentoff)
Sep 16 1989: Huettengelaende, Neunkirchen, Germany (TV)

Jack Bruce Band with Ginger Baker, Bernie Worrell, Blues Saraceno, Gary 'Mudbone, Cooper, Tom Goss
Nov 29 1989: The Bayou, Washington DC, USA
Nov 30 1989: The Chance, Poughkeepsie, NY, USA
Dec 1 1989: The Living Room, Providence, RI, USA
Dec 2 1989: Saratoga Winners, Albany, NY, USA
Dec 3 1989: Toads Place, New Haven, CT, USA
Dec 4 1989: Hammerjacks, Baltimore, MA, USA
Dec 6 1989: Paradise, Boston, MA, USA
Dec 7 1989: Bottom Line, New York, NY, USA (radio)
Dec 8 1989: 23 East, Ardmore, PA, USA
Dec 10 1989: Newport, Columbus, OH, USA
Dec 11 1989: Bogarts, Cincinnati, OH, USA
Dec 13 1989: Peabody's Down Under, Cleveland, OH, USA
Dec 14 1989: The Ritz, Roseville, MI, USA
Dec 15 1989: Biddy Mulligans, Chicago, IL, USA
Dec 16 1989: Zivkos, Milwaukee, WI, USA
Dec 19 1989: The Bacchanal, San Diego, CA, USA
Dec 20 1989: The Coach House, San Juan Capistrano, CA, USA
Dec 21 1989: The Palace, Hollywood, CA, USA
Dec 22 1989: The Omni, Oakland, CA, USA
Jan 19 1990: N.A.M.M. Show, Disneyland Hotel, Anaheim, CA, USA
Jan 20 1990: Ventura Theatre, Ventura, CA, USA
Jan 21 1990: The Coach House, San Juan Capistrano, CA, USA
Jan 22 1990: Belly-Up, Solana Beach, CA, USA
Jan 23 1990: The Strand, Redondo Beach, CA, USA
Jan 24 1990: Calamity Jane's, Las Vegas, NV, USA
Jan 26 1990: Arcadia Theatre, Dallas, TX, USA
Jan 27 1990: Fitzgeralds, Houston, TX, USA
Jan 29 1990: Center Stage Theatre, Atlanta, GA, USA
Feb 1 1990: Orlando, Florida, USA
Feb 2 1990: Floodzone, Richmond, VA, USA
Feb 3 1990: The Boathouse, Norfolk, VA, USA
Feb 4 1990: The Bayou, Washington DC, USA
Feb 5 1990: Charlotte, NC, USA
Feb 6 1990: Hammerjacks, Baltimore, MD, USA
Feb 7 1990: Chestnut Cabaret, Philadelphia, PA, USA
Feb 8 1990: Club Bene Dinner Club, Saryeville, South Amboy, NJ, USA
Feb 9 1990: Late Night With David Letterman, NBC TV, New York, NY, USA

Feb 9 1990: The Ritz, New York, NY, USA
Feb 10 1990: The Living Room, Providence, RI, USA
Feb 11 1990: Toads Place, New Haven, CT, USA

Kip Hanrahan's *Look, The Moon*
June 3 1990: unknown venue, Bremen, Germany (radio)
June 4 1990: 29th Internationales New Jazz Festival
Moers, Moers Festival, Moers, Germany
June ? 1990: unknown venue, France
June ? 1990: unknown venue, Italy

Norman Beaker Band
Sep 15 1990: Salerno Festival, Salerno, Italy

Jack Bruce
Oct 17 1990: *Rocklife*, Live Music Hall, Cologne, Germany
(TV; Jack also sat in with Rory Gallagher)
Nov 3 1990: Town Hall, Falkirk, Scotland

Norman Beaker Band
Dec 7 1990: Exhibition Centre, Thessaloniki, Greece
Dec 8 1990: The Rodon, Athens, Greece

Jack Bruce *with Rainer Baumann, Zabba Lindner, Dick Heckstall-Smith, Zoot Money*
Apr 12 1991: Fabrik, Hamburg, Germany

The Jimi Hendrix Concert
Apr 25 1991: *Rocklife*, E-Werk, Cologne, Germany (TV)

Jack Bruce Blues Band *with Jonas Bruce, Dick Heckstall-Smith, Tim Franks, Norman Beaker*
May 4 1991: Assembly Arms, Derby, England
? ? 1991: San Remo Blues Festival, San Remo, Italy (TV)

Many Have No Speech
June 4–5 1991: Danau Festival, Stadsaal, St Polten, Austria

The New Generation Band *with Jonas Bruce, Malcolm Bruce, Koffi Baker, Norman Beaker*
July 6 1991: unknown venue, Budapest, Hungary

Kip Hanrahan's *... then she turned so that ...*
July 9 1991: Umbria Jazz Festival, Perugia, Italy (radio)
July 11 1991: Copenhagen Jazz Festival, Copenhagen, Denmark (radio)
July 12 1991: North Sea Jazz Festival, The Hague, Holland (radio)
July 14 1991: Liederhalle, Stuttgart, Germany (TV)
July ? 1991: Pori Jazz Festival, Porissa, Finland
July 18 1991: Fasching, Stockholm, Sweden (radio)
July 20–21 1991: New Morning, Paris, France

Jack Bruce Band *with Ginger Baker, Blues Saraceno*
Aug 8 1991: Park Hayarkon, Open Air Festival, Tel Aviv, Israel

The Jack Bruce Blues Band *with Jonas Bruce, Malcolm Bruce, Dick Heckstall-Smith, Tim Franks, Norman Beaker*
Aug 23 1991: The Great British Rhythm & Blues Festival, Municipal Hall, Colne, England

Guitar Legends Festival
Oct 17 1991: Cartouges Stadium, Seville, Spain (radio & TV)

Jack Bruce Band *with Blues Saraceno, Simon Phillips*
Mar 16 1992: The Penny Lane Club, Sapporo, Japan
Mar 18 1992: unknown venue, Nagoya, Japan
Mar 19 1992: unknown venue, Osaka, Japan
Mar 20–21 1992: Club Citta, Kawasaki, Japan

Jack Bruce Band *with Clem Clempson, Ronnie Leahy, Gary Husband*
Apr 26 1992: Bull's Head, Barnes, London, England

Jack Bruce *with Alex Conti, Zabba Lindner*
? ? 1992: Hamburg, Germany

Kip Hanrahan's Conjure Band
July 3 1992: New Morning, Paris, France
July 6 1992: Westport Jazz Festival, Festival-Zelt Deichtorplatz, Hamburg, Germany
July 7 1992: Kulturzentrum, Mainz, Germany
July ? 1992: Wien Jazz Festival, Vienna, Austria

Jack Bruce Band *with Blues Saraceno, Simon Phillips*
Aug 20 1992: Grand Theatre, Clapham, London, England
Aug 31 1992: Sala Kongress, Warsaw, Poland

Kip Hanrahan's *Imagining New Orleans*
Oct ? 1992: unknown venue, Skopje, Macedonia
Oct ? 1992: unknown venue, Brussels, Belgium
Oct 30 1992: Bockenheimer Depot, Frankfurt, Germany (radio & TV)
Nov 1 1992: unknown venue, Nijmegen, Holland (radio)

Cream
Jan 12 1993: Rock & Roll Hall Of Fame Induction Ceremony, Century Plaza Hotel Ballroom, Los Angeles, CA, USA

Jack Bruce Band *with Blues Saraceno, Gary Husband*
Mar 21 1993: The Stone, San Francisco, CA, USA
Mar 22 1993: The Strand, Redondo Beach, CA, USA
Mar 23 1993: The Coach House, San Juan Capistrano, CA, USA
Mar 25 1993: Paradise, Boston, MA, USA
Mar 26 1993: Chestnut Cabaret, Philadelphia, PA, USA
Mar 27 1993: The Ritz, New York, NY, USA
Mar 30 1993: Grand Theatre, Clapham, London, England (TV)
Apr 4 1993: Fabrik, Hamburg, Germany
Apr 5 1993: Metropolis, Munich, Germany
June 28–30 1993: Ronnie Scott's, Birmingham, England
July 1 1993: The Irish Centre, Leeds, England
July 2 1993: Glasgow Jazz Festival, Old Fruitmarket, Glasgow, Scotland

July 4 1993: Pistoia Blues Festival, Pistoia, Italy
July 30 1993: unknown venue, Rudkobing, Denmark

Jack Bruce Trio with *Steve Topping, Gary Husband*
Aug 14 1993: unknown venue, Kerpen, Germany

Jack Bruce Trio with *Gary Moore, Gary Husband*
Aug 15 1993: Zelt Am Marktplatz, Esslingen, Germany

Jack Bruce, Mick Taylor, Richard Thompson, and others
Aug 17 1993: San Remo Festival, San Remo, Italy (radio)

Jack Bruce, Dick Heckstall-Smith, John Stevens
Sep 4 1993: Outside In Festival, Crawley, West Sussex, England

The 50th Birthday Party Concerts with *Gary Moore, Ginger Baker, Simon Phillips, Gary Husband, Clem Clempson, Pete Brown, Dick Heckstall-Smith, Art Themen, Henry Lowther, John Mumford, Jonas Bruce, Malcolm Bruce, Gary 'Mudbone, Cooper, Maggie Reilly, Bernie Worrell, Francois Garny, Kip Hanrahan*
Nov 2–3 1993: E-Werk, Cologne, Germany

BBM
May 16 1994: Muziekcentrum Vredenburg, Utrecht, Holland (cancelled)
May 18 1994: Terminal One, Munich, Germany (cancelled)
May 19 1994: Marquee Club, London, England
May 22 1994: Ulster Hall, Belfast, Northern Ireland (cancelled)
May 23 1994: Barrowlands, Glasgow, Scotland
May 26 1994: The Manor, Virgin Records 21st Anniversary Show, London, England (TV)
May 31 1994: Falkoner Theatre, Copenhagen, Denmark
June 1 1994: Cirkus, Stockholm, Sweden
June 5 1994: Academy, Brixton, London, England
June 7 1994: Le Zenith, Paris, France (postponed)
June 16 1994: Sports Palace, Barcelona, Spain
June 18 1994: Cyclodrome, San Sebastian, Spain
June 20 1994: Sports Palace, Madrid, Spain
June 25 1994: Midtfyns Festival, Ringe Fyn, Denmark
June 28 1994: Le Zenith, Paris, France
July 2 1994: Schuettorf Festival, Vechtewiese, Germany
July 3 1994: Berlin Festival, Freilichtbuehne, Germany (cancelled)
July 6 1994: Montreux Jazz Festival, Montreux, Switzerland (cancelled)
July 9 1994: Balingen Festival, Messegelaende, Germany (cancelled)
July 21 1994: Pori Jazz Festival, Porissa, Finland (cancelled)
July 22 1994: Molde Jazz Festival, Molde, Norway (cancelled)

Kip Hanrahan's *Casual Hit*
Nov 13 1994: Sounds Of Brazil, New York, NY, USA

Alexis Korner Tribute Concert
May 21 1995: Buxton Opera House, Buxton, England

Jack Bruce with *Rainer Baumann, Zabba Lindner*
May 29 1995: Fabrik, Hamburg, Germany

The Universe Of Jimi Hendrix
July 23 1995: Liederhalle, Stuttgart, Germany (TV)

Jack Bruce, Bernie Worrell
Sep 2 1995: Queens Hall, Edinburgh, Scotland
Sep 4 1995: Queen Elizabeth Hall, London, England

Jack Bruce, Chaka Khan, and others
Aug ? 1996: unknown venue, Lichtenstein (with Jimmy Griego and Michael Tovar)
Aug ? 1996: unknown venue, Switzerland
Aug ? 1996: unknown venue, Germany

The School Of Languages
Aug 31 1996: Arken Museum Of Modern Art, Copenhagen, Denmark
Sep 1 1996: Arken Museum Of Modern Art, Copenhagen, Denmark

Fender 50th Anniversary Concert: A Tribute To Rory Gallagher
Nov 30 1996: Wembley Conference Centre, London, England

Ringo Starr And The All-Starrs
Apr 28 1997: Moore Theatre, Seattle, WA, USA
Apr 29 1997: Hult Center For Performing Arts, Eugene, OR, USA
Apr 30 1997: Arlene Schnitzer Concert Hall, Portland, OR, USA
May 2 1997: Concord Pavilion, Concord, CA, USA
May 3 1997: Universal Amphitheatre, Los Angeles, CA, USA
May 4 1997: Humphrey's, San Diego, CA, USA
May 5 1997: Mesa Amphitheatre, Phoenix, AZ, USA
May 7 1997: Fiddler's Green Amphitheatre, Denver, CO, USA (with Ginger Baker)
May 9 1997: Rosemont Horizon, Chicago, IL, USA
May 10 1997: Riverport Amphitheatre, St Louis, MO, USA
May 11 1997: State Theatre, Minneapolis, MN, USA
May 13 1997: Eagles Ballroom, Milwaukee, WI, USA
May 14 1997: Breslin Center, East Lansing, MI, USA
May 16 1997: Chastain Park Amphitheatre, Atlanta, GA, USA
May 17 1997: Sunrise Theatre, Miami, FL, USA
May 18 1997: Ruth Eckerd Hall, Tampa, FL, USA
May 20 1997: The Palace Theatre, Myrtle Beach, SC, USA
May 21 1997: Wolf Trap Auditorium, Vienna, VA, USA
May 23 1997: Billy Bob's, Fort Worth, TX, USA
May 24 1997: Six Flags Fiesta Texas, San Antonio, TX, USA
May 25 1997: Six Flags Astroworld, Houston, TX, USA
May 28 1997: Bob Carpenter Center, Newark, DE, USA
May 29 1997: I.C. Light Amphitheatre, Pittsburg, PA, USA

May 30 1997: Pine Knob Amphitheatre, Detroit, MI, USA
May 31 1997: Rubber Bowl, Akron, OH, USA
June 2 1997: Mohegan Sun Casino, Uncasville, CT, USA
June 3 1997: PNC Bank Arts Center, Holmdel, NJ, USA
(with Bernie Worrell)
June 5 1997: Harborlights Pavilion, Boston, MA, USA
June 6 1997: Resorts International, Atlantic City, NJ, USA
June 7 1997: Jones Beach Amphitheatre, Wantaugh, NY,
USA

The School Of Understanding
Nov 21–23 1997: Hebbel Theatre, Berlin, Germany

Jack Bruce, Gary Moore, Gary Husband
Apr 6–7 1998: Angel Studios, Islington, London, England
(band performances and interview session for *The
Cream Of Cream*)

Jack Bruce *with Norman Beaker, Tim Franks, David
Bainbridge, Lennie Crookes*
June 13 1998: Live In The Marquee, Stockport Rugby Club,
Stockport, England

Jack Bruce & Friends *with Gary Moore, Gary Husband*
July 14 1998: Cellar Bar, South Shields, England
July 15 1998: Cellar Bar, South Shields, England
July 18 1998: Ashburnham Centre, Chelsea, England
(charity concert)

Ringo Starr And The All-Starrs
Aug 7 1998: Helsingin Jaahalli (Helsinki Icehall), Helsinki,
Finland
Aug 8 1998: Festival, Zurich, Switzerland
Aug 9 1998: Skanderborg Festivalen, Skanderborg,
Denmark
Aug 12 1998: Freilichtbuehne Killesberg, Stuttgart, Germany
Aug 13 1998: Theaterplatz, Chemnitz, Germany
Aug 15 1998: Centre Sportif, Luxembourg City,
Luxembourg (cancelled)
Aug 16 1998: Marktrock Festival, Leuven, Belgium
Aug 18 1998: World Expo 98, Lisbon, Portugal
Aug 20 1998: The Point, Dublin, Ireland
Aug 21–22 1998: Shepherds Bush Empire, London,
England (second show cancelled)
Aug 25 1998: Sports Complex, Moscow, Russia
Aug 26 1998: Jubilee Complex, St Petersburg, Russia
Aug 28–30 1998: Sporting Club, Monte Carlo
Sep 1 1998: Grugahalle, Essen, Germany
Sep 2 1998: Stadtpark, Hamburg, Germany
Sep 3 1998: Museumshof, Bonn, Germany
Sep 5 1998: Benefit Concert, Wintershall, England

Ringo Starr And The All-Starrs
Feb 12–14 1999: Trump Taj Mahal, The Mark Etess Arena,
Atlantic City, NJ, USA
Feb 16–17 1999: Beacon Theatre, New York, NY, USA
Feb 19–20 1999: Mohegan Sun Resort and Casino,
Uncasville, CT, USA

Feb 21 1999: Westbury Music Fair, Westbury, NY, USA
Feb 22 1999: Schottenstein Center, Columbus, OH, USA
Feb 24 1999: Westbury Music Fair, Westbury, NY, USA
Feb 26 1999: Star Plaza Theatre, Merrillville, IN, USA
Feb 28 1999: Park West, Chicago, IL, USA
Mar 1 1999: Palace Theatre, Detroit, MI, USA
Mar 4 1999: Eureka Municipal Auditorium, Eureka, CA, USA
Mar 5–6 1999: Konocti Harbor Resort, Kelseyville, CA, USA
Mar 7 1999: Berkeley Community Theatre, Berkeley, CA,
USA
Mar 11 1999: Bank America Center, Boise, ID, USA
Mar 12 1999: Dee Events Center, Ogden, UT, USA
Mar 13 1999: Hard Rock Hotel & Casino, The Joint, Las
Vegas, NV, USA
Mar 14 1999: 4th & B, San Diego, CA, USA
Mar 18 1999: Universal Amphitheatre, Los Angeles, CA,
USA
Mar 19 1999: Silver Legacy Casino, Reno, NV, USA
Mar 20 1999: Silver Legacy Casino, Reno, NV, USA
Mar 21 1999: Harrah's Casino, Lake Tahoe, NV, USA
Mar 25 1999: Horseshoe Casino, Tunica, MS, USA
Mar 26 1999: Florida Theatre, Jacksonville, FL, USA
Mar 27 1999: Sunrise Musical Theatre, Ft. Lauderdale, FL,
USA
Mar 28 1999: Hard Rock Cafe, Orlando, FL, USA

**Michael Jackson & Friends: A Concert To Benefit The
Children Of The World**
June 27 1999: Olympic Stadium, Munich, Germany (TV)

Ringo Starr And The All-Starrs
May 12–13 2000: Trump Taj Mahal, Xanadu Showroom,
Atlantic City, NJ, USA
May 15 2000: Mid Hudson Civic Center, Poughkeepsie,
New York, USA
May 16–17 2000: Westbury Music Fair, Westbury, New
York, USA
May 19 2000: *The Late Night With David Letterman*, NBC
TV, New York, NY, USA
May 19–20 2000: Mohegan Sun Casino, Uncasville, CT,
USA
May 21 2000: I Center, Salem, NH, USA
May 23 2000: Beacon Theatre, New York, NY, USA
May 24 2000: State Theatre, New Brunswick, NJ, USA
May 26 2000: Norva Theatre, Norfolk, VA, USA
May 27 2000: Festival, Cleveland, OH, USA
May 28 2000: Riverport Amphitheatre, St Louis, MO, USA
May 30 2000: Wolf Trap Auditorium, Washington DC, USA
May 31 2000: Nashville Arena, Nashville, TN, USA
June 1 2000: Horseshoe Casino, Robinsonville, MS, USA
June 3 2000: Sunrise Musical Theatre, Fort Lauderdale, FL,
USA
June 4 2000: Chastain Park Amphitheatre, Atlanta, GA, USA
June 5 2000: IC Light Amphitheatre, Pittsburgh, PA, USA
(cancelled)
June 7 2000: Casino Rama, Orillia, Ontario, Canada, USA
(cancelled)
June 8 2000: House of Blues, Chicago, IL, USA

June 10 2000: Landmark Theatre, Syracuse, NY, USA
June 11 2000: Pine Knob Amphitheatre, Detroit, MI, USA
June 14–15 2000: Montalvo Center for the Arts, Saratoga, CA, USA
June 16 2000: Harrah's Casino, Lake Tahoe, NV, USA
June 17 2000: Hard Rock Hotel and Casino - The Joint, Las Vegas, NV, USA
June 19–20 2000: The Sun Theatre, Anaheim, CA, USA (cancelled)
June 22–23 2000: House of Blues, Los Angeles, CA, USA
June 25–26 2000: Humphrey's, San Diego, CA, USA
June 28 2000: Red Rocks Amphitheatre, Denver, CO, USA
June 30 2000: State Capitol Grounds, St Paul, MN, USA
July 1 2000: SummerFest, Miller Oasis, Milwaukee, WI, USA

Jack Bruce & The Cuicoland Express with Vernon Reid, Alfredo Triff, Bernie Worrell, Milton Cardona, Richie Flores, Robby Ameen, El Negro Horacio Hernandez, Mick Hutton
June 18 2001: Jazz Cafe, London, England

Uli Jon Roth
June 23 2001: Castle Donington, Donington Park, England

Jack Bruce & The Cuicoland Express with Vernon Reid, Bernie Worrell, Richie Flores, Robby Ameen, El Negro Horacio Hernandez
July 14 2001: North Sea Jazz Festival, The Hague, Holland (radio broadcast also featuring Alfredo Triff, Milton Cardona, Andy Gonzalez)
Oct 1 2001: Shepherds Bush Empire, London, England
Oct 2 2001: Pavilion Theatre, Bournemouth, England (cancelled)
Oct 3 2001: Royal Centre, Nottingham, England
Oct 4 2001: Royal Opera House, Newcastle, England
Oct 6 2001: The Old Fruitmarket, Glasgow, Scotland
Oct 7 2001: Bridgewater Hall, Manchester, England
Oct 9 2001: Schlachthof, Bremen, Germany (radio)
Oct 10 2001: Fabrik, Hamburg, Germany
Oct 11 2001: Arnager Bio, Copenhagen, Denmark
Oct 13 2001: Bruckenforum, Bonn, Germany
Oct 14 2001: Kulturfabrik, Roth, Germany
Oct 15 2001: Bataclan, Paris, France (cancelled)
Oct 16 2001: Frankfurter Hof, Mainz, Germany
Oct 18 2001: Alcatraz, Milan, Italy
Oct 19 2001: Konzert Fabrik Z7, Prattein, Switzerland
Oct 20 2001: Melkweg, Amsterdam, Holland
Oct 21 2001: Hof Ter Lo, Antwerp, Belgium
Oct 26 2001: Later With Jools Holland, BBC TV, London, England
Dec 12 2001: B.B. King's, New York, NY, USA
Dec 14 2001: Park West, Chicago, IL, USA
Dec 16 2001: Galaxy Theatre, Santa Ana, CA, USA
Dec 17 2001: House Of Blues, Los Angeles, CA, USA
Apr 4–6 2002: Blue Note, Fukuoka, Japan
Apr 8–10 2002: Blue Note, Osaka, Japan
June 14–15 2002: B.B. King's, New York, NY, USA (cancelled)

A Walk Down Abbey Road: A Tribute To The Beatles
June 15 2002: Maui Arts & Cultural Center Amphitheatre, Maui, HI, USA
June 16 2002: Neil Blaisdell Center Arena, Honolulu, HI, USA
June 24 2002: Humphrey's Concerts By The Bay, San Diego, CA, USA
June 26 2002: Radisson Hotel, Sacramento, CA, USA
June 27 2002: Mountain Winery, Saratoga, CA, USA
June 28 2002: Chronicle Pavilion, Concord, CA, USA
June 29 2002: Greek Theatre, Los Angeles, CA, USA
June 30 2002: Celebrity Theatre, Phoenix, AZ, USA
July 3 2002: Summerfest, Briggs & Stratton Stage, Milwaukee, WI, USA
July 6 2002: Taste Of Chicago, Petrillo Music Shell, Grant Park, Chicago, IL, USA
July 10 2002: DTE Energy Music Theatre, Clarkston, MI, USA
July 12 2002: Columbus Zoo & Aquarium Amphitheatre, Columbus, OH, USA
July 14 2002: Memorial Auditorium, Burlington, IA, USA
July 16 2002: Massey Hall, Toronto, Ontario, Canada
July 18 2002: Seaside Music Festival, Brooklyn, NY, USA
July 19 2002: Mohegan Sun Casino, Uncasville, CT, USA
July 21 2002: Cape Cod Melody Tent, Hyannis, MA, USA
July 23 2002: Hampton Beach Casino, Hampton Beach, NH, USA
July 24 2002: Keswick Theatre, Glenside, PA, USA
July 25 2002: Westbury Music Fair, Westbury, NY, USA
July 26 2002: AC Hilton, Grand Theatre, Atlantic City, NJ, USA
July 27 2002: Wolf Trap Filene Center, Vienna, VA, USA
July 28 2002: AC Hilton, Grand Theatre, Atlantic City, NJ, USA

Jack Bruce & The Cuicoland Express as above
Aug 24 2002: Canterbury Fayre 2002, Mount Ephraim Gardens, Hernhill, Faversham, Kent, England
Aug 30 2002: Kunsfest, Weimer, Germany

Leslie Mandoki
Sep 21 2002: Urania Theatre, Budapest, Hungary

Jack Bruce, Bernie Worrell, Godfrey Townsend, Steve Murphy
Oct 18 2002: B.B. King's, New York, NY, USA

Jack Bruce & The Cuicoland Express as above, but with Godfrey Townsend in place of Vernon Reid
Oct 19 2002: B.B. King's, New York, NY, USA

Legends Of Rock
Nov 13 2002: Arts Centre, Aberystwyth, Wales
Nov 14 2002: Wulfrun Hall, Wolverhamton, England
Nov 15 2002: St Georges Hall, Bradford, England
Nov 17 2002: Shepherds Bush Empire, London, England
Nov 18 2002: Apollo, Manchester, England
Nov 19 2002: Guildhall, Portsmouth, England

Nov 20 2002: Cliffs Pavilion, Southend, England
Nov 21 2002: Victoria Hall, Stoke-on-Trent, England
Nov 22 2002: City Hall, Newcastle, England
Nov 23 2002: Usher Hall, Edinburgh, Scotland
Nov 24 2002: Royal Concert Hall, Nottingham, England
Nov 25 2002: Corn Exchange, Cambridge, England
Nov 26 2002: St Davids Hall, Cardiff, Wales

Cream
May 2–6 2005: Royal Albert Hall, London, England

A Story Ended: A Tribute To Dick Heckstall-Smith
June 6 2005: Astoria, London, England

Cream
Oct 24–26 2005: Madison Square Garden, New York, NY, USA

More Jack Than Blues with The Hessischer Rundfunk Big Band; conducted by Jörg Achim Keller
Oct 26 2006: Deutsches Jazzfestival Frankfurt, Frankfurt, Germany (radio)

Jack Bruce Zone with Clem Clempson, Gary Husband, Ronnie Leahy, Natascha Eleonore
May 17 2007: Royal Scottish Academy Of Music And Drama, Glasgow, Scotland

Motown Night
Dec 7 2007: Pavillion, Bisley, England

Jeff Healy: A Celebration
May 3 2008: Sound Academy, Toronto, Ontario, Canada (CBC Radio)

Hippiefest 2008
July 11 2008: The Dodge Theater, Phoenix, AZ, USA
July 12 2008: Chateau St Michelle Winery, Seattle, WA, USA
July 13 2008: The Mountain Winery, Saratoga, CA, USA
July 16 2008: The Greek Theater, Los Angeles, CA, USA
July 17–18 2008: Humphrey's By The Bay, San Diego, CA, USA
July 19 2008: The Fantasy Springs Casino, Palm Springs, CA, USA
July 20 2008: Nokia Live, Grand Prairie, TX, USA
July 22 2008: Fiddler's Green, Denver, CO, USA
July 25 2008: Molson Amphitheatre, Toronto, Ontario, Canada
July 26 2008: Fraze Pavilion, Kettering, OH, USA
July 29 2008: Mann Music Center, Philadelphia, PA, USA
July 30 2008: Wolftrap, Vienna, Virginia, USA
July 31 2008: North Fork Theater, Westbury, NY, USA

Aug 1 2008: The Meadowbrook US Cellular Pavilion, Gilford, NH, USA
Aug 2 2008: DTE Energy Music Theater, Detroit, MI, USA
Aug 3 2008: Bethel Woods, Bethel, NY, USA
Aug 5 2008: Bergen Performance Arts Center, Englewood, NJ, USA
Aug 8 2008: Chastain Park Amphitheatre, Atlanta, GA, USA
Aug 9 2008: Ruth Eckerd Hall, Clearwater, FL, USA
Aug 10 2008: Pompano Beach Amphitheatre, Pompano Beach, FL, USA

Rock And Roll Benefit
Sep 20 2008: Koka Booth Amphitheatre, Raleigh, NC, USA (with The John Entwistle Band)

Jack Bruce & The BBC Big Band conducted by Jörg Achim Keller
Nov 14 2008: Town Hall, Birmingham, England

Zildjian's Drummers Achievement Awards with Ginger Baker, Tony Allen
Dec 7 2008: Shepherds Bush Empire, London, England

Tribute To Tony Williams
Dec 14 2008: Motion Blue, Yokohama, Japan
Dec 15–19 2008: Blue Note, Tokyo, Japan

Jack Bruce, Robin Trower, Gary Husband
Feb 25 2009: Tollhaus, Karlsruhe, Germany
Feb 26 2009: Kantine, Cologne, Germany
Feb 28 2009: Concertgebouw De Vereeniging, Nijmegen, Holland
Mar 1 2009: Music Hall, Worpswede, Germany
July 23 2009: Savona Summer Festival, Savona, Italy
July 24 2009: Trasimeno Blues Festival, Perugia, Italy
July 25 2009: Villa Ada: Roma Incontra il Mondo, Rome, Italy
July 26 2009: Live Summer Festival, Padova, Italy (cancelled)
July 30–Aug 1 2009: Notodden Blues Festival, Notodden, Norway
Aug 5 2009: Shepherds Bush Empire, London, England
Aug 6 2009: Glasgow Academy, Glasgow, Scotland
Aug 7 2009: Queen's Hall, Rock & Blues Festival, Edinburgh, Scotland
Aug 8 2009: Westmid Showground: Memories of Woodstock, Shrewsbury, England (cancelled)

Jack Bruce, Clem Clempson, Gary Husband
Sep 11 2009: Burgkultur, St Veit, Austria

Ronnie Scott's Blues Experience
Oct 25 2009: Ronnie Scott's, London, England

Index

Words *in italics* indicate album titles unless otherwise stated. Words 'in quotes' indicate song titles. Page numbers in **bold** indicate illustrations.

PICTURE CREDITS

Many of the pictures used in this book came from Jack's own archives, and we are grateful to Jack and his wife, Margrit, for their help. The rest came from the following sources. We have tried to contact all copyright holders, but if you feel there has been a mistaken attribution please contact the publisher. **Jacket** Chuck Stewart; **2–3** Kees Tabak/Sunshine International/Retna; **6** young Jack: Charlie Bruce; **7** Cream: Keith Morris/Redfern's; **8** WBL: Jorgen Angel/Redfern's; **9** OWGT: Alan Messer/Rex Features; **10** Jack and Ginger: Margrit Seyffer; **11** Jack with Walter and Kurt: Josef Goertz; Jack and John Belushi: Margrit Seyffer; **13** Jack with Gary Moore and Dick Heckstall-Smith: Nanna Botsch; **14** Cream reunited: Brian Rasic/Rex Features; backstage: Margrit Seyffer; **15** Jack with Bernie Worrell and Jo Bruce: Margrit Seyffer; **16** BMI and Zildjian Awards: Brian Rasic/Rex Features.